The Book of OHDSI

Observational Health Data Sciences and Informatics

2019-08-29

Contents

Preface

This is a book about the Observational Health Data Sciences and Informatics (OHDSI) collaborative. The OHSDI community wrote the book to serve as a central knowledge repository for all things OHDSI. The Book is a living document, community-maintained through open-source development tools, and evolves continuously. The online version, available for free at http://book.ohdsi.org, always represents the latest version. A physical copy of the book is available from Amazon at cost price.

Goals of this Book

This book aims to be a central knowledge repository for OHDSI, and it focuses on describing the OHDSI community, OHDSI data standards, and OHDSI tools. It is intended both for both OHDSI newcomers and veterans alike, and aims to be practical, providing the necessary theory and subsequent instructions on how to do things. After reading this book you will understand what OHDSI is, and how you can join the journey. You will learn what the common data model and standard vocabularies are, and how they can be used to standardize an observational healthcare database. You will learn the three main use cases for these data: characterization, population-level estimation, and patient-level prediction. You will read about OHDSI's open-source tools that support all three activities and how to use those tools. Chapters on data quality, clinical validity, software validity, and method validity will explain how to establish the quality of the generated evidence. Lastly, you will learn how to use the OHDSI tools to execute these studies in a distributed research network.

Structure of the Book

This book is organized in five major sections:

I) The OHDSI Community
II) Uniform data representation
III) Data Analytics
IV) Evidence Quality
V) OHDSI Studies

Each section has multiple chapters, and, as appropriate, each chapter follows the sequence: Introduction, Theory, Practice, Summary, and Exercises.

Contributors

Each chapter lists one or more chapter leads. These are the people who lead the writing of the chapter. However, there are many others that have contributed to the book, whom we would like to acknowledge here:

Hamed Abedtash	Mustafa Ascha	Mark Beno
Clair Blacketer	David Blatt	Brian Christian
Gino Cloft	Frank DeFalco	Sara Dempster
Jon Duke	Sergio Eslava	Clark Evans
Thomas Falconer	George Hripcsak	Vojtech Huser
Mark Khayter	Greg Klebanov	Kristin Kostka
Bob Lanese	Wanda Lattimore	Chun Li
David Madigan	Sindhoosha Malay	Harry Menegay
Akihiko Nishimura	Ellen Palmer	Nirav Patil
Jose Posada	Nicole Pratt	Dani Prieto-Alhambra
Christian Reich	Jenna Reps	Peter Rijnbeek
Patrick Ryan	Craig Sachson	Izzy Saridakis
Paula Saroufim	Martijn Schuemie	Sarah Seager
Anthony Sena	Chan Seng You	Sunah Song
Matt Spotnitz	Marc Suchard	Joel Swerdel
Devin Tian	Don Torok	Kees van Bochove
Mui Van Zandt	Erica Voss	Kristin Waite
Mike Warfe	Jamie Weaver	James Wiggins
Andrew Williams	Chan You Seng	

Software Versions

A large part of this book is about the open-source software of OHDSI, and this software will evolve over time. Although the developers do their best to offer a consistent and stable experience to the users, it is inevitable that over time improvements to the software will render some of the instructions in this book outdated. The community will update the online version of the book to reflect those changes, and new editions of the hard copy will be released over time. For reference, these are the version numbers of the software used in this version of the book:

- ACHILLES: version 1.6.6
- ATLAS: version 2.7.3
- EUNOMIA: version 1.0.0

Table 1: Versions of packages in the Methods Library used in this book.

Package	Version
CaseControl	1.6.0
CaseCrossover	1.1.0
CohortMethod	3.1.0
Cyclops	2.0.2
DatabaseConnector	2.4.1
EmpiricalCalibration	2.0.0
EvidenceSynthesis	0.0.4
FeatureExtraction	2.2.4
MethodEvaluation	1.1.0
ParallelLogger	1.1.0
PatientLevelPrediction	3.0.6
SelfControlledCaseSeries	1.4.0
SelfControlledCohort	1.5.0
SqlRender	1.6.2

- Methods Library packages: see Table 1

License

This book is licensed under the Creative Commons Zero v1.0 Universal license.

How the Book Is Developed

The book is written in RMarkdown using the bookdown package. The online version is automatically rebuilt from the source repository at https://github.com/OHDSI/TheBookOfOhdsi through the continuous integration system "travis". At regular intervals a snapshot is taken of the state of the book and marked as an "edition." These editions will be available as physical copies from Amazon.

Part I

The OHDSI Community

Chapter 1

The OHDSI Community

Chapter leads: Patrick Ryan & George Hripcsak

> Coming together is a beginning; staying together is progress; working together is success. *Henry Ford*

1.1 The Journey from Data to Evidence

Everywhere in healthcare, all across the world, within academic medical centers and private practices, regulatory agencies and medical product manufacturers, insurance companies and policy centers, and at the heart of every patient-provider interaction, there is a common challenge: how do we apply what we've learned from the past to make better decisions for the future?

For more than a decade, many have argued for the vision of a **learning healthcare system**, "designed to generate and apply the best evidence for the collaborative healthcare choices of each patient and provider; to drive the process of discovery as a natural outgrowth of patient care; and to ensure innovation, quality, safety, and value in healthcare". (Olsen et al., 2007) A chief component of this ambition rests on the exciting prospect that patient-level data captured during the routine course of clinical care could be analyzed to produce **real-world evidence**, which in turn could be disseminated across the healthcare system to inform clinical practice. In 2007, the Institute of Medicine Roundtable on Evidence-Based Medicine issued a report which established a goal that "By the year 2020, 90 percent of clinical decisions will be supported by accurate, timely, and up-to-date clinical information, and will reflect the best available evidence." (Olsen et al., 2007) While tremendous progress has been made on many different fronts, we still fall well short of these laudable aspirations.

Why? In part, because the journey from patient-level data to reliable evidence is an arduous one. There is no single defined path from data to evidence, and no single map that can help to navigate along the way. In fact, there is no single notion of "data," nor is there a singular notion of "evidence."

3

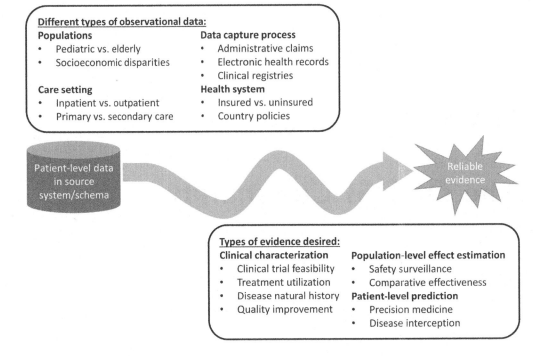

Figure 1.1: The journey from data to evidence

There are different types of observational databases which capture disparate patient-level data in source systems. These databases are as diverse as the healthcare system itself, reflecting different populations, care settings, and data capture processes. There are also different types of evidence that could be useful to inform decision-making, which can be classified by the analytic use cases of clinical characterization, population-level effect estimation, and patient-level prediction. Independent from the origin (source data) and desired destination (evidence), the challenge is further complicated by the breadth of clinical, scientific, and technical competencies that are required to undertake the journey. It requires a thorough understanding of health informatics, including its full provenance of the source data from the point-of-care interaction between a patient and provider through the administrative and clinical systems and into final repository, with an appreciation of the biases that can arise as part of the health policies and behavioral incentives associated with the data capture and curation processes. It requires mastery of epidemiologic principles and statistical methods to translate a clinical question into an observational study design properly suited to produce a relevant answer. It requires the technical ability to implement and execute computationally-efficient data science algorithms to datasets containing millions of patients with billions of clinical observations over years of longitudinal follow-up. It requires the clinical knowledge to synthesize what has been learned across an observational data network with evidence from other information sources, and to determine how this new knowledge should impact health policy and clinical practice. Accordingly, it is quite rare that any one individual would possess the requisite skills and resources to successfully trek from data to evidence alone. Instead, the journey often requires collaboration across multiple individuals and organizations to ensure that the best available data are analyzed using the most appropriate methods to produce the evidence that all stakeholders can trust and use in their decision-making processes.

1.2 Observational Medical Outcomes Partnership

A notable example of collaboration in observational research was the Observational Medical Outcomes Partnership (OMOP). OMOP was a public-private partnership, chaired by the US Food and Drug Administration, administered by the Foundation for the National Institutes of Health, and funded by a consortium of pharmaceutical companies that collaborated with academic researchers and health data partners to establish a research program that sought to advance the science of active medical product safety surveillance using observational health-care data. (Stang et al., 2010) OMOP established a multi-stakeholder governance structure and designed a series of methodological experiments to empirically test the performance of alternative epidemiologic designs and statistical methods when applied to an array of administrative claims and electronic health records databases for the task of identifying true drug safety associations and discriminating them from false positive findings.

Recognizing the technical challenges of conducting research across disparate observational databases in both a centralized environment and a distributed research network, the team designed the OMOP Common Data Model (CDM) as a mechanism to standardize the structure, content and semantics of observational data and to make it possible to write statistical analysis code once that could be re-used at every data site. (Overhage et al., 2012) The OMOP experiments demonstrated it was feasible to establish a common data model and standardized vocabularies that could accommodate different data types from different care settings and represented by different source vocabularies in a manner that could facilitate cross-institutional collaboration and computationally-efficient analytics.

From its inception, OMOP adopted an open-science approach, placing all of its work products, including study designs, data standards, analysis code, and empirical results, in the public domain to promote transparency, build confidence in the research that OMOP was conducting, but also to provide a community resource that could be repurposed to advance others' research objectives. While OMOP's original focus was drug safety, the OMOP CDM continually evolved to support an expanded set of analytical use cases, including comparative effectiveness of medical interventions and health system policies.

And while OMOP was successful in completing its large-scale empirical experiments, (Ryan et al., 2012, 2013b) developing methodological innovations, (Schuemie et al., 2014) and generating useful knowledge that has informed the appropriate use of observational data for safety decision-making, (Madigan et al., 2013b,a) the legacy of OMOP may be more remembered for its early adoption of open-science principles and its stimulus that motivated the formation of the OHDSI community.

When the OMOP project had completed, having fulfilled its mandate to perform methodological research to inform the FDA's active surveillance activities, the team recognized the end of the OMOP journey needed to become the start of a new journey together. In spite of OMOP's methodological research providing tangible insights into scientific best practices that could demonstrably improve the quality of evidence generated from observational data, adoption of those best practices was slow. Several barriers were identified, including: 1) fundamental concerns about observational data quality that were felt to be higher priority to address before analytics innovations; 2) insufficient conceptual understanding of the methodological problems and solutions; 3) inability to independently implement solutions within their local environment; 4) uncertainty over whether these approaches were applicable to their clinical problems of interest. The one common thread to every barrier was the sense that one person alone didn't have everything they needed to enact change by themselves, but with some collaborative support all issues could be overcome. But several areas of collaboration were needed:

- Collaboration on establishing open-community data standards, standardized vocabularies and ETL (Extract-Transform-Load) conventions that would increase confidence in the underlying data quality and promote consistency in structure, content, and semantics to enable standardized analytics.
- Collaboration on methodological research beyond drug safety to establish best practices more broadly for clinical characterization, population-level effect estimation, and patient-level prediction. Collaboration on open-source analytics development, to codify the scientific best practices proven through methodological research and make accessible as publicly available tools that can be easily adopted by the research community.
- Collaboration on clinical applications that address important health questions of shared interest across the community by collectively navigating the journey from data to evidence.

From this insight, OHDSI was born.

1.3   OHDSI as an Open-Science Collaborative

Observational Health Data Sciences and Informatics (OHDSI, pronounced "Odyssey") is an open-science community that aims to improve health by empowering the community to collaboratively generate the evidence that promotes better health decisions and better care. (Hripcsak et al., 2015) OHDSI conducts methodological research to establish scientific best practices for the appropriate use of observational health data, develops open-source analytics software that codify these practices into consistent, transparent, reproducible solutions, and applies these tools and practices to clinical questions to generate evidence that can guide healthcare policy and patient care.

1.3.1   Our Mission

> To improve health by empowering a community to collaboratively generate the evidence that promotes better health decisions and better care.

1.3.2 Our Vision

A world in which observational research produces a comprehensive understanding of health and disease.

1.3.3 Our Objectives

- **Innovation**: Observational research is a field which will benefit greatly from disruptive thinking. We actively seek and encourage fresh methodological approaches in our work.

- **Reproducibility**: Accurate, reproducible, and well-calibrated evidence is necessary for health improvement.

- **Community**: Everyone is welcome to actively participate in OHDSI, whether you are a patient, a health professional, a researcher, or someone who simply believes in our cause.

- **Collaboration**: We work collectively to prioritize and address the real-world needs of our community's participants.

- **Openness**: We strive to make all our community's proceeds open and publicly accessible, including the methods, tools and the evidence that we generate.

- **Beneficence**: We seek to protect the rights of individuals and organizations within our community at all times.

1.4 OHDSI's Progress

OHDSI has grown since its inception in 2014 to include over 2,500 collaborators on its online forums from different stakeholders, including academia, medical product industry, regulators, government, payers, technology providers, health systems, clinicians, patients, and representing different disciplines, including computer science, epidemiology, statistics, biomedical informatics, health policy, and clinical sciences. A listing of self-identified OHDSI collaborators is available on the OHDSI website. [1] The OHDSI collaborator map (Figure 1.2) highlights the breadth and diversity of the international community.

As of August, 2019, OHDSI has also established a data network of over 100 different healthcare databases from over 20 countries, collectively capturing over one billion patient records by applying a distributed network approach using an open-community data standard it maintains, the OMOP CDM. A distributed network means that patient-level data are not required to be shared between individuals or organizations. Instead, research questions are asked by individuals within the community in the form of a study protocol and accompanied by analysis code that generates evidence as a set of aggregated summary statistics, and only

---

[1] https://www.ohdsi.org/who-we-are/collaborators/

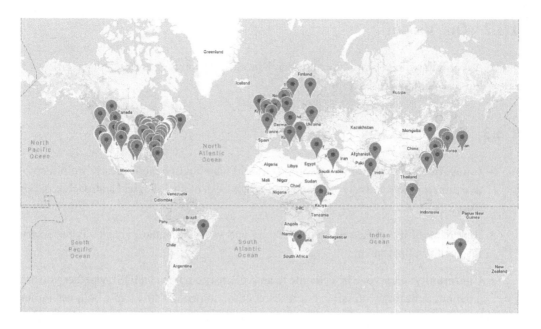

Figure 1.2: Map of OHDSI collaborators as of August, 2019

these summary statistics are shared amongst the partners who opt to collaborate in the study. With the OHDSI distributed network, each data partner retains full autonomy over the use of their patient-level data, and continues to observe the data governance policies within their respective institutions.

The OHDSI developer community has created a robust library of open-source analytics tools atop the OMOP CDM to support 3 use cases: 1) clinical characterization for disease natural history, treatment utilization, and quality improvement; 2) population-level effect estimation to apply causal inference methods for medical product safety surveillance and comparative effectiveness; and 3) patient-level prediction to apply machine learning algorithms for precision medicine and disease interception. OHDSI developers have also developed applications to support adoption of the OMOP CDM, data quality assessment, and facilitation of OHDSI network studies. These tools include back-end statistical packages built in R and Python, and front-end web applications developed in HTML and Javascript. All OHDSI tools are open source and publicly available via Github.[2]

OHDSI's open science community approach, coupled with its open-source tools, has enabled tremendous advances in observational research. One of the first OHDSI network analyses examined treatment pathways across three chronic diseases: diabetes, depression, and hypertension. Published in the Proceedings of the National Academy of Science, it was one of the largest observational studies ever conducted, with results from 11 data sources covering more than 250 million patients and revealed tremendous geographic differences and patient heterogeneity in treatment choices that had never been previously observable. (Hripcsak et al., 2016) OHDSI has developed new statistical methods for confounding adjustment (Tian et al.,

---

[2]https://github.com/OHDSI

2018) and evaluating the validity of observational evidence for causal inference, (Schuemie et al., 2018a) and it has applied these approaches in multiple contexts, from an individual safety surveillance question in epilepsy (Duke et al., 2017) to comparative effectiveness of second-line diabetes medications (Vashisht et al., 2018) to a large-scale population-level effect estimation study for comparative safety of depression treatments. (Schuemie et al., 2018b) The OHDSI community has also established a framework for how to responsibly apply machine learning algorithms to observational healthcare data, (Reps et al., 2018) which has been applied across various therapeutic areas. (Johnston et al., 2019; Cepeda et al., 2018; Reps et al., 2019)

1.5   Collaborating in OHDSI

Since OHDSI is a community aimed to empower collaboration to generate evidence, what does it mean to be an OHDSI collaborator? If you are someone who believes in OHDSI's mission and is interested in making a contribution anywhere along the journey from data to evidence, then OHDSI can be the community for you. Collaborators can be individuals who have access to patient-level data who are interested in seeing that data put to use to generate evidence. Collaborators can be methodologists interested in establishing scientific best practices and evaluating alternative approaches. Collaborators can be software developers who are interested in applying their programming skills to create tools that can be used by the rest of the community. Collaborators can be clinical researchers who have important public health questions and are seeking to provide the evidence to those questions to the broader healthcare community through publication and other forms of dissemination. Collaborators can be individuals or organizations who believe in this common cause for public health and wish to provide resources to ensure that the community can sustain itself and continue its mission, including hosting community activities and training sessions around the world. No matter your disciplinary background or stakeholder affiliation, OHDSI seeks to be a place where individuals can work together towards a common purpose, each making their individual contributions which collectively can advance healthcare. If you are interested in joining the journey, check out Chapter 2 ("Where To Begin") for how to get started.

1.6   Summary

- OHDSI's mission is to improve health by empowering a community to collaboratively generate the evidence that promotes better health decisions and better care.

- Our vision is a world in which observational research produces a comprehensive understanding of health and disease, which will be achieved through our objectives of innovation, reproducibility, community, collaboration, openness, and beneficence.

– OHDSI collaborators are focused on open-community data standards, methodological research, open-source analytics development, and clinical applications to improve the journey from data to evidence.

Chapter 2

Where to Begin

Chapter leads: Hamed Abedtash & Kristin Kostka

"A journey of a thousand miles begins with a single step." - Lao Tzu

The OHDSI community represents a mosaic of stakeholders across academia, industry and government-entities. Our work benefits a range of individuals and organizations, including patients, providers, and researchers, as well as health care systems, industry, and government agencies. This benefit is achieved by improving both the quality of healthcare data analytics as well as the usefulness of healthcare data to these stakeholders. We believe observational research is a field which benefits greatly from disruptive thinking. We actively seek and encourage fresh methodological approaches in our work.

2.1 Join the Journey

Everyone is welcome to actively participate in OHDSI, whether you are a patient, a health professional, a researcher, or someone who simply believes in our cause. OHDSI maintains an inclusive membership model. To become an OHDSI collaborator requires no membership fee. Collaboration is as simple as raising a hand to be included in the yearly OHDSI membership count. Involvement is entirely at-will. A collaborator can have any level of contribution within the community, ranging from someone who attends weekly community calls to leading network studies or OHDSI working groups. Collaborators do not have to be data holders to be considered active members of the community. The OHDSI community aims to serve data holders, researchers, health care providers and patients & consumers alike. A record of collaborator profiles are maintained and periodically updated on the OHDSI website. Membership is fostered via OHDSI community calls, workgroups and regional chapters.

Join the OHDSI forum

OHDSI Tip: Follow topics to receive emails when new posts are added

Introduce yourself!

Let the community know you're here by introducing yourself in the forum or at a community meeting

Join an OHDSI meeting

Sit in on our weekly community meetings

Join the OHDSI research network

By leading a study across the network

OR

By converting data to the OMOP Common Data Model

Join an working group

Or start your own work group!

Join the Journey

Help improve medical decision making today!

Provide feedback

Identify and evaluate ways to use real-world evidence to inform decision making

Figure 2.1: Join the journey - How to become an OHDSI collaborator.

2.1.1 OHDSI Forums

The OHDSI Forums[1] is an online discussion site where OHDSI Community Collaborators can hold conversations in the form of posted messages. The forums consist of a tree-like directory structure. The top end is "Categories". The forums can be divided into categories for the relevant discussions. Under the categories are sub-forums and these sub-forums can further have more sub-forums. The topics (commonly called threads) come under the lowest level of sub-forums and these are the places under which forums members can start their discussions or posts.

In the OHDSI forums, you can find categories of content including:

- **General:** for general discussion about the OHDSI community and how to get involved
- **Implementers:** for discussion about how to implement the Common Data Model and OHDSI analytics framework in your local environment
- **Developers:** for discussion around open-sourced development of OHDSI applications and other tools that leverage the OMOP CDM
- **Researchers:** for discussion around CDM-based research, including evidence generation, collaborative research, statistical methods and other topics of interest to the OHDSI Research Network
- **CDM Builders:** for discussion of ongoing CDM development, including requirements, vocabulary, and technical aspects
- **Vocabulary Users:** for discussion around vocabulary content
- **Regional Chapters (e.g. Korea, China, Europe):** for regional discussions in their native languages related to local OMOP implementations and OHDSI community activities

To being posting your own topics, you will need to sign up for an account. Once you have a forums account, you are encouraged to introduce yourself on the General Topic under the thread called "Welcome to OHDSI! - Please introduce yourself". You are invited to reply and 1) Introduce yourself and tell us a bit about what you do and 2) Let us know how you'd like to help out in the community (ex. software development, run studies, write research papers, etc). Now you are on your OHDSI Journey! From here, you are encouraged to join in the discussion. The OHDSI Community encourages using the Forums as your way to ask questions, discuss new ideas and collaborate.

 You can select topics to "watch." What this means is whenever a new post is added in a topic you're watching, you will receive an email and be able to reply to the post directly through your email. Watch the general thread to recieve details about upcoming meeting agendas, collaboration opportunities and have the weekly OHDSI digest delivered directly to your inbox!

---

[1]http://forum.ohdsi.org

2.1.2 OHDSI Events

OHDSI regularly holds in-person events to provide opportunities for collaborators to learn from each other and connect to foster future collaborations. These events are communicated on the OHDSI website, and are free for anyone interested in attending.

OHDSI Symposia are scientific conferences, held annually in US, Europe, and Asia, where collaborators can present their latest research through plenary talks, poster presentations, and software demonstrations. OHDSI Symposia provide a great venue for networking and to learn about the most recent progress across the community. OHDSI Symposia are generally accompanied by OHDSI tutorials, taught by fellow OHDSI collaborators as the course faculty, which provide community newcomers the opportunity for hands-on engagement on topics around data standards and analysis best practices. These tutorials are generally video-recorded and made available on the OHDSI website after the events for those who can't make it in person.

OHDSI Collaborator face-to-face events are smaller fora which are typically centered on a problem of shared interest to focus on during the time together. Past events have included a phenotype hack-a-thon, and data quality hack-a-thon, and open-source software documentation-a-thon. OHDSI has hosted multiple Study-a-thon events, where the goal of the multi-day session is to collaborate as a team on a particular research question by designing and implementing an appropriate observational analysis, executing the study across the OHDSI network, and synthesizing the evidence for public dissemination. In all of these events, there is a shared desire to solve a common problem but also a shared interest in providing a welcoming environment that encourages learning and continuous improvement on the process of collaborative problem-solving.

Learn more about the power of the OHDSI Community. Explore past symposiums, face-to-face meetings and watch OHDSI tutorials by visiting the OHDSI Past Events section on the OHDSI website. Past Events is updated regularly to archive community events.

2.1.3 OHDSI Community Calls

OHDSI Community Calls are a weekly opportunity to spotlight ongoing activity within the OHDSI community. Held every Tuesday from 12-1pm ET, these teleconferences are a time for the OHDSI community to come together to share recent developments and recognize the accomplishments of individual collaborators, working groups and the community as a whole. Each week's meeting is recorded, and presentations are archived in the OHDSI website resources.

All OHDSI Collaborators are welcome to participate in this weekly teleconference and encouraged to propose topics for community discussion. OHDSI Community Calls can be a forum to share research findings, present and seek feedback for active works-in-progress, demonstrate open-source software tools under development, debate community best practices for data modeling and analytics, and brainstorm future collaborative opportunities for grants/publications/conference workshops. If you are a Collaborator with a topic for an up-coming OHDSI Collaborator meeting, you are invited to post your thoughts on the OHDSI Forums.

As a newcomer to the OHDSI community, it is encouraged to add this call series to your calendar to get acquainted with what is happening across the OHDSI network. If you would like to join an OHDSI call, please consult the OHDSI wiki. Community call topics vary from week-to-week. You can also consult the OHDSI Weekly Digest on the OHDSI forum for more information on weekly presentation topics. Newcomers are invited to introduce themselves on their first call and tell the community about themselves, their background and what brought them to OHDSI.

2.1.4 OHDSI Workgroups

OHDSI has a variety of ongoing projects lead by workgroup teams. Each workgroup has its own leadership team which determine the project's objectives, goals and artifacts to be contributed to the community. Workgroup participation is open to all who have an interest in contributing to the project objectives and goals. Workgroups may be long-standing, strategic objectives or short-term projects to accomplish a specific need in the community. Workgroup meeting cadence is determined by the project leadership and will vary from group to group. A list of the active workgroups is maintained on the OHDSI Wiki.

Table 2.1 provides a quick reference to active OHDSI workgroups. You are encouraged to join a call and learn more.

Table 2.1: Notable OHDSI Workgroups

Workgroup Name	Objective	Target Audience
Atlas & WebAPI	Atlas and WebAPI are part of the OHDSI open-source software architecture that aim to provide standardized analytic capabilities built on the foundation of the OMOP Common Data Model.	Java & JavaScript software developers aiming to improve and contribute to the open-source Atlas/WebAPI platform
CDM & Vocabulary	To continue to develop the OMOP Common Data Model for the purpose of systematic, standardized and large-scale analytics applied to clinical patient data. To improve the quality of the Standardized Vocabularies by increasing their coverage of international coding systems and clinical aspects of patient care in order to support the standardized analytics developed by other working groups.	Any who has an interest in improving the OMOP Common Data Model and Standardized Vocabularies to meet all needs and use cases

Workgroup Name	Objective	Target Audience
Genomics	Expand the OMOP CDM to incorporate genomic data from patients. The group will define a CDM-compatible schema that can store information for genetic variants from various sequencing process.	Open to all
Population-Level Estimation	Develop scientific methods for observational research leading to population level estimates of effects that are accurate, reliable, and reproducible, and facilitate the use of these methods by the community.	Open to all
Natural Language Processing	To promote the use of textual information from Electronic Health Records (EHRs) for observational studies under the OHDSI umbrella. To facilitate this objective, the group will develop methods and software that can be implemented to utilize clinical text for studies by the OHDSI community.	Open to all
Patient-Level Prediction	establish a standardized process for developing accurate and well-calibrated patient-centered predictive models that can be utilized for multiple outcomes of interest and can be applied to observational healthcare data from any patient subpopulation of interest	Open to all
Gold Standard Phenotype Library	To enable members of the OHDSI community to find, evaluate, and utilize community-validated cohort definitions for research and other activities	Open to all with an interest in curation and validation of phenotypes
FHIR Workgroup	To establish the roadmap for the OHDSI FHIR integration and to make recommendations to the broader community for leveraging the FHIR implementation and data in EHR community for the OHDSI-based observation studies and for disseminating the OHDSI data and research results through the FHIR-based tools and APIs.	Open to all with an interest in interoperability
GIS	Expand the OMOP CDM and leverage OHDSI tools so that patients' environmental exposure histories can be related to their clinical phenotypes	Open to all with an interest in health-related geographic attributes

Workgroup Name	Objective	Target Audience
Clinical Trials	Understand clinical trial use cases where the OHDSI platform & ecosystem can aid trials in any aspect, and assist in driving updates in OHDSI tools to support.	Open to all with an interest in clinical trials
THEMIS	The objective of THEMIS is to develop standard conventions, above and beyond the OMOP CDM conventions, to ensure ETL protocols designed at each OMOP site are of highest quality, reproducible and efficient.	
Metadata & Annotations	Our goal is to define a standard process for storing human- and machine-authored metadata and annotations in the Common Data Model to ensure researchers can consume and create useful data artifacts about observational data sets.	Open to all
Patient Generated Health Data (PGHD)	The goal of this WG would be developing ETL conventions, integration process with clinical data, and analytic process for PGHD, which is generated through Smart Phone/App/Wearable devices.	Open to all
Women of OHDSI	To provide a forum for women within the OHDSI community to come together and discuss challenges they face as women working in science, technology, engineering and mathematics (STEM). We aim to facilitate discusses where women can share their perspectives, raise concerns, propose ideas on how the OHDSI community can support women in STEM, and ultimately inspire women to become leaders within the community and their respective fields.	Open to all who identify with this mission
Steering Committee	To uphold OHDSI's mission vision and values by ensuring all OHDSI activities and events are aligned with the needs of our growing community. In addition, the group serves as an advisory group for the OHDSI coordinating center based at Columbia by providing guidance for OHDSI's future direction.	Leaders within the community

2.1.5   OHDSI Regional Chapters

An OHDSI regional chapter represents a group of OHDSI collaborators located in a geographic area who wish to hold local networking events and meetings to address problems specific to their geographic location. Today, OHDSI regional chapters include OHDSI in Europe[2], OHDSI in South Korea[3] and OHDSI in China.[4] If you would like to set-up an OHDSI regional chapter in your region, you may do so by following the OHDSI regional chapter process outlined on the OHDSI website.

2.1.6   OHDSI Research Network

Many OHDSI collaborators are interested in converting their data into the OMOP Common Data Model. The OHDSI research network represents a diverse, global community of observational databases that have undergone Extract-Transform-Load (ETL) processes to become OMOP compliant. If your journey in the OHDSI community includes transforming data, there are numerous community resources available to aid you in your journey including tutorials on the OMOP CDM and Vocabularies, freely available tools to assist with conversion, and workgroups targeting specific domains or types of data conversions. The OHDSI collaborators are encouraged to utilize the OHDSI forum to discuss and troubleshoot challenges that arise during CDM conversions.

2.2   Where You Fit In

By now, you may be wondering: *where do I fit into the OHDSI Community?*

I am a clinical researcher looking to start a study. If you are a clinical researcher interesting in using the OHDSI Research Network to answer a specific question – maybe even publish a paper – you're in the right place. You can start by posting your idea to the OHDSI Researchers Topic on the OHDSI Forum. This will help you connect with researchers of similar interest. OHDSI loves to publish and has many resources available to expedite turning your research question into an analysis and a paper. You can find more information in Chapters 11, 12, and 13.

I want to read and consume the information the OHDSI community is produce. Whether you're a patient, a practicing clinician or subject matter expertise in healthcare, OHDSI wants to provide you with high quality evidence to help you better understand health outcomes. Maybe it's been a while since you have written code. Maybe you never program. You have a place in this community. We call you an *evidence consumer* – you are the individuals who are turning OHDSI research into action. You are sifting through to know what evidence OHDSI has generated and is generating, possibly also wanting to suggest questions relevant for you.

---

[2]https://www.ohdsi-europe.org/
[3]http://forums.ohdsi.org/c/For-collaborators-wishing-to-communicate-in-Korean
[4]https://ohdsichina.org/

We welcome you to join the discussion. Start asking questions on the OHDSI Forum. Attend Community Calls and hear about the latest research. Attend the OHDSI Symposiums and Face-to-Face Meetings to engage directly with the community. Your questions are an important part of the OHDSI community. Speak up and help us learn more about what evidence you are searching for!

I work in a healthcare leadership role. I may be a data owner and/or represent one. I am evaluating the utility of the OMOP CDM and OHDSI analytical tools for my organization. As an administrator/leader of an organization, you may have heard about OHDSI and are curious to know the OMOP CDM could work for your use cases. You may start by looking through OHDSI Past Events materials to see the body of research. You may join a Community Call and simply listen in. You may also find that Chapter 7 (Data Analytics Use Cases) helps you understand the kind of research the OMOP CDM and OHDSI analytics tools can enable. The OHDSI Community is here for you in your journey. Don't be afraid to speak up and ask for examples if you have specific areas you're interested in. More than 200 organizations around the world are collaborating in OHDSI, there's plenty of success stories to help showcase the value of this community.

I am a database administrator looking to ETL/convert my institution's data to the OMOP CDM. Choosing to "OMOP" your data is a novel and worthwhile undertaking. If you're just starting out on your ETL process, consult the OHDSI Community ETL Tutorial Slides or sign-up for the next offering at an upcoming OHDSI Symposium. Consider dialing into the THEMIS workgroup calls and engaging the OHDSI Forum with your questions. You will find a wealth of knowledge in the community who are interested in helping your successful implementation of the OMOP CDM. Don't be shy!

I am a biostatistician and/or methods developer interested in contributing to the OHDSI tool stack. You're savvy in R. You know how to commit to Git. Most of all, you're eager to bring your expertise to the OHDSI Methods Library and further develop these methodologies. You'll want to start by joining either the Population-Level Estimation or Patient Level Prediction workgroup calls to hear more about current community priorities. As you're using the OHDSI tools, you can also file Issues under the respective GitHub repo (e.g. if it is a SQL Render package problem, you would file under the GitHub Repo for OHDSI/SqlRender). We welcome your contributions!

I am a software developer interested in building a tool that complements the OHDSI tool stack. Welcome to the community! As part of the OHDSI mission, our tools are open source and governed under Apache licenses. You are welcome to develop solutions that complement the OHDSI tool stack. Feel free to join a workgroup and pitch your ideas. Please be mindful that OHDSI is heavily invested in open-science and open collaboration. Proprietary algorithms and software solutions are welcome but are not the main focus of our software development efforts.

I am a consultant looking to advise the OHDSI Community. Welcome to the community! Your expertise is valuable and appreciated. You are welcome to promote your services on the OHDSI Forum, as appropriate. You're invited to join us at OHDSI Tutorials and consider giving back by contributing your expertise in the Symposium proceedings and OHDSI face-to-face meetings throughout the year.

I am a student looking to learn more about OHDSI. You're in the right place! Consider joining an OHDSI Community Call and introducing yourself. You are encouraged to delve into the OHDSI tutorials, attend OHDSI Symposiums and face-to-face meetings to learn more about the methods and tools the OHDSI community offers. If you have a specific research interest, let us know by posting in the Researcher topic on the OHDSI Forum. Many organizations offer OHDSI sponsored research opportunities (e.g. post-Doc, research fellowships). The OHDSI Forum will give you the latest information on these opportunities and more.

2.3   Summary

- Getting started in the OHDSI Community is as easy as saying hello! Post on the **OHDSI Forum** and join a Community Call.
- Post your research or ETL questions to the OHDSI Forum.

Chapter 3

Open Science

Chapter lead: Kees van Bochove

From the inception of the OHDSI community, the goal was to establish an international collaborative by building on open-science values, such as the use of open-source software, public availability of all conference proceedings and materials, and transparent, open-access publication of generated medical evidence. But what exactly is open-science? And how could OHDSI build an open-science or open-data strategy around medical data, which is very privacy-sensitive and typically not open for good reasons? Why is it so important to have reproducibility of analysis, and how does the OHDSI community aim to achieve this? These are some of the questions that we touch on in this chapter.

3.1 Open Science

The term 'open science' has been used since the nineties, but it really gained traction in the 2010s, during the same period OHDSI was born. Wikipedia (Wikipedia, 2019a) defines it as "the movement to make scientific research (including publications, data, physical samples, and software) and its dissemination accessible to all levels of an inquiring society, amateur or professional," and goes on to state that it is typically developed through collaborative networks. Although the OHDSI community never positioned itself explicitly as an 'open-science' collective or network, the term is frequently used to explain the driving concepts and principles behind OHDSI. For example, in 2015, Jon Duke presented OHDSI as "An Open Science Approach to Medical Evidence Generation,"[1] and in 2019, the EHDEN consortium's introductory webinar hailed the OHDSI network approach as "21st Century Real World Open Science."[2] Indeed, as we shall see in this chapter, many of the practices of open-science can be found in today's OHDSI community. One could argue that the OHDSI community is a

---

[1] https://www.ohdsi.org/wp-content/uploads/2014/07/ARM-OHDSI_Duke.pdf
[2] https://www.ehden.eu/webinars/

grassroots open-science collective driven by a shared desire for improving the transparency and reliability of medical evidence generation.

Open-science or "Science 2.0" (Wikipedia, 2019b) approaches mean to address a number of perceived problems within the current scientific practice. Information technology has led to an explosion of data generation and analysis methods, and for individual researchers, it is very hard to keep up with all literature published in their area of expertise. This holds even more true for medical doctors who have a practice to run as their day job, but still need to keep abreast of the latest medical evidence. In addition, there is growing concern that many experiments may suffer from poor statistical designs, publication bias, p-hacking and similar statistical problems, and are hard to reproduce. The traditional method of correcting these concerns, peer review of published articles, often fails to identify and tackle these problems. The special 2018 Nature edition on "Challenges in irreproducible research"[3] includes several examples of this. A group of authors attempting to apply systematic peer review on the articles in their field found that, for various reasons, it was very hard to get the errors they identified rectified. Experiments that have a flawed design to begin with are especially hard to correct. In the words of Ronald Fisher: "To consult the statistician after an experiment is finished is often merely to ask him to conduct a post mortem examination. He can perhaps say what the experiment died of." (Wikiquote, 2019) The authors encountered common statistical problems such as poor randomization designs leading to false conclusions about statistical significance, miscalculations in meta-analyses, and inappropriate baseline comparisons. (Allison et al., 2016) Another paper from the same collection, taking experiences from physics as an example, argues that it is critical to not only provide access to the underlying data, but also to publish and properly document the data processing and analysis scripts to achieve full reproducibility. (Chen et al., 2018)

The OHDSI community addresses these challenges in its own way, and it puts significant emphasis on the importance of generating medical evidence at scale. As stated in Schuemie et al. (2018b), while the current paradigm "centers on generating one estimate at a time using a unique study design with unknown reliability and publishing (or not) one estimate at a time," the OHDSI community "advocates for high-throughput observational studies using consistent and standardized methods, allowing evaluation, calibration and unbiased dissemination to generate a more reliable and complete evidence base." This is achieved by a combination of a network of medical data sources that map their data to the OMOP common data model, open source analytics code that can be used and verified by all, and large-scale baseline data such as the condition occurrences published at howoften.org. In the following paragraphs, concrete examples are provided and the open-science approach of OHDSI is detailed further using the four principles of Open Standards, Open Source, Open Data and Open Discourse as a guide. The chapter is concluded with a brief reference to the FAIR principles and outlook for OHDSI from an open-science perspective.

---

[3]https://www.nature.com/collections/prbfkwmwvz

3.2 Open-Science in Action: the Study-a-Thon

A recent development in the community is the emergence of 'study-a-thons': short, concentrated face-to-face gatherings of a multidisciplinary group of scientists aimed at answering an important, clinically relevant research question using the OMOP data model and the OHDSI tools. A nice example is the 2018 Oxford study-a-thon, which is explained in an EHDEN webinar[4] that provides a walkthrough of the process and also highlights the openly available results. In the period leading up to the study-a-thon, the participants propose medically relevant research questions to study, and one or more research questions are selected to study during the study-a-thon itself. Data is provided through participants that have access to patient-level data in OMOP format and are able to run queries on these data sources. Much of the actual study-a-thon time is devoted to discussing the statistical approach (see also chapter 2), the suitability of the data sources, the results which are interactively produced and the follow-up questions that are inevitably raised by these results. In the case of the Oxford study-a-thon, the questions centered around studying adverse post-surgical effects of different knee replacement methods, and the results were published interactively during the study-a-thon using the OHDSI forums and tools (see chapter 8). The OHDSI tools such as ATLAS facilitate rapid creation, exchange, discussion and tests of cohort definitions, which greatly speeds up the initial process of achieving consensus on problem definition and choice of methods. Thanks to the usage of the OMOP Common Data Model by the involved data sources and the availability of the OHDSI open source patient level prediction packages 13, it was possible to create a prediction model for 90-day post-operative mortality in one day, and validate the model externally in several large data sources the day after. The study-a-thon also resulted in a traditional scholarly paper (Development and validation of patient-level prediction models for adverse outcomes following total knee arthroplasty, Ross Williams, Daniel Prieto-Alhambra et al., manuscript in preparation), which took months to process through peer review. But the fact that the analysis scripts and results for several healthcare databases covering hundreds of millions of patient records were conceived, produced and published from scratch within a week illustrates the fundamental improvements OHDSI can bring to medical science, reducing the turnaround time for evidence to become available from months to days.

3.3 Open Standards

A very significant community resource that is maintained in the OHDSI community is the OMOP Common Data Model (see chapter 4) and associated Standardized Vocabularies (see chapter 5). The model itself is scoped to capture observational healthcare data, and it was originally meant to analyze associations between exposures such as drugs, procedures, devices, etc., and outcomes such as conditions and measurements. It has been extended for various analysis use cases (see also 7). However, harmonizing healthcare data worldwide from a wide variety of coding systems, healthcare paradigm and different types of healthcare

---

[4]https://youtu.be/X5yuoJoL6xs

sources requires a massive amount of 'mappings' between source codes and their closest standardized counterparts. The OMOP Standardized Vocabulary is further described in chapter
7 and includes mappings from hundreds of medical coding systems that are used worldwide,
and is browsable through the OHDSI Athena tool. By providing these vocabularies and mappings as a freely available community resource, OMOP and the OHDSI community make a
significant contribution to healthcare data analytics and is, by several accounts, the most comprehensive model for this purpose, representing approximately 1.2 billion healthcare records
worldwide.[5] (Garza et al., 2016)

3.4   Open Source

Another key resource the OHDSI community provides are open source programs. These can
be divided in several categories, such as the helper tools to map data to OMOP (see chapter
6), the OHDSI Methods Library which contain a powerful suite of commonly used statistical
methods, open source code for published observational studies, and ATLAS, Athena and
other infrastructure-related software which underpins the OHDSI ecosystem (see chapter
8). From an open-science perspective, one of the most important resources is the code for
the actual execution of studies, such as studies from the OHDSI Research Network (see
chapter 20). In turn, these programs leverage the fully open source OHDSI stack, which
can be inspected, reviewed and contributed to via GitHub. For example, network studies
often build on the Methods Library, which ensures a consistent re-use of statistical methods
across analytical use cases. See chapter 17 for a more detailed overview of how the use of
and collaboration on open source software in OHDSI ultimately underpins the quality and
reliability of the generated evidence.

3.5   Open Data

Because of the privacy-sensitive nature of healthcare data, fully open, comprehensive patient-
level datasets are typically not available. However, it is possible to leverage OMOP mapped
datasets to publish important aggregated data and results sets, such as the earlier mentioned
http://howoften.org and other public result sets that are published to http://data.ohdsi.org.
Also, the OHDSI community provides simulated datasets such as SynPUF for testing and
development purposes, and the OHDSI Research Network (see 20) can be leveraged to run
studies in a network of available datasources that have mapped their data to OMOP. In order to
make the mapping between the source data and the OMOP CDM transparent, it is encouraged
for data sources to re-use the OHDSI ETL or 'mapping' tools and publish their mapping code
as open source as well.

---

[5] https://www.ema.europa.eu/en/events/common-data-model-europe-why-which-how

3.6 Open Discourse

Open standards, open source and open data are great assets, but left by themselves, they will not impact medical practice. Key to the open-science practice and impact of OHDSI is the implementation of medical evidence generation and the translation of the science to medical practice. The OHDSI community has several annual OHDSI Symposia, held in the United States, Europe, and Asia as well as dedicated communities of practice in, amongst others, China and Korea. These symposia discuss the advancements in statistical methods, data and software tooling, the standardized vocabularies, and all other aspects of the OHDSI open source community. The OHDSI forums[6] and wiki[7] facilitate thousands of researchers worldwide in practicing observational research. The community calls[8] and the code, issues and pull requests in Github[9] constantly evolve the open-community assets such as code and the CDM, and in the OHDSI Network Studies, global observational research is practiced in an open and transparent way using hundreds of millions of patient records worldwide. Openness and open discourse is encouraged throughout the community, and this very book is written via an open process facilitated by the OHDSI wiki, community calls and a GitHub repository.[10] It needs to be stressed however that without all the OHDSI collaborators, the processes and tools would be empty shells. Indeed, one could argue that the true value of the OHDSI community is with its members, who share a vision of improving health through collaborative and open-science, as discussed in Chapter 1.

3.7 OHDSI and the FAIR Guiding Principles

3.7.1 Introduction

This last paragraph of the chapter takes a look at the current state of the OHDSI community and tooling, using the FAIR Data Guiding Principles published in Wilkinson et al. (2016).

3.7.2 Findability

Any healthcare database that is mapped to OMOP and used for analytics should, from a scientific perspective, persist for future reference and reproducibility. The use of persistent identifiers for OMOP databases is not yet widespread, partly because these databases are often contained behind firewalls and on internal networks and not necessarily connected to the internet. However, it is entirely possible to publish summaries of the databases as a descriptor record that can be referenced for e.g. citation purposes. This method is followed

---

[6] https://forums.ohdsi.org

[7] https://www.ohdsi.org/web/wiki

[8] https://www.ohdsi.org/web/wiki/doku.php?id=projects:overview

[9] https://github.com/ohdsi

[10] https://github.com/OHDSI/TheBookOfOhdsi

in for example the EMIF catalog[11], which provides a comprehensive record of the database in terms of data-gathering purpose, sources, vocabularies and terms, access control mechanisms, license, consents, etc. (Oliveira et al., 2019) This approach is further developed in the IMI EHDEN project.

3.7.3 Accessibility

Accessibility of OMOP mapped data through an open protocol is typically achieved through the SQL interface, which combined with the OMOP CDM provides a standardized and well-documented method for accessing OMOP data. However, as discussed above, OMOP sources are often not directly available over the internet for security reasons. Creating a secure worldwide healthcare data network that is accessible for researchers is an active research topic and operational goal of projects like IMI EHDEN. However, results of analyses in multiple OMOP databases, as shown through OHDSI initiatives such as LEGEND and http://howoften.org, can be openly published.

3.7.4 Interoperability

Interoperability is arguably the strong suit of the OMOP data model and OHDSI tooling. In order to build a strong network of medical data sources worldwide which can be leveraged for evidence generation, achieving interoperability between healthcare data sources is key, and this is achieved through the OMOP model and Standardized Vocabularies. However, by sharing cohort definitions and statistical approaches, the OHDSI community goes beyond code mapping and also provides a platform to build an interoperable understanding of the analysis methods for healthcare data. Since healthcare systems such as hospitals are often the source of record for OMOP data, the interoperability of the OHDSI approach could be further enhanced by alignment with operational healthcare interoperability standards such as HL7 FHIR, HL7 CIMI and openEHR. The same is true for alignment with clinical interoperability standards such as CDISC and biomedical ontologies. Especially in areas such as oncology, this is an important topic, and the Oncology Working Group and Clinical Trials Working Group in the OHDSI community provide good examples of forums where these issues are actively discussed. In terms of references to other data and specifically ontology terms, ATLAS and OHDSI Athena are important tools, as they allow the exploration of the OMOP Standardized Vocabularies in the context of other available medical coding systems.

3.7.5 Reusability

The FAIR principles around reusability focus on important issues such as the data license, provenance (clarifying how the data came in existence) and the link to relevant community standards. Data licensing is a complicated topic, especially across jurisdictions, and it would fall outside of the scope of this book to cover it extensively. However, it is important to

---

[11] https://emif-catalogue.eu

state that if you intend for your data (e.g. analysis results) to be freely used by others, it is good practice to explicitly provide these permissions via a data license. This is not yet a common practice for most data that can be found on the internet, and the OHDSI community is unfortunately not an exception here. Concerning the data provenance of OMOP databases, potential improvements exist for making meta-data available in an automated way, including, for example, CDM version, Standardized Vocabularies release, custom code lists, etc. The OHDSI ETL tools do not currently produce this information automatically, but working groups such as the Data Quality Working Group and Metadata Working Group actively work on these. Another important aspect is the provenance of the underlying databases itself; it is important to know if a hospital or GP information system was replaced or changed, and when known data omissions or other data issues occurred historically. Exploring ways to attach this metadata systematically in the OMOP CDM is the domain of the Metadata Working Group.

– The OHDSI community can be seen as an open-science community that is actively pursuing the interoperability and reproducibility of medical evidence generation.

– It also advocates a paradigm shift from single study and single estimate medical research to large-scale systematic evidence generation, where facts such as baseline occurrence are known and the evidence focuses on statistically estimating the effects of interventions and treatments from real world healthcare sources.

Part II

Uniform Data Representation

Chapter 4

The Common Data Model

Chapter lead: Clair Blacketer

Observational data provides a view of what happens to a patient while receiving healthcare. Data are collected and stored for increasingly large numbers of patients all over the world creating what is often called Big Health Data. The purpose of these collections are threefold: (i) directly to facilitate research (often in the form of survey or registry data), or (ii) to support the conduct of healthcare (usually called EHR - Electronic Health Records) or (iii) to manage the payment for healthcare (usually called claims data). All three are routinely used for clinical research, the latter two as secondary use data, and all three typically have their unique formating and encoding of the content.

Why do we need a Common Data Model for observational healthcare data?

Depending on their primary needs none of the observational databases capture all clinical events equally well. Therefore, research results must be drawn from many disparate data sources and compared and contrasted to understand the effect of potential capture bias. In addition, in order to draw conclusions with statistical power we need large numbers of observed patients. That explains the need for assessing and analyzing multiple data sources concurrently. In order to do that, data need to be harmonized into a common data standard. In addition, patient data require a high level of protection. To extract data for analysis purposes as it is done traditionally requires strict data use agreements and complex access control. A common data standard can alleviate this need by omitting the extraction step and allowing a standardized analytic to be executed on the data in it's native environment - the analytic comes to the data instead of the data to the analytic.

This standard is provided by the Common Data Model (CDM). The CDM, combined with its standardized content (see Chapter 5), will ensure that research methods can be systematically applied to produce meaningfully comparable and reproducible results. In this chapter we provide an overview of the data model itself, design, conventions, and discussion of select tables.

An overview of all the tables in the CDM is provided in Figure 4.1.

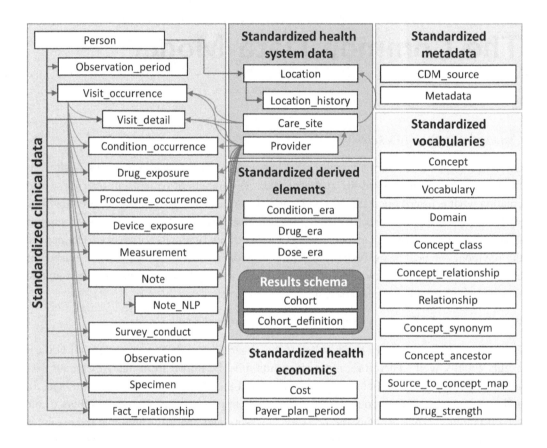

Figure 4.1: Overview of all tables in the CDM version 6.0. Note that not all relationships between tables are shown.

4.1 Design Principles

The CDM is optimized for typical observational research purposes of

- Identifying patient populations with certain healthcare interventions (drug exposure, procedures, healthcare policy changes etc.) and outcomes (conditions, procedures, other drug exposures etc.),
- Characterization of these patient populations for various parameters like demographic information, disease natural history, healthcare delivery, utilization and cost, morbidities, treatments and sequence of treatment etc.,
- Predicting the occurrence of these outcomes in individual patients - see Chapter 13,
- Estimating the effect these interventions have a population - see Chapter 12,

To achieve this goal, the development of the CDM follows the following design elements:

- **Suitability for purpose**: The CDM aims to provide data organized in a way optimal for analysis, rather than for the purpose of addressing the operational needs of health care providers or payers.
- **Data protection**: All data that might jeopardize the identity and protection of patients, such as names, precise birthdays etc. are limited. Exceptions are possible when the research expressly requires more detailed information, such as precise birth dates for the study of infants.
- **Design of domains**: The domains are modeled in a person-centric relational data model, where for each record the identity of the person and a date is captured as a minimum. Here, a relational data model is one where the data is represented as a collection of tables linked by primary and foreign keys.
- **Rationale for domains**: Domains are identified and separately defined in an entity-relationship model if they have an analysis use case (conditions, for example) and the domain has specific attributes that are not otherwise applicable. All other data can be preserved as an observation in the observation table in an entity-attribute-value structure.
- **Standardized Vocabularies**: To standardize the content of those records, the CDM relies on the Standardized Vocabularies containing all necessary and appropriate corresponding standard healthcare concepts.
- **Reuse of existing vocabularies**: If possible, these concepts are leveraged from national or industry standardization or vocabulary definition organizations or initiatives, such as the National Library of Medicine, the Department of Veterans' Affairs, the Center of Disease Control and Prevention, etc.
- **Maintaining source codes**: Even though all codes are mapped to the Standardized Vocabularies, the model also stores the original source code to ensure no information is lost.
- **Technology neutrality**: The CDM does not require a specific technology. It can be realized in any relational database, such as Oracle, SQL Server etc., or as SAS analytical datasets.
- **Scalability**: The CDM is optimized for data processing and computational analysis to

accommodate data sources that vary in size, including databases with up to hundreds of millions of persons and billions of clinical observations.

- **Backwards compatibility**: All changes from previous CDMs are clearly delineated in the github repository (https://github.com/OHDSI/CommonDataModel). Older versions of the CDM can be easily created from the current version, and no information is lost that was present previously.

4.2   Data Model Conventions

There are a number of implicit and explicit conventions that have been adopted in the CDM. Developers of methods that run against the CDM need to understand these conventions.

4.2.1   General Conventions of the Model

The CDM is considered a "person-centric" model, meaning that all clinical Event tables are linked to the PERSON table. Together with the date or start date this allows for a longitudinal view on all healthcare-relevant Events by person. The exceptions from this rule are the standardized health system data tables, which are linked directly to Events of the various domains.

4.2.2   General Conventions of Schemas

Schemas, or database users in some systems, allow for separation between read-only and read-write tables. The clinical Event and vocabulary tables are in the "CDM" schema and are considered read-only to the end user or analytic tool. Tables that need to be manipulated by web-based tools or end users are stored in the "Results" schema. The two tables in the "Results" schema are COHORT and COHORT_DEFINITON. These tables are meant to describe groups of interest that the user might define, as detailed in Chapter 10. These tables can be written to, meaning that a cohort can be stored in the COHORT table at run time. Since there is only one read-write schema for all users it is up to the implementation of the CDM how multiple user access is organized and controlled.

4.2.3   General Conventions of Data Tables

The CDM is platform-independent. Data types are defined generically using ANSI SQL data types (VARCHAR, INTEGER, FLOAT, DATE, DATETIME, CLOB). Precision is provided only for VARCHAR. It reflects the minimal required string length, but can be expanded within a concrete CDM instantiation. The CDM does not prescribe the date and datetime format. Standard queries against CDM may vary for local instances and date/datetime configurations.

Note: While the data model itself is platform-independent, many of the tools that have been built to work with it require certain specifications. For more about this please see Chapter 8.

4.2.4 General Conventions of Domains

Events of different nature are organized into Domains. These Events are stored in tables and fields which are Domain-specific, and represented by Standard Concepts that are also Domain-specific as defined in the Standardized Vocabularies (see section 5.2.3). Each Standard Concept has a unique Domain assignment, which defines which table they are recorded in. Even though the correct Domain assignment is subject for debate in the community, this strict Domain-table-field correspondence rule assures that there is always an unambiguous location for any code or concept. For example, signs, symptoms and diagnosis Concepts are of the Condition Domain, and are recorded in the CONDITION_CONCEPT_ID of the CONDITION_OCCURRENCE table. So-called Procedure Drugs are typically recorded as procedure codes in a procedure table in the source data. In an CDM, these records are found in the DRUG_EXPOSURE table because the mapped Standard Concepts have the Domain assignment Drug. There is a total of 30 Domains, as shown in table 4.1.

Table 4.1: Number of standard concepts belonging to each domain.

Concept Count	Domain ID	Concept Count	Domain ID
1731378	Drug	183	Route
477597	Device	180	Currency
257000	Procedure	158	Payer
163807	Condition	123	Visit
145898	Observation	51	Cost
89645	Measurement	50	Race
33759	Spec Anatomic Site	13	Plan Stop Reason
17302	Meas Value	11	Plan
1799	Specimen	6	Episode
1215	Provider Specialty	6	Sponsor
1046	Unit	5	Meas Value Operator
944	Metadata	3	Spec Disease Status
538	Revenue Code	2	Gender
336	Type Concept	2	Ethnicity
194	Relationship	1	Observation Type

4.2.5 Representation of Content Through Concepts

In CDM data tables the content of each record is fully normalized and represented through Concepts. Concepts are stored in Event tables with their CONCEPT_ID values, which are foreign keys to the CONCEPT table, which serves as the general reference table. All CDM instances use the same CONCEPT table as a reference of the Concepts, which together with the Common Data Model is a key mechanism of interoperability and the foundation of the OHDSI research network. If a Standard Concept does not exist or cannot be identified, the value of the CONCEPT_ID is set to 0, representing a non-existing concept, an unknown or un-mappable value.

Records in the CONCEPT table contain detailed information about each concept (name, domain, class etc.). Concepts, Concept Relationships, Concept Ancestors and other information relating to Concepts is contained in the tables of the Standardized Vocabularies (see Chapter 5).

4.2.6   General Naming Conventions of Fields

Variable names across all tables follow one convention:

Table 4.2: Field name conventions.

Notation	Description
[Event]_ID	Unique identifier for each record, which serves as a foreign keys establishing relationships across Event tables. For example, PERSON_ID uniquely identifies each individual. VISIT_OCCURRENCE_ID uniquely identifies a Visit.
[Event]_CONCEPT_ID	Foreign key to a Standard Concept record in the CONCEPT reference table. This is the main representation of the Event, serving as the primary basis for all standardized analytics. For example, CONDITION_CONCEPT_ID = 31967 contains the reference value for the SNOMED concept of "Nausea".
[Event]_SOURCE _CONCEPT_ID	Foreign key to a record in the CONCEPT reference table. This Concept is the equivalent of the Source Value (below), and it may happen to be a Standard Concept, at which point it would be identical to the [Event]_CONCEPT_ID, or another non-standard concept. For example, CONDITION_SOURCE_CONCEPT_ID = 45431665 denotes the concept of "Nausea" in the Read terminology, and the analogous CONDITION_CONCEPT_ID is the Standard SNOMED-CT Concept 31967. The use of Source Concepts for standard analytics applications is discouraged since only Standard Concepts represent the semantic content of an Event in a unambiguous way and therefore Source Concepts are not interoperable.

Notation	Description
[Event]_TYPE_CONCEPT_ID	Foreign key to a record in the CONCEPT reference table, representing the origin of the source information, standardized within the Standardized Vocabularies. Note that despite the field name this is not a type of an Event, or type of a Concept, but declares the capture mechanism that created this record. For example, DRUG_TYPE_CONCEPT_ID discriminates if a Drug record was derived from a dispensing Event in the pharmacy ("Pharmacy dispensing") or from an e-prescribing application ("Prescription written")
[Event]_SOURCE_VALUE	Verbatim code or free text string reflecting how this Event was represented in the source data. Its use is discouraged for standard analytics applications, as these Source Values are not harmonized across data sources. For example, CONDITION_SOURCE_VALUE might contain a record of "78702", corresponding to ICD-9 code 787.02 written in a notation omitting the dot.

4.2.7   Difference Between Concepts and Source Values

Many tables contain equivalent information in multiple places: as a Source Value, a Source Concept and as a Standard Concept.

- **Source Values** are the original representation of an Event record in the source data. They can be codes from widely used coding systems, which are often public domain, such as ICD9CM, NDC or Read, proprietary coding systems like CPT4, GPI or Med-DRA, or controlled vocabularies used only in the source data, such as F for female and M for male. They can also be short free text phrases that are not standardized and controlled. Source Values are stored in the [Event]_SOURCE_VALUE fields in the data tables.
- **Concepts** are CDM-specific entities that normalize the meaning of a clinical fact. Most Concepts are based on existing public or proprietary coding systems in healthcare, while others were created de-novo (CONCEPT_CODE starts with "OMOP"). Concepts have unique IDs across all domains.
- **Source Concepts** are the Concepts that represent the code used in the source. Source Concepts are only used for existing public or proprietary coding systems, not for OMOP-generated Concepts. Source Concepts are stored in the [Event]_SOURCE_CONCEPT_ID field in the data tables.
- **Standard Concepts** are those Concepts that are used to define the meaning of a clinical entity uniquely across all databases and independent from the coding system used in the sources. Standard Concepts are typically drawn from existing public or proprietary vocabulary sources. Non-standard Concepts that have the equivalent meaning

Figure 4.2: ICD9CM code for Pulmonary Tuberculosis

to a Standard Concept have a mapping to the Standard Concept in the Standardized Vocabularies. Standard Concepts are referred to in the [Event]_CONCEPT_ID field of the data tables.

Source Values are only provided for convenience and quality assurance (QA) purposes. They may contain information that is only meaningful in the context of a specific data source. The use of Source Values and Source Concepts is optional, even though **strongly recommended** if the source data make use of coding systems. Standard Concepts **are mandatory** however. This mandatory use of Standard Concepts is what allows all CDM instances to speak the same language. For example, the condition "Pulmonary Tuberculosis" (TB, Figure 4.2) shows that the ICD9CM code for TB is 011.

Without context, the code 011 could be interpreted as "Hospital Inpatient (Including Medicare Part A)" from the UB04 vocabulary, or as "Nervous System Neoplasms without Complications, Comorbidities" from the DRG vocabulary. This is where Concept IDs, both Source and Standard, are valuable. The CONCEPT_ID value that represents the 011 ICD9CM code is 44828631. This differentiates the ICD9CM from the UBO4 and DRG. The ICD9CM TB Source Concept maps to Standard Concept 253954 from the SNOMED vocabulary through the relationship "Non-standard to Standard map (OMOP)" as shown in figure 4.3. This same

TERM CONNECTIONS (82)

RELATIONSHIP	RELATES TO	CONCEPT ID	VOCABULARY
ICD-9-CM to MedDRA (MSSO)	Pulmonary tuberculosis	36110777	MedDRA
Non-standard to Standard map (OMOP)	Pulmonary tuberculosis	253954	SNOMED
Subsumes	Other specified pulmonary tuberculosis	44830894	ICD9CM
	Other specified pulmonary tuberculosis, bacteriological or histological examination not done	44836741	ICD9CM
	Other specified pulmonary tuberculosis, bacteriological or histological examination unknown (at present)	44836742	ICD9CM
	Other specified pulmonary tuberculosis, tubercle bacilli found (in sputum) by microscopy	44821641	ICD9CM
	Other specified pulmonary tuberculosis, tubercle bacilli not found (in sputum) by microscopy, but found by bacterial culture	44833188	ICD9CM

Figure 4.3: SNOMED code for Pulmonary Tuberculosis

mapping relationships exists for Read, ICD10, CIEL, and MeSH codes, among others, so that any research that references the standard SNOMED concept is sure to include all supported source codes.

An example of how the Standard Concept to Source Concept relationship is depicted is shown in Table 4.7.

4.3 CDM Standardized Tables

The CDM contains 16 Clinical Event tables, 10 Vocabulary tables, 2 metadata tables, 4 health system data tables, 2 health economics data tables, 3 standardized derived elements, and 2 Results schema tables. These tables are fully specified in the CDM Wiki.[1]

To illustrate how these tables are used in practice, the data of one person will be used as a common thread throughout the rest of the chapter.

4.3.1 Running Example: Endometriosis

Endometriosis is a painful condition whereby cells normally found in the lining of a woman's uterus occur elsewhere in the body. Severe cases can lead to infertility, bowel, and bladder problems. The following sections will detail one patient's experience with this disease and how it might be represented in the Common Data Model.

---

[1]https://github.com/OHDSI/CommonDataModel/wiki

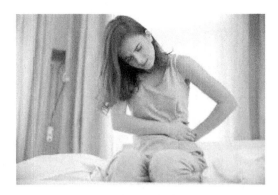

Every step of this painful journey I had to convince everyone how much pain I was in.

Lauren had been experiencing endometriosis symptoms for many years; however, it took a ruptured cyst in her ovary before she was diagnosed. You can read more about Lauren at https://www.endometriosis-uk.org/laurens-story.

4.3.2   PERSON Table

What Do We Know About Lauren?

- She is a 36-year-old woman
- Her birthday is 12-March-1982
- She is white
- She is English

With that in mind, her PERSON table might look something like this:

Table 4.3: The PERSON table.

Column name	Value	Explanation
PERSON_ID	1	The PERSON_ID should be an integer, either directly from the source or generated as part of the build process.
GENDER_CONCEPT_ID	8532	The concept ID referring to female gender is 8532.
YEAR_OF_BIRTH	1982	
MONTH_OF_BIRTH	3	
DAY_OF_BIRTH	12	
BIRTH_DATETIME	1982-03-12 00:00:00	When the time is not known midnight is used.
DEATH_DATETIME		

Column name	Value	Explanation
RACE_CONCEPT_ID	8527	The concept ID referring to white race is 8527. English ethnicity is 4093769. Either one is correct, the latter will roll up to the former. Notice that ethnicities are stored here as part of Races, not in the ETHNICITY_CONCEPT_ID
ETHNICITY_CONCEPT_ID	38003564	This is a US-typical notation to distinguish Hispanics from the rest. Ethnicities, in this case English, is stored in the RACE_CONCEPT_ID. Outside the US this is not used. 38003564 refers to "Not hispanic".
LOCATION_ID		Her address is not known.
PROVIDER_ID		Her primary care Provider is not known.
CARE_SITE		Her primary Care Site is not known.
PERSON_SOURCE_VALUE	1	Typically this would be her identifier in the source data, though often it is the same as the PERSON_ID.
GENDER_SOURCE_VALUE	F	The gender value as it appears in the source is stored here.
GENDER_SOURCE_CONCEPT_ID	0	If the gender value in the source was coded using a coding scheme supported by OHDSI that Concept would go here. For example, if her gender was "sex-F" in the source and it was stated to be in the PCORNet vocabulary concept 44814665 would go in this field.
RACE_SOURCE_VALUE	white	The race value as it appears in the source is stored here.
RACE_SOURCE_CONCEPT_ID	0	Same principle as GENDER_CONCEPT_ID.
ETHNICITY_SOURCE_VALUE	english	The ethnicity value as it appears in the source is stored here.
ETHNICITY_SOURCE_CONCEPT_ID	0	Same principle as GENDER_SOURCE_CONCEPT_ID.

4.3.3   OBSERVATION_PERIOD Table

The OBSERVATION_PERIOD table is designed to define the amount of time for which at least a patient's demographics, conditions, procedures and drugs are recorded in the source system with the expectation of a reasonable sensitivity and specificity. For insurance data this is typically the enrollment period of the patient. It's trickier in electronic health records (EHR), as most healthcare systems do not determine which healthcare institution or provider is visited. As a next best solution, often the first record in the system is considered the Start Date of the Observation Period and the latest record is considered the End Date.

How Is Lauren's Observation Period Defined?

Let's say Lauren's information as shown in Table 4.4 is recorded like in an EHR system. Her encounters from which the Observation Period was derived are:

Table 4.4: Lauren's healthcare encounters.

Encounter ID	Start date	Stop date	Type
70	2010-01-06	2010-01-06	outpatient
80	2011-01-06	2011-01-06	outpatient
90	2012-01-06	2012-01-06	outpatient
100	2013-01-07	2013-01-07	outpatient
101	2013-01-14	2013-01-14	ambulatory
102	2013-01-17	2013-01-24	inpatient

Based on the encounter records her OBSERVATION_PERIOD table might look something like this:

Table 4.5: The OBSERVATION_PERIOD table.

Column name	Value	Explanation
OBSERVATION_ PERIOD_ID	1	This is typically an autogenerated value creating a unique identifier for each record in the table.
PERSON_ID	1	This is a foreign key to Laura's record in the PERSON table and links PERSON to OBSERVATION_PERIOD table.
OBSERVATION_PERIOD_ START_DATE	2010-01-06	This is the start date of her earliest encounter on record.
OBSERVATION_PERIOD_ END_DATE	2013-01-24	This is the end date of her latest encounter on record.
PERIOD_TYPE_ CONCEPT_ID	44814725	The best option in the Vocabulary with the concept class "Obs Period Type" is 44814724, which stands for "Period covering healthcare encounters".

4.3.4 VISIT_OCCURRENCE

the VISIT_OCCURRENCE table houses information about a patient's encounters with the health care system. Within the OHDSI vernacular these are referred to as Visits and are considered to be discreet events. There are 12 top categories of Visits with an extensive hierarchy, depicting the many different circumstances healthcare might be delivered. The most common Visits recorded are inpatient, outpatient, emergency department and non-medical institution Visits.

How Are Lauren's Encounters Represented As Visits?

As an example let's represent the inpatient encounter in Table 4.4 in the VISIT_OCCURRENCE table.

Table 4.6: the VISIT_OCCURRENCE table.

Column name	Value	Explanation
VISIT_OCCURRENCE_ ID	514	This is typically an autogenerated value creating a unique identifier for each record.
PERSON_ID	1	This is a foreign key to Laura's record in the PERSON table and links PERSON to VISIT_OCCURRENCE.
VISIT_CONCEPT_ID	9201	A foreign key referring to an Inpatient Visit is 9201.
VISIT_START_DATE	2013-01-17	The start date of the Visit.
VISIT_START_ DATETIME	2013-01-17 00:00:00	The date and time of the Visit. The time is unknown, so midnight is used.
VISIT_END_DATE	2013-01-24	The end date of the Visit. If this is a one-day Visit the end date should match the start date.
VISIT_END_DATETIME	2013-01-24 00:00:00	The date and time of the Visit end. The time is unknown, so midnight is used.
VISIT_TYPE_ CONCEPT_ID	32034	This provides information about the provenance of the Visit record, i.e. does it come from an insurance claim, hospital billing, EHR record, etc. For this example the concept ID 32035 ("Visit derived from EHR encounter record") is used as the encounters are similar to Electronic Health Records
PROVIDER_ID*	NULL	If the encounter record has a provider associated the ID for that provider goes into this field. This should be the content of the PROVIDER_ID field from the PROVIDER table.

Column name	Value	Explanation
CARE_SITE_ID	NULL	If the encounter record has a Care Site associated, the ID for that Care Site goes into this field. This should be the CARE_SITE_ID from the CARE_SITE table.
VISIT_SOURCE_VALUE	inpatient	The Visit value as it appears in the source goes here. Lauren's data do not have that.
VISIT_SOURCE_CONCEPT_ID	0	If the Visit value from the source is coded using a vocabulary that is recognized by OHDSI the CONCEPT_ID value representing the source code would be found here. Lauren's data do not have that.
ADMITTED_FROM_CONCEPT_ID	0	If known, this is contains a Concept representing where the patient was admitted from. This concept should have the domain "Visit". For example, if the patient were admitted to the hospital from home it would contain 8536 ("Home").
ADMITTED_FROM_SOURCE_CONCEPT_ID	NULL	This is the value from the source that represents where the patient was admitted from. Using the above example, this would be "home".
DISCHARGE_TO_CONCEPT_ID	0	If known, this refers to a Concept representing where the patient was discharged to. This concept should have domain "Visit". For example, if a patient was released to an assisted living facility, the concept ID would be 8615 ("Assisted Living Facility").
DISCHARGE_TO_SOURCE_VALUE	0	This is the value from the source that represents where the patient was discharged to. Using the above example, this would be "Assisted living facility".
PRECEDING_VISIT_OCCURRENCE_ID	NULL	This denotes the Visit immediately preceding the current one. In contrast to ADMITTED_FROM_CONCEPT_ID this links to the actual Visit Occurrence record rather than a Visit Concept. Also, note there is no record for the following Visit Occurrence, Visit Occurrences are only linked through this field.

- A patient may interact with multiple health care Providers during one visit, as is often the case with inpatient stays. These interactions can be recorded in the VISIT_DETAIL table. While not covered in depth in this chapter, you can read more about the VISIT_DETAIL table in the CDM wiki.

4.3.5 CONDITION_OCCURRENCE

Records in the CONDITION_OCCURRENCE table are diagnoses, signs, or symptoms of a condition either observed by a Provider or reported by the patient.

What Are Lauren's Conditions?

Revisiting her account she says:

> About 3 years ago I noticed my periods, which had also been painful, were getting increasingly more painful. I started becoming aware of a sharp jabbing pain right by my colon and feeling tender and bloated around my tailbone and lower pelvis area. My periods had become so painful that I was missing 1-2 days of work a month. Painkillers sometimes dulled the pain, but usually they didn't do much.

The SNOMED code for painful menstruation cramps, otherwise known as dysmenorrhea, is 266599000. Table 4.7 shows how that would be represented in the CONDITION_OCCURRENCE table:

Table 4.7: The CONDITION_OCCURRENCE table.

Column name	Value	Explanation
CONDITION_ OCCURRENCE_ID	964	This is typically an autogenerated value creating a unique identifier for each record.
PERSON_ID	1	This is a foreign key to Laura's record in the PERSON table and links PERSON to CONDITION_OCCURRENCE.
CONDITION_ CONCEPT_ID	194696	A foreign key referring to the SNOMED code 266599000: 194696.
CONDITION_START_ DATE	2010-01-06	The date when the instance of the Condition is recorded.
CONDITION_START_ DATETIME	2010-01-06 00:00:00	The date and time when the instance of the Condition is recorded. Midnight is used since the time is unknown.
CONDITION_END_ DATE	NULL	This is the date when the instance of the Condition is considered to have ended, but this is rarely recorded.

Column name	Value	Explanation
CONDITION_END_ DATETIME	NULL	If known, this is the date and time when the instance of the Condition is considered to have ended.
CONDITION_TYPE_ CONCEPT_ID	32020	This column is intended to provide information about the provenance of the record, i.e. that it comes from an insurance claim, hospital billing record, EHR record, etc. For this example the concept 32020 ("EHR encounter diagnosis") is used as the encounters are similar to electronic health records. Concepts in this field should be in the "Condition Type" vocabulary.
CONDITION_STATUS_ CONCEPT_ID	0	If known, the this tells the circumstance and . For example, a condition could be an admitting diagnosis, in which case the concept ID 4203942 was used.
STOP_REASON	NULL	If known, the reason that the Condition was no longer present, as indicated in the source data.
PROVIDER_ID	NULL	If the condition record has a diagnosing provider listed, the ID for that provider goes in this field. This should be the provider_id from the PROVIDER table that represents the provider on the encounter.
VISIT_OCCURRENCE_ ID	509	The Visit (foreign key to the VISIT_OCCURRENCE_ID in the VISIT_OCCURRENCE table) during which the Condition was diagnosed.
CONDITION_SOURCE_ VALUE	266599000	This is the original source value representing the Condition. In Lauren's case of dysmenorrhea the SNOMED code for that Condition is stored here, while the Concept representing the code went to the CONDITION_SOURCE_CONCEPT_ID and the Standard Concept mapped from that is stored in the CONDITION_CONCEPT_ID field.

Column name	Value	Explanation
CONDITION_SOURCE_ CONCEPT_ID	194696	If the condition value from the source is coded using a vocabulary that is recognized by OHDSI, the concept ID that represents that value would go here. In the example of dysmennorhea the source value is a SNOMED code so the Concept representing that code is 194696. In this case it has the same value as the CONDITION_CONCEPT_ID field.
CONDITION_STATUS_ SOURCE_VALUE	0	If the Condition Status value from the source is coded using a coding scheme supported by OHDSI that concept would go here.

4.3.6 DRUG_EXPOSURE

The DRUG_EXPOSURE table captures records about the intent or actual introduction of a drug into the body of the patient. Drugs include prescription and over-the-counter medicines, vaccines, and large-molecule biologic therapies. Drug exposures are inferred from clinical events associated with orders, prescriptions written, pharmacy dispensings, procedural administrations, and other patient-reported information.

How Are Lauren's Drug Exposures Represented?

To help with her dysmenorrhea pain, Lauren was given 60 oral tablets with 375 mg Acetaminophen (aka Paracetamol, e.g. sold in the US under NDC code 69842087651) each for 30 days at her Visit on 2010-01-06. Here's how that might look in the DRUG_EXPOSURE table:

Table 4.8: The DRUG_EXPOSURE table.

Column name	Value	Explanation
DRUG_EXPOSURE_ID	1001	This is typically an autogenerated value creating a unique identifier for each record.
PERSON_ID	1	This is a foreign key to Laura's record in the PERSON table and links PERSON to DRUG_EXPOSURE.
DRUG_CONCEPT_ID	1127433	The Concept for the Drug product. The NDC code for acetaminophen maps to the RxNorm code 313782 which is represented by the Concept 1127433.

Column name	Value	Explanation
DRUG_EXPOSURE_START_DATE	2010-01-06	The start date of the exposure to the Drug.
DRUG_EXPOSURE_START_DATETIME	2010-01-06 00:00:00	The start date and time of the drug exposure. Midnight is used as the time is not known.
DRUG_EXPOSURE_END_DATE	2010-02-05	The end date of the Drug Exposure. Depending on different sources, it could be a known or an inferred date and denotes the last day at which the patient was still exposed to the drug. In this case this date is inferred since we know Lauren had a 30 days supply.
DRUG_EXPOSURE_END_DATETIME	2010-02-05 00:00:00	The end date and time of the drug exposure. Similar rules apply as to DRUG_EXPOSURE_END_DATE. Midnight is used as time is unknown.
VERBATIM_END_DATE	NULL	If the source recorded an explicit actual end date. The inferred end date banks on the assumption that the full range of days supply was utilized by the patient.
DRUG_TYPE_CONCEPT_ID	38000177	This column is intended to provide information about the provenance of the record, i.e. does it come from an insurance claim, prescription record, etc. For this example the concept 38000177 ("Prescription written") is used.
STOP_REASON	NULL	The reason the administration of the Drug was stopped. Reasons include regimen completed, changed, removed, etc. This information is very rarely captured.
REFILLS	NULL	The number of automatic refills after the initial prescription that are part of the prescription system in many countries. The initial prescription is not counted, values start with NULL. In the case of Lauren's acetaminophen she did not have any refills so the value is NULL.
QUANTITY	60	The quantity of drug as recorded in the original prescription or dispensing record.
DAYS_SUPPLY	30	The number of days of supply of the medication as prescribed.

Column name	Value	Explanation
SIG	NULL	The directions ("signetur") on the Drug prescription as recorded in the original prescription or dispensing record (and printed on the container in the US drug prescription system). Signeturs are not yet standardized in the CDM, and provided verbatim.
ROUTE_CONCEPT_ID	4132161	This concept is meant to represent the route of administration of the Drug the patient was exposed to. Lauren took her acetaminophen orally so the concept ID 4132161 ("Oral") is used.
LOT_NUMBER	NULL	An identifier assigned to a particular quantity or lot of Drug product from the manufacturer. This information is rarely captured.
PROVIDER_ID	NULL	If the drug record has a prescribing Provider listed, the ID for that Provider goes in this field. In that case this contains the PROVIDER_ID from the PROVIDER table.
VISIT_OCCURRENCE_ ID	509	A foreign key to the VISIT_OCCURRENCE table during which the Drug was prescribed.
VISIT_DETAIL_ID	NULL	A foreign key to the VISIT_DETAIL table during which the Drug was prescribed.
DRUG_SOURCE_ VALUE	69842087651	This is the source code for the Drug as it appears in the source data. In Lauren's case the NDC code is stored here.
DRUG_SOURCE_ CONCEPT_ID	750264	This is the Concept that represents the drug source value. The Concept 750264 standing for the NDC code for "Acetaminophen 325 MG Oral Tablet".
ROUTE_SOURCE_ VALUE	NULL	The verbatim information about the route of administration as detailed in the source.

4.3.7 PROCEDURE_OCCURRENCE

The PROCEDURE_OCCURRENCE table contains records of activities or processes ordered or carried out by a healthcare Provider on the patient with a diagnostic or therapeutic purpose. Procedures are present in various data sources in different forms with varying levels of standardization. For example:

- Medical Claims include procedure codes that are submitted as part of a claim for health services rendered, including procedures performed.

- Electronic Health Records that capture procedures as orders.

What Procedures Did Lauren Have?

From her description we know she had an ultrasound of her left ovary on 2013-01-14 that showed a 4x5cm cyst. Here's how that would look in the PROCEDURE_OCCURRENCE table:

Table 4.9: The PROCEDURE_OCCURRENCE table.

Column name	Value	Explanation
PROCEDURE_ OCCURRENCE_ID	1277	This is typically an autogenerated value creating a unique identifier for each record.
PERSON_ID	1	This is a foreign key to Laura's record in the PERSON table and links PERSON to PROCEDURE_OCCURRENCE
PROCEDURE_ CONCEPT_ID	4127451	The SNOMED procedure code for a pelvic ultrasound is 304435002 which is represented by Concept 4127451.
PROCEDURE_DATE	2013-01-14	The date on which the Procedure was performed.
PROCEDURE_ DATETIME	2013-01-14 00:00:00	The date and time on which the procedure was performed. Midnight is used as time is unknown.
PROCEDURE_TYPE_ CONCEPT_ID	38000275	This column is intended to provide information about the provenance of the procedure record, i.e. does it come from an insurance claim, EHR order, etc. For this example the concept ID 38000275 ("EHR order list entry") is used as the procedure record is from an EHR record.
MODIFIER_CONCEPT_ ID	0	This is meant for a concept ID representing the modifier on the procedure. For example, if the record indicated that a CPT4 procedure was performed bilaterally then the concept ID 42739579 ("Bilateral procedure") would be used.
QUANTITY	0	The quantity of Procedures ordered or administered. A missing Quantity, the numbers 0 and 1 all mean the same thing.
PROVIDER_ID	NULL	If the Procedure record has a Provider listed, the ID for that Provider goes in this field. This should be a foreign key to the PROVIDER_ID from the PROVIDER table.

Column name	Value	Explanation
VISIT_OCCURRENCE_ID	740	If known, this is the Visit (represented as VISIT_occurrence_id taken from the VISIT_OCCURRENCE table) during which the procedure was performed.
VISIT_DETAIL_ID	NULL	If known, this is the Visit detail (represented as VISIT_detail_id taken from the VISIT_DETAIL table) during which the procedure was performed.
PROCEDURE_SOURCE_VALUE	304435002	The code or information for the Procedure as it appears in the source data.
PROCEDURE_SOURCE_CONCEPT_ID	4127451	This is the Concept that represents the procedure source value.
MODIFIER_SOURCE_VALUE	NULL	The source code for the modifier as it appears in the source data.

4.4 Additional Information

This chapter covers only a portion of the tables available in the CDM as examples of how data is represented. You are encouraged to visit the wiki site[2] for more information.

4.5 Summary

- The CDM is designed to support a wide range of observational research activities.

- The CDM is a person-centric model.

- The CDM not only standardizes the structure of the data, but through the Standardized Vocabularies it also standardizes the representation of the content.

- Source codes are maintained in the CDM for full traceability.

---

[2]https://github.com/OHDSI/CommonDataModel/wiki

4.6   Exercises

Prerequisites

For these first exercises you will need to review the CDM tables discussed earlier, and you will have to look up concepts in the Vocabulary, which can be done through ATHENA[3] or ATLAS.[4]

Exercise 4.1. John is an African American man born on August 4, 1974. Define an entry in the PERSON table that encodes this information.

Exercise 4.2. John enrolled in his current insurance on January 1st, 2015. The data from his insurance database were extracted on July 1st, 2019. Define an entry in the OBSERVA-TION_PERIOD table that encodes this information.

Exercise 4.3. John was prescribed a 30-day supply of Ibuprofen 200 MG Oral tablets (NDC code: 76168009520) on May 1st, 2019. Define an entry in the DRUG_EXPOSURE table that encodes this information.

Prerequisites

For these last three exercises we assume R, R-Studio and Java have been installed as described in Section 8.4.5. Also required are the SqlRender, DatabaseConnector, and Eunomia packages, which can be installed using:

```
install.packages(c("SqlRender", "DatabaseConnector", "devtools"))
devtools::install_github("ohdsi/Eunomia", ref = "v1.0.0")
```

The Eunomia package provides a simulated dataset in the CDM that will run inside your local R session. The connection details can be obtained using:

```
connectionDetails <- Eunomia::getEunomiaConnectionDetails()
```

The CDM database schema is "main".

Exercise 4.4. Using SQL and R, retrieve all records of the condition "Gastrointestinal hemorrhage" (with concept ID 192671).

Exercise 4.5. Using SQL and R, retrieve all records of the condition "Gastrointestinal hemorrhage" using source codes. This database uses ICD-10, and the relevant ICD-10 code is "K92.2".

Exercise 4.6. Using SQL and R, retrieve the observation period of the person with PER-SON_ID 61.

---

[3] http://athena.ohdsi.org/
[4] http://atlas-demo.ohdsi.org

Suggested answers can be found in Appendix E.1.

Chapter 5

Standardized Vocabularies

Chapter leads: Christian Reich & Anna Ostropolets

The OMOP Standardized Vocabularies, often referred to simply as "the Vocabulary", are a foundational part of the OHDSI research network, and an integral part of the Common Data Model (CDM). They allow standardization of methods, definitions and results by defining the content of the data, paving the way for true remote (behind the firewall) network research and analytics. Usually, finding and interpreting the content of observational healthcare data, whether it is structured data using coding schemes or laid down in free text, is passed all the way through to the researcher, who is faced with a myriad of different ways to describe clinical events. OHDSI requires harmonization not only to a standardized format, but also to a rigorous standard content.

In this chapter we first describe the main principles of the Standardized Vocabularies, their components, and the relevant rules, conventions and some typical situations, all of which are necessary to understand and utilizing this foundational resource. We also point out where the support of the community is required to continuously improve it.

5.1 Why Vocabularies, and Why Standardizing

Medical vocabularies go back to the Bills of Mortality in medieval London to manage outbreaks of the plague and other diseases (see Figure 5.1).

Since then, the classifications have greatly expanded in size and complexity and spread into other aspects of healthcare, such as procedures and services, drugs, medical devices, etc. The main principles have remained the same: they are controlled vocabularies, terminologies, hierarchies or ontologies that some healthcare communities agree upon for the purpose of capturing, classifying and analyzing patient data. Many of these vocabularies are maintained by public and government agencies with a long-term mandate for doing so. For example, the World Health Organization (WHO) produces the International Classification of Disease (ICD) with the recent addition of its 11th revision (ICD11). Local governments

1660.

A General BILL for this prefent Year,

Ending the 11th Day of December 1660.

According to the Report made to the King's moft excellent Majefty,

By the Company of Parifh Clerks of LONDON, &c.

DISEASES and CASUALTIES.

ABortive and Stillborn —— 421	Flox and Small Pox ——— —1523	Palfy ——— ——— ——— 17
Aged ——— ——— 909	Found dead in the Streets, } 2	Plague ——— ——— ——— 36
Ague and Fever —— ——2303	Fields, &c. — }	Plurify ——— ——— ——— 12
Apoplexy and Suddenly — — 91	French Pox — ——— ——— 51	Quinfy and fore Throat — — 21
Blafted and Planet — ——— 3	Gout ——— ——— ——— 4	Rickets ——— ——— — 441
Bleeding and bloody Iffue —— 7	Grief ——— ——— ——— 13	Rifing of the Lights ——— — 210
Bloody Flux, Scowring, and } 346	Griping in the Guts ——— — 253	Rupture ——— ——— ——— 12
Flux —— }	Hanged and made away them- } 11	Scurvy ——— ——— ——— 82
Burnt and Scalded — —— 6	felves ——— }	Shot ——— ——— ——— 7
Cancer, Gangrene and Fiftula 63	Head-ach and Headmouldfhot 35	Shingles ——— ——— ——— 1
Canker, fore Mouth and Thrufh 73	Jaundies ——— ——— 102	Sores, Ulcers, broken and } 61
Childbed ——— — —— 226	Impofthume ——— ——— 105	bruifed Limbs — }
Chrifomes and Infants ——— 858	Killed by feveral Accidents—— 55	Spleen ——— ——— ——— 7
Cold, Cough and Hiccough — 33	King's Evil ——— ——— 28	Spotted Fever and Purples —— 368
Colick and Wind — —— 116	Lethargy ——— ——— — 6	Starved ——— ——— ——— 7
Confumption and Tiffick ——2982	Livergrown ——— ——— 8	Strangury ——— ——— —— 22
Convulfion ——— ——— 742	Lunatick and Frenzy ——— 14	Stopping of the Stomach — — 186
Cut of the Stone and Stone — 46	Megrims ——— ——— 5	Surfeit ——— — ——— 202
Dropfy and Tympany ——— 646	Meafles ——— ——— — 6	Swine Pox ——— ——— — 2
Drowned ——— ——— 57	Mother ——— ——— — 1	Teeth and Worms ——— —— 839
Executed ——— ——— —— 7	Murthered ——— ——— 7	Vomiting ——— ——— —— 8
Falling Sicknefs ——— —— 4	Overlaid and Starved at Nurfe 46	Wen ——— ——— ——— 1

Figure 5.1: 1660 London Bill of Mortality, showing the cause of death for deceased inhabitants using a classification system of 62 diseases known at the time.

create country-specific versions, such as ICD10CM (USA), ICD10GM (Germany), etc. Governments also control the marketing and sale of drugs and maintain national repositories of such certified drugs. Vocabularies are also used in the private sector, either as commercial products or for internal use, such as electronic health record (EHR) systems or for medical insurance claim reporting.

As a result, each country, region, healthcare system and institution tends to have their own classifications that would most likely only be relevant where it is used. This myriad of vocabularies prevents interoperability of the systems they are used in. Standardization is the key that enables patient data exchange, unlocks health data analysis on a global level and allows systematic and standardized research, including performance characterization and quality assessment. To address that problem, multinational organizations have sprung up and started creating broad standards, such as the WHO mentioned above and the Standard Nomenclature of Medicine (SNOMED) or Logical Observation Identifiers Names and Codes (LOINC). In the US, the Health IT Standards Committee (HITAC) recommends the use of SNOMED, LOINC and the drug vocabulary RxNorm as standards to the National Coordinator for Health IT (ONC) for use in a common platform for nationwide health information exchange across diverse entities.

OHDSI developed the OMOP CDM, a global standard for observational research. As part of the CDM, the OMOP Standardized Vocabularies are available for two main purposes:

- Common repository of all vocabularies used in the community
- Standardization and mapping for use in research

The Standardized Vocabularies are available to the community free of charge and **must be used** for OMOP CDM instance **as its mandatory reference table**.

5.1.1 Building the Standardized Vocabularies

All vocabularies of the Standardized Vocabularies are consolidated into the same common format. This relieves the researchers from having to understand and handle multiple different formats and life-cycle conventions of the originating vocabularies. All vocabularies are regularly refreshed and incorporated using the Pallas system.[1] It is built and run by the OHDSI Vocabulary Team, which is part of the overall OMOP CDM Workgroup. If you find mistakes please report and help improve our resource by posting in either the OHDSI Forums[2] or CDM Github page.[3]

---

[1] https://github.com/OHDSI/Vocabulary-v5.0
[2] https://forums.ohdsi.org
[3] https://github.com/OHDSI/CommonDataModel/issues

5.1.2   Access to the Standardized Vocabularies

In order to obtain the Standardized Vocabularies, you do not have to run Pallas yourself. Instead, you can download the latest version from ATHENA[4] and load it into your local database. ATHENA also allows faceted search of the Vocabularies.

To download a zip file with all Standardized Vocabularies tables select all the vocabularies you need for your OMOP CDM. Vocabularies with Standard Concepts (see Section 5.2.6) and very common usage are preselected. Add vocabularies that are used in your source data. Vocabularies that are proprietary have no select button. Click on the "License required" button to incorporate such a vocabulary into your list. The Vocabulary Team will contact you and request you demonstrate your license or help you connect to the right folks to obtain one.

5.1.3   Source of Vocabularies: Adopt Versus Build

OHDSI generally prefers adopting existing vocabularies, rather than de-novo construction, because (i) many vocabularies have already been utilized in observational data in the community, and (ii) construction and maintenance of vocabularies is complex and requires the input of many stakeholders over long periods of time to mature. For that reason, dedicated organizations provide vocabularies, which are subject to a life-cycle of generation, deprecation, merging and splitting (see Section 5.2.10). Currently, OHDSI only produces internal administrative vocabularies like Type Concepts (e.g. condition type concepts). The only exception is RxNorm Extension, a vocabulary covering drugs that are only used outside the United States (see Section 5.6.9).

5.2   Concepts

All clinical events in the OMOP CDM are expressed as concepts, which represent the semantic notion of each event. They are the fundamental building blocks of the data records, making almost all tables fully normalized with few exceptions. Concepts are stored in the CONCEPT table (see Figure 5.2).

This system is meant to be **comprehensive**, i.e. there are enough concepts to cover any event relevant to the patient's healthcare experience (e.g. conditions, procedures, exposures to drug, etc.) as well as some of the administrative information of the healthcare system (e.g. visits, care sites, etc.).

---

[4]http://athena.ohdsi.org

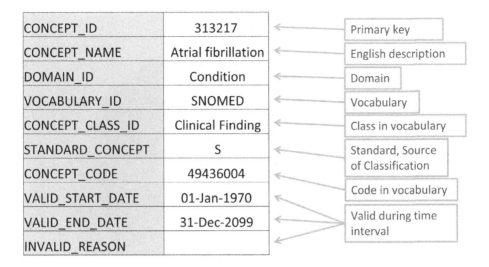

Figure 5.2: Standard representation of vocabulary concepts in the OMOP CDM. The example provided is the CONCEPT table record for the SNOMED code for Atrial Fibrillation.

5.2.1   Concept IDs

Each concept is assigned a concept ID to be used as a primary key. This meaningless integer ID, rather than the original code from the vocabulary, is used to record data in the CDM event tables.

5.2.2   Concept Names

Each concept has one name. Names are always in English. They are imported from the source of the vocabulary. If the source vocabulary has more than one name, the most expressive is selected and the remaining ones are stored in the CONCEPT_SYNONYM table under the same CONCEPT_ID key. Non-English names are recorded in CONCEPT_SYNONYM as well, with the appropriate language concept ID in the LANGUAGE_CONCEPT_ID field. The name is 255 characters long, which means that very long names get truncated and the full-length version recorded as another synonym, which can hold up to 1000 characters.

5.2.3   Domains

Each concept is assigned a domain in the DOMAIN_ID field, which in contrast to the numerical CONCEPT_ID is a short case-sensitive unique alphanumeric ID for the domain. Examples of such domain identifiers are "Condition," "Drug," "Procedure," "Visit," "Device," "Specimen," etc. Ambiguous or pre-coordinated (combination) concepts can belong to a combination domain, but Standard Concepts (see Section 5.2.6) are always assigned a singular domain. Domains also direct to which CDM table and field a clinical event or event

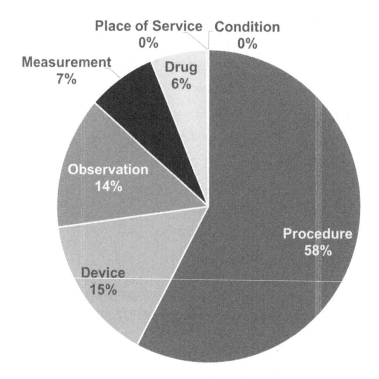

Figure 5.3: Domain assignment in procedure vocabularies CPT4 and HCPCS. By intuition, these vocabularies should contain codes and concepts of a single domain, but in reality they are mixed.

attribute is recorded. Domain assignments are an OMOP-specific feature done during vocabulary ingestion using a heuristic laid out in Pallas. Source vocabularies tend to combine codes of mixed domains, but to a varying degree (see Figure 5.3).

The domain heuristic follows the definitions of the domains. These definitions are derived from the table and field definitions in the CDM (see Chapter 4). The heuristic is not perfect; there are grey zones (see Section 5.6 "Special Situations"). If you find concept domains assigned incorrectly please report and help improve the process through a Forums or CDM issue post.

5.2.4   Vocabularies

Each vocabulary has a short case-sensitive unique alphanumeric ID, which generally follows the abbreviated name of the vocabulary, omitting dashes. For example, ICD-9-CM has the vocabulary ID "ICD9CM". There are 111 vocabularies currently supported by OHDSI, of which 78 are adopted from external sources, while the rest are OMOP-internal vocabularies. These vocabularies are typically refreshed at a quarterly schedule. The source and the version of the vocabularies is defined in the VOCABULARY reference file.

5.2.5 Concept Classes

Some vocabularies classify their codes or concepts, denoted through their case-sensitive unique alphanumerical IDs. For example, SNOMED has 33 such concept classes, which SNOMED refers to as "semantic tags": clinical finding, social context, body structure, etc. These are vertical divisions of the concepts. Others, such as MedDRA or RxNorm, have concept classes classifying horizontal levels in their stratified hierarchies. Vocabularies without any concept classes, such as HCPCS, use the vocabulary ID as the Concept Class ID.

Table 5.1: Vocabularies with or without horizontal and vertical sub-classification principles in concept class.

Concept class subdivision principle	Vocabulary
Horizontal	all drug vocabularies, ATC, CDT, Episode, HCPCS, HemOnc, ICDs, MedDRA, OSM, Census
Vertical	CIEL, HES Specialty, ICDO3, MeSH, NAACCR, NDFRT, OPCS4, PCORNET, Plan, PPI, Provider, SNOMED, SPL, UCUM
Mixed	CPT4, ISBT, LOINC
None	APC, all Type Concepts, Ethnicity, OXMIS, Race, Revenue Code, Sponsor, Supplier, UB04s, Visit

Horizontal concept classes allow you to determine a specific hierarchical level. For example, in the drug vocabulary RxNorm the concept class "Ingredient" defines the top level of the hierarchy. In the vertical model, members of a concept class can be of any hierarchical level from the top to the very bottom.

5.2.6 Standard Concepts

One concept representing the meaning of each clinical event is designated the Standard. For example, MESH code D001281, CIEL code 148203, SNOMED code 49436004, ICD9CM code 427.31 and Read code G573000 all define "Atrial fibrillation" in the condition domain, but only the SNOMED concept is Standard and represents the condition in the data. The others are designated non-standard or source concepts and mapped to the Standard ones. Standard Concepts are indicated through an "S" in the STANDARD_CONCEPT field. And only these Standard Concepts are used to record data in the CDM fields ending in "_CONCEPT_ID".

5.2.7 Non-Standard Concepts

Non-standard concepts are not used to represent the clinical events, but they are still part of the Standardized Vocabularies, and are often found in the source data. For that reason, they

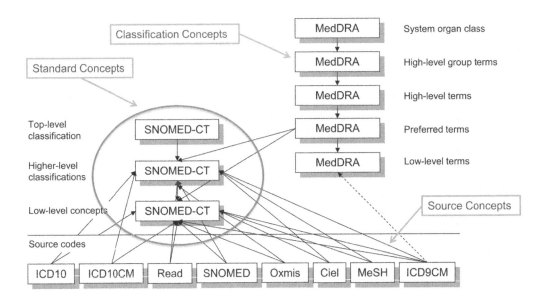

Figure 5.4: Standard, non-standard source and classification concepts and their hierarchical relationships in the condition domain. SNOMED is used for most standard condition concepts (with some oncology-related concepts derived from ICDO3), MedDRA concepts are used for hierarchical classification concepts, and all other vocabularies contain non-standard or source concepts, which do not participate in the hierarchy.

are also called "source concepts". The conversion of source concepts to Standard Concepts is a process called "mapping" (see Section 5.3.1). Non-standard concepts have no value (NULL) In the STANDARD_CONCEPT field.

5.2.8   Classification Concepts

These concepts are not Standard, and hence cannot be used to represent the data. But they are participating in the hierarchy with the Standard Concepts, and can therefore be used to perform hierarchical queries. For example, querying for all descendants of MedDRA code 10037908 (not visible for users who have not obtained a MedDRA license, see Section 5.1.2 for access restrictions) will retrieve the Standard SNOMED concept for Atrial Fibrillation (see Section 5.4 for hierarchical queries using the CONCEPT_ANCESTOR table) - see Figure 5.4.

The choice of concept designation as Standard, non-standard and classification is typically done for each domain separately at the vocabulary level. This is based on the quality of the concepts, the built-in hierarchy and the declared purpose of the vocabulary. Also, not all concepts of a vocabulary are used as Standard Concepts. The designation is separate for each domain, each concept has to be active (see Section 5.2.10) and there might be an order of precedence if more than one concept from different vocabularies compete for the same meaning. In other words, there is no such a thing as a "standard vocabulary." See Table 5.2 for examples.

Table 5.2: List of vocabularies to utilize for Standard/non-standard/classification concept assignments.

Domain	for Standard Concepts	for source concepts	for classification concepts
Condition	SNOMED, ICDO3	SNOMED Veterinary	MedDRA
Procedure	SNOMED, CPT4, HCPCS, ICD10PCS, ICD9Proc, OPCS4	SNOMED Veterinary, HemOnc, NAACCR	None at this point
Measurement	SNOMED, LOINC	SNOMED Veterinary, NAACCR, CPT4, HCPCS, OPCS4, PPI	None at this point
Drug	RxNorm, RxNorm Extension, CVX	HCPCS, CPT4, HemOnc, NAAACCR	ATC
Device	SNOMED	Others, currently not normalized	None at this point
Observation	SNOMED	Others	None at this point
Visit	CMS Place of Service, ABMT, NUCC	SNOMED, HCPCS, CPT4, UB04	None at this point

5.2.9 Concept Codes

Concept codes are the identifiers used in the source vocabularies. For example, ICD9CM or NDC codes are stored in this field, while the OMOP tables use the concept ID as a foreign key into the CONCEPT table. The reason is that the name space overlaps across vocabularies, i.e. the same code can exist in different vocabularies with completely different meanings (see Table 5.3)

Table 5.3: Concepts with identical concept code 1001, but different vocabularies, domains and concept classes.

Concept ID	Concept Code	Concept Name	Domain ID	Vocabulary ID	Concept Class
35803438	1001	Granulocyte colony-stimulating factors	Drug	HemOnc	Component Class
35942070	1001	AJCC TNM Clin T	Measurement	NAACCR	NAACCR Variable
1036059	1001	Antipyrine	Drug	RxNorm	Ingredient
38003544	1001	Residential Treatment - Psychiatric	Revenue Code	Revenue Code	Revenue Code

Concept ID	Concept Code	Concept Name	Domain ID	Vocabulary ID	Concept Class
43228317	1001	Aceprometazine maleate	Drug	BDPM	Ingredient
45417187	1001	Brompheniramine Maleate, 10 mg/mL injectable solution	Drug	Multum	Multum
45912144	1001	Serum	Specimen	CIEL	Specimen

5.2.10 Life-Cycle

Vocabularies are rarely permanent corpora with a fixed set of codes. Instead, codes and concepts are added and get deprecated. The OMOP CDM is a model to support longitudinal patient data, which means it needs to support concepts that were used in the past and might no longer be active, as well as supporting new concepts and placing them into context. There are three fields in the CONCEPT table that describe the possible life-cycle statuses: VALID_START_DATE, VALID_END_DATE, and INVALID_REASON. Their values differ depending on the concept life-cycle status:

- **Active or new concept**
  - Description: Concept in use.
  - VALID_START_DATE: Day of instantiation of concept, if that is not known day of incorporation of concept in Vocabularies, if that is not known 1970-1-1.
  - VALID_END_DATE: Set to 2099-12-31 as a convention to indicate "Might become invalid in an undefined future, but active right now".
  - INVALID_REASON: NULL
- **Deprecated Concept with no successor**
  - Description: Concept inactive and cannot be used as Standard (see Section 5.2.6).
  - VALID_START_DATE: Day of instantiation of concept, if that is not known day of incorporation of concept in Vocabularies, if that is not known 1970-1-1.
  - VALID_END_DATE: Day in the past indicating deprecation, or if that is not known day of vocabulary refresh where concept in vocabulary went missing or set to inactive.
  - INVALID_REASON: "D"
- **Upgraded Concept with successor**
  - Description: Concept inactive, but has defined successor. These are typically concepts which went through de-duplication.
  - VALID_START_DATE: Day of instantiation of concept, if that is not known day of incorporation of concept in Vocabularies, if that is not known 1970-1-1.
  - VALID_END_DATE: Day in the past indicating an upgrade, or if that is not

known day of vocabulary refresh where the upgrade was included.
    – INVALID_REASON: "U"
- **Reused code for another new concept**
    – Description: The vocabulary reused the concept code of this deprecated concept for a new concept.
    – VALID_START_DATE: Day of instantiation of concept, if that is not known day of incorporation of concept in Vocabularies, if that is not known 1970-1-1.
    – VALID_END_DATE: Day in the past indicating deprecation, or if that is not known day of vocabulary refresh where concept in vocabulary went missing or set to inactive.
    – INVALID_REASON: "R"

In general, concept codes are not reused. But there are a few vocabularies that deviate from this rule, in particular HCPCS, NDC and DRG. For those, the same concept code appears in more than one concept of the same vocabulary. Their CONCEPT_ID value stays unique. These reused concept codes are marked with an "R" in the INVALID_REASON field, and the VALID_START_DATE to VALID_END_DATE period should be used to distinguish concepts with the same concept codes.

5.3 Relationships

Any two concepts can have a defined relationship, regardless of whether the two concepts belong to the same domain or vocabulary. The nature of the relationships is indicated in its short case-sensitive unique alphanumeric ID in the RELATIONSHIP_ID field of the CONCEPT_RELATIONSHIP table. Relationships are symmetrical, i.e. for each relationship an equivalent relationship exists, where the content of the fields CONCEPT_ID_1 and CONCEPT_ID_2 are swapped, and the RELATIONHSIP_ID is changed to its opposite. For example, the "Maps to" relationship has an opposite relationship "Mapped from."

CONCEPT_RELATIONSHIP table records also have life-cycle fields RELATIONSHIP_START_DATE, RELATIONSHIP_END_DATE and INVALID_REASON. However, only active records with INVALID_REASON = NULL are available through ATHENA. Inactive relationships are kept in the Pallas system for internal processing only. The RELATIONSHIP table serves as the reference with the full list of relationship IDs and their reverse counterparts.

5.3.1 Mapping Relationships

These relationships provide translations from non-standard to Standard concepts, supported by two relationship ID pairs (see Table 5.4).

Table 5.4: Type of mapping relationships.

Relationship ID pair	Purpose
"Maps to" and "Mapped from"	Mapping to Standard Concepts. Standard Concepts are mapped to themselves, non-standard concepts to Standard Concepts. Most non-standard and all Standard Concepts have this relationship to a Standard Concept. The former are stored in *_SOURCE_CONCEPT_ID, and the latter in the *_CONCEPT_ID fields. Classification concepts are not mapped.
"Maps to value" and "Value mapped from"	Mapping to a concept that represents a Value to be placed into the VALUE_AS_CONCEPT_ID fields of the MEASUREMENT and OBSERVATION tables.

The purpose of these mapping relationships is to allow a crosswalk between equivalent concepts to harmonize how clinical events are represented in the OMOP CDM. This is a main achievement of the Standardized Vocabularies.

"Equivalent concepts" means it carries the same meaning, and, importantly, the hierarchical descendants cover the same semantic space. If an equivalent concept is not available and the concept is not Standard, it is still mapped, but to a slightly broader concept (so-called "up-hill mappings"). For example, ICD10CM W61.51 "Bitten by goose" has no equivalent in the SNOMED vocabulary, which is generally used for standard condition concepts. Instead, it is mapped to SNOMED 217716004 "Peck by bird," losing the context of the bird being a goose. Up-hill mappings are only used if the loss of information is considered irrelevant to standard research use cases.

Some mappings connect a source concept to more than one Standard Concept. For example, ICD9CM 070.43 "Hepatitis E with hepatic coma" is mapped to both SNOMED 235867002 "Acute hepatitis E" as well as SNOMED 72836002 "Hepatic Coma." The reason for this is that the original source concept is a pre-coordinated combination of two conditions, hepatitis and coma. SNOMED does not have that combination, which results in two records written for the ICD9CM record, one with each mapped Standard Concept.

Relationships "Maps to value" have the purpose of splitting of a value for OMOP CDM tables following an entity-attribute-value (EAV) model. This is typically the case in the following situations:

- Measurements consisting of a test and a result value
- Personal or family disease history
- Allergy to substance
- Need for immunization

In these situations, the source concept is a combination of the attribute (test or history) and the value (test result or disease). The "Maps to" relationship maps this source to the attribute concept, and the "Maps to value" to the value concept. See Figure 5.5 for an example.

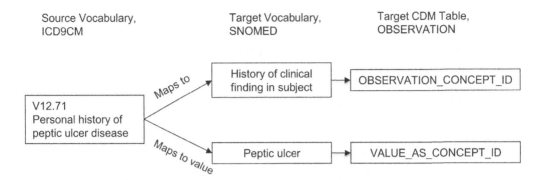

Figure 5.5: One-to-many mapping between source concept and Standard Concepts. A pre-coordinated concept is split into two concepts, one of which is the attribute (here history of clinical finding) and the other one is the value (peptic ulcer). While "Maps to" relationship will map to concepts of the measurement or observation domains, the 'Maps to value" concepts have no domain restriction.

Mapping of concepts is another central feature of the OMOP Standardized Vocabularies provided for free and supporting the efforts of the community conducting Network Studies. Mapping relationships are derived from external sources or maintained manually by the Vocabulary Team. This means they are not perfect. If you find wrong or objectionable mapping relationships it is crucial that you report and help improve the process through a Forums or CDM issue post.

A more detailed description of mapping conventions can be found in the OHDSI Wiki.[5]

5.3.2 Hierarchical Relationships

Relationships which indicate a hierarchy are defined through the "Is a" - "Subsumes" relationship pair. Hierarchical relationships are defined such that the child concept has all the attributes of the parent concept, plus one or more additional attributes or a more precisely defined attribute. For example, SNOMED 49436004 "Atrial fibrillation" is related to SNOMED 17366009 "Atrial arrhythmia" through a "Is a" relationship. Both concepts have an identical set of attributes except the type of arrhythmia, which is defined as fibrillation in one but not the other. Concepts can have more than one parent and more than one child concept. In this example, SNOMED 49436004 "Atrial fibrillation" is also an "Is a" to SNOMED 40593004 "Fibrillation."

5.3.3 Relationships Between Concepts of Different Vocabularies

These relationships are typically of the type "Vocabulary A - Vocabulary B equivalent", which is either supplied by the original source of the vocabulary or is built by the OHDSI

---

[5]https://www.ohdsi.org/web/wiki/doku.php?id=documentation:vocabulary:mapping

Vocabulary team. They may serve as approximate mappings but often times are less precise than the better curated mapping relationships. High-quality equivalence relationships (such as "Source - RxNorm equivalent") are always duplicated by "Maps to" relationship.

5.3.4 Relationships Between Concepts of the Same Vocabulary

Internal vocabulary relationships are usually supplied by the vocabulary provider. Full descriptions can be found in the vocabulary documentation under the individual vocabulary at the OHDSI Wiki.[6]

Many of these define relationships between clinical events and can be used for information retrieval. For example, disorders of the urethra can be found by following the "Finding site of" relationship (see Table 5.5):

Table 5.5: "Finding site of" relationship of the "Urethra," indicating conditions that are situated all in the this anatomical structure.

CONCEPT_ID_1	CONCEPT_ID_2
4000504 "Urethra part"	36713433 "Partial duplication of urethra"
4000504 "Urethra part"	433583 "Epispadias"
4000504 "Urethra part"	443533 "Epispadias, male"
4000504 "Urethra part"	4005956 "Epispadias, female"

The quality and comprehensiveness of these relationships varies depending on the quality in the original vocabulary. Generally, vocabularies that are used to draw Standard Concepts from, such as SNOMED, are chosen for the reason of their better curation and therefore tend to have higher quality internal relationships as well.

5.4 Hierarchy

Within a domain, standard and classification concepts are organized in a hierarchical structure and stored in the CONCEPT_ANCESTOR table. This allows querying and retrieving concepts and all their hierarchical descendants. These descendants have the same attributes as their ancestor, but also additional or more defined ones.

The CONCEPT_ANCESTOR table is built automatically from the CONCEPT_RELATIONSHIP table traversing all possible concepts connected through hierarchical relationships. These are the "Is a" - "Subsumes" pairs (see Figure 5.6), and other relationships connecting hierarchies across vocabularies. The choice whether a relationship participates in the hierarchy constructor is defined for each relationship ID by the flag DEFINES_ANCESTRY in the RELATIONSHIP reference table.

---

[6]https://www.ohdsi.org/web/wiki/doku.php?id=documentation:vocabulary

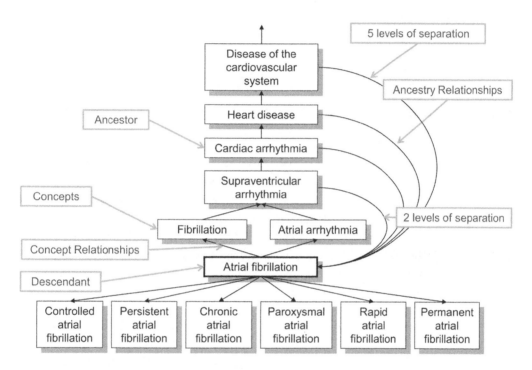

Figure 5.6: Hierarchy of the condition "Atrial fibrillation." First degree ancestry is defined through "Is a" and "Subsumes" relationships, while all higher degree relations are inferred and stored in the CONCEPT_ANCESTOR table. Each concept is also its own descendant with both levels of separation equal to 0.

The ancestral degree, or the number of steps between ancestor and descendant, is captured in the MIN_LEVELS_OF_SEPARATION and MAX_LEVELS_OF_SEPARATION fields, defining the shortest or longest possible connection. Not all hierarchical relationships contribute equally to the levels-of-separation calculation. A step counted for the degree is determined by the IS_HIERARCHICAL flag in the RELATIONSHIP reference table for each relationship ID.

At the moment, a high-quality comprehensive hierarchy exists only for two domains: drug and condition. Procedure, measurement and observation domains are only partially covered and in the process of construction. The ancestry is particularly useful for the drug domain as it allows browsing all drugs with a given ingredient or members of drug classes irrespective of the country of origin, brand name or other attributes.

5.5   Internal Reference Tables

DOMAIN_ID, VOCABULARY_ID, CONCEPT_CLASS_ID (all in CONCEPT records) and CONCEPT_RELATIONSHIP_ID (in CONCEPT_RELATIONSHIP) are all controlled by their own vocabularies. They are defined in the four reference tables DOMAIN, VOCABULARY, CONCEPT_CLASS and RELATIONSHIP, containing the *_ID fields as primary keys, a more detailed *_NAME field and a *_CONCEPT_ID field with a reference back to the CONCEPT table, which contains a concept for each of the reference table records. The purpose of these duplicate records is to support an information model allowing for automatic navigation engines.

The VOCABULARY table also contains the VOCABULARY_REFERENCE and VOCABULARY_VERSION fields referring to the source and version of the original vocabulary. The RELATIONSHIP table has the additional fields DEFINES_ANCESTRY, IS_HIERARCHICAL and REVERSE_RELATIONSHIP_ID. The latter defines the counter relationship ID for a pair of relationships.

5.6   Special Situations

5.6.1   Gender

Gender in the OMOP CDM and Standardized Vocabularies denotes the biological sex at birth. Often, questions are posed how to define alternative genders. These use cases have to be covered through records in the OBSERVATION table, where the self-defined gender of a person is stored (if the data asset contains such information).

5.6.2 Race and Ethnicity

These follow the definitions of how the US government defines this. Ethnicity is a differentiation of Hispanic or non-Hispanic populations, which can have any race. Race is divided into the common 5 top races, which have ethnicities as their hierarchical descendants. Mixed races are not included.

5.6.3 Diagnostic Coding Schemes and OMOP Conditions

Commonly used coding schemes such as ICD-9 or ICD-10 define more or less well-defined diagnoses based on a proper diagnostic work-up. The condition domain is not identical with this semantic space, but partially overlapping. For example, conditions also contain signs and symptoms that are recorded before a diagnosis is derived, and ICD codes contain concepts that belong to other domains (e.g. procedures).

5.6.4 Procedure Coding Systems

Similarly, coding schemes like HCPCS and CPT4 are thought to be listings of medical procedures. In reality, they are more like a menu of justifications for payment for medical service. Many of these services are subsumed under the procedure domain, but many concepts fall outside this realm.

5.6.5 Devices

Device concepts have no standardized coding scheme that could be used to source Standard Concepts. In many source data, devices are not even coded or contained in an external coding scheme. For this same reason, there is currently no hierarchical system available.

5.6.6 Visits and Services

Visits concepts define the nature of healthcare encounters. In many source systems they are called Place of Service, denoting some organization or physical structure, such as a hospital. In others, they are called services. These also differ between countries, and their definition is hard to obtain. Care sites are often specializing on one of few visits (XYZ Hospital), but still should not be defined by them (even in XYZ hospital patients might encounter non-hospital visits).

5.6.7 Providers and Specialties

Any human provider is defined in the provider domain. These can be medical professionals such as doctors and nurses, but also non-medical providers like optometrists or shoemakers.

Specialties are descendants of the provider "Physician." Care Sites cannot carry a specialty, even though they are often defined by the specialty of their main staff ("Surgical department").

5.6.8 Therapeutic Areas With Special Requirements

The Standardized Vocabularies cover all aspects of healthcare in a comprehensive fashion. However, some therapeutic areas have special needs and require special vocabularies. Examples are oncology, radiology, and genomics. Special OHDSI Working Groups develop these extensions. As a result, the OMOP Standardized Vocabularies constitutes an integrated system, where concepts from different origins and purposes all reside in the same domain-specific hierarchies.

5.6.9 Standard Concepts in the Drug Domain

Many concepts of the drug domain are sourced from RxNorm, a publicly available vocabulary produced by the US National Library of Medicine. However, drugs outside the US may or may not be covered, depending on whether or not the combination of ingredient, form and strength is marketed in the US. Drugs that are not on the US market are added by the OHDSI Vocabulary Team under a vocabulary called RxNorm Extension, which is the only large domain vocabulary produced by OHDSI.

5.6.10 Flavors of NULL

Many vocabularies contain codes about absence of information. For example, of the five gender concepts 8507 "Male," 8532 "Female," 8570 "Ambiguous," 8551 "Unknown," and 8521 "Other", only the first two are Standard, and the other three are source concepts with no mapping. In the Standardized Vocabularies, there is no distinction made why a piece of information is not available; it might be because of an active withdrawal of information by the patient, a missing value, a value that is not defined or standardized in some way, or the absence of a mapping record in CONCEPT_RELATIONSHIP. Any such concept is not mapped, which corresponds to a default mapping to the Standard Concept with the concept ID = 0.

5.7 Summary

- All events and administrative facts are represented in the OMOP Standardized Vocabularies as concepts, concept relationships, and concept ancestor hierarchy.
- Most of these are adopted from existing coding schemes or vocabularies, while some of them are curated de-novo by the OHDSI Vocabulary Team.

– All concepts are assigned a domain, which controls where the fact represented by the concept is stored in the CDM.

– Concepts of equivalent meaning in different vocabularies are mapped to one of them, which is designated the Standard Concept. The others are source concepts.

– Mapping is done through the concept relationships "Maps to" and "Maps to value".

– There is an additional class of concepts called classification concepts, which are non-standard, but in contrast to source concepts they participate in the hierarchy.

– Concepts have a life-cycle over time.

– Concepts within a domain are organized into hierarchies. The quality of the hierarchy differs between domains, and the completion of the hierarchy system is an ongoing task.

– You are strongly encouraged to engage with the community if you believe you found a mistake or inaccuracy.

5.8 Exercises

Prerequisites

For these first exercises you will need to look up concepts in the Standardized Vocabularies, which can be done through ATHENA[7] or ATLAS.[8]

Exercise 5.1. What is the Standard Concept ID for "Gastrointestinal hemorrhage"?

Exercise 5.2. Which ICD-10CM codes map to the Standard Concept for "Gastrointestinal hemorrhage"? Which ICD-9CM codes map to this Standard Concept?

Exercise 5.3. What are the MedDRA preferred terms that are equivalent to the Standard Concept for "Gastrointestinal hemorrhage"?

Suggested answers can be found in Appendix E.2.

---

[7]http://athena.ohdsi.org/
[8]http://atlas-demo.ohdsi.org

Chapter 6

Extract Transform Load

Chapter leads: Clair Blacketer & Erica Voss

6.1 Introduction

In order to get from the native/raw data to the OMOP Common Data Model (CDM) we have to create an extract, transform, and load (ETL) process. This process should restructure the data to the CDM, and add mappings to the Standardized Vocabularies, and is typically implemented as a set of automated scripts, for example SQL scripts. It is important that this ETL process is repeatable, so that it can be rerun whenever the source data is refreshed.

Creating an ETL is usually a large undertaking. Over the years, we have developed best practices, consisting of four major steps:

1. Data experts and CDM experts together design the ETL.
2. People with medical knowledge create the code mappings.
3. A technical person implements the ETL.
4. All are involved in quality control.

In this chapter we will discuss each of these steps in detail. Several tools have been developed by the OHDSI community to support some of these steps, and these will be discussed as well. We close this chapter with a discussion of CDM and ETL maintenance.

6.2 Step 1: Design the ETL

It is important to clearly separate the design of the ETL from the implementation of the ETL. Designing the ETL requires extensive knowledge of both the source data, as well as the CDM. Implementing the ETL on the other hand typically relies mostly on technical expertise on how to make the ETL computationally efficient. If we try to do both at once, we are likely to get stuck in nitty-gritty details, while we should be focusing on the overall picture.

Two closely-integrated tools have been developed to support the ETL design process: White Rabbit, and Rabbit-in-a-Hat.

6.2.1   White Rabbit

To initiate an ETL process on a database you need to understand your data, including the tables, fields, and content. This is where the White Rabbit tool comes in. White Rabbit is a software tool to help prepare for ETLs of longitudinal healthcare databases into the OMOP CDM. White Rabbit scans your data and creates a report containing all the information necessary to begin designing the ETL. All source code and installation instructions, as well as a link to the manual, are available on GitHub.[1]

Scope and Purpose

White Rabbit's main function is to perform a scan of the source data, providing detailed information on the tables, fields, and values that appear in a field. The source data can be in comma-separated text files, or in a database (MySQL, SQL Server, Oracle, PostgreSQL, Microsoft APS, Microsoft Access, Amazon RedShift). The scan will generate a report that can be used as a reference when designing the ETL, for instance by using it in conjunction with the Rabbit-In-a-Hat tool. White Rabbit differs from standard data profiling tools in that it attempts to prevent the display of personally identifiable information (PII) data values in the generated output data file.

Process Overview

The typical sequence for using the software to scan source data:

1. Set working folder, the location on the local desktop computer where results will be exported.
2. Connect to the source database or CSV text file and test connection.
3. Select the tables of interest for the scan and scan the tables.
4. White Rabbit creates an export of information about the source data.

Setting a Working Folder

After downloading and installing the White Rabbit application, the first thing you need to do is set a working folder. Any files that White Rabbit creates will be exported to this local folder. Use the "Pick Folder" button shown in Figure 6.1 to navigate in your local environment where you would like the scan document to go.

---

[1] https://github.com/OHDSI/WhiteRabbit.

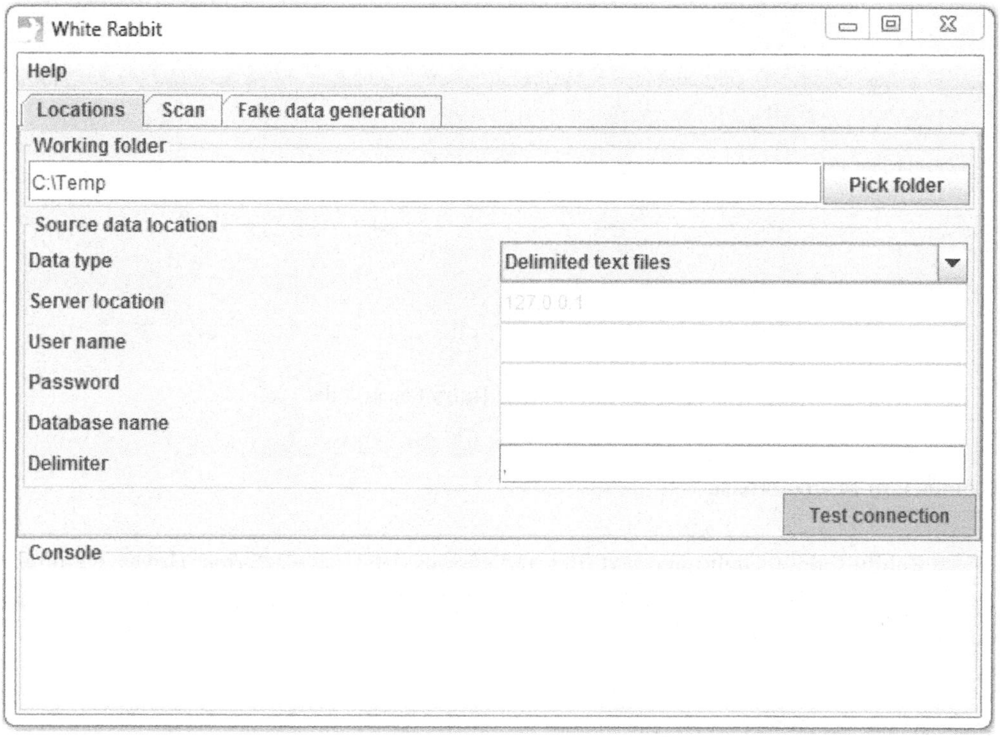

Figure 6.1: The "Pick Folder" button allows the specification of a working folder for the White Rabbit application.

Figure 6.2: White Rabbit Scan tab.

Connection to a Database

White Rabbit supports delimited text files and various database platforms. Hover the mouse over the various fields to get a description of what is required. More detailed information can be found in the manual.

Scanning the Tables in a Database

After connecting to a database, you can scan the tables contained therein. A scan generates a report containing information on the source data that can be used to help design the ETL. Using the Scan tab shown in Figure 6.2 you can either select individual tables in the selected source database by clicking on "Add" (Ctrl + mouse click), or automatically select all tables in the database by clicking on "Add all in DB".

There are a few setting options as well with the scan:

- Checking the "Scan field values" tells WhiteRabbit that you would like to investigate which values appear in the columns.
- "Min cell count" is an option when scanning field values. By default, this is set to 5, meaning values in the source data that appear less than 5 times will not appear in the report. Individual data sets may have their own rules about what this minimum cell

	A	B	C	D	E	F	G	
1	Table	Field	Type	Max length	N rows	N rows checked	Fraction empty	
2	dbo.allergies	start	date	10	3184	3184	0	
3	dbo.allergies	stop	date	10	3184	3184	0.725188442	
4	dbo.allergies	patient	varchar	36	3184	3184	0	
5	dbo.allergies	encounter	varchar	36	3184	3184	0	
6	dbo.allergies	code	varchar	9	3184	3184	0	
7	dbo.allergies	description	varchar	24	3184	3184	0	
8								
9	dbo.careplans	id	varchar	36	30199	30199	0	
10	dbo.careplans	start	date	10	30199	30199	0	
11	dbo.careplans	stop	date	10	30199	30199	0.057849598	
12	dbo.careplans	patient	varchar	36	30199	30199	0	
13	dbo.careplans	encounter	varchar	36	30199	30199	0	
14	dbo.careplans	code	varchar	15	30199	30199	0	
15	dbo.careplans	description	varchar	62	30199	30199	0	
16	dbo.careplans	reasoncode	varchar	9	30199	30199	0.050796384	
17	dbo.careplans	reasondescription	varchar	56	30199	30199	0.050796384	
18								

Overview | dbo.allergies | dbo.carepla ... (+)

Figure 6.3: Example overview tab from a scan report.

count can be.

- "Rows per table" is an option when scanning field values. By default, White Rabbit will scan 100,000 randomly selected rows in the table.

Once all settings are completed, press the "Scan tables" button. After the scan is completed the report will be written to the working folder.

Interpreting the Scan Report

Once the scan is complete, an Excel file is generated in the selected folder with one tab present for each table scanned as well as an overview tab. The overview tab lists all tables scanned, each field in each table, the data type of each field, the maximum length of the field, the number of rows in the table, the number of rows scanned, and how often each field was found to be empty. Figure 6.3. shows an example overview tab.

The tabs for each of the tables show each field, the values in each field, and the frequency of each value. Each source table column will generate two columns in the Excel. One column will list all distinct values that have a "Min cell count" greater than what was set at time of the scan. If a list of unique values was truncated, the last value in the list will be "List truncated"; this indicates that there are one or more additional unique source values that appear less than the number entered in the "Min cell count". Next to each distinct value will be a second column that contains the frequency (the number of times that value occurs in the sample). These two columns (distinct values and frequency) will repeat for all the source columns in the table profiled in the workbook.

The report is powerful in understanding your source data by highlighting what exists. For

	A	B
1	Sex	Frequency
2	2	61491
3	1	35401
4	List truncated...	

Figure 6.4: Example values for a single column.

example, if the results shown in Figure 6.4 were given back on the "Sex" column within one of the tables scanned, we can see that there were two common values (1 and 2) that appeared 61,491 and 35,401 times respectively. White Rabbit will not define 1 as male and 2 as female; the data holder will typically need to define source codes unique to the source system. However, these two values (1 & 2) are not the only values present in the data because we see this list was truncated. These other values appear with very low frequency (defined by "Min cell count") and often represent incorrect or highly suspicious values. When generating an ETL we should not only plan to handle the high-frequency gender concepts 1 and 2 but the other low-frequency values that exist within this column. For example, if those lower frequency genders were "NULL" we want to make sure the ETL can handle processing that data and knows what to do in that situation.

6.2.2   Rabbit-In-a-Hat

With the White Rabbit scan in hand, we have a clear picture of the source data. We also know the full specification of the CDM. Now we need to define the logic to go from one to the other. This design activity requires thorough knowledge of both the source data and the CDM. The Rabbit-in-a-Hat tools that comes with the White Rabbit software is specifically designed to support a team of experts in these areas. In a typical setting, the ETL design team sits together in a room, while Rabbit-in-a-Hat is projected on a screen. In a first round, the table-to-table mappings can be collaboratively decided, after which field-to-field mappings can be designed, while defining the logic by which values will be transformed.

Scope and Purpose

Rabbit-In-a-Hat is designed to read and display a White Rabbit scan document. White Rabbit generates information about the source data while Rabbit-In-a-Hat uses that information and through a graphical user interface to allow a user to connect source data to tables and columns within the CDM. Rabbit-In-a-Hat generates documentation for the ETL process, it does not generate code to create an ETL.

Process Overview

The typical sequence for using this software to generate documentation of an ETL:

1. Scanned results from WhiteRabbit completed.
2. Open scanned results; interface displays source tables and CDM tables.
3. Connect source tables to CDM tables where the source table provides information for that corresponding CDM table.
4. For each source table to CDM table connection, further define the connection with source column to CDM column detail.
5. Save Rabbit-In-a-Hat work and export to a MS Word document.

Writing ETL Logic

Once you have opened your White Rabbit scan report in Rabbit-In-a-Hat you are ready to begin designing and writing the logic for how to convert the source data to the OMOP CDM. As an example, the next few sections will depict how some of the tables in the Synthea[2] database might look during conversion.

General Flow of an ETL

Since the CDM is a person-centric model it is always a good idea to start mapping the PERSON table first. Every clinical event table (CONDITION_OCCURRENCE, DRUG_EXPOSURE, PROCEDURE_OCCURRENCE, etc.) refers to the PERSON table by way of the person_id so working out the logic for the PERSON table first makes it easier later on. After the PERSON table a good rule of thumb is to convert the OBSERVATION_PERIOD table next. Each person in a CDM database should have at least one OBSERVATION_PERIOD and, generally, most events for a person fall within this timeframe. Once the PERSON and OBSERVATION_PERIOD tables are done the dimensional tables like PROVIDER, CARE_SITE, and LOCATION are typically next. The final table logic that should be worked out prior to the clinical tables is VISIT_OCCURRENCE. Often this is the most complicated logic in the entire ETL and it is some of the most crucial since most events that occur during the course of a person's patient journey will happen during visits. Once those tables are finished it is your choice which CDM tables to map and in which order.

It is often the case that, during CDM conversion, you will need to make provisions for intermediate tables. This could be for assigning the correct VISIT_OCCURRENCE_IDs to events, or for mapping source codes to standard concepts (doing this step on the fly is often very slow). Intermediate tables are 100% allowed and encouraged. What is discouraged is the persistence and reliance on these intermediate tables once the conversion is complete.

---

[2] Synthea[TM] is a patient generator that aims to model real patients. Data are created based on parameters passed to the application. The structure of the data can be found here: https://github.com/synthetichealth/synthea/wiki.

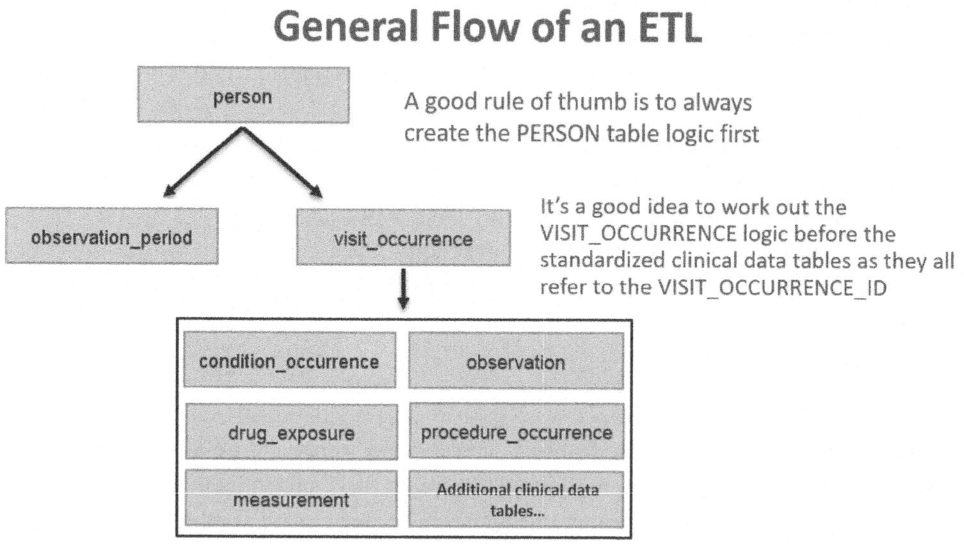

General Flow of an ETL

Figure 6.5: General flow of an ETL and which tables to map first.

Mapping Example: Person Table

The Synthea data structure contains 20 columns in the patients table but not all were needed to populate the PERSON table, as seen in Figure 6.6. This is very common and should not be cause for alarm. In this example many of the data points in the Synthea patients table that were not used in the CDM PERSON table were additional identifiers like patient name, driver's license number, and passport number.

Table 6.1 below shows the logic that was imposed on the Synthea patients table to convert it to the CDM PERSON table. The 'Destination Field' discusses where in the CDM data is being mapped to. The 'Source field' highlights the column from the source table (in this case patients) that will be used to populate the CDM column. Finally, the 'Logic & comments' column gives explanations for the logic.

Destination Field	Source field	Logic & comments

Table 6.1: ETL logic to convert the Synthea Patients table to CDM PERSON table.

Destination Field	Source field	Logic & comments
PERSON_ID		Autogenerate. The PERSON_ID will be generated at the time of implementation. This is because the id value from the source is a varchar value while the PERSON_ID is an integer. The id field from the source is set as the PERSON_SOURCE_VALUE to preserve that value and allow for error-checking if necessary.
GENDER_CONCEPT_ID	gender	When gender = 'M' then set GENDER_CONCEPT_ID to 8507, when gender = 'F' then set to 8532. Drop any rows with missing/unknown gender. These two concepts were chosen as they are the only two standard concepts in the gender domain. The choice to drop patients with unknown genders tends to be site-based, though it is recommended they are removed as people without a gender are excluded from analyses.
YEAR_OF_BIRTH	birthdate	Take year from birthdate
MONTH_OF_BIRTH	birthdate	Take month from birthdate
DAY_OF_BIRTH	birthdate	Take day from birthdate
BIRTH_DATETIME	birthdate	With midnight as time 00:00:00. Here, the source did not supply a time of birth so the choice was made to set it at midnight.
RACE_CONCEPT_ID	race	When race = 'WHITE' then set as 8527, when race = 'BLACK' then set as 8516, when race = 'ASIAN' then set as 8515, otherwise set as 0. These concepts were chosen because they are the standard concepts belonging to the race domain that most closely align with the race categories in the source.

Destination Field	Source field	Logic & comments
ETHNICITY_ CONCEPT_ID	race ethnicity	When race = 'HISPANIC', or when ethnicity in ('CENTRAL_AMERICAN', 'DOMINICAN', 'MEXICAN', 'PUERTO_RICAN', 'SOUTH_AMERICAN') then set as 38003563, otherwise set as 0. This is a good example of how multiple source columns can contribute to one CDM column. In the CDM ethnicity is represented as either Hispanic or not Hispanic so values from both the source column race and source column ethnicity will determine this value.
LOCATION_ID PROVIDER_ID CARE_SITE_ID		
PERSON_SOURCE_ VALUE	id	
GENDER_SOURCE_ VALUE	gender	
GENDER_SOURCE_ CONCEPT_ID		
RACE_SOURCE_ VALUE	race	
RACE_SOURCE_ CONCEPT_ID		
ETHNICITY_ SOURCE_VALUE	ethnicity	In this case the ETHNICITY_SOURCE_VALUE will have more granularity than the ETHNICITY_CONCEPT_ID.
ETHNICITY_ SOURCE_CONCEPT_ID		

For more examples on how the Synthea dataset was mapped to the CDM please see the full specification document.[3]

6.3   Step 2: Create the Code Mappings

More and more source codes are being added to the OMOP Vocabulary all the time. This means that the coding systems in the data being transformed to the CDM may already be

---

[3] https://ohdsi.github.io/ETL-Synthea/

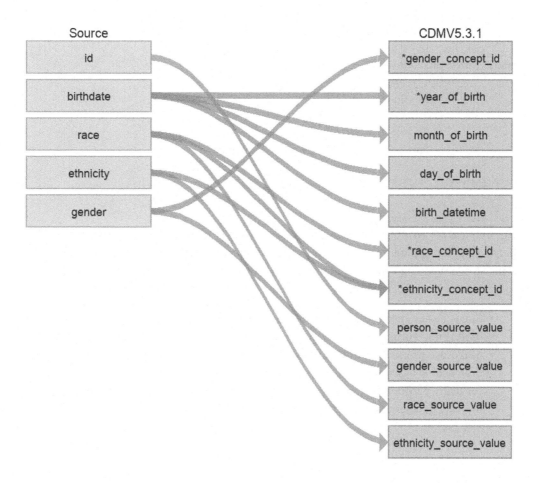

Figure 6.6: Mapping of Synthea Patients table to CDM PERSON table.

included and mapped. Check the VOCABULARY table in the OMOP Vocabulary to see which vocabularies are included. To extract the mapping from non-standard source codes (e.g. ICD-10CM codes) to standard concepts (e.g. SNOMED codes), we can use the records in the CONCEPT_RELATIONSHIP table having relationship_id = "Maps to". For example, to find the standard concept ID for the ICD-10CM code 'I21' ("Acute Myocardial Infarction"), we can use the following SQL:

```
SELECT concept_id_2 standard_concept_id
FROM concept_relationship
INNER JOIN concept source_concept
  ON concept_id = concept_id_1
WHERE concept_code = 'I21'
  AND vocabulary_id = 'ICD10CM'
  AND relationship_id = 'Maps to';
```

STANDARD_CONCEPT_ID
312327

Unfortunately, sometimes the source data uses coding systems that are not in the Vocabulary. In this case, a mapping must be created from the source coding system to the Standard Concepts. Code mapping can be a daunting task, especially when there are many codes in the source coding system. There are several things that can be done to make the task easier:

- Focus on the most frequently used codes. A code that is never used or infrequently used is not worth the effort of mapping, since it will never be used in a real study.
- Make use of existing information whenever possible. For example, many national drug coding systems have been mapped to ATC. Although ATC is not detailed enough for many purposes, the concept relationships between ATC and RxNorm can be used to make good guesses of what the right RxNorm codes are.
- Use Usagi.

6.3.1 Usagi

Usagi is a tool to aid the manual process of creating a code mapping. It can make suggested mappings based on textual similarity of code descriptions. If the source codes are only available in a foreign language, we have found that Google Translate[4] often gives surprisingly good translation of the terms into English. Usagi allows the user to search for the appropriate target concepts if the automated suggestion is not correct. Finally, the user can indicate which mappings are approved to be used in the ETL. Usagi is available on GitHub.[5]

---

[4]https://translate.google.com/
[5]https://github.com/OHDSI/Usagi

Scope and Purpose

Source codes that need mapping are loaded into the Usagi (if the codes are not in English additional translations columns are needed). A term similarity approach is used to connect source codes to Vocabulary concepts. However, these code connections need to be manually reviewed and Usagi provides an interface to facilitate that. Usagi will only propose concepts that are marked as Standard concepts in the Vocabulary.

Process Overview

The typical sequence for using this software is:

1. Load codes from your sources system ("source codes") that you would like to map to Vocabulary concepts.
2. Usagi will run term similarity approach to map source codes to Vocabulary concepts.
3. Leverage Usagi interface to check, and where needed, improve suggested mappings. Preferably an individual who has experience with the coding system and medical terminology should be used for this review.
4. Export mapping to the Vocabulary's SOURCE_TO_CONCEPT_MAP.

Importing Source Codes into Usagi

Export source codes from source system into a CSV or Excel (.xlsx) file. This should at least have columns containing the source code and an English source code description, however additional information about codes can be brought over as well (e.g. dose unit, or the description in the original language if translated). In addition to information about the source codes, the frequency of the code should preferably also be brought over, since this can help prioritize which codes should receive the most effort in mapping (e.g. you can have 1,000 source codes but only 100 are truly used within the system). If any source code information needs translating to English, use Google Translate to do that.

Note: source code extracts should be broken out by domain (i.e. drugs, procedures, conditions, observations) and not lumped into one large file.

Source codes are loaded into Usagi from the File –> Import codes menu. From here an "Import codes …" will display as seen in Figure 6.7. In this figure, the source code terms were in Dutch and were also translated into English. Usagi will leverage the English translations to map to the standard vocabulary.

The "Column mapping" section (bottom left) is where you define for Usagi how to use the imported table. If you mouse hover over the drop downs, a pop-up will appear defining each column. Usagi will not use the "Additional info" column(s) as information to associate source codes to Vocabulary concept codes; however, this additional information may help the individual reviewing the source code mapping and should be included.

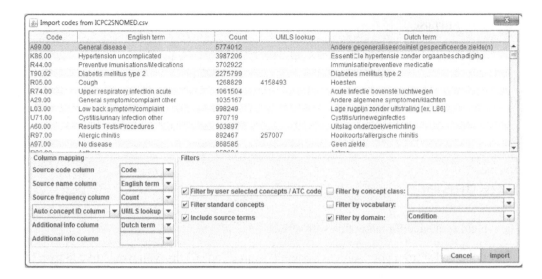

Figure 6.7: Usagi source code input screen.

Finally, in the "Filters" section (bottom right) you can set some restrictions for Usagi when mapping. For example, in Figure 6.7, the user is mapping the source codes only to concepts in the Condition domain. By default, Usagi only maps to Standard Concepts, but if the option "Filter standard concepts" is turned off, Usagi will also consider Classification Concepts. Hover your mouse over the different filters for additional information about the filter.

One special filter is "Filter by automatically selected concepts / ATC code". If there is information that you can use to restrict the search, you can do so by providing a list of CONCEPT_IDs or an ATC code in the column indicated in the Auto concept ID column (semicolon-delimited). For example, in the case of drugs there might already be ATC codes assigned to each drug. Even though an ATC code does not uniquely identify a single RxNorm drug code, it does help limit the search space to only those concepts that fall under the ATC code in the Vocabulary. To use the ATC code, follow these steps:

1. In the Column mapping section, switch from "Auto concept ID column" to "ATC column"
2. In the Column mapping section, select the column containing the ATC code as "ATC column".
3. Turn on the "Filter by user selected concepts / ATC code" on in the Filters section.

You can also use other sources of information than the ATC code to restrict as well. In the example shown in the figure above, we used a partial mapping derived from UMLS to restrict the Usagi search. In that case we will need to use "Auto concept ID column".

Once all your settings are finalized, click the "Import" button to import the file. The file import will take a few minutes as it is running the term similarity algorithm to map source codes.

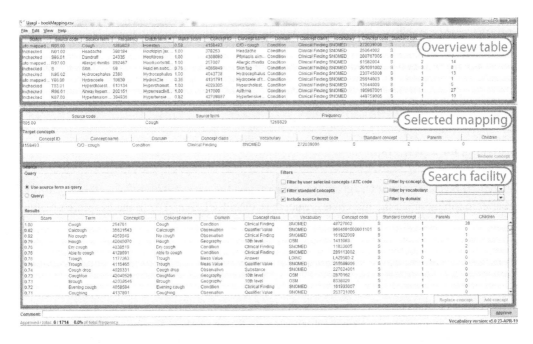

Figure 6.8: Usagi source code input screen.

Reviewing Source Code to Vocabulary Concept Maps

Once you have imported your input file of source codes, the mapping process begins. In Figure 6.8, you see the Usagi screen is made up of 3 main sections: an overview table, the selected mapping section, and place to perform searches. Note that in any of the tables, you can right-click to select the columns that are shown or hidden to reduce the visual complexity.

Approving a Suggested Mapping

The "Overview Table" shows the current mapping of source codes to concepts. Right after importing source codes, this mapping contains the automatically generated suggested mappings based on term similarity and any search options. In the example in Figure 6.8, the English names of Dutch condition codes were mapped to standard concepts in the Condition domain, because the user restricted the search to that domain. Usagi compared the source code descriptions to concept names and synonyms to find the best match. Because the user had selected "Include source terms" Usagi also considered the names and synonyms of all source concepts in the vocabulary that map to a particular concept. If Usagi is unable to make a mapping, it will map to the CONCEPT_ID = 0.

It is suggested that someone with experience with coding systems help map source codes to their associated standard vocabulary. That individual will work through code by code in the "Overview Table" to either accept the mapping Usagi has suggested or choose a new mapping. For example in Figure 6.8 we see that the Dutch term "Hoesten" which was translated to the English term "Cough". Usagi used "Cough" and mapped it to the Vocabulary concept of

"4158493-C/O - cough". There was a matching score of 0.58 associated to this matched pair (matching scores are typically 0 to 1 with 1 being a confident match), a score of 0.58 signifies that Usagi is not very sure of how well it has mapped this Dutch code to SNOMED. Let us say in this case, we are okay with this mapping, we can approve it by hitting the green "Approve" button in the bottom right hand portion of the screen.

Searching for a New Mapping

There will be cases where Usagi suggests a map and the user will be left to either try to find a better mapping or set the map to no concept (CONCEPT_ID = 0). In the example given in Figure 6.8, we see for the Dutch Term "Hoesten", which was translated to "Cough". Usagi's suggestion was restricted by the concept identified in our automatically derived mapping from UMLS, and the result might not be optimal. In the Search Facility, we could search for other concepts using either the actual term itself or a search box query.

When using the manual search box, one should keep in mind that Usagi uses a fuzzy search, and does not support structured search queries, so for example not supporting Boolean operators like AND and OR.

To continue our example, suppose we used the search term "Cough" to see if we could find a better mapping. On the right of the Query section of the Search Facility, there is a Filters section, this provides options to trim down the results from the Vocabulary when searching for the search term. In this case we know we want to only find standard concepts, and we allow concepts to be found based on the names and synonyms of source concepts in the vocabulary that map to those standard concepts.

When we apply these search criteria we find "254761-Cough" and feel this may be an appropriate Vocabulary concept to map to our Dutch code. In order to do that we can hit the "Replace concept" button, which you will see in the "Selected Source Code" section update, followed by the "Approve" button. There is also an "Add concept" button, this allows for multiple standardized Vocabulary concepts to map to one source code (e.g. some source codes may bundle multiple diseases together while the standardized vocabulary may not).

Concept Information

When looking for appropriate concepts to map to, it is important to consider the "social life" of a concept. The meaning of a concept might depend partially on its place in the hierarchy, and sometimes there are "orphan concepts" in the vocabulary with few or no hierarchical relationships, which would be ill-suited as target concepts. Usagi will often report the number of parents and children a concept has, and it also possible to show more information by pressing ALT + C or selecting view –> Concept information in the top menu bar.

Figure 6.9 shows the concept information panel. It shows general information about a concept, as well as its parents, children, and other source codes that map to the concept. Users can use this panel to navigate the hierarchy and potentially choose a different target concept.

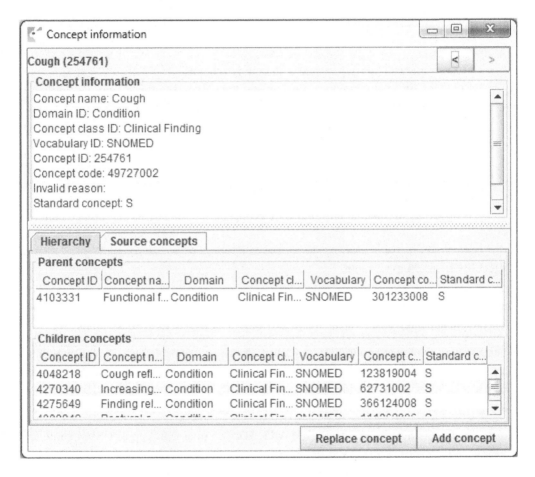

Figure 6.9: Usagi concept information panel.

Continue to move through this process, code by code, until all codes have been checked. In the list of source codes at the top of the screen, by selecting the column heading you can sort the codes. Often, we suggest going from the highest frequency codes to the lowest. In the bottom left of the screen you can see the number of codes that have approved mappings, and how many code occurrences that corresponds to.

It is possible to add comments to mappings, which could be used to document why a mapping decision was made.

Best Practices

- Use someone who has experience with coding schemes.
- By clicking on a column name, you can sort the columns in the "Overview Table". It may be valuable to sort on "Match Score"; reviewing codes that Usagi is most confident on first may quickly knock out a significant chunk of codes. Also sorting on "Frequency" is valuable, spending more effort on frequent codes versus non-frequent is important.
- It is okay to map some codes to CONCEPT_ID = 0, some codes may not be worth it to find a good map and others may just lack a proper map.
- It is important to consider the context of a concept, specifically its parents and children.

Export the Usagi Map Created

Once you have created your map within USAGI, the best way to use it moving forward is to export it and append it to the Vocabulary SOURCE_TO_CONCEPT_MAP table.

To export your mappings, go to File –> Export source_to_concept_map. A pop-up will appear asking you which SOURCE_VOCABULARY_ID you would like to use, type in a short identifier. Usagi will use this identifier. as the SOURCE_VOCABULARY_ID which will allow you to identify your specific mapping in the SOURCE_TO_CONCEPT_MAP table.

After selecting the SOURCE_VOCABULARY_ID, you give your export CSV a name and save to location. The export CSV structure is in that of the SOURCE_TO_CONCEPT_MAP table. This mapping could be appended to the Vocabulary's SOURCE_TO_CONCEPT_MAP table. It would also make sense to append a single row to the VOCABULARY table defining the SOURCE_VOCABULARY_ID you defined in the step above. Finally, it is important to note that only mappings with the "Approved" status will be exported into the CSV file; the mapping needs to be completed in USAGI in order to export it.

Updating an Usagi Mapping

Often a mapping is not a one-time effort. As data is updated perhaps new source codes are added, and the vocabulary is updated regularly, perhaps requiring an update of the mapping.

When the set of source codes is updated the following steps can be followed to support the update:

1. Import the new source code file
2. Choose File –> Apply previous mapping, and select the old Usagi mapping file
3. Identify codes that haven't inherited approved mappings from the old mapping, and map them as usual.

When the vocabulary is updated, follow these steps:

1. Download the new vocabulary files from Athena
2. Rebuild the Usagi index (Help –> Rebuild index)
3. Open the mapping file
4. Identify codes that map to concepts that in the new vocabulary version no longer are Standard concepts, and find more appropriate target concepts.

6.4 Step 3: Implement the ETL

Once the design and code mappings are completed, the ETL process can be implemented in a piece of software. When the ETL was being designed we recommended that people who are knowledgeable about the source and CDM work together on the task. Similarly, when the ETL is being implemented it is preferred to use people who have experience with working with data (particularly large data) and experience with implementing ETLs. This may mean working with individuals outside of your immediate group or hiring technical consultants to execute the implementation. It is also important to note that this is not a one-time expense. Moving forward it would be good to have someone or a team who spends at least some dedicated time to maintaining and running the ETL (this will become clearer in Section 6.7).

Implementation usually varies site to site and it largely depends on many factors including infrastructure, size of the database, the complexity of the ETL, and the technical expertise available. Because it depends on many factors the OHDSI community does not make a formal recommendation on how best to implement an ETL. There have been groups that use simple SQL builders, SAS, C#, Java, and Kettle. All have their advantages and disadvantages, and none are usable if there is nobody at the site who is familiar with the technology.

A few examples of different ETLs (listed in order of complexity):

- ETL-Synthea - A SQL builder written to convert the Synthea database
    - https://github.com/OHDSI/etl-synthea
- ETL-CDMBuilder - A .NET application designed to transform multiple databases
    - https://github.com/OHDSI/etl-cdmbuilder
- ETL-LambdaBuilder - A builder using the AWS lambda functionality
    - https://github.com/OHDSI/etl-lambdabuilder

It should be noted that after several independent attempts, we have given up on developing the 'ultimate' user-friendly ETL tool. It is always the case that tools like that work well for

80% of the ETL, but for the remaining 20% of the ETL some low-level code needs to be written that is specific to a source database

Once the technical individuals are ready to start implementing, the ETL design document should be shared with them. There should be enough information in the documentation for them to get started however it should be expected that the developers have access to the ETL designers to ask questions during their development process. Logic that may be clear to the designers may be less clear to an implementer who might not be familiar with the data and CDM. The implementation phase should remain a team effort. It is considered acceptable practice to go through the process of CDM creation and testing between the implementers and designers, respectively, until both groups are in agreement that all logic has been executed correctly.

6.5   Step 4: Quality Control

For the extract, transform, load process, quality control is iterative. The typical pattern is to write logic -> implement logic -> test logic -> fix/write logic. There are many ways to go about testing a CDM but below are recommend steps that have been developed across the community through years of ETL implementation.

- Review of the ETL design document, computer code, and code mappings. Any one person can make mistakes, so always at least one other person should review what the what was done.
  - The largest issues in the computer code tend to come from how the source codes in the native data are mapped to Standard Concepts. Mapping can get tricky, especially when it comes to date-specific codes like NDCs. Be sure to double check any area where mappings are done to ensure the correct source vocabularies are translated to the proper concept id.

- Manually compare all information on a sample of persons in the source and target data.
  - It can be helpful to walk through one person's data, ideally a person with a large number of unique records. Tracing through a single person can highlight issues if the data in the CDM is not how you expect it to look based on the agreed upon logic.
- Compare overall counts in the source and target data.
  - There may be some expected differences in counts depending on how you chose to address certain issues. For instance, some collaborators choose to drop any people with a NULL gender since those people will not be included in analyses anyway. It may also be the case that visits in the CDM are constructed differently than visits or encounters in the native data. Therefore, when comparing overall counts between the source and CDM data be sure to account for and expect these differences.

- Replicate a study that has already been performed on the source data on the CDM version.
  - This is a good way to understand any major differences between the source data and CDM version, though it is a little more time-intensive.
- Create unit tests meant to replicate a pattern in the source data that should be addressed in the ETL. For example, if your ETL specifies that patients without gender information should be dropped, create a unit test of a person without a gender and assess how the builder handles it.
  - Unit testing is very handy when evaluating the quality and accuracy of an ETL conversion. It usually involves creating a much smaller dataset that mimics the structure of the source data you are converting. Each person or record in the dataset should test a specific piece of logic as written in the ETL document. Using this method, it is easy to trace back issues and to identify failing logic. The small size also enables the computer code to execute very quickly allowing for faster iterations and error identification.

These are high-level ways to approach quality control from an ETL standpoint. For more detail on the data quality efforts going on within OHDSI, please see Chapter 15.

6.6 ETL Conventions and THEMIS

As more groups converted data to the CDM it became apparent that conventions needed to be specified. For example, what should the ETL do in a situation where a person record lacks a birth year? The goal of the CDM is to standardized healthcare data however if every group handles data specific scenarios differently it makes it more difficult to systematically use data across the network.

The OHDSI community started documenting conventions to improve consistency across CDMs. These defined conventions, that the OHDSI community has agreed upon, can be found on the CDM Wiki.[6] Each CDM table has its own set of conventions that can be referred to when designing an ETL. For example, persons are allowed to be missing a birth month or day, but if they lack a birth year the person should be dropped. In designing an ETL, refer to the conventions to help make certain design decisions that will be consistent with the community.

While it will never be possible to document all possible data scenarios that exist and what to do when they occur, there is an OHDSI work group trying to document common scenarios. THEMIS[7] is made up of individuals in the community who gather conventions, clarify them, share them with the community for comment, and then document finalized conventions in the CDM Wiki. Themis is an ancient Greek Titaness of divine order, fairness, law, natural law, and custom which seemed a good fit for this groups remit. When performing an ETL, if there is a scenario that you are unsure how to handle, THEMIS recommends that a question about

---

[6]https://github.com/OHDSI/CommonDataModel/wiki].

[7]https://github.com/OHDSI/Themis

the scenario is posed on the OHDSI Forums.[8] Most likely if you have a question, others in the community probably have it as well. THEMIS uses these discussions, as well as work group meetings and face-to-face discussions, to help inform what other conventions need to be documented.

6.7   CDM and ETL Maintenance

It is no small effort to design the ETL, create the mappings, implement the ETL, and build out quality control measures. Unfortunately, the effort does not stop there. There is a cycle of ETL maintenance that is a continuous process after the first CDM is built. Some common triggers that require maintenance are: changes in the source data, a bug in the ETL, a new OMOP Vocabulary is released, or the CDM itself has changed or updated. If one of these triggers occur the following might need updating: the ETL documentation, the software programming running the ETL, and test cases and quality controls.

Often a healthcare data source is forever changing. New data might be available (e.g. a new column in the data might exist). Patience scenarios that never existed before suddenly do (e.g. a new patient who has a death record before they were born). Your understanding of the data may improve (e.g. some of the records around inpatient child birth come across as outpatient due to how claims are processed). Not all changes in the source data my trigger a change in the ETL processing of it, however at a bare minimum the changes that break the ETL processing will need to be addressed.

If bugs are found, they should be addressed. However, it is important to keep in mind that not all bugs are created equal. For example, let say in the COST table the column cost was being rounded to a whole digit (e.g. the source data had \$3.82 and this became \$4.00 in the CDM). If the primary researchers using the data were mostly performing characterizations of patient's drug exposures and conditions, a bug such as this is of little importance and can be addressed in the future. If the primary researchers using the data also included health economists, this would be a critical bug that need to be addressed immediately.

The OMOP Vocabulary is also ever changing just as our source data may be. In fact, the Vocabulary can have multiple releases in one given month as vocabularies update. Each CDM is run on a specific version of a Vocabulary and running on a newer improved Vocabulary could result in changes in how sources codes get mapped to in the standardized vocabularies. Often differences between Vocabularies are minor, so building a new CDM every time a new Vocabulary is release is not necessary. However, it is good practice to adopt a new Vocabulary once or twice a year which would require reprocessing the CDM again. It is rare are there changes in a new version of a Vocabulary that would require the ETL code itself to be updated.

The final trigger that could require CDM or ETL maintenance is when the common data model itself updates. As the community grows and new data requirements are found this may lead to additional data being stored in the CDM. This might mean data that you previously

---

[8]http://forums.ohdsi.org/

were not storing in the CDM might have a location in a new CDM version. Less frequently are changes to existing CDM structure, however it is a possibility. For example, the CDM is moved to adopting DATETIME fields over the original DATE fields would could cause an error in ETL processing. CDM versions are not released often and sites can choose when they migrate.

6.8   Final Thoughts on ETL

The ETL process is a difficult one to master for many reasons, not the least of which the fact that we are all working off unique source data, making it hard to create a "one-size-fits-all" solution. However, there are some hard won lessons we have learned over the years.

- The 80/20 rule. If you can avoid it do not spend too much time manually mapping source codes to concepts sets. Ideally, map the source codes that cover the majority of your data. This should be enough to get you started and you can address any remaining codes in the future based on use cases.
- It's ok if you lose data that is not of research quality. Often these are the records that would be discarded before starting an analysis anyway, we just remove them during the ETL process instead.
- A CDM requires maintenance. Just because you complete an ETL does not mean you do not need to touch it ever again. Your raw data might change, there might be a bug in the code, there may be new vocabulary or an update to the CDM. Plan for an allocate resources to these changes so your ETL is always up-to-date.
- For support with getting started with the OHDSI CDM, performing your database conversion, or running the analytics tools, please visit our Implementers Forum.[9]

6.9   Summary

- There is a generally agreed upon process for how to approach an ETL, including

  * Data experts and CDM experts together design the ETL
  * People with medical knowledge create the code mappings
  * A technical person implements the ETL
  * All are involved in quality control

- Tools have been developed by the OHDSI community to facilitate these steps and are freely available for use

- There are many ETL examples and agreed upon conventions you can use as a guide

---

[9]https://forums.ohdsi.org/c/implementers

6.10   Exercises

Exercise 6.1. Put the steps of the ETL process in the proper order:

   A) Data experts and CDM experts together design the ETL
   B) A technical person implements the ETL
   C) People with medical knowledge create the code mappings
   D) All are involved in quality control

Exercise 6.2. Using OHDSI resources of your choice, spot four issues with the PERSON record show in Table 6.3 (table abbreviated for space):

Table 6.3: A PERSON table.

Column	Value
PERSON_ID	A123B456
GENDER_CONCEPT_ID	8532
YEAR_OF_BIRTH	NULL
MONTH_OF_BIRTH	NULL
DAY_OF_BIRTH	NULL
RACE_CONCEPT_ID	0
ETHNICITY_CONCEPT_ID	8527
PERSON_SOURCE_VALUE	A123B456
GENDER_SOURCE_VALUE	F
RACE_SOURCE_VALUE	WHITE
ETHNICITY_SOURCE_VALUE	NONE PROVIDED

Exercise 6.3. Let us try to generate VISIT_OCCURRENCE records. Here is some example logic written for Synthea: Sort data in ascending order by PATIENT, START, END. Then by PERSON_ID, collapse lines of claim as long as the time between the END of one line and the START of the next is <=1 day. Each consolidated inpatient claim is then considered as one inpatient visit, set:

   • MIN(START) as VISIT_START_DATE
   • MAX(END) as VISIT_END_DATE
   • "IP" as PLACE_OF_SERVICE_SOURCE_VALUE

If you see a set of visits as shown in Figure 6.10 in your source data, how would you expect the resulting VISIT_OCCURRENCE record(s) to look in the CDM?

Suggested answers can be found in Appendix E.3.

Data Output Explain Messages Notifications Query History

	id character varying (1000)	start date	stop date	patient character varying (1000)	encounterclass character varying (1000)
1	12	2004-09-26	2004-09-27	11	inpatient
2	13	2004-09-27	2004-09-30	11	inpatient

Figure 6.10: Example source data.

Part III

Data Analytics

Chapter 7

Data Analytics Use Cases

Chapter lead: David Madigan

The OHDSI collaboration focuses on generating reliable evidence from real-world healthcare data, typically in the form of claims databases or electronic health record databases. The use cases that OHDSI focuses on fall into three major categories:

- Characterization
- Population-level estimation
- Patient-level prediction

We describe these in detail below. Note, for all the use cases, the evidence we generate inherits the limitations of the data; we discuss these limitations at length in the book section on Evidence Quality (Chapters 14 - 18)

7.1   Characterization

Characterization attempts to answer the question

> What happened to them?

We can use the data to provide answers to questions about the characteristics of the persons in a cohort or the entire database, the practice of healthcare, and study how these things change over time.

The data can provide answers to questions like:

- For patients newly diagnosed with atrial fibrillation, how many receive a prescription for warfarin?
- What is the average age of patients who undergo hip arthroplasty?
- What is the incidence rate of pneumonia in patients over 65 years old?

Typical characterization questions are formulated as:

- How many patients…?
- How often does…?
- What proportion of patients…?
- What is the distribution of values for lab…?
- What are the HbA1c levels for patients with…?
- What are the lab values for patients…?
- What is the median length of exposure for patients on….?
- What are the trends over time in…?
- What are other drugs that these patients are using?
- What are concomitant therapies?
- Do we have enough cases of…?
- Would it be feasible to study X…?
- What are the demographics of…?
- What are the risk factors of…? (if identifying a specific risk factor, maybe estimation, not prediction)
- What are the predictors of…?

And the desired output is:

- Count or percentage
- Averages
- Descriptive statistics
- Incidence rate
- Prevalence
- Cohort
- Rule-based phenotype
- Drug utilization
- Disease natural history
- Adherence
- Co-morbidity profile
- Treatment pathways
- Line of therapy

7.2 Population-Level Estimation

To a limited extent, the data can support causal inferences about the effects of healthcare interventions, answering the question

> What are the causal effects?

We would like to understand causal effects to understand consequences of actions. For example, if we decide to take some treatment, how does that change what happens to us in the future?

The data can provide answers to questions like:

- For patients newly diagnosed with atrial fibrillation, in the first year after therapy initiation, does warfarin cause more major bleeds than dabigatran?
- Does the causal effect of metformin on diarrhea vary by age?

Typical population-level effect estimation questions are formulated as:

- What is the effect of...?
- What if I do intervention...?
- Which treatment works better?
- What is the risk of X on Y?
- What is the time-to-event of...?

And the desired output is:

- Relative risk
- Hazards ratio
- Odds ratio
- Average treatment effect
- Causal effect
- Association
- Correlation
- Safety surveillance
- Comparative effectiveness

7.3 Patient-Level Prediction

Based on the collected patient health histories in the database, we can make patient-level predictions about future health events, answering the question

What will happen to me?

The data can provide answers to questions like:

- For a specific patient newly diagnosed with major depressive disorder, what is the probability the patient will attempt suicide in the first year following diagnosis?
- For a specific patient newly diagnosed with atrial fibrillation, in the first year after therapy initiation with warfarin, what is the probability the patient suffers an ischemic stroke?

Typical patient-level prediction questions are formulated as:

- What is the chance that this patient will...?
- Who are candidates for...?

And the desired output is:

- Probability for an individual
- Prediction model
- High/low risk groups

• Probabilistic phenotype

Population-level estimation and patient-level prediction overlap to a certain extent. For example, an important use case for prediction is to predict an outcome for a specific patient had drug A been prescribed and also predict the same outcome had drug B been prescribed. Let's assume that in reality only one of these drugs is prescribed (say drug A) so we get to see whether the outcome following treatment with A actually occurs. Since drug B was not prescribed, the outcome following treatment B, while predictable, is "counterfactual" since it is not ever observed. Each of these prediction tasks falls under patient-level prediction. However, the difference between (or ratio of) the two outcomes is a unit-level *causal* effect, and should be estimated using causal effect estimation methods instead.

> People have a natural tendency to erroneously interpret predictive models as if they are causal models. But a predictive model can only show correlation, never causation. For example, diabetic drug use might be a strong predictor for myocardial infarction (MI) because diabetes is a strong risk factor for MI. However, that does not mean that stopping the diabetic drugs will prevent MI!

7.4   Example Use Cases in Hypertension

You're a researcher interested in studying the effects of ACE inhibitor monotherapy vs. thiazide diuretic monotherapy on the outcomes of acute myocardial infarction and angioedema as first-line treatment for hypertension. You understand that based on the OHDSI literature, you are asking a population-level effect estimation question but first, you need to do some homework on how to characterize this particular treatment of interest.

7.4.1   Characterization Questions

Acute myocardial infarction is a cardiovascular complication that can occur in patients with high blood pressure, so effective treatment for hypertension should reduce the risk. Angioedema is a known side effect of ACE inhibitors, which is rare but potentially serious. You start by creating cohorts (see Chapter 10) for the exposures of interest (new users of ACE inhibitors and new users of thiazide diuretics). You perform a characterization (see Chapter 11) analysis to summarize baseline characteristics of these exposure populations, including demographics, co morbid conditions, and concomitant medications. You perform another characterization analysis to estimate the incidence of selected outcomes within these exposure populations. Here, you ask 'how often does 1) acute myocardial infarction and 2) angioedema occur during the period of exposure to ACE inhibitors and thiazide diuretics?' These characterizations allow us to assess the feasibility of conducting a population-level estimation study, to evaluate whether the two treatment groups are comparable, and to identify 'risk factors' that might predict which treatment choice that patients made.

7.4.2 Population-Level Estimation Question

The population-level effect estimation study (see Chapter 12) estimates the relative risk of ACE inhibitor vs, thiazide use for the outcomes of AMI and angioedema. Here, you further evaluate through study diagnostics and negative controls whether we can produce a reliable estimate of the average treatment effect.

7.4.3 Patient-Level Prediction Question

Independent of whether there is a causal effect of the exposures, you are also interested in trying to determine which patients are at highest risk of the outcomes. This is a patient-level prediction problem (see Chapter 13). Here, you develop a prediction model that evaluates: amongst the patients who are new users of ACE inhibitors, which patients are at highest risk of developing acute myocardial infarction during the 1 year after starting treatment. The model allows us to predict, for a patient who has just been prescribed ACE for the first time, based on events observed from their medical history, what is the chance that they will experience AMI in the next 1 year.

7.5 Limitations of Observational Research

There are many important healthcare questions for which OHDSI databases cannot provide answers. These include:

- Causal effects of interventions compared to placebo. Sometimes it is possible to consider the causal effect of a treatment as compared with non-treatment but not placebo treatment.
- Anything related to over-the-counter medications.
- Many outcomes and other variables are sparsely recorded if at all. These include mortality, behavioral outcomes, lifestyle, and socioeconomic status.
- Since patients tend to encounter the healthcare system only when they are unwell, measurement of the benefits of treatments can prove elusive.

7.5.1 Erroneous Data

Clinical data recorded in OHDSI databases can deviate from clinical reality. For example, a patient's record may include a code for myocardial infarction even though the patient never experienced a myocardial infarction. Similarly, a lab value may be erroneous or an incorrect code for a procedure may appear in the database. Chapters 15 and 16 discuss several of these issues and good practice aims to identify and correct for as many of these kinds of issues as possible. Nonetheless, erroneous data inevitably persist to some extent and can undermine the validity of subsequent analyses. An extensive literature focuses on adjustment of statistical inferences to account for errors-in-data - see, for example, Fuller (2009).

7.5.2 Missing Data

Missingness in OHDSI databases presents subtle challenges. A health event (e.g., prescription, laboratory value, etc.) that should be recorded in a database, but isn't, is "missing." The statistics literature distinguishes between types of missingness such as "missing completely at random," "missing at random," and "missing not at random" and methods of increasing complexity attempt to address these types. Perkins et al. (2017) provide a useful introduction to this topic.

7.6 Summary

- In observational research we distinguish three large categories of uses cases.

- **Characterization** aims to answer the questions "What happened to them?"

- **Population-level estimation** attempts to answer the question "What are the causal effects?"

- **Patient-level prediction** tries to answer "What will happen to me?"

- Prediction models are not causal models; There is no reason to believe that intervening on a strong predictor will impact the outcome.

- There are questions that cannot be answered using observational healthcare data.

7.7 Exercises

Exercise 7.1. Which use case categories do these questions belong to?

1. Compute the rate of gastrointestinal (GI) bleeding in patients recently exposed to NSAIDs.

2. Compute the probability that a specific patient experiences a GI bleed in the next year, based on their baseline characteristics.

3. Estimate the increased risk of GI bleeding due to diclofenac compared to celecoxib.

Exercise 7.2. You wish to estimate the increased risk of GI bleeding due to diclofenac compared to no exposure (placebo). Can this be done using observational healthcare data?

Suggested answers can be found in Appendix E.4.

Chapter 8

OHDSI Analytics Tools

Chapter leads: Martijn Schuemie & Frank DeFalco

OHDSI offers a wide range of open source tools to support various data-analytics use cases on observational patient-level data. What these tools have in common is that they can all interact with one or more databases using the Common Data Model (CDM). Furthermore, these tools standardize the analytics for various use cases; Rather than having to start from scratch, an analysis can be implemented by filling in standard templates. This makes performing analysis easier, and also improves reproducibility and transparency. For example, there appear to be a near-infinite number of ways to compute an incidence rate, but these can be specified in the OHDSI tools with a few choices, and anyone making those same choices will compute incidence rates the same way.

In this chapter we first describe various ways in which we can choose to implement an analysis, and what strategies the analysis can employ. We then review the various OHDSI tools and how they fit the various use cases.

8.1 Analysis Implementation

Figure 8.1 shows the various ways in which we can choose to implement a study against a database using the CDM.

There are three main approaches to implementing a study. The first is to write custom code that does not make use of any of the tools OHDSI has to offer. One could write a de novo analysis in R, SAS, or any other language. This provides the maximum flexibility, and may in fact be the only option if the specific analysis is not supported by any of our tools. However, this path requires a lot of technical skill, time, and effort, and as the analysis increases in complexity it becomes harder to avoid errors in the code.

The second approach involves developing the analysis in R, and making use of the packages in the OHDSI Methods Library. At a minimum, one could use the SqlRender and DatabaseC-

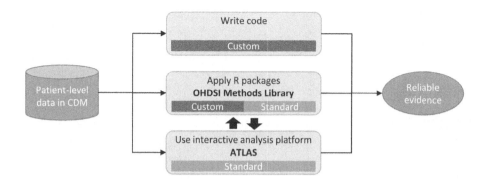

Figure 8.1: Different ways to implement an analysis against data in the CDM.

onnector packages described in more detail in Chapter 9 that allow the same code to be executed on various database platforms, such as PostgreSQL, SQL Server, and Oracle. Other packages such as CohortMethod and PatientLevelPrediction offer R functions for advanced analytics against the CDM that can be called on in one's code. This still requires a lot of technical expertise, but by re-using the validated components of the Methods Library we can be more efficient and less prone to error than when using completely custom code.

The third approach relies on our interactive analysis platform ATLAS, a web-based tool that allows non-programmers to perform a wide range of analyses efficiently. ATLAS makes use of the Methods Libraries but provides a simple graphical interface to design analyses and in many cases generate the necessary R code to run the analysis. However, ATLAS does not support all options available in the Methods Library. While it is expected that the majority of studies can be performed through ATLAS, some studies may require the flexibility offered by the second approach.

ATLAS and the Methods Library are not independent. Some of the more complicated analytics that can be invoked in ATLAS are executed through calls to the packages in the Methods Library. Similarly, cohorts used in the Methods Library are often designed in ATLAS.

8.2   Analysis Strategies

In addition to the strategy used to implement our analysis against the CDM, for example through custom coding or use of standard analytic code in the Methods Library, there are also multiple strategies for using those analytic techniques to generate evidence. Figure 8.2 highlights three strategies that are employed in OHDSI.

The first strategy views every analysis as a single individual study. The analysis must be pre-specified in a protocol, implemented as code, executed against the data, after which the result can be compiled and interpreted. For every question, all steps must be repeated. An example of such an analysis is the OHDSI study into the risk of angioedema associated with levetiracetam compared with phenytoin. (Duke et al., 2017) Here, a protocol was first written,

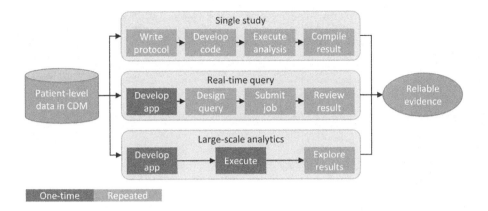

Figure 8.2: Strategies for generating evidence for (clinical) questions.

analysis code using the OHDSI Methods Library was developed and executed across the OHDSI network, and results were compiled and disseminated in a journal publication.

The second strategy develops an application that allows users to answer a specific class of questions in real time or near-real time. Once the application has been developed, users can interactively define queries, submit them, and view the results. An example of this strategy is the cohort definition and generation tool in ATLAS. This tool allows users to specify cohort definitions of varying complexity, and execute the definition against a database to see how many people meet the various inclusion and exclusion criteria.

The third strategy similarly focuses on a class of questions, but then attempts to exhaustively generate all the evidence for the questions within the class. Users can then explore the evidence as needed through a variety of interfaces. One example is the OHDSI study into the effects of depression treatments. (Schuemie et al., 2018b) In this study all depression treatments are compared for a large set of outcomes of interest across four large observational databases. The full set of results, including 17,718 empirically calibrated hazard ratios along with extensive study diagnostics, is available in an interactive web app.[1]

8.3 ATLAS

ATLAS is a free, publicly available, web-based tool developed by the OHDSI community that facilitates the design and execution of analyses on standardized, patient-level, observational data in the CDM format. ATLAS is deployed as a web application in combination with the OHDSI WebAPI and is typically hosted on Apache Tomcat. Performing real time analyses requires access to the patient-level data in the CDM and is therefore typically installed behind an organization's firewall. However, there is also a public ATLAS[2], and although this ATLAS instance only has access to a few small simulated datasets, it can still be used for many

---

[1] http://data.ohdsi.org/SystematicEvidence/
[2] http://www.ohdsi.org/web/atlas

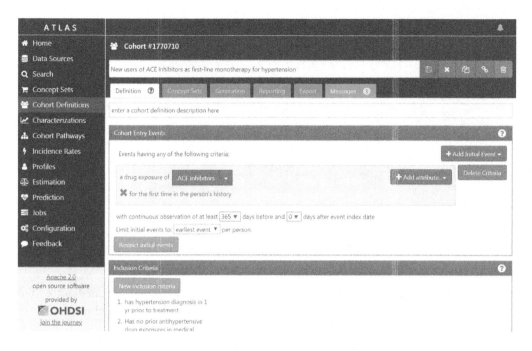

Figure 8.3: ATLAS user interface.

purposes including testing and training. It is even possible to fully define an effect estimation or prediction study using the public instance of ATLAS, and automatically generate the R code for executing the study. That code can then be run in any environment with an available CDM without needing to install ATLAS and the WebAPI.

A screenshot of ATLAS is provided in Figure 8.3. On the left is a navigation bar showing the various functions provided by ATLAS:

Data Sources Data sources provides the capability review descriptive, standardized reporting for each of the data sources that you have configured within your Atlas platform. This feature uses the large-scale analytics strategy: all descriptives have been precomputed. Data sources is discussed in Chapter 11.

Vocabulary Search Atlas provides the ability to search and explore the OMOP standardized vocabulary to understand what concepts exist within those vocabularies and how to apply those concepts in your standardized analysis against your data sources. This feature is discussed in Chapter 5.

Concept Sets Concept sets provides the ability to create collections of logical expressions that can be used to identify a set of concepts to be used throughout your standardized analyses. Concept sets provide more sophistication than a simple list of codes or values. A concept set is comprised of multiple concepts from the standardized vocabulary in combination with logical indicators that allow a user to specify that they are interested in including or excluding related concepts in the vocabulary hierarchy. Searching the vocabulary, identifying the set of concepts, and specifying the logic to be used to resolve a concept set provides a powerful mechanism for defining the often obscure medical language used in analysis plans. These concept sets can be saved within ATLAS and then used throughout your analysis as part of cohort definitions or analysis specifications.

Cohort Definitions   Cohort definitions is the ability to construct a set of persons who satisfy one or more criteria for a duration of time and these cohorts can then serve as the basis of inputs for all of your subsequent analyses. This feature is discussed in Chapter 10.

Characterizations   Characterizations is an analytic capability that allows you to look at one or more cohorts that you've defined and to summarize characteristics about those patient populations. This feature uses the real-time query strategy, and is discussed in Chapter 11.

Cohort Pathways   Cohort pathways is an analytic tool that allows you to look at the sequence of clinical events that occur within one or more populations. This feature uses the real-time query strategy, and is discussed in Chapter 11.

Incidence Rates   Incidence rates is a tool that allows you to estimate the incidence of outcomes within target populations of interest. This feature uses the real-time query strategy, and is discussed in Chapter 11.

Profiles   Profiles is a tool that allows you to explore an individual patients longitudinal observational data to summarize what is going on within a given individual. This feature uses the real-time query strategy.

Population Level Estimation   Estimation is a capability to allow you to define a population level effect estimation study using a comparative cohort design whereby comparisons between one or more target and comparator cohorts can be explored for a series of outcomes. This feature can be said to implement the real-time query strategy, as no coding is required, and is discussed in Chapter 12.

Patient Level Prediction   Prediction is a capability to allow you to apply machine learning algorithms to conduct patient level prediction analyses whereby you can predict an outcome within any given target exposures. This feature can be said to implement the real-time query strategy, as no coding is required, and is discussed in Chapter 13.

Jobs   Select the Jobs menu item to explore the state of processes that are running through the WebAPI. Jobs are often long running processes such as generating a cohort or computing cohort characterization reports.

Configuration   Select the Configuration menu item to review the data sources that have been configured in the source configuration section.

Feedback   The Feedback link will take you to the issue log for Atlas so that you can log a new issue or to search through existing issues. If you have ideas for new features or enhancements, this is also a place note these for the development community.

8.3.1   Security

ATLAS and the WebAPI provide a granular security model to control access to features or data sources within the overall platform. The security system is built leveraging the Apache Shiro library. Additional information on the security system can be found in the online WebAPI security wiki.[3]

---

[3]https://github.com/OHDSI/WebAPI/wiki/Security-Configuration

8.3.2 Documentation

Documentation for ATLAS can be found online in the ATLAS GitHub repository wiki.[4] This wiki includes information on the various application features as well as links to online video tutorials.

8.3.3 How to Install

Installation of ATLAS is done in combination with the OHDSI WebAPI. Installation guides for each component are available online in the ATLAS GitHub repository Setup Guide[5] and WebAPI GitHub repository Installation Guide.[6]

8.4 Methods Library

The OHDSI Methods Library is the collection of open source R packages show in Figure 8.4.

The packages offer R functions that together can be used to perform a complete observational study, starting from data in the CDM, and resulting in estimates and supporting statistics, figures, and tables. The packages interact directly with observational data in the CDM, and can be used simply to provide cross-platform compatibility to completely custom analyses as described in Chapter 9, or can provide advanced standardized analytics for population characterization (Chapter 11), population-level effect estimation (Chapter 12), and patient-level prediction (Chapter 13). The Methods Library supports best practices for use of observational data and observational study design as learned from previous and ongoing research, such as transparency, reproducibility, as well as measuring of the operating characteristics of methods in a particular context and subsequent empirical calibration of estimates produced by the methods.

The Methods Library has already been used in many published clinical studies (Boland et al., 2017; Duke et al., 2017; Ramcharran et al., 2017; Weinstein et al., 2017; Wang et al., 2017; Ryan et al., 2017, 2018; Vashisht et al., 2018; Yuan et al., 2018; Johnston et al., 2019), as well as methodological studies. (Schuemie et al., 2014, 2016; Reps et al., 2018; Tian et al., 2018; Schuemie et al., 2018a,b; Reps et al., 2019) The validity of the implementations of methods in the Methods library is described in Chapter 17.

8.4.1 Support for Large-Scale Analytics

One key feature incorporated in all packages is the ability to efficiently run many analyses. For example, when performing population-level estimation, the CohortMethod package al-

---

[4] https://github.com/OHDSI/ATLAS/wiki
[5] https://github.com/OHDSI/Atlas/wiki/Atlas-Setup-Guide
[6] https://github.com/OHDSI/WebAPI/wiki/WebAPI-Installation-Guide

Figure 8.4: Packages in the OHDSI Methods Library.

lows for computing effect-size estimates for many exposures and outcomes, using various analysis settings, and the package will automatically choose the optimal way to compute all the required intermediary and final data sets. Steps that can be re-used, such as extraction of covariates, or fitting a propensity model that is used for one target-comparator pair but multiple outcomes, will be executed only once. Where possible, computations will take place in parallel to maximize the use of computational resources.

This computational efficiency allows for large-scale analytics, answering many questions at once, and is also essential for including control hypotheses (e.g. negative controls) to measure the operating characteristics of our methods, and perform empirical calibration as described in Chapter 18.

8.4.2   Support for Big Data

The Methods Library is also designed to run against very large databases and be able to perform computations involving large amounts of data. This achieved in three ways:

1. Most data manipulation is performed on the database server. An analysis usually only requires a small fraction of the entire data in the database, and the Methods Library, through the SqlRender and DatabaseConnector packages, allows for advanced operations to be performed on the server to preprocess and extract the relevant data.
2. Large local data objects are stored in a memory-efficient manner. For the data that is downloaded to the local machine, the Methods Library uses the ff package to store and work with large data objects. This allows us to work with data much larger than fits in memory.
3. High-performance computing is applied where needed. For example, the Cyclops package implements a highly efficient regression engine that is used throughout the Methods Library to perform large-scale regressions (large number of variables, large number of observations) that would not be possible to fit otherwise.

8.4.3   Documentation

R provides a standard way to document packages. Each package has a *package manual* that documents every function and data set contained in the package. All package manuals are available online through the Methods Library website[7], through the package GitHub repositories, and for those packages available through CRAN they can be found in CRAN. Furthermore, from within R the package manual can be consulted by using the question mark. For example, after loading the DatabaseConnector package, typing the command ?connect brings up the documentation on the "connect" function.

In addition to the package manual, many packages provide *vignettes*. Vignettes are long-form documentation that describe how a package can be used to perform certain tasks. For

---

[7]https://ohdsi.github.io/MethodsLibrary

example, one vignette[8] describes how to perform multiple analyses efficiently using the CohortMethod package. Vignettes can also be found through the Methods Library website, through the package GitHub repositories, and for those packages available through CRAN they can be found in CRAN.

8.4.4 System Requirements

Two computing environments are relevant when discussing the system requirements: The database server, and the analytics workstation.

The database server must hold the observational healthcare data in CDM format. The Methods Library supports a wide array of database management systems including traditional database systems (PostgreSQL, Microsoft SQL Server, and Oracle), parallel data warehouses (Microsoft APS, IBM Netezza, and Amazon RedShift), as well as Big Data platforms (Hadoop through Impala, and Google BigQuery).

The analytics workstation is where the Methods Library is installed and run. This can either be a local machine, such as someone's laptop, or a remote server running RStudio Server. In all cases the requirements are that R is installed, preferably together with RStudio. The Methods Library also requires that Java is installed. The analytics workstation should also be able to connect to the database server, specifically, any firewall between them should have the database server access ports opened the workstation. Some of the analytics can be computationally intensive, so having multiple processing cores and ample memory can help speed up the analyses. We recommend having at least four cores and 16 gigabytes of memory.

8.4.5 How to Install

Here are the steps for installing the required environment to run the OHDSI R packages. Four things need to be installed:

1. **R** is a statistical computing environment. It comes with a basic user interface that is primarily a command-line interface.
2. **RTools** is a set of programs that is required on Windows to build R packages from source.
3. **RStudio** is an IDE (Integrated Development Environment) that makes R easier to use. It includes a code editor, debugging and visualization tools. Please use it to obtain a nice R experience.
4. **Java** is a computing environment that is needed to run some of the components in the OHDSI R packages, for example those needed to connect to a database.

Below we describe how to install each of these in a Windows environment.

---

[8]https://ohdsi.github.io/CohortMethod/articles/MultipleAnalyses.html

R-3.6.1 for Windows (32/64 bit)

Download R 3.6.1 for Windows (81 megabytes, 32/64 bit) ◀

Installation and other instructions
New features in this version

CRAN
Mirrors
What's new?
Task Views
Search

If you want to double-check that the package you have downloaded matches the package distributed by CRAN, you can compare the md5sum of the .exe to the fingerprint on the master server. You will need a version of md5sum for windows: both graphical and command line versions are available.

Figure 8.5: Downloading R from CRAN.

 In Windows, both R and Java come in 32-bit and 64-bits architectures. If you install R in both architectures, you **must** also install Java in both architectures. It is recommended to only install the 64-bit version of R.

Installing R

1. Go to https://cran.r-project.org/, click on "Download R for Windows", then "base", then click the Download link indicated in Figure 8.5.

2. After the download has completed, run the installer. Use the default options everywhere, with two exceptions: First, it is better not to install into program files. Instead, just make R a subfolder of your C drive as shown in Figure 8.6. Second, to avoid problems due to differing architectures between R and Java, disable the 32-bit architecture as shown in Figure 8.7.

Once completed, you should be able to select R from your Start Menu.

Installing RTools

1. Go to https://cran.r-project.org/, click on "Download R for Windows", then "Rtools", and select the very latest version of RTools to download.

2. After downloading has completed run the installer. Select the default options everywhere.

Installing RStudio

1. Go to https://www.rstudio.com/, select "Download RStudio" (or the "Download" button under "RStudio"), opt for the free version, and download the installer for Windows as shown in Figure 8.8.

2. After downloading, start the installer, and use the default options everywhere.

Figure 8.6: Settings the destination folder for R.

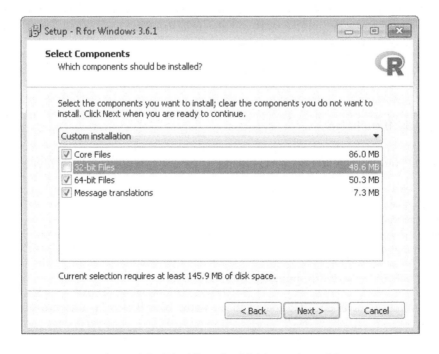

Figure 8.7: Disabling the 32-bit version of R.

Installers for Supported Platforms

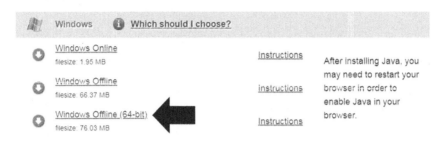

Installers	Size	Date	MD5
RStudio 1.2.1335 - Windows 7+ (64-bit)	126.9 MB	2019-04-08	d0e2470f1
RStudio 1.2.1335 - Mac OS X 10.12+ (64-bit)	121.1 MB	2019-04-08	6c570b0e2
RStudio 1.2.1335 - Ubuntu 14/Debian 8 (64-bit)	92.2 MB	2019-04-08	c1b07d051

Figure 8.8: Downloading RStudio.

Figure 8.9: Downloading Java.

Installing Java

1. Go to https://java.com/en/download/manual.jsp, and select the Windows 64-bit installer as shown in Figure 8.9. If you also installed the 32-bit version of R, you *must* also install the other (32-bit) version of Java.

2. After downloading just run the installer.

Verifying the Installation

You should now be ready to go, but we should make sure. Start RStudio, and type

```
install.packages("SqlRender")
library(SqlRender)
translate("SELECT TOP 10 * FROM person;", "postgresql")
```

```
## [1] "SELECT  * FROM person LIMIT 10;"
```

This function uses Java, so if all goes well we know both R and Java have been installed correctly!

Another test is to see if source packages can be built. Run the following R code to install the CohortMethod package from the OHDSI GitHub repository:

```
install.packages("drat")
drat::addRepo("OHDSI")
install.packages("CohortMethod")
```

8.5 Deployment Strategies

Deploying the entire OHDSI tool stack, including ATLAS and the Methods Library, in an organization is a daunting task. There are many components with dependencies that have to be considered, and configurations to set. For this reason, two initiatives have developed integrated deployment strategies that allow the entire stack to be installed as one package, using some forms of virtualization: Broadsea and Amazon Web Services (AWS).

8.5.1 Broadsea

Broadsea[9] uses Docker container technology.[10] The OHDSI tools are packaged along with dependencies into a single portable binary file called a Docker Image. This image can then be run on a Docker engine service, creating a virtual machine with all the software installed and ready to run. Docker engines are available for most operating systems, including Microsoft Windows, MacOS, and Linux. The Broadsea Docker image contains the main OHDSI tools, including the Methods Library and ATLAS.

8.5.2 Amazon AWS

Amazon has prepared two environments that can be instantiated in the AWS cloud computing environment with a click of the button: OHDSI-in-a-Box[11] and OHDSIonAWS.[12]

OHDSI-in-a-Box is specifically created as a learning environment, and is used in most of the tutorials provided by the OHDSI community. It includes many OHDSI tools, sample data sets, RStudio and other supporting software in a single, low cost Windows virtual machine. A PostgreSQL database is used to store the CDM and also to store the intermediary results from ATLAS. The OMOP CDM data mapping and ETL tools are also included in OHDSI-in-a-Box. The architecture for OHDSI-in-a-Box is depicted in Figure 8.10.

OHDSIonAWS is a reference architecture for enterprise class, multi-user, scalable and fault tolerant OHDSI environments that can be used by organizations to perform their data analytics. It includes several sample datasets and can also automatically load your organization's real healthcare data. The data is placed in the Amazon Redshift database platform, which is supported by the OHDSI tools. Intermediary results of ATLAS are stored in a PostgreSQL

---

[9]https://github.com/OHDSI/Broadsea

[10]https://www.docker.com/

[11]https://github.com/OHDSI/OHDSI-in-a-Box

[12]https://github.com/OHDSI/OHDSIonAWS

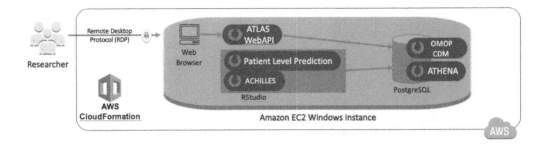

Figure 8.10: The Amazon Web Services architecture for OHDSI-in-a-Box.

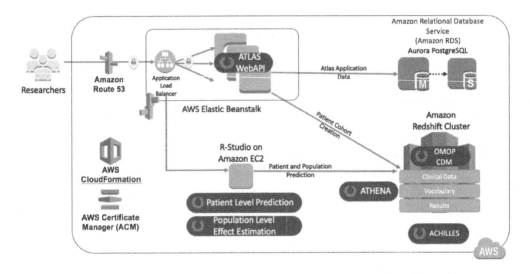

Figure 8.11: The Amazon Web Services architecure for OHDSIonAWS.

database. On the front end, users have access to ATLAS and to RStudio through a web interface (leveraging RStudio Server). In RStudio the OHDSI Methods Library has already been installed, and can be used to connect to the databases. The automation to deploy OHDSIonAWS is open-source, and can be customized to include your organization's management tools and best practices. The architecture for OHDSIonAWS is depicted in Figure 8.11.

8.6 Summary

- We can perform analyses against data in the CDM by
  * writing custom code
  * writing code that uses the R packages in the OHDSI Methods Library
  * using the interactive analysis platform ATLAS
- OHDSI tools use different analysis strategies
  * Single studies

        * Real-time queries
        * Large-scale analytics
    – The majority of OHDSI analytics tool are embedded in
        * The interactive analysis platform ATLAS
        * The OHDSI Methods Library R packages
    – Several strategies exist facilitating the deployment of the OHDSI tools.

Chapter 9

SQL and R

Chapter leads: Martijn Schuemie & Peter Rijnbeek

The Common Data Model (CDM) is a relational database model (all data is represented as records in tables that have fields), which means that the data will typically be stored in a relational database using a software platform like PostgreSQL, Oracle, or Microsoft SQL Server. The various OHDSI tools such as ATLAS and the Methods Library work by querying the database behind the scene, but we can also query the database directly ourselves if we have appropriate access rights. The main reason to do this is to perform analyses that currently are not supported by any existing tool. However, directly querying the database also comes with greater risk of making mistakes, as the OHDSI tools are often designed to help guide the user to appropriate analysis of the data. Direct queries do not provide such guidance.

The standard language for querying relational databases is SQL (Structured Query Language), which can be used both to query the database as well as to make changes to the data. Although the basic commands in SQL are indeed standard, meaning the same across software platforms, each platform has its own dialect, with subtle changes. For example, to retrieve the top 10 rows of the PERSON table on SQL Server, one would type:

```
SELECT TOP 10 * FROM person;
```

Whereas the same query on PostgreSQL would be:

```
SELECT * FROM person LIMIT 10;
```

In OHDSI, we would like to be agnostic to the specific dialect a platform uses; we would like to 'speak' the same SQL language across all OHDSI databases. For this reason OHDSI developed the SqlRender package, an R package that can translate from one standard dialect to any of the supported dialects that will be discussed later in this chapter. This standard dialect - **OHDSI SQL** - is mainly a subset of the SQL Server SQL dialect. The example SQL statements provided throughout this chapter will all use OHDSI SQL.

Each database platform also comes with its own software tools for querying the database using SQL. In OHDSI we developed the DatabaseConnector package, one R package that can connect to many database platforms. DatabaseConnector will also be discussed later in this chapter.

So although one can query a database that conforms to the CDM without using any OHDSI tools, the recommended path is to use the DatabaseConnector and SqlRender packages. This allows queries that are developed at one site to be used at any other site without modification. R itself also immediately provides features to further analyze the data extracted from the database, such as performing statistical analyses and generating (interactive) plots.

In this chapter we assume the reader has a basic understanding of SQL. We first review how to use SqlRender and DatabaseConnector. If the reader does not intend to use these packages these sections can be skipped. In Section 9.3 we discuss how to use SQL (in this case OHDSI SQL) to query the CDM. The following section highlights how to use the OHDSI Standardized Vocabulary when querying the CDM. We highlight the QueryLibrary, a collection of commonly-used queries against the CDM that is publicly available. We close this chapter with an example study estimating incidence rates, and implement this study using SqlRender and DatabaseConnector.

9.1   SqlRender

The SqlRender package is available on CRAN (the Comprehensive R Archive Network), and can therefore be installed using:

```
install.packages("SqlRender")
```

SqlRender supports a wide array of technical platforms including traditional database systems (PostgreSQL, Microsoft SQL Server, SQLite, and Oracle), parallel data warehouses (Microsoft APS, IBM Netezza, and Amazon RedShift), as well as Big Data platforms (Hadoop through Impala, and Google BigQuery). The R package comes with a package manual and a vignette that explores the full functionality. Here we describer some of the main features.

9.1.1   SQL Parameterization

One of the functions of the package is to support parameterization of SQL. Often, small variations of SQL need to be generated based on some parameters. SqlRender offers a simple markup syntax inside the SQL code to allow parameterization. Rendering the SQL based on parameter values is done using the `render()` function.

Substituting Parameter Values

The @ character can be used to indicate parameter names that need to be exchanged for actual parameter values when rendering. In the following example, a variable called a is mentioned in the SQL. In the call to the render function the value of this parameter is defined:

```
sql <- "SELECT * FROM concept WHERE concept_id = @a;"
render(sql, a = 123)
```

```
## [1] "SELECT * FROM concept WHERE concept_id = 123;"
```

Note that, unlike the parameterization offered by most database management systems, it is just as easy to parameterize table or field names as values:

```
sql <- "SELECT * FROM @x WHERE person_id = @a;"
render(sql, x = "observation", a = 123)
```

```
## [1] "SELECT * FROM observation WHERE person_id = 123;"
```

The parameter values can be numbers, strings, booleans, as well as vectors, which are converted to comma-delimited lists:

```
sql <- "SELECT * FROM concept WHERE concept_id IN (@a);"
render(sql, a = c(123, 234, 345))
```

```
## [1] "SELECT * FROM concept WHERE concept_id IN (123,234,345);"
```

If-Then-Else

Sometimes blocks of codes need to be turned on or off based on the values of one or more parameters. This is done using the {Condition} ? {if true} : {if false} syntax. If the *condition* evaluates to true or 1, the *if true* block is used, else the *if false* block is shown (if present).

```
sql <- "SELECT * FROM cohort {@x} ? {WHERE subject_id = 1}"
render(sql, x = FALSE)
```

```
## [1] "SELECT * FROM cohort "
```

```
render(sql, x = TRUE)
```

```
## [1] "SELECT * FROM cohort WHERE subject_id = 1"
```

Simple comparisons are also supported:

```
sql <- "SELECT * FROM cohort {@x == 1} ? {WHERE subject_id = 1};"
render(sql, x = 1)
```

```
## [1] "SELECT * FROM cohort WHERE subject_id = 1;"
```

```
render(sql, x = 2)
```

```
## [1] "SELECT * FROM cohort ;"
```

As well as the `IN` operator:

```
sql <- "SELECT * FROM cohort {@x IN (1,2,3)} ? {WHERE subject_id = 1};"
render(sql, x = 2)
```

```
## [1] "SELECT * FROM cohort WHERE subject_id = 1;"
```

9.1.2   Translation to Other SQL Dialects

Another function of the SqlRender package is to translate from OHDSI SQL to other SQL dialects. For example:

```
sql <- "SELECT TOP 10 * FROM person;"
translate(sql, targetDialect = "postgresql")
```

```
## [1] "SELECT  * FROM person LIMIT 10;"
```

The `targetDialect` parameter can have the following values: "oracle", "postgresql", "pdw", "redshift", "impala", "netezza", "bigquery", "sqlite", and "sql server".

 There are limits to what SQL functions and constructs can be translated properly, both because only a limited set of translation rules have been implemented in the package, but also some SQL features do not have an equivalent in all dialects. This is the primary reason why OHDSI SQL was developed as its own, new SQL dialect. However, whenever possible we have kept to the SQL Server syntax to avoid reinventing the wheel.

Despite our best efforts, there are quite a few things to consider when writing OHDSI SQL that will run without error on all supported platforms. In what follows we discuss these considerations in detail.

Functions and Structures Supported By Translate

These SQL Server functions have been tested and were found to be translated correctly to
the various dialects:

Table 9.1: Functions supported by translate.

Function	Function	Function
ABS	EXP	RAND
ACOS	FLOOR	RANK
ASIN	GETDATE	RIGHT
ATAN	HASHBYTES*	ROUND
AVG	ISNULL	ROW_NUMBER
CAST	ISNUMERIC	RTRIM
CEILING	LEFT	SIN
CHARINDEX	LEN	SQRT
CONCAT	LOG	SQUARE
COS	LOG10	STDEV
COUNT	LOWER	SUM
COUNT_BIG	LTRIM	TAN
DATEADD	MAX	UPPER
DATEDIFF	MIN	VAR
DATEFROMPARTS	MONTH	YEAR
DATETIMEFROMPARTS	NEWID	
DAY	PI	
EOMONTH	POWER	

* Requires special privileges on Oracle. Has no equivalent on SQLite.

Similarly, many SQL syntax structures are supported. Here is a non-exhaustive list of expressions that we know will translate well:

```
-- Simple selects:
SELECT * FROM table;

-- Selects with joins:
SELECT * FROM table_1 INNER JOIN table_2 ON a = b;

-- Nested queries:
SELECT * FROM (SELECT * FROM table_1) tmp WHERE a = b;

-- Limiting to top rows:
SELECT TOP 10 * FROM table;

-- Selecting into a new table:
```

```
SELECT * INTO new_table FROM table;

-- Creating tables:
CREATE TABLE table (field INT);

-- Inserting verbatim values:
INSERT INTO other_table (field_1) VALUES (1);

-- Inserting from SELECT:
INSERT INTO other_table (field_1) SELECT value FROM table;

-- Simple drop commands:
DROP TABLE table;

-- Drop table if it exists:
IF OBJECT_ID('ACHILLES_analysis', 'U') IS NOT NULL
  DROP TABLE ACHILLES_analysis;

-- Drop temp table if it exists:
IF OBJECT_ID('tempdb..#cohorts', 'U') IS NOT NULL
  DROP TABLE #cohorts;

-- Common table expressions:
WITH cte AS (SELECT * FROM table) SELECT * FROM cte;

-- OVER clauses:
SELECT ROW_NUMBER() OVER (PARTITION BY a ORDER BY b)
  AS "Row Number" FROM table;

-- CASE WHEN clauses:
SELECT CASE WHEN a=1 THEN a ELSE 0 END AS value FROM table;

-- UNIONs:
SELECT * FROM a UNION SELECT * FROM b;

-- INTERSECTIONs:
SELECT * FROM a INTERSECT SELECT * FROM b;

-- EXCEPT:
SELECT * FROM a EXCEPT SELECT * FROM b;
```

String Concatenation

String concatenation is one area where SQL Server is less specific than other dialects. In SQL Server, one would write SELECT first_name + ' ' + last_name AS full_name FROM table, but this should be SELECT first_name || ' ' || last_name AS full_name FROM table in PostgreSQL and Oracle. SqlRender tries to guess when values that are being concatenated are strings. In the example above, because we have an explicit string (the space surrounded by single quotation marks), the translation will be correct. However, if the query had been SELECT first_name + last_name AS full_name FROM table, SqlRender would have had no clue the two fields were strings, and would incorrectly leave the plus sign. Another clue that a value is a string is an explicit cast to VARCHAR, so SELECT last_name + CAST(age AS VARCHAR(3)) AS full_name FROM table would also be translated correctly. To avoid ambiguity altogether, it is probable best to use the CONCAT() function to concatenate two or more strings.

Table Aliases and the AS Keyword

Many SQL dialects allow the use of the AS keyword when defining a table alias, but will also work fine without the keyword. For example, both these SQL statements are fine for SQL Server, PostgreSQL, RedShift, etc.:

```
-- Using AS keyword
SELECT *
FROM my_table AS table_1
INNER JOIN (
  SELECT * FROM other_table
) AS table_2
ON table_1.person_id = table_2.person_id;

-- Not using AS keyword
SELECT *
FROM my_table table_1
INNER JOIN (
  SELECT * FROM other_table
) table_2
ON table_1.person_id = table_2.person_id;
```

However, Oracle will throw an error when the AS keyword is used. In the above example, the first query will fail. It is therefore recommended to not use the AS keyword when aliasing tables. (Note: we can't make SqlRender handle this, because it can't easily distinguish between table aliases where Oracle doesn't allow AS to be used, and field aliases, where Oracle requires AS to be used.)

Temp Tables

Temp tables can be very useful to store intermediate results, and when used correctly can dramatically improve performance of queries. On most database platforms temp tables have very nice properties: they're only visible to the current user, are automatically dropped when the session ends, and can be created even when the user has no write access. Unfortunately, in Oracle temp tables are basically permanent tables, with the only difference that the data inside the table is only visible to the current user. This is why, in Oracle, SqlRender will try to emulate temp tables by

1. Adding a random string to the table name so tables from different users will not conflict.
2. Allowing the user to specify the schema where the temp tables will be created.

For example:

```
sql <- "SELECT * FROM #children;"
translate(sql, targetDialect = "oracle", oracleTempSchema = "temp_schema")
```

```
## [1] "SELECT * FROM temp_schema.r4z6nb9rchildren ;"
```

Note that the user will need to have write privileges on `temp_schema`.

Also note that because Oracle has a limit on table names of 30 characters. **Temp table names are only allowed to be at most 22 characters long**, because else the name will become too long after appending the session ID.

Furthermore, remember that temp tables are not automatically dropped on Oracle, so you will need to explicitly `TRUNCATE` and `DROP` all temp tables once you're done with them to prevent orphan tables accumulating in the Oracle temp schema.

Implicit Casts

One of the few points where SQL Server is less explicit than other dialects is that it allows implicit casts. For example, this code will work on SQL Server:

```
CREATE TABLE #temp (txt VARCHAR);

INSERT INTO #temp
SELECT '1';

SELECT * FROM #temp WHERE txt = 1;
```

Even though `txt` is a VARCHAR field and we are comparing it with an integer, SQL Server will automatically cast one of the two to the correct type to allow the comparison. In contrast, other dialects such as PostgreSQL will throw an error when trying to compare a VARCHAR with an INT.

You should therefore always make casts explicit. In the above example, the last statement should be replaced with either

```
SELECT * FROM #temp WHERE txt = CAST(1 AS VARCHAR);
```

or

```
SELECT * FROM #temp WHERE CAST(txt AS INT) = 1;
```

Case Sensitivity in String Comparisons

Some DBMS platforms such as SQL Server always perform string comparisons in a case-insensitive way, while others such as PostgreSQL are always case sensitive. It is therefore recommended to always assume case-sensitive comparisons, and to explicitly make comparisons case-insensitive when unsure about the case. For example, instead of

```
SELECT * FROM concept WHERE concep_class_id = 'Clinical Finding'
```

it is preferred to use

```
SELECT * FROM concept WHERE LOWER(concep_class_id) = 'clinical finding'
```

Schemas and Databases

In SQL Server, tables are located in a schema, and schemas reside in a database. For example, cdm_data.dbo.person refers to the person table in the dbo schema in the cdm_data database. In other dialects, even though a similar hierarchy often exists they are used very differently. In SQL Server, there is typically one schema per database (often called dbo), and users can easily use data in different databases. On other platforms, for example in PostgreSQL, it is not possible to use data across databases in a single session, but there are often many schemas in a database. In PostgreSQL one could say that the equivalent of SQL Server's database is the schema.

We therefore recommend concatenating SQL Server's database and schema into a single parameter, which we typically call @databaseSchema. For example, we could have the parameterized SQL

```
SELECT * FROM @databaseSchema.person
```

where on SQL Server we can include both database and schema names in the value: databaseSchema = "cdm_data.dbo". On other platforms, we can use the same code, but now only specify the schema as the parameter value: databaseSchema = "cdm_data".

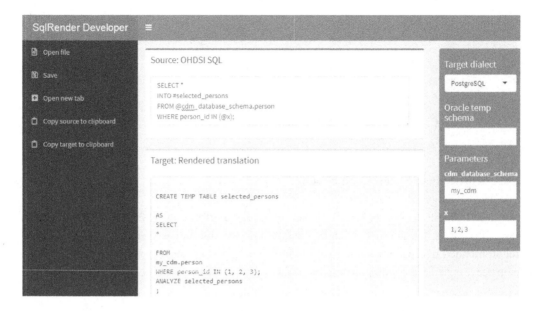

Figure 9.1: The SqlDeveloper Shiny app.

The one situation where this will fail is the USE command, since USE `cdm_data.dbo;` will throw an error. It is therefore preferred not to use the USE command, but always specify the database / schema where a table is located.

Debugging Parameterized SQL

Debugging parameterized SQL can be a bit complicated. Only the rendered SQL can be tested against a database server, but changes to the code should be made in the parameterized (pre-rendered) SQL.

A Shiny app is included in the SqlRender package for interactively editing source SQL and generating rendered and translated SQL. The app can be started using:

```
launchSqlRenderDeveloper()
```

That will open the default browser with the app shown in Figure 9.1. The app is also publicly available on the web.[1]

In the app you can enter OHDSI SQL, select the target dialect as well as provide values for the parameters that appear in your SQL, and the translation will automatically appear at the bottom.

---

[1] http://data.ohdsi.org/SqlDeveloper/

9.2 DatabaseConnector

DatabaseConnector is an R package for connecting to various database platforms using Java's JDBC drivers. The DatabaseConnector package is available on CRAN (the Comprehensive R Archive Network), and can therefore be installed using:

```
install.packages("DatabaseConnector")
```

DatabaseConnector supports a wide array of technical platforms including traditional database systems (PostgreSQL, Microsoft SQL Server, SQLite, and Oracle), parallel data warehouses (Microsoft APS, IBM Netezza, and Amazon RedShift), as well as Big Data platforms (Hadoop through Impala, and Google BigQuery). The package already contains most drivers, but because of licensing reasons the drivers for BigQuery, Netezza and Impala are not included but must be obtained by the user. Type ?jdbcDrivers for instructions on how to download these drivers. Once downloaded, you can use the pathToDriver argument of the connect, dbConnect, and createConnectionDetails functions.

9.2.1 Creating a Connection

To connect to a database a number of details need to be specified, such as the database platform, the location of the server, the user name, and password. We can call the connect function and specify these details directly:

```
conn <- connect(dbms = "postgresql",
                server = "localhost/postgres",
                user = "joe",
                password = "secret",
                schema = "cdm")
```

```
## Connecting using PostgreSQL driver
```

See ?connect for information on which details are required for each platform. Don't forget to close any connection afterwards:

```
disconnect(conn)
```

Note that, instead of providing the server name, it is also possible to provide the JDBC connection string if this is more convenient:

```
connString <- "jdbc:postgresql://localhost:5432/postgres"
conn <- connect(dbms = "postgresql",
                connectionString = connString,
                user = "joe",
```

```
                    password = "secret",
                    schema = "cdm")
```

Connecting using PostgreSQL driver

Sometimes we may want to first specify the connection details, and defer connecting until later. This may be convenient for example when the connection is established inside a function, and the details need to be passed as an argument. We can use the createConnectionDetails function for this purpose:

```
details <- createConnectionDetails(dbms = "postgresql",
                                   server = "localhost/postgres",
                                   user = "joe",
                                   password = "secret",
                                   schema = "cdm")
conn <- connect(details)
```

Connecting using PostgreSQL driver

9.2.2   Querying

The main functions for querying database are the querySql and executeSql functions. The difference between these functions is that querySql expects data to be returned by the database, and can handle only one SQL statement at a time. In contrast, executeSql does not expect data to be returned, and accepts multiple SQL statements in a single SQL string.

Some examples:

```
querySql(conn, "SELECT TOP 3 * FROM person")
```

```
##   person_id gender_concept_id year_of_birth
## 1         1              8507          1975
## 2         2              8507          1976
## 3         3              8507          1977
```

```
executeSql(conn, "TRUNCATE TABLE foo; DROP TABLE foo;")
```

Both functions provide extensive error reporting: When an error is thrown by the server, the error message and the offending piece of SQL are written to a text file to allow better debugging. The executeSql function also by default shows a progress bar, indicating the percentage of SQL statements that has been executed. If those attributes are not desired, the package also offers the lowLevelQuerySql and lowLevelExecuteSql functions.

9.2.3 Querying Using Ffdf Objects

Sometimes the data to be fetched from the database is too large to fit into memory. As mentioned in Section 8.4.2, in such a case we can use the ff package to store R data objects on file, and use them as if they are available in memory. DatabaseConnector can download data directly into ffdf objects:

```
x <- querySql.ffdf(conn, "SELECT * FROM person")
```

x is now an ffdf object.

9.2.4 Querying Different Platforms Using the Same SQL

The following convenience functions are available that first call the render and translate functions in the SqlRender package: renderTranslateExecuteSql, renderTranslateQuerySql, renderTranslateQuerySql.ffdf. For example:

```
x <- renderTranslateQuerySql(conn,
                    sql = "SELECT TOP 10 * FROM @schema.person",
                    schema = "cdm_synpuf")
```

Note that the SQL Server-specific 'TOP 10' syntax will be translated to for example 'LIMIT 10' on PostgreSQL, and that the SQL parameter @schema will be instantiated with the provided value 'cdm_synpuf'.

9.2.5 Inserting Tables

Although it is also possible to insert data in the database by sending SQL statements using the executeSql function, it is often more convenient and faster (due to some optimization) to use the insertTable function:

```
data(mtcars)
insertTable(conn, "mtcars", mtcars, createTable = TRUE)
```

In this example, we're uploading the mtcars data frame to a table called 'mtcars' on the server, which will be automatically created.

9.3 Querying the CDM

In the following examples we use OHDSI SQL to query a database that adheres to the CDM. These queries use @cdm to denote the database schema where the data in CDM can be found.

We can start by just querying how many people are in the database:

```
SELECT COUNT(*) AS person_count FROM @cdm.person;
```

PERSON_COUNT
26299001

Or perhaps we're interested in the average length of an observation period:

```
SELECT AVG(DATEDIFF(DAY,
                    observation_period_start_date,
                    observation_period_end_date) / 365.25) AS num_years
FROM @cdm.observation_period;
```

NUM_YEARS
1.980803

We can join tables to produce additional statistics. A join combines fields from multiple tables, typically by requiring specific fields in the tables to have the same value. For example, here we join the PERSON table to the OBSERVATION_PERIOD table on the PERSON_ID fields in both tables. In other words, the result of the join is a new table-like set that has all the fields of the two tables, but in all rows the PERSON_ID fields from the two tables must have the same value. We can now for example compute the maximum age at observation end by using the OBSERVATION_PERIOD_END_DATE field from the OBSERVATION_PERIOD table together with the year_of_birth field of the PERSON table:

```
SELECT MAX(YEAR(observation_period_end_date) -
           year_of_birth) AS max_age
FROM @cdm.person
INNER JOIN @cdm.observation_period
  ON person.person_id = observation_period.person_id;
```

MAX_AGE
90

A much more complicated query is needed to determine the distribution of age at the start of observation. In this query, we first join the PERSON to the OBSERVATION_PERIOD table to compute age at start of observation. We also compute the ordering for this joined set based on age, and store it as order_nr. Because we want to use the result of this join multiple times, we define it as a common table expression (CTE) (defined using WITH ... AS) that we call "ages," meaning we can refer to ages as if it is an existing table. We count the number of rows in ages to produce "n," and then for each quantile find the minimum age where the order_nr is smaller than the fraction times n. For example, to find the median we use the minimum age where $order\_nr < .50 * n$. The minimum and maximum age are computed separately:

```
WITH ages
AS (
    SELECT age,
        ROW_NUMBER() OVER (
            ORDER BY age
            ) order_nr
    FROM (
        SELECT YEAR(observation_period_start_date) - year_of_birth AS age
        FROM @cdm.person
        INNER JOIN @cdm.observation_period
            ON person.person_id = observation_period.person_id
        ) age_computed
    )
SELECT MIN(age) AS min_age,
    MIN(CASE
            WHEN order_nr < .25 * n
                THEN 9999
            ELSE age
            END) AS q25_age,
    MIN(CASE
            WHEN order_nr < .50 * n
                THEN 9999
            ELSE age
            END) AS median_age,
    MIN(CASE
            WHEN order_nr < .75 * n
                THEN 9999
            ELSE age
            END) AS q75_age,
    MAX(age) AS max_age
FROM ages
CROSS JOIN (
    SELECT COUNT(*) AS n
    FROM ages
    ) population_size;
```

MIN_AGE	Q25_AGE	MEDIAN_AGE	Q75_AGE	MAX_AGE
0	6	17	34	90

More complex computations can also be performed in R instead of using SQL. For example, we can get the same answer using this R code:

```
sql <- "SELECT YEAR(observation_period_start_date) -
                year_of_birth AS age
FROM @cdm.person
INNER JOIN @cdm.observation_period
  ON person.person_id = observation_period.person_id;"
age <- renderTranslateQuerySql(conn, sql, cdm = "cdm")
quantile(age[, 1], c(0, 0.25, 0.5, 0.75, 1))
```

```
##    0%  25%  50%  75% 100%
##    0    6   17   34   90
```

Here we compute age on the server, download all ages, and then compute the age distribution. However, this requires millions of rows of data to be downloaded from the database server, and is therefore not very efficient. You will need to decide on a case-by-case basis whether a computation is best performed in SQL or in R.

Queries can use the source values in the CDM. For example, we can retrieve the top 10 most frequent condition source codes using:

```
SELECT TOP 10 condition_source_value,
  COUNT(*) AS code_count
FROM @cdm.condition_occurrence
GROUP BY condition_source_value
ORDER BY -COUNT(*);
```

CONDITION_SOURCE_VALUE	CODE_COUNT
4019	49094668
25000	36149139
78099	28908399
319	25798284
31401	22547122
317	22453999
311	19626574
496	19570098
110	19453451
3180	18973883

Here we grouped records in the CONDITION_OCCURRENCE table by values of the CONDITION_SOURCE_VALUE field, and counted the number of records in each group. We retrieve the CONDITION_SOURCE_VALUE and the count, and reverse-order it by the count.

9.4 Using the Vocabulary When Querying

Many operations require the vocabulary to be useful. The Vocabulary tables are part of the CDM, and are therefore available using SQL queries. Here we show how queries against the Vocabulary can be combined with queries against the CDM. Many fields in the CDM contain concept IDs which can be resolved using the CONCEPT table. For example, we may wish to count the number of persons in the database stratified by gender, and it would be convenient to resolve the GENDER_CONCEPT_ID field to a concept name:

```
SELECT COUNT(*) AS subject_count,
  concept_name
FROM @cdm.person
INNER JOIN @cdm.concept
  ON person.gender_concept_id = concept.concept_id
GROUP BY concept_name;
```

SUBJECT_COUNT	CONCEPT_NAME
14927548	FEMALE
11371453	MALE

A very powerful feature of the Vocabulary is its hierarchy. A very common query looks for a specific concept *and all of its descendants*. For example, imagine we wish to count the number of prescriptions containing the ingredient ibuprofen:

```
SELECT COUNT(*) AS prescription_count
FROM @cdm.drug_exposure
INNER JOIN @cdm.concept_ancestor
  ON drug_concept_id = descendant_concept_id
INNER JOIN @cdm.concept ingredient
  ON ancestor_concept_id = ingredient.concept_id
WHERE LOWER(ingredient.concept_name) = 'ibuprofen'
  AND ingredient.concept_class_id = 'Ingredient'
  AND ingredient.standard_concept = 'S';
```

PRESCRIPTION_COUNT
26871214

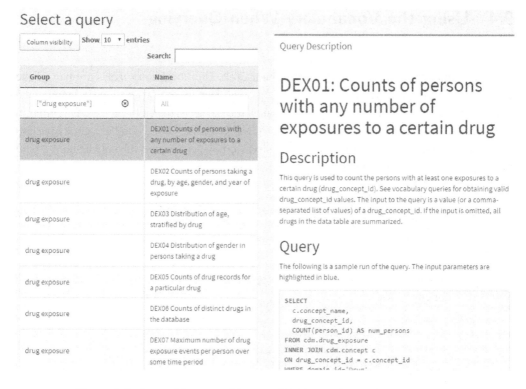

Figure 9.2: QueryLibrary: a library of SQL queries against the CDM.

9.5   QueryLibrary

QueryLibrary is a library of commonly-used SQL queries for the CDM. It is available as an online application[2] shown in Figure 9.2, and as an R package.[3]

The purpose of the library is to help new users learn how to query the CDM. The queries in the library have been reviewed and approved by the OHDSI community. The query library is primarily intended for training purposes, but it is also a valuable resource for experienced users.

The QueryLibrary makes use of SqlRender to output the queries in the SQL dialect of choice. Users can also specify the CDM database schema, vocabulary database schema (if separate), and the Oracle temp schema (if needed), so the queries will be automatically rendered with these settings.

---

[2]http://data.ohdsi.org/QueryLibrary
[3]https://github.com/OHDSI/QueryLibrary

9.6 Designing a Simple Study

9.6.1 Problem Definition

Angioedema is a well-known side-effect of ACE inhibitors (ACEi). Slater et al. (1988) estimate the incidence rate of angioedema in the first week of ACEi treatment to be one case per 3,000 patients per week. Here we seek to replicate this finding, and stratify by age and gender. For simplicity, we focus on one ACEi: lisinopril. We thus answer the question

> What is the rate of angioedema in the first week following lisinopril treatment initiation, stratified by age and gender?

9.6.2 Exposure

We'll define exposure as first exposure to lisinopril. By first we mean no earlier exposure to lisinopril. We require 365 days of continuous observation time prior to the first exposure.

9.6.3 Outcome

We define angioedema as any occurrence of an angioedema diagnosis code during an inpatient or emergency room (ER) visit.

9.6.4 Time-At-Risk

We will compute the incidence rate in the first week following treatment initiation, irrespective of whether patients were exposed for the full week.

9.7 Implementing the Study Using SQL and R

Although we are not bound to any of the OHDSI tool conventions, it is helpful to follow the same principles. In this case, we will use SQL to populate a cohort table, similarly to how the OHDSI tools work. The COHORT table is defined in the CDM, and has a predefined set of fields that we will also use. We first must create the COHORT table in a database schema where we have write access, which likely is not the same as the database schema that holds the data in CDM format.

```
library(DatabaseConnector)
conn <- connect(dbms = "postgresql",
                server = "localhost/postgres",
                user = "joe",
                password = "secret")
```

```
cdmDbSchema <- "cdm"
cohortDbSchema <- "scratch"
cohortTable <- "my_cohorts"

sql <- "
CREATE TABLE @cohort_db_schema.@cohort_table (
  cohort_definition_id INT,
  cohort_start_date DATE,
  cohort_end_date DATE,
  subject_id BIGINT
);
"

renderTranslateExecuteSql(conn, sql,
                          cohort_db_schema = cohortDbSchema,
                          cohort_table = cohortTable)
```

Here we have parameterized the database schema and table names, so we can easily adapt them to different environments. The result is an empty table on the database server.

9.7.1 Exposure Cohort

Next we create our exposure cohort, and insert it into our COHORT table:

```
sql <- "
INSERT INTO @cohort_db_schema.@cohort_table (
  cohort_definition_id,
  cohort_start_date,
  cohort_end_date,
  subject_id
)
SELECT 1 AS cohort_definition_id,
  cohort_start_date,
  cohort_end_date,
  subject_id
FROM (
  SELECT drug_era_start_date AS cohort_start_date,
    drug_era_end_date AS cohort_end_date,
    person_id AS subject_id
  FROM (
    SELECT drug_era_start_date,
      drug_era_end_date,
      person_id,
      ROW_NUMBER() OVER (
        PARTITION BY person_id
          ORDER BY drug_era_start_date
      ) order_nr
    FROM @cdm_db_schema.drug_era
```

```
      WHERE drug_concept_id = 1308216 -- Lisinopril
  ) ordered_exposures
  WHERE order_nr = 1
) first_era
INNER JOIN @cdm_db_schema.observation_period
  ON subject_id = person_id
    AND observation_period_start_date < cohort_start_date
    AND observation_period_end_date > cohort_start_date
WHERE DATEDIFF(DAY,
              observation_period_start_date,
              cohort_start_date) >= 365;
"

renderTranslateExecuteSql(conn, sql,
                    cohort_db_schema = cohortDbSchema,
                    cohort_table = cohortTable,
                    cdm_db_schema = cdmDbSchema)
```

Here we use the DRUG_ERA table, a standard table in the CDM that is automatically derived from the DRUG_EXPOSURE table. The DRUG_ERA table contains eras of continuous exposure at the ingredient level. We can thus search for lisinopril, and this will automatically identify all exposures to drugs containing lisinopril. We take the first drug exposure per person, and then join to the OBSERVATION_PERIOD table, and because a person can have several observation periods we must make sure we only join to the period containing the drug exposure. We then require at least 365 days between the OBSERVATION_PERIOD_START_DATE and the COHORT_START_DATE.

9.7.2 Outcome Cohort

Finally, we must create our outcome cohort:

```
sql <- "
INSERT INTO @cohort_db_schema.@cohort_table (
 cohort_definition_id,
 cohort_start_date,
 cohort_end_date,
subject_id
)
SELECT 2 AS cohort_definition_id,
  cohort_start_date,
  cohort_end_date,
  subject_id
FROM (
  SELECT DISTINCT person_id AS subject_id,
    condition_start_date AS cohort_start_date,
    condition_end_date AS cohort_end_date
```

```
  FROM @cdm_db_schema.condition_occurrence
  INNER JOIN @cdm_db_schema.concept_ancestor
    ON condition_concept_id = descendant_concept_id
  WHERE ancestor_concept_id = 432791 -- Angioedema
) distinct_occurrence
INNER JOIN @cdm_db_schema.visit_occurrence
  ON subject_id = person_id
  AND visit_start_date <= cohort_start_date
  AND visit_end_date >= cohort_start_date
WHERE visit_concept_id IN (262, 9203,
    9201) -- Inpatient or ER;
"

renderTranslateExecuteSql(conn, sql,
                          cohort_db_schema = cohortDbSchema,
                          cohort_table = cohortTable,
                          cdm_db_schema = cdmDbSchema)
```

Here we join the CONDITION_OCCURRENCE table to the CONCEPT_ANCESTOR table to find all occurrences of angioedema or any of its descendants. We use DISTINCT to make sure we only select one record per day, as we believe multiple angioedema diagnoses on the same day are more likely to be the same occurrence rather than multiple angioedema events. We join these occurrences to the VISIT_OCCURRENCE table to ensure the diagnosis was made in and inpatient or ER setting.

9.7.3 Incidence Rate Calculation

Now that our cohorts are in place, we can compute the incidence rate, stratified by age and gender:

```
sql <- "
WITH tar AS (
  SELECT concept_name AS gender,
    FLOOR((YEAR(cohort_start_date) -
         year_of_birth) / 10) AS age,
    subject_id,
    cohort_start_date,
    CASE WHEN DATEADD(DAY, 7, cohort_start_date) >
      observation_period_end_date
    THEN observation_period_end_date
    ELSE DATEADD(DAY, 7, cohort_start_date)
    END AS cohort_end_date
  FROM @cohort_db_schema.@cohort_table
  INNER JOIN @cdm_db_schema.observation_period
    ON subject_id = observation_period.person_id
      AND observation_period_start_date < cohort_start_date
```

```
        AND observation_period_end_date > cohort_start_date
  INNER JOIN @cdm_db_schema.person
    ON subject_id = person.person_id
  INNER JOIN @cdm_db_schema.concept
    ON gender_concept_id = concept_id
  WHERE cohort_definition_id = 1 -- Exposure
)
SELECT days.gender,
    days.age,
    days,
    CASE WHEN events IS NULL THEN 0 ELSE events END AS events
FROM (
  SELECT gender,
    age,
    SUM(DATEDIFF(DAY, cohort_start_date,
      cohort_end_date)) AS days
  FROM tar
  GROUP BY gender,
    age
) days
LEFT JOIN (
  SELECT gender,
      age,
      COUNT(*) AS events
  FROM tar
  INNER JOIN @cohort_db_schema.@cohort_table angioedema
    ON tar.subject_id = angioedema.subject_id
      AND tar.cohort_start_date <= angioedema.cohort_start_date
      AND tar.cohort_end_date >= angioedema.cohort_start_date
  WHERE cohort_definition_id = 2 -- Outcome
  GROUP BY gender,
    age
) events
ON days.gender = events.gender
  AND days.age = events.age;
"


results <- renderTranslateQuerySql(conn, sql,
                                   cohort_db_schema = cohortDbSchema,
                                   cohort_table = cohortTable,
                                   cdm_db_schema = cdmDbSchema,
                                   snakeCaseToCamelCase = TRUE)
```

We first create "tar," a CTE that contains all exposures with the appropriate time-at-risk.
Note that we truncate the time-at-risk at the OBSERVATION_PERIOD_END_DATE. We
also compute the age in 10-year bins, and identify the gender. The advantage of using a CTE
is that we can use the same set of intermediate results several times in a query. In this case we
use it to count the total amount of time-at-risk, as well as the number of angioedema events

that occur during the time-at-risk.

We use `snakeCaseToCamelCase` = `TRUE` because in SQL we tend to use snake_case for field names (because SQL in case-insensitive), whereas in R we tend to use camelCase (because R is case-sensitive). The `results` data frame column names will now be in camel-Case.

With the help of the ggplot2 package we can easily plot our results:

```
# Compute incidence rate (IR) :
results$ir <- 1000 * results$events / results$days / 7

# Fix age scale:
results$age <- results$age * 10

library(ggplot2)
ggplot(results, aes(x = age, y = ir, group = gender, color = gender)) +
  geom_line() +
  xlab("Age") +
  ylab("Incidence (per 1,000 patient weeks)")
```

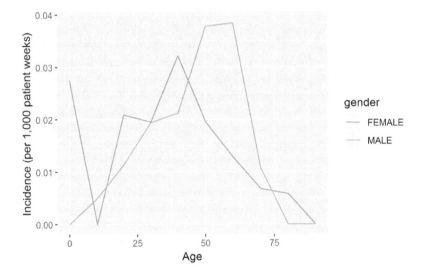

9.7.4   Clean Up

Don't forget to clean up the table we created, and to close the connection:

```
sql <- "
TRUNCATE TABLE @cohort_db_schema.@cohort_table;
DROP TABLE @cohort_db_schema.@cohort_table;
"

renderTranslateExecuteSql(conn, sql,
```

```
                              cohort_db_schema = cohortDbSchema,
                              cohort_table = cohortTable)

disconnect(conn)
```

9.7.5 Compatibility

Because we use OHDSI SQL together with DatabaseConnector and SqlRender throughout, the code we reviewed here will run on any database platform supported by OHDSI.

Note that for demonstration purposes we chose to create our cohorts using hand-crafted SQL. It would probably have been more convenient to construct cohort definition in ATLAS, and use the SQL generated by ATLAS to instantiate the cohorts. ATLAS also produced OHDSI SQL, and can therefore easily be used together with SqlRender and DatabaseConnector.

9.8 Summary

- **SQL** (Structured Query Language) is a standard language for querying databases, including those that conform to the Common Data Model (CDM).

- Different database platforms have different SQL dialects, and require different tools to query them.

- The **SqlRender** and **DatabaseConnector** R packages provide a unified way to query data in the CDM, allowing the same analysis code to be run in different environments without modification.

- By using R and SQL together we can implement custom analyses that are not supported by the OHDSI tools.

- The **QueryLibrary** provides a collection of re-usable SQL queries for the CDM.

9.9 Exercises

Prerequisites

For these exercises we assume R, R-Studio and Java have been installed as described in Section 8.4.5. Also required are the SqlRender, DatabaseConnector, and Eunomia packages, which can be installed using:

```
install.packages(c("SqlRender", "DatabaseConnector", "devtools"))
devtools::install_github("ohdsi/Eunomia", ref = "v1.0.0")
```

The Eunomia package provides a simulated dataset in the CDM that will run inside your local R session. The connection details can be obtained using:

```
connectionDetails <- Eunomia::getEunomiaConnectionDetails()
```

The CDM database schema is "main".

Exercise 9.1. Using SQL and R, compute how many people are in the database.

Exercise 9.2. Using SQL and R, compute how many people have at least one prescription of celecoxib.

Exercise 9.3. Using SQL and R, compute how many diagnoses of gastrointestinal hemorrhage occur during exposure to celecoxib. (Hint: the concept ID for gastrointestinal hemorrhage is 192671.)

Suggested answers can be found in Appendix E.5.

Chapter 10

Defining Cohorts

Chapter lead: Kristin Kostka

Observational health data, also referred to *real world data*, are the data related to patient health status and/or the delivery of health care routinely collected from a variety of sources. As such, OHDSI data stewards (OHDSI collaborators who maintain data in CDM for their sites) may capture data from a number of sources including Electronic Health Records (EHR), health insurance claims and billing activities, product and disease registries, patient-generated data including in home-use settings, and data gathered from other sources that can inform on health status, such as mobile devices. As these data were not collected for research purposes, the data may not explicitly capture the clinical data elements we are interested in.

For example, a health insurance claims database is designed to capture all care provided for some condition (e.g. angioedema) so the associated costs can appropriately be reimbursed, and information on the actual condition is captured only as part of this aim. If we wish to use such observational data for research purposes, we will often have to write some logic that uses *what is captured in the data* to infer *what we are really interested in.* In other words, we often need to create a cohort using some definition of how a clinical event manifests. Thus, if we want to identify angioedema events in an insurance claims database, we may define logic requiring an angioedema diagnose code recorded in an emergency room setting, to distinguish from claims that merely describe follow-up care for some past angioedema occurrence. Similar considerations may apply for data captured during routine healthcare interactions logged in an EHR. As data are being used for a secondary purpose, we must be cognizant of what each database was originally designed to do. Each time we design a study, we must think through the nuances of how our cohort exists in a variety of healthcare settings.

The chapter serves to explain what is meant by creating and sharing cohort definitions, the methods for developing cohorts, and how to build your own cohorts using ATLAS or SQL.

10.1   What Is a Cohort?

In OHDSI research, we define a cohort as a set of persons who satisfy one or more inclusion criteria for a duration of time. The term cohort is often interchanged with the term *phenotype*. Cohorts are used throughout OHDSI analytical tools and network studies as the primary building blocks for executing a research question. For instance, in a study aiming to predict the risk of angioedema in a group of people initiation ACE inhibitors, we define two cohorts: the outcome cohort (angioedema), and the target cohort (people initiating ACE inhibitors). An important aspect of cohorts in OHDSI is that they are typically defined independently from the other cohorts in the study, thus allowing re-use. For example, in our example the angioedema cohort would identify all angioedema events in the population, including those outside the target population. Our analytics tools will take the intersection of these two cohorts when needed at analysis time. The advantage of this is that the same angioedema cohort definition can now also be used in other analyses, for example an estimation study comparing ACE inhibitors to some other exposure. Cohort definitions can vary from study to study depending on the research question of interest.

 A cohort is a set of persons who satisfy one or more inclusion criteria for a duration of time.

It is important to realize that this definition of a cohort used in OHDSI might differ from that used by others in the field. For example, in many peer-reviewed scientific manuscripts, a cohort is suggested to be analogous to a code set of specific clinical codes (e.g. ICD-9/ICD-10, NDC, HCPCS, etc). While code sets are an important piece in assembling a cohort, a cohort is not defined by code set. A cohort requires specific logic for how to use the code set for the criteria (e.g. is it the first occurrence of the ICD-9/ICD-10 code? any occurrence?). A well-defined cohort specifies how a patient enters a cohort and how a patient exits a cohort.

There are unique nuances to utilizing OHDSI's definition of a cohort, including:

- One person may belong to multiple cohorts
- One person may belong to the same cohort for multiple different time periods
- One person may not belong to the same cohort multiple times during the same period of time
- A cohort may have zero or more members

There are two main approaches to constructing a cohort:

1. **Rule-based cohort definitions** use explicit rules to describe when a patient is in the cohort. Defining these rules typically relies heavily on the domain expertise of the individual designing the cohort to use their knowledge of the therapeutic area of interest to build rules for cohort inclusion criteria.
2. **Probabilistic cohort definitions** use a probabilistic model to compute a probability between 0 and 100% of the patient being in the cohort. This probability can be turned into a yes-no classification using some threshold, or in some study designs can be used as is. The probabilistic model is typically trained using machine learning (e.g. lo-

gistic regression) on some example data to automatically identify the relevant patient characteristics that are predictive.

The next sections will discuss these approaches in further detail.

10.2 Rule-Based Cohort Definitions

A rule-based cohort definition begins with explicitly stating one or more inclusion criteria (e.g. "people with angioedema") in a specific duration of time (e.g. "who developed this condition within the last 6 months").

The standard components we use to assemble these criteria are:

- **Domain**: The CDM domain(s) where the data are stored (e.g. "Procedure Occurrence", "Drug Exposure") define the type of clinical information and the allowable concepts that can be represented inside that CDM table. Domains are discussed in more detail in Section 4.2.4.

- **Concept set**: A data-agnostic expression that defines one or more Standard Concepts encompassing the clinical entity of interest. These concept sets are interoperable across different observational health data as they represent the standard terms the clinical entity maps to in the Vocabulary. Concept sets are discussed in Section 10.3.

- **Domain-specific attribute**: Additional attributes related to the clinical entity of interest (E.g. DAYS_SUPPLY for a DRUG_EXPOSURE, or VALUE_AS_NUMBER or RANGE_HIGH for a MEASUREMENT.)

- **Temporal logic**: The time intervals within which the relationship between an inclusion criteria and an event is evaluated (E.g. Indicated condition must occur during 365 days prior to or on exposure start.)

As you are building your cohort definition, you may find it helpful to think of Domains analogous to building blocks (see Figure 10.1) that represent cohort attributes. If you are confused about allowable content in each domain, you can always refer to the Common Data Model chapter (Chapter 4) for help.

When creating a cohort definition, you need to ask yourself the following questions:

- *What initial event defines the time of cohort entry?*
- *What inclusion criteria are applied to the initial events?*
- *What defines the time of cohort exit?*

Cohort entry event: The cohort entry event (initial event) defines the time when people enter the cohort, called the **cohort index date**. A cohort entry event can be any event recorded in the CDM such as drug exposures, conditions, procedures, measurements and visits. Initial events are defined by the CDM domain where the data are stored (e.g. PROCEDURE_OCCURRENCE, DRUG_EXPOSURE, etc), the concept sets built to identify the clinical activity (e.g. SNOMED codes for conditions, RxNorm codes for drugs) as well as

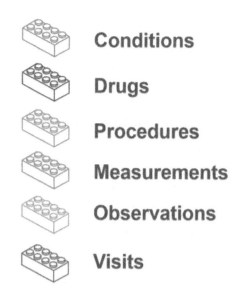

Conditions

Drugs

Procedures

Measurements

Observations

Visits

Figure 10.1: Building Blocks of Cohort definitions.

any other specific attributes (e.g. age at occurrence, first diagnosis/procedure/etc, specifying start and end date, specifying visit type or criteria, days supply, etc). The set of people having an entry event is referred to as the **initial event cohort**.

Inclusion criteria: Inclusion criteria are applied to the initial event cohort to further restrict the set of people. Each inclusion criterion is defined by the CDM domain(s) where the data are stored, concept set(s) representing the clinical activity, domain-specific attributes (e.g. days supply, visit type, etc), and the temporal logic relative to the cohort index date. Each inclusion criterion can be evaluated to determine the impact of the criteria on the attrition of persons from the initial event cohort. The **qualifying cohort** is defined as all people in the initial event cohort that satisfy all inclusion criteria.

Cohort exit criteria: The cohort exit event signifies when a person no longer qualifies for cohort membership. Cohort exit can be defined in multiple ways such as the end of the observation period, a fixed time interval relative to the initial entry event, the last event in a sequence of related observations (e.g. persistent drug exposure) or through other censoring of observation period. Cohort exit strategy will impact whether a person can belong to the cohort multiple times during different time intervals.

In the OHDSI tools there is no distinction between inclusion and exclusion criteria. All criteria are formulated as inclusion criteria. For example, the exclusion criterium "Exclude people with prior hypertension" can be formulated as the inclusion criterium "Include people with 0 occurrences of prior hypertension".

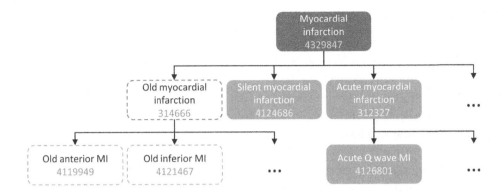

Figure 10.2: A concept set including "Myocardial infaction" (with descendants), but excluding "Old myocardial infarction" (with descendants).

10.3   Concept Sets

A concept set is an expression representing a list of concepts that can be used as a reusable component in various analyses. It can be thought of as a standardized, computer-executable equivalent of the code lists often used in observational studies. A concept set expression consists of a list of concepts with the following attributes:

- **Exclude**: Exclude this concept (and any of its descendants if selected) from the concept set.
- **Descendants**: Consider not only this concept, but also all of its descendants.
- **Mapped**: Allow to search for non-standard concepts.

For example, a concept set expression could contains two concepts as depicted in Table 10.1. Here we include concept 4329847 ("Myocardial infarction") and all of its descendants, but exclude concept 314666 ("Old myocardial infarction") and all of its descendants.

Table 10.1: An example concept set expression.

Concept Id	Concept Name	Excluded	Descendants	Mapped
4329847	Myocardial infarction	NO	YES	NO
314666	Old myocardial infarction	YES	YES	NO

As shown in Figure 10.2, this will include "Myocardial infarction" and all of its descendants except "Old myocardial infarction" and its descendants. In total, this concept set expression implies nearly a hundred Standard Concepts. These Standard Concepts in turn reflect hundreds of source codes (e.g. ICD-9 and ICD-10 codes) that may appear in the various databases.

10.4   Probabilistic Cohort Definitions

Rule-based cohort definitions are a popular method for assembling cohort definitions. However, assembling necessary expert consensus to create a study cohort can be prohibitively time consuming. Probabilistic cohort design is an alternative, machine-driven method to expedite the selection of cohort attributes. In this approach, supervised machine learning allows a phenotyping algorithm to learn from a set of labeled examples (cases) of what attributes contribute to cohort membership. This algorithm can then be used to better ascertain the defining characteristics of a phenotype and what trade-offs occur in overall study accuracy when choosing to modify phenotype criteria.

An example of applying this approach on data in the CDM is the APHRODITE (Automated PHenotype Routine for Observational Definition, Identification, Training and Evaluation) R-package[1] . This package provides a cohort building framework that combines the ability of learning from imperfectly labeled data. (Banda et al., 2017)

10.5   Cohort Definition Validity

When you are building a cohort, you should consider which of these is more important to you: *finding all the eligible patients?* versus *Getting only the ones you are confident about?*

Your strategy to construct your cohort will depend on the clinical stringency of how your expert consensus defines the disease. This is to say, the right cohort design will depend on the question you're trying to answer. You may opt to build a cohort definition that uses everything you can get, uses the lowest common denominator so you can share it across OHDSI sites or is a compromise of the two. It is ultimately at the researcher's discretion what threshold of stringency is necessary to adequately study the cohort of interest.

As mentioned at the beginning of the chapter, a cohort definition is an attempt to infer something we would like to observe from the data that is recorded. This begs the question how well we succeeded in that attempt. In general, the validation of a rule-based cohort definition or probabilistic algorithm can be thought of as a test of the proposed cohort compared to some form of "gold standard" reference (e.g. manual chart review of cases). This is discussed in detail in Chapter 16 ("Clinical Validity").

10.5.1   OHDSI Gold Standard Phenotype Library

To assist the community in the inventory and overall evaluation of existing cohort definitions and algorithms, the OHDSI Gold Standard Phenotype Library (GSPL) Workgroup was formed. The purpose of the GSPL workgroup is to develop a community-backed phenotype library from rules-based and probabilistic methods. The GSPL enable members of the OHDSI community to find, evaluate, and utilize community-validated cohort definitions for

---

[1]https://github.com/OHDSI/Aphrodite

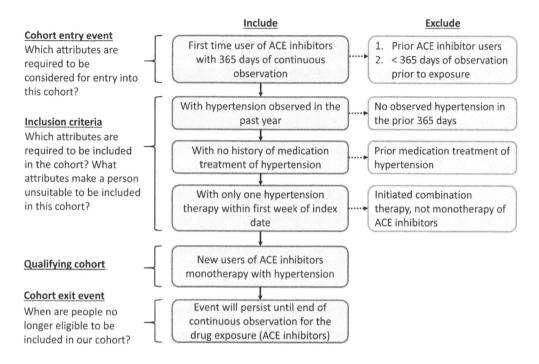

Figure 10.3: Logical Diagram of Intended Cohort

research and other activities. These "gold standard" definitions will reside in a library, the entries of which are held to specific standards of design and evaluation. For additional information related to the GSPL, consult the OHDSI workgroup page.[2] Research within this workgroup includes APHRODITE (Banda et al., 2017) and the PheValuator tool (Swerdel et al., 2019) , discussed in the prior section, as well as work done to share the Electronic Medical Records and Genomics eMERGE Phenotype Library across the OHDSI network (Hripcsak et al., 2019). If phenotype curation is your interest, consider contributing to this workgroup.

10.6 Defining a Cohort for Hypertension

We begin to practice our cohort skills by putting together a cohort definition using a rule-based approach. In this example, we want to find *patients who initiate ACE inhibitors monotherapy as first-line treatments for hypertension*

With this context in mind, we are now going to build our cohort. As we go through this exercise, we will approach building our cohort similar to standard attrition chart. Figure 10.3 shows the logical framework for how we want to build this cohort.

You can build a cohort in the user interface of ATLAS or you can write a query directly against your CDM. We will briefly discuss both in this chapter.

---

[2]https://www.ohdsi.org/web/wiki/doku.php?id=projects:workgroups:gold-library-wg

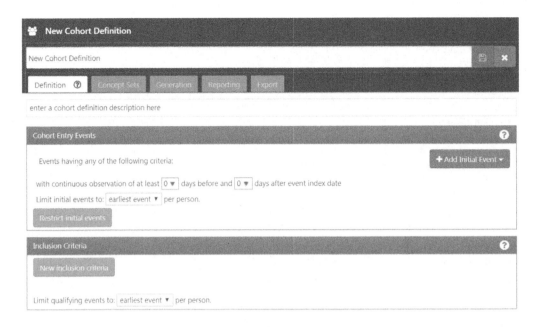

Figure 10.4: New Cohort Definition

10.7   Implementing a Cohort Using ATLAS

To begin in ATLAS, click on the █ Cohort Definitions module. When the module loads, click on "New cohort". The next screen you will see will be an empty cohort definition. Figure 10.4 shows what you will see on your screen.

Before you do anything else, you are encouraged to change the name of the cohort from "New Cohort Definition" to your own unique name for this cohort. You may opt for a name like "New users of ACE inhibitors as first-line monotherapy for hypertension".

> ATLAS will not allow two cohorts to have the same exact names. ATLAS will give you a pop-up error message if you choose a name already used by another ATLAS cohort.

Once you have chosen a name, you can save the cohort by clicking 🖫.

10.7.1   Initial Event Criteria

Now we can proceed with defining the initial cohort event. You will click "Add initial event". You now have to pick which domain you are building a criteria around. You may ask yourself, "how do I know which domain is the initial cohort event?" Let's figure that out.

As we see in Figure 10.5, ATLAS provides descriptions below each criteria to help you. If we were building a CONDITION_OCCURRENCE based criteria, our question would be look-

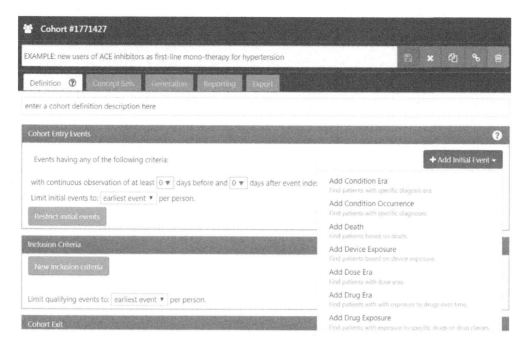

Figure 10.5: Adding an Initial Event

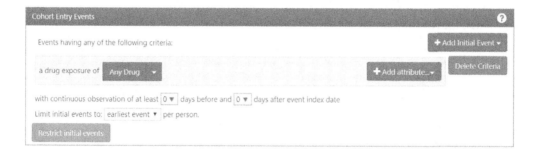

Figure 10.6: Defining a Drug Exposure

ing for patients with a specific diagnosis. If we were building a DRUG_EXPOSURE based criteria, our question would be looking for patients with a specific drug or drug class. Since we want to find patients who initiate ACE inhibitors monotherapy as first-line treatments for hypertension, we want to choose a DRUG_EXPOSURE criteria. You may say, "but we also care about hypertension as a diagnosis". You are correct. Hypertension is another criterion we will build. However, the cohort start date is defined by the initiation of the ACE inhibitor treatment, which is therefore the initial event. The diagnosis of hypertension is what we call an *additional qualifying criteria*. We will return to this once we build this criteria. We will click "Add Drug Exposure".

The screen will update with your selected criteria but you are not done yet. As we see in Figure 10.6, ATLAS does not know what drug we are looking for. We need to tell ATLAS which concept set is associated to ACE inhibitors.

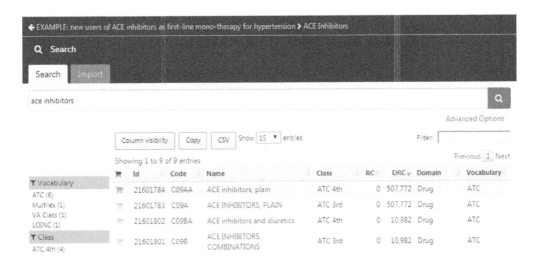

Figure 10.7: Searching the Vocabulary - ACE Inhibitors

10.7.2   Defining the Concept Set

You will need to click ![icon] to open the dialogue box that will allow you to retrieve a concept set to define ACE Inhibitors.

Scenario 1: You Have Not Built a Concept Set

If you have not assembled your concept sets to apply to your criteria, you will need to do so before you move forward. You may build a concept set within the cohort definition by navigating to the "Concept set" tab and clicking "New Concept Set". You will need to rename the concept set from "Unnamed Concept Set" to a name of your choosing. From there you can use the **Q Search** module to look for clinical concepts that represent ACE inhibitors (Figure 10.7).

When you have found terms that you would like to use to define this drug exposure, you can select the concept by clicking on ![icon] . You can return to your cohort definition by using the left arrow in the top left of Figure 10.7. You can refer back to Chapter 5 (Standardized Vocabularies) on how to navigate the vocabularies to find clinical concepts of interest.

Figure 10.8 shows our concept set expression. We selected all ACE inhibitor ingredients we are interested in, and include all their descendants, thus including all drugs that contain any of these ingredients. We can click on "Included concepts" to see all 21,536 concepts implied by this expression, or we can click on "Included Source Codes" to explore all source codes in the various coding systems that are implied.

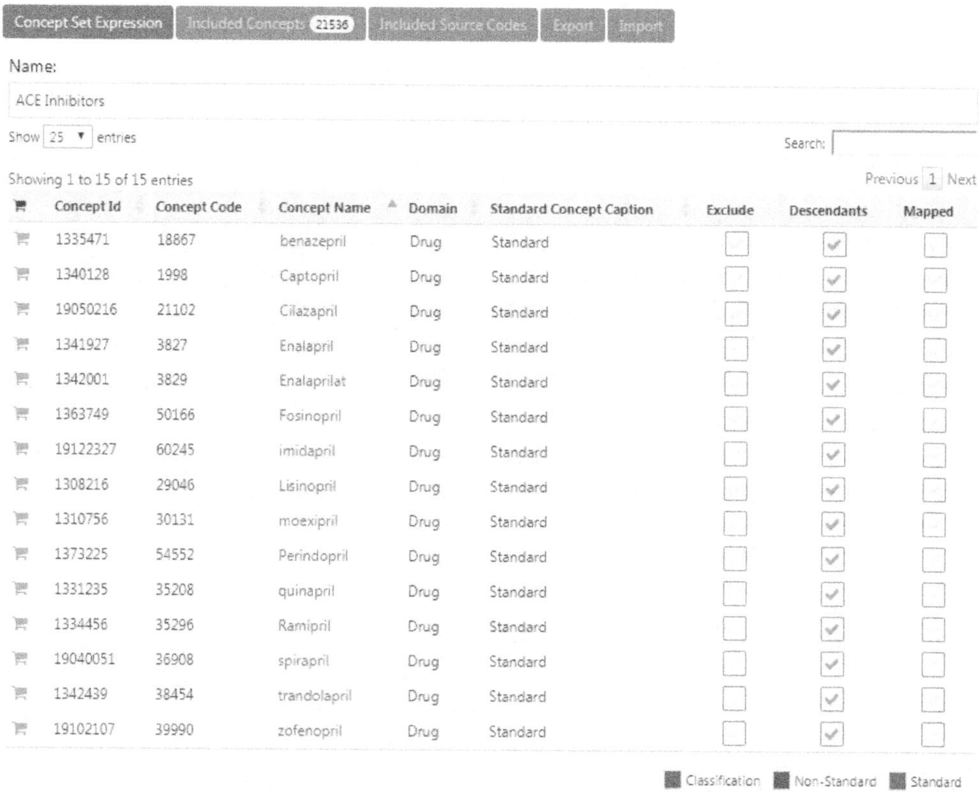

	Concept Id	Concept Code	Concept Name ▲	Domain	Standard Concept Caption	Exclude	Descendants	Mapped
🛒	1335471	18867	benazepril	Drug	Standard	☐	☑	☐
🛒	1340128	1998	Captopril	Drug	Standard	☐	☑	☐
🛒	19050216	21102	Cilazapril	Drug	Standard	☐	☑	☐
🛒	1341927	3827	Enalapril	Drug	Standard	☐	☑	☐
🛒	1342001	3829	Enalaprilat	Drug	Standard	☐	☑	☐
🛒	1363749	50166	Fosinopril	Drug	Standard	☐	☑	☐
🛒	19122327	60245	imidapril	Drug	Standard	☐	☑	☐
🛒	1308216	29046	Lisinopril	Drug	Standard	☐	☑	☐
🛒	1310756	30131	moexipril	Drug	Standard	☐	☑	☐
🛒	1373225	54552	Perindopril	Drug	Standard	☐	☑	☐
🛒	1331235	35208	quinapril	Drug	Standard	☐	☑	☐
🛒	1334456	35296	Ramipril	Drug	Standard	☐	☑	☐
🛒	19040051	36908	spirapril	Drug	Standard	☐	☑	☐
🛒	1342439	38454	trandolapril	Drug	Standard	☐	☑	☐
🛒	19102107	39990	zofenopril	Drug	Standard	☐	☑	☐

Figure 10.8: A concept set containing ACE inhibitor drugs.

Import Concept Set From Repository...				

New Concept Set

Show 10 ▼ entries   Filter Repository Concept Sets: |ace inhibitors|

Id	Title	Created	Modified	Author
1794480	[OHDSI EU 2019] Excluded concepts of ACE inhibitors or Thiazide diuretics	03/28/2019 11:04 AM	03/28/2019 11:04 AM	anonymous
963	ACE Inhibitors			anonymous
3268	COPY OF: ACE Inhibitors			anonymous
99283	Ace Inhibitors			anonymous
142965	PheKB ACE-I ACE inhibitors			anonymous

Showing 1 to 5 of 5 entries (filtered from 11,667 total entries)   Previous 1 Next

Figure 10.9: Importing a Concept Set from ATLAS Repository

Scenario 2: You Have Already Built a Concept Set

If you have already created a concept set and saved it in ATLAS, you can click to "Import Concept Set". A dialogue box will open that will be prompt you to find your concept in the concept set repository of your ATLAS as shown in Figure 10.9. In the example figure the user is retrieving concept sets stored in ATLAS. The user typed in the name given to this concept set "ace inhibitors" in the right hand search. This shortened the concept set list to only concepts with matching names. From there, the user can click on the row of the concept set to select it. (Note: the dialogue box will disappear once you have selected a concept set.) You will know this action is successful when the Any Drug box is updated with the name of the concept set you selected.

10.7.3   Additional Initial Event Criteria

Now that you've attached a concept set, you are not done yet. Your question is looking for new users or the first time in someone's history they are exposed to ACE inhibitors. This translates to the *first exposure* of ACE inhibitors in the patient's record. To specify this, you need to click "+Add attribute". You will want to select the "Add first exposure criteria". Notice, you could specify other attributes of a criteria you build. You could specify an attribute of age at occurrence, the date of occurrence, gender or other attributes related to the drug. Criteria available for selection will look different for each domain.

From there, the window will automatically close. Once selected, this additional attribute will show up in the same box as the initial criteria (see Figure 10.10).

 The current design of ATLAS may confuse some. Despite its appearance, the ✖ is not intended to mean "No". It is an actionable feature to allow the user to delete the criteria. If you click ✖, this criteria will go away. Thus, you need to leave the criteria

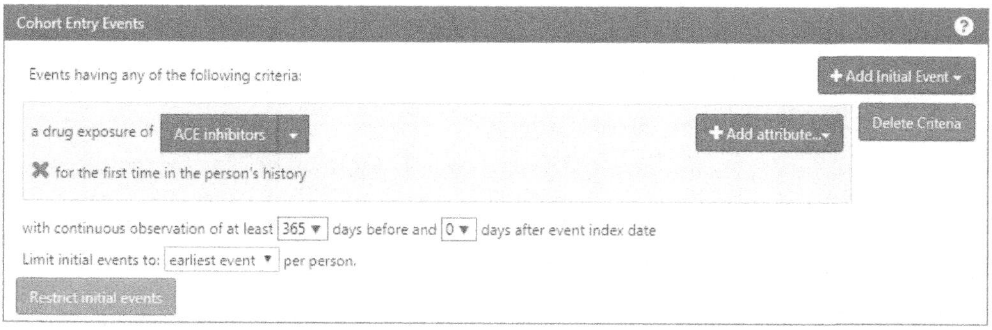

Figure 10.10: Setting the required continuous observation before the index date.

with the ✖ to keep the criteria active.

Now you have built an initial qualifying event. To ensure you are capturing the first observed drug exposure, you will want to add a look-back window to know that you are looking at enough of the patient's history to know what comes first. It is possible that a patient with a short observation period may have received an exposure elsewhere that we do not see. We cannot control this but we can mandate a minimum amount of time the patient must be in the data prior to the index date You can do this by adjusting the continuous observation drop downs. You could also click the box and type in a value to these windows. We will require 365 days of continuous observation prior to the initial event. You will update your observation period to: *with continuous observation of 365 days before*, as shown in Figure 10.10. This look-back window is the discretion of your study team. You may choose differently in other cohorts. This creates, as best as we are able, a minimum period of time we see the patient to ensure we are capturing the first record. This criteria is about prior history and does not involve time after the index event. Therefore, we require 0 days after the index event. Our qualifying event is the first-ever use of ACE inhibitors. Thus, we limit initial events to the "earliest event" per person.

To further explain how this logic comes together, you can think about assembling patient timelines.

In Figure 10.11, each line represents a single patient that may be eligible to join the cohort. The filled in stars represent a time the patient fulfills the specified criteria. As additional criteria is applied, you may see some stars are a lighter shade. This means that these patients have other records that satisfy the criteria but there is another record that proceeds that. By the time we get to the last criteria, we are looking at the cumulative view of patients who have ACE inhibitors for the first time and have 365 days prior to the first-time occurrence. Logically, limiting to the initial event is redundant though it is helpful to maintain our explicit logic in every selection we make. When you are building your own cohorts, you may opt to engage the Researchers section of the OHDSI Forum to get a second opinion on how to construct your cohort logic.

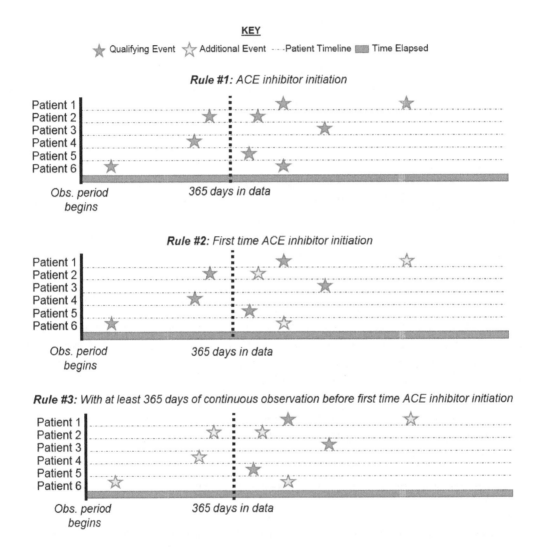

Figure 10.11: Explaining patient eligibility by criteria applied

10.7.4 Inclusion Criteria

Once we have specified a cohort entry event, you could proceed to one of two places to add your additional qualifying events: "Restrict initial events" and "New inclusion criteria". The fundamental difference between these two options is what interim information you want ATLAS to serve back to you. If you add additional qualifying criteria into the Cohort Entry Event box by selecting "Restrict initial events", when you choose to generate a count in ATLAS, you will only get back the number of people who meet ALL of these criteria. If you opt to add criteria into the "New inclusion criteria", you will get an attrition chart to show you how many patients are lost by applying additional inclusion criteria. It is highly encouraged to utilize the Inclusion Criteria section so you can understand the impact of each rule on the overall success of the cohort definition. You may find a certain inclusion criteria severely limits the number of people who end up in the cohort. You may choose to relax this criterion to get a larger cohort. This will ultimately be at the discretion of the expert consensus assembling this cohort.

You will now want to click "New inclusion criteria" to add a subsequent piece of logic about membership to this cohort. The functionality in this section is identical to the way we discussed building cohort criteria above. You may specific the criteria and add specific attributes. Our first additional criteria is to subset the cohort to only patients: *With at least 1 occurrence of hypertension disorder between 365 and 0 days after index date (first initiation of an ACE inhibitor)*. You will click "New inclusion criteria" to add a new criteria. You should name your criteria and, if desired, put a little description of what you are looking for. This is for your own purposes to recall what you build – it will not impact the integrity of the cohort you are defining.

Once you have annotated this new criteria, you will click on the "+Add criteria to group" button to build your actual criteria for this rule. This button functions similar to the "Add Initial Event" except we are no longer specifying an initial event. We could add multiple criteria to this – which is why it specifies "add criteria to group". An example would be if you have multiple ways of finding a disease (e.g. logic for a CONDITION_OCCURRENCE, logic using a DRUG_EXPOSURE as a proxy for this condition, logic for using a MEASUREMENT as a proxy for this condition). These would be separate domains and require different criteria but can be grouped into one criteria looking for this condition. In this case, we want to find a diagnosis of hypertension so we "Add condition occurrence". We will follow similar steps as we did with the initial event by attaching a concept set to this record. We also want to specify the event starts between 365 days before and 0 days after the index date (the occurrence of the first ACE inhibitor use). Now check your logic against Figure 10.12.

You will then want to add another criterion to look for patients: *with exactly 0 occurrences of hypertension drugs ALL days before and 1 day before index start date (no exposure to HT drugs before an ACE inhibitor)*. This process begins as we did before by clicking the "New inclusion criteria" button, adding your annotations to this criterion and then clicking "+Add criteria to group". This is a DRUG_EXPOSURE so you will click "Add Drug Exposure", attach a concept set for hypertensive drugs, and will specify ALL days before and 0 days after the index date. Make sure to confirm you have *exactly 0* occurrence selected. Now

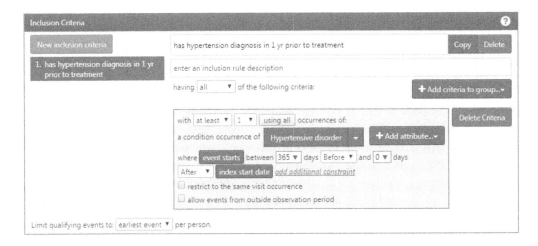

Figure 10.12: Additional Inclusion criteria 1

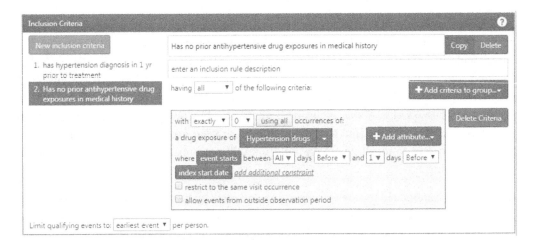

Figure 10.13: Additional Inclusion Criteria 2

check your logic against Figure 10.13.

You may be confused why "having no occurrences" is coded as "exactly 0 occurrences." This is a nuance of how ATLAS consumes knowledge. ATLAS only consumes inclusion criteria. You must use logical operators to indicate when you want the absence of a specific attribute such as: "Exactly 0." Over time you will become more familiar with the logical operators available in ATLAS criteria.

Lastly, you will want to add your another criterion to look for patients: *with exactly 1 occurrence of hypertension drugs between 0 days before and 7 days after index start date AND can only start one HT drug (an ACE inhibitor)* . This process begins as we did before by clicking the "New inclusion criteria" button, adding your annotations to this criterion and then clicking "+Add criteria to group". This is a DRUG_EXPOSURE so you will click "Add Drug Exposure", attach a concept set for hypertensive drugs, and will specify 0 days before

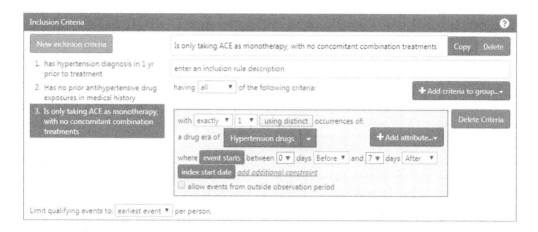

Figure 10.14: Additional Inclusion Criteria 3

and 7 days after the index date. Now check your logic against Figure 10.14.

10.7.5   Cohort Exit Criteria

You have now added all of your qualifying inclusion criteria. You must now specify your cohort exit criteria. You will ask yourself, "when are people no longer eligible to be included in this cohort?" In this cohort, we are following new-users of a drug exposure. We want to look at continuous observation period as it relates to the drug exposure. As such, the exit criterion is specified to follow for the entirety of the continuous drug exposure. If there is a subsequent break in the drug exposure, the patient will exit the cohort at this time. We do this as we cannot determine what happened to the person during the break in the drug exposure. We can also set a criteria on the persistence window to specify an allowable gap between drug exposures. In this case, our experts leading this study concluded that a maximum of 30 days between exposure records is allowable when inferring the era of persistence exposure.

Why are gaps allowed? In some data sets, we see only portions of clinical interactions. Drug exposures, in particular, may represent a dispense of a prescription that can cover a certain period of time. Thus, we allow a certain amount of time between drug exposures as we know the patient may logically still have access to the initial drug exposure because the unit of dispense exceeded one day.

We can configure this by selecting the Event will persist "end of a continuous drug exposure". We then will add our persistence window to "allow for a maximum of 30 days" and append the concept set for "ACE inhibitors". Now check your logic against Figure 10.15.

In the case of this cohort, there are no other censoring events. However, you may build other cohorts where you need to specify this criteria. You would proceed similarly to the way we have added other attributes to this cohort definition. You have now successfully finished creating your cohort. Make sure to hit the 🖫 button. Congratulations! Building a cohort is the most important building block of answering a question in the OHDSI tools. You can

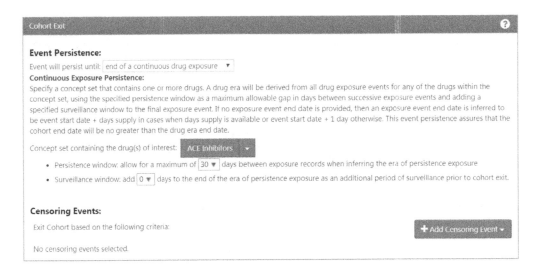

Figure 10.15: Cohort Exit Criteria

now use the "Export" tab to share your cohort definition to other collaborators in the form of SQL code or JSON files to load into ATLAS.

10.8   Implementing the Cohort Using SQL

Here we describe how to create the same cohort, but using SQL and R. As discussed in Chapter 9, OHDSI provides two R packages, called SqlRender and DatabaseConnector, which together allow writing SQL code that can be automatically translated and executed against a wide variety of database platforms.

For clarity, we will split the SQL into several chunks, each chunk generating a temp table that is used in the next. This is likely not the most computationally efficient way to do it, but it is easier to read than a single very long statement.

10.8.1   Connecting to the Database

We first need to tell R how to connect to the server.   We use the DatabaseConnector package, which provides a function called `createConnectionDetails`.   Type `?createConnectionDetails` for the specific settings required for the various database management systems (DBMS). For example, one might connect to a PostgreSQL database using this code:

```
library(CohortMethod)
connDetails <- createConnectionDetails(dbms = "postgresql",
                                       server = "localhost/ohdsi",
```

```
                                     user = "joe",
                                     password = "supersecret")

cdmDbSchema <- "my_cdm_data"
cohortDbSchema <- "scratch"
cohortTable <- "my_cohorts"
```

The last three lines define the `cdmDbSchema`, `cohortDbSchema`, and `cohortTable` variables. We will use these later to tell R where the data in CDM format live, and where the cohorts of interest have to be created. Note that for Microsoft SQL Server, database schemas need to specify both the database and the schema, so for example `cdmDbSchema <- "my_cdm_data.dbo"`.

10.8.2 Specifying the Concepts

For readability we will define the concept IDs we need in R, and pass them to the SQL:

```
aceI <- c(1308216, 1310756, 1331235, 1334456, 1335471, 1340128, 1341927,
          1342439, 1363749, 1373225)

hypertension <- 316866

allHtDrugs <- c(904542, 907013, 932745, 942350, 956874, 970250, 974166,
                978555, 991382, 1305447, 1307046, 1307863, 1308216,
                1308842, 1309068, 1309799, 1310756, 1313200, 1314002,
                1314577, 1317640, 1317967, 1318137, 1318853, 1319880,
                1319998, 1322081, 1326012, 1327978, 1328165, 1331235,
                1332418, 1334456, 1335471, 1338005, 1340128, 1341238,
                1341927, 1342439, 1344965, 1345858, 1346686, 1346823,
                1347384, 1350489, 1351557, 1353766, 1353776, 1363053,
                1363749, 1367500, 1373225, 1373928, 1386957, 1395058,
                1398937, 40226742, 40235485)
```

10.8.3 Finding First Use

We will first find first use of ACE inhibitors for each patient:

```
conn <- connect(connectionDetails)

sql <- "SELECT person_id AS subject_id,
  MIN(drug_exposure_start_date) AS cohort_start_date
INTO #first_use
FROM @cdm_db_schema.drug_exposure
INNER JOIN @cdm_db_schema.concept_ancestor
```

```
   ON descendant_concept_id = drug_concept_id
WHERE ancestor_concept_id IN (@ace_i)
GROUP BY person_id;"

renderTranslateExecuteSql(conn,
                          sql,
                          cdm_db_schema = cdmDbSchema,
                          ace_i = aceI)
```

Note that we join the DRUG_EXPOSURE table to the CONCEPT_ANCESTOR table to find all drugs that contain an ACE inhibitor.

10.8.4   Require 365 Days of Prior Observation

Next, we require 365 of continuous prior observation by joining to the OBSERVA-TION_PERIOD table:

```
sql <- "SELECT subject_id,
  cohort_start_date
INTO #has_prior_obs
FROM #first_use
INNER JOIN @cdm_db_schema.observation_period
  ON subject_id = person_id
    AND observation_period_start_date <= cohort_start_date
    AND observation_period_end_date >= cohort_start_date
WHERE DATEADD(DAY, 365, observation_period_start_date) < cohort_start_date;"

renderTranslateExecuteSql(conn, sql, cdm_db_schema = cdmDbSchema)
```

10.8.5   Require Prior Hypertension

We require a hypertension diagnosis in the 365 days prior:

```
sql <- "SELECT DISTINCT subject_id,
  cohort_start_date
INTO #has_ht
FROM #has_prior_obs
INNER JOIN @cdm_db_schema.condition_occurrence
  ON subject_id = person_id
    AND condition_start_date <= cohort_start_date
    AND condition_start_date >= DATEADD(DAY, -365, cohort_start_date)
INNER JOIN @cdm_db_schema.concept_ancestor
  ON descendant_concept_id = condition_concept_id
WHERE ancestor_concept_id = @hypertension;"
```

```
renderTranslateExecuteSql(conn,
                          sql,
                          cdm_db_schema = cdmDbSchema,
                          hypertension = hypertension)
```

Note that we SELECT DISTINCT, because else if a person has multiple hypertension diagnoses in their past, we would create duplicate cohort entries.

10.8.6   No Prior Treatment

We require no prior exposure to any hypertension treatment:

```
sql <- "SELECT subject_id,
  cohort_start_date
INTO #no_prior_ht_drugs
FROM #has_ht
LEFT JOIN (
  SELECT *
  FROM @cdm_db_schema.drug_exposure
  INNER JOIN @cdm_db_schema.concept_ancestor
    ON descendant_concept_id = drug_concept_id
  WHERE ancestor_concept_id IN (@all_ht_drugs)
) ht_drugs
  ON subject_id = person_id
    AND drug_exposure_start_date < cohort_start_date
WHERE person_id IS NULL;"

renderTranslateExecuteSql(conn,
                          sql,
                          cdm_db_schema = cdmDbSchema,
                          all_ht_drugs = allHtDrugs)
```

Note that we use a left join, and only allow rows where the person_id, which comes from the DRUG_EXPOSURE table is NULL, meaning no matching record was found.

10.8.7   Monotherapy

We require there to be only one exposure to hypertension treatment in the first seven days of the cohort entry:

```
sql <- "SELECT subject_id,
  cohort_start_date
INTO #monotherapy
FROM #no_prior_ht_drugs
```

```
INNER JOIN @cdm_db_schema.drug_exposure
  ON subject_id = person_id
    AND drug_exposure_start_date >= cohort_start_date
    AND drug_exposure_start_date <= DATEADD(DAY, 7, cohort_start_date)
INNER JOIN @cdm_db_schema.concept_ancestor
  ON descendant_concept_id = drug_concept_id
WHERE ancestor_concept_id IN (@all_ht_drugs)
GROUP BY subject_id,
  cohort_start_date
HAVING COUNT(*) = 1;"

renderTranslateExecuteSql(conn,
                          sql,
                          cdm_db_schema = cdmDbSchema,
                          all_ht_drugs = allHtDrugs)
```

10.8.8 Cohort Exit

We have now fully specified our cohort except the cohort end date. The cohort is defined to end when the exposure stops, allowing for a maximum 30-day gap between subsequent exposures. This means we need to not only consider the first drug exposure, but also subsequent drug exposures to ACE inhibitors. The SQL for combining subsequent exposures into eras can be highly complex. Luckily, standard code has been defined that can efficiently create eras. (This code was written by Chris Knoll, and is often referred to within OHDSI as 'the magic'). We first create a temp table containing all exposures we wish to merge:

```
sql <- "
  SELECT person_id,
    CAST(1 AS INT) AS concept_id,
    drug_exposure_start_date AS exposure_start_date,
    drug_exposure_end_date AS exposure_end_date
  INTO #exposure
  FROM @cdm_db_schema.drug_exposure
  INNER JOIN @cdm_db_schema.concept_ancestor
    ON descendant_concept_id = drug_concept_id
  WHERE ancestor_concept_id IN (@ace_i);"
renderTranslateExecuteSql(conn,
                          sql,
                          cdm_db_schema = cdmDbSchema,
                          ace_i = aceI)
```

We then run the standard code for merging sequential exposures:

```
sql <- "
SELECT ends.person_id AS subject_id,
```

```
    ends.concept_id AS cohort_definition_id,
  MIN(exposure_start_date) AS cohort_start_date,
  ends.era_end_date AS cohort_end_date
INTO #exposure_era
FROM (
  SELECT exposure.person_id,
    exposure.concept_id,
    exposure.exposure_start_date,
    MIN(events.end_date) AS era_end_date
  FROM #exposure exposure
  JOIN (
--cteEndDates
    SELECT person_id,
      concept_id,
      DATEADD(DAY, - 1 * @max_gap, event_date) AS end_date
    FROM (
      SELECT person_id,
        concept_id,
        event_date,
        event_type,
        MAX(start_ordinal) OVER (
          PARTITION BY person_id ,concept_id ORDER BY event_date,
              event_type ROWS UNBOUNDED PRECEDING
        ) AS start_ordinal,
        ROW_NUMBER() OVER (
          PARTITION BY person_id, concept_id ORDER BY event_date,
            event_type
        ) AS overall_ord
      FROM (
-- select the start dates, assigning a row number to each
        SELECT person_id,
          concept_id,
          exposure_start_date AS event_date,
          0 AS event_type,
          ROW_NUMBER() OVER (
            PARTITION BY person_id, concept_id ORDER BY exposure_start_date
          ) AS start_ordinal
        FROM #exposure exposure

        UNION ALL
-- add the end dates with NULL as the row number, padding the end dates by
-- @max_gap to allow a grace period for overlapping ranges.

        SELECT person_id,
          concept_id,
          DATEADD(day, @max_gap, exposure_end_date),
          1 AS event_type,
          NULL
        FROM #exposure exposure
```

```
            ) rawdata
        ) events
    WHERE 2 * events.start_ordinal - events.overall_ord = 0
    ) events
    ON exposure.person_id = events.person_id
        AND exposure.concept_id = events.concept_id
        AND events.end_date >= exposure.exposure_end_date
    GROUP BY exposure.person_id,
        exposure.concept_id,
        exposure.exposure_start_date
    ) ends
GROUP BY ends.person_id,
    concept_id,
    ends.era_end_date;"

renderTranslateExecuteSql(conn,
                          sql,
                          cdm_db_schema = cdmDbSchema,
                          max_gap = 30)
```

This code merges all subsequent exposures, allowing for a gap between exposures as defined by the `max_gap` argument. The resulting drug exposure eras are written to a temp table called `#exposure_era`.

Next, we simply join these ACE inhibitor exposure eras to our original cohort to use the era end dates as our cohort end dates:

```
sql <- "SELECT ee.subject_id,
  CAST(1 AS INT) AS cohort_definition_id,
  ee.cohort_start_date,
  ee.cohort_end_date
INTO @cohort_db_schema.@cohort_table
FROM #monotherapy mt
INNER JOIN #exposure_era ee
  ON mt.subject_id = ee.subject_id
    AND mt.cohort_start_date = ee.cohort_start_date;"

renderTranslateExecuteSql(conn,
                          sql,
                          cohort_db_schema = cohortDbSchema,
                          cohort_table = cohortTable)
```

Here we store the final cohort in schema and table we defined earlier. We assign it a cohort definition ID of 1, to distinguish it from other cohorts we may wish to store in the same table.

10.8.9 Cleanup

Finally, it is always recommend to clean up any temp tables that were created, and disconnect from the database server:

```
sql <- "TRUNCATE TABLE #first_use;
DROP TABLE #first_use;

TRUNCATE TABLE #has_prior_obs;
DROP TABLE #has_prior_obs;

TRUNCATE TABLE #has_ht;
DROP TABLE #has_ht;

TRUNCATE TABLE #no_prior_ht_drugs;
DROP TABLE #no_prior_ht_drugs;

TRUNCATE TABLE #monotherapy;
DROP TABLE #monotherapy;

TRUNCATE TABLE #exposure;
DROP TABLE #exposure;

TRUNCATE TABLE #exposure_era;
DROP TABLE #exposure_era;"

renderTranslateExecuteSql(conn, sql)

disconnect(conn)
```

10.9 Summary

- A cohort is set of persons who satisfy one or more inclusion criteria for a duration of time.

- A cohort definition is the description of logic used for identifying a particular cohort.

- Cohorts are used (and re-used) throughout the OHDSI analytics tools to define for example the exposures and outcomes of interest.

- There are two major approaches to building a cohort: rule-based and probabilistic.

- Rule-based cohort definitions can be created in ATLAS, or using SQL

10.10   Exercises

Prerequisites

For the first exercise, access to an ATLAS instance is required. You can use the instance at http://atlas-demo.ohdsi.org, or any other instance you have acces to.

Exercise 10.1. Use ATLAS to create a cohort definition following these criteria:

- New users of diclofenac
- Ages 16 or older
- With at least 365 days of continuous observation prior to exposure
- Without prior exposure to any NSAID (Non-Steroidal Anti-Inflammatory Drug)
- Without prior diagnosis of cancer
- With cohort exit defined as discontinuation of exposure (allowing for a 30-day gap)

Prerequisites

For the second exercise we assume R, R-Studio and Java have been installed as described in Section 8.4.5. Also required are the SqlRender, DatabaseConnector, and Eunomia packages, which can be installed using:

```
install.packages(c("SqlRender", "DatabaseConnector", "devtools"))
devtools::install_github("ohdsi/Eunomia", ref = "v1.0.0")
```

The Eunomia package provides a simulated dataset in the CDM that will run inside your local R session. The connection details can be obtained using:

```
connectionDetails <- Eunomia::getEunomiaConnectionDetails()
```

The CDM database schema is "main".

Exercise 10.2. Use SQL and R to create a cohort for acute myocardial infarction (AMI) in the existing COHORT table, following these criteria:

- An occurrence of a myocardial infarction diagnose (concept 4329847 "Myocardial infarction" and all of its descendants, excluding concept 314666 "Old myocardial infarction" and any of its descendants).
- During an inpatient or ER visit (concepts 9201, 9203, and 262 for "Inpatient visit", "Emergency Room Visit", and "Emergency Room and Inpatient Visit", respectively).

Suggested answers can be found in Appendix E.6.

Chapter 11

Characterization

Chapter leads: Anthony Sena & Daniel Prieto-Alhambra

Observational healthcare databases provide a valuable resource to understand variations in populations based on a host of characteristics. Characterizing populations through the use of descriptive statistics is an important first step in generating hypotheses about the determinants of health and disease. In this chapter we cover methods for characterization:

- **Database-level characterization**: provides a top-level set of summary statistics to understand the data profile of a database in its totality.
- **Cohort characterization**: describes a population in terms of its aggregate medical history.
- **Treatment pathways**: describes the sequence of interventions a person received for a duration of time.
- **Incidence**: measures the occurrence rate of an outcome in a population for a time at risk.

With the exception of database-level characterization, these methods aim to describe a population relative to an event referred to as the index date. This population of interest is defined as a cohort as described in chapter 10. The cohort defines the index date for each person in the population of interest. Using the index date as an anchor, we define the time preceding the index date as **baseline** time. The index date and all time after is called the **post-index** time.

Use-cases for characterization include disease natural history, treatment utilization and quality improvement. In this chapter will describe the methods for characterization. We will use a population of hypertensive persons to demonstrate how to use ATLAS and R to perform these characterization tasks.

11.1   Database Level Characterization

Before we can answer any characterization question about a population of interest, we must first understand the characteristics of the database we intend to utilize. Database level characterization seeks to describe the totality of a database in terms of the temporal trends and distributions. This quantitative assessment of a database will typically include questions such as:

- What is the total count of persons in this database?
- What is the distribution of age for persons?
- How long are persons in this database observed for?
- What is the proportion of persons having a {treatment, condition, procedure, etc} recorded/prescribed over time?

These database-level descriptive statistics also help a researcher to understand what data may be missing in a database. Chapter 15 goes into further detail on data quality.

11.2   Cohort Characterization

Cohort characterization describes the baseline and post-index characteristics of people in a cohort. OHDSI approaches characterization through descriptive statistics of all conditions, drug and device exposures, procedures and other clinical observations that are present in the person's history. We also summarize the socio-demographics of members of the cohort at the index date. This approach provides a complete summary of the cohort of interest. Importantly, this enables a full exploration of the cohort with an eye towards variation in the data while also allowing for identification of potentially missing values.

Cohort characterization methods can be used for person-level drug utilization studies (DUS) to estimate the prevalence of indications and contraindications amongst users of a given treatment. The dissemination of this cohort characterization is a recommended best practice for observational studies as detailed in the Strengthening the Reporting of Observation Studies in Epidemiology (STROBE) guidelines. (von Elm et al., 2008)

11.3   Treatment Pathways

Another method to characterize a population is to describe the treatment sequence during the post-index time window. For example, Hripcsak et al. (2016) utilized the OHDSI common data standards to create descriptive statistics to characterize treatment pathways for type 2 diabetes, hypertension and depression. By standardizing this analytic approach, Hripcsak and colleagues were able to run the same analysis across the OHDSI network to describe the characteristics of these populations of interest.

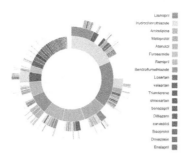

Figure 11.1: OHDSI Treatment Pathways "sunburst" visualization for hypertension

The pathway analysis aims to summarize the treatments (events) received by persons diagnosed with a specific condition from the first drug prescription/dispensation. In this study, treatments were described after the diagnosis of type 2 diabetes, hypertension and depression respectively. The events for each person were then aggregated to a set of summary statistics and visualized for each condition and for each database.

As an example, figure 11.1 represents a population of persons initiating treatment for hypertension. The first ring in the center shows the proportion of persons based on their first-line therapy. In this example, Hydrochlorothiazide is the most common first-line therapy for this population. The boxes that extend from the Hydrochlorothiazide section represent the 2nd and 3rd line therapies recorded for persons in the cohort.

A pathways analysis provides important evidence about treatment utilization amongst a population. From this analysis we can describe the most prevalent first-line therapies utilized, the proportion of persons that discontinue treatment, switch treatments or augment their therapy. Using the pathway analysis, Hripcsak et al. (2016) found that metformin is the most commonly prescribed medication for diabetes thus confirming general adoption of the first-line recommendation of the American Association of Clinical Endocrinologists diabetes treatment algorithm. Additionally, they noted that 10% of diabetes patients, 24% of hypertension patients, and 11% of depression patients followed a treatment pathway that was shared with no one else in any of the data sources.

In classic DUS terminology, treatment pathway analyses include some population-level DUS estimates such as prevalence of use of one or more medications in a specified population, as well as some person-level DUS including measures of persistence and switching between different therapies.

11.4   Incidence

Incidence rates and proportions are statistics that are used in public health to assess the occurrence of a new outcome in a population during a time-at-risk (TAR). Figure 11.2 aims to show the components of an incidence calculation for a single person:

In figure 11.2, a person has a period of time where they are observed in the data denoted by

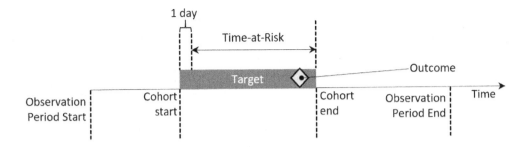

Figure 11.2: Person-level view of incidence calculation components. In this example, time-at-risk is defined to start one day after cohort start, and end at cohort end.

their observation start and end time. Next, the person has a point in time where they enter and exit a cohort by meeting some eligibility criteria. The time at risk window then denotes when we seek to understand the occurrence of an outcome. If the outcome falls into the TAR, we count that as an incidence of the outcome.

There are two metrics for calculating incidence:

$$Incidence\ Proportion = \frac{\#\ persons\ in\ cohort\ with\ new\ outcome\ during\ TAR}{\#\ persons\ in\ cohort\ with\ TAR}$$

An incidence proportion provides a measure of the new outcomes per person in the population during the time-at-risk. Stated another way, this is the proportion of the population of interest that developed the outcome in a defined timeframe.

$$Incidence\ Rate = \frac{\#\ persons\ in\ cohort\ with\ new\ outcome\ during\ TAR}{person\ time\ at\ risk\ contributed\ by\ persons\ in\ cohort}$$

An incidence rate is a measure of the number of new outcomes during the cumulative TAR for the population. When a person experiences the outcome in the TAR, their contribution to the total person-time stops at the occurrence of the outcome event. The cumulative TAR is referred to as **person-time** and is expressed in days, months or years.

When calculated for therapies, incidence proportions and incidence rates of use of a given therapy are classic population-level DUS.

11.5   Characterizing Hypertensive Persons

Per the World Health Organization's (WHO) global brief on hypertension (Who, 2013), there are significant health and economic gains attached to early detection, adequate treatment and good control of hypertension. The WHO brief provides an overview of hypertension

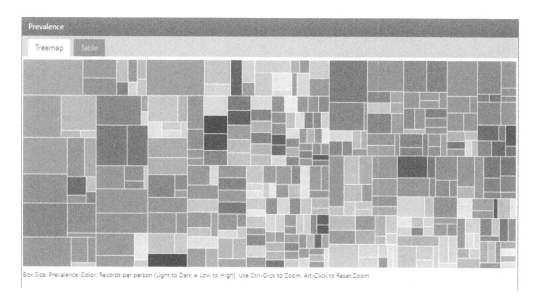

Figure 11.3: Atlas Data Sources: Condition Occurrence Treemap

and characterizes the burden of the disease across different countries. The WHO provides descriptive statistics around hypertension for geographic regions, socio-economic class and gender.

Observational data sources provide a way to characterize hypertensive populations as was done by the WHO. In the subsequent sections of this chapter, we'll explore the ways that we make use of ATLAS and R to explore a database to understand its composition for studying hypertensive populations. Then, we will use these same tools to describe the natural history and treatment patterns of hypertensive populations.

11.6 Database Characterization in ATLAS

Here we demonstrate how to use the data sources module in ATLAS to explore database characterization statistics created with ACHILLES to find database level characteristics related to hypertensive persons. Start by clicking on ▤ Data Sources in the left bar of ATLAS to start. In the first drop down list shown in ATLAS, select the database to explore. Next, use the drop down below the database to start exploring reports. To do this, select the Condition Occurrence from the report drop down which will reveal a treemap visualization of all conditions present in the database:

To search for a specific condition of interest, click on the Table tab to reveal the full list of conditions in the database with person count, prevalence and records per person. Using the filter box on the top, we can filter down the entries in the table based on concept name containing the term "hypertension":

We can explore a detailed drill-down report of a condition by clicking on a row. In this case,

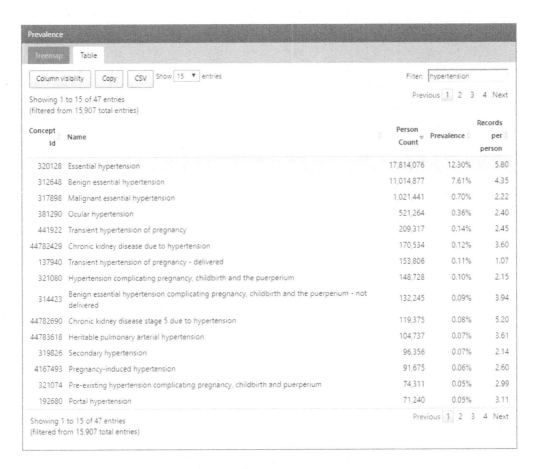

Figure 11.4: Atlas Data Sources: Conditions with "hypertension" found in the concept name

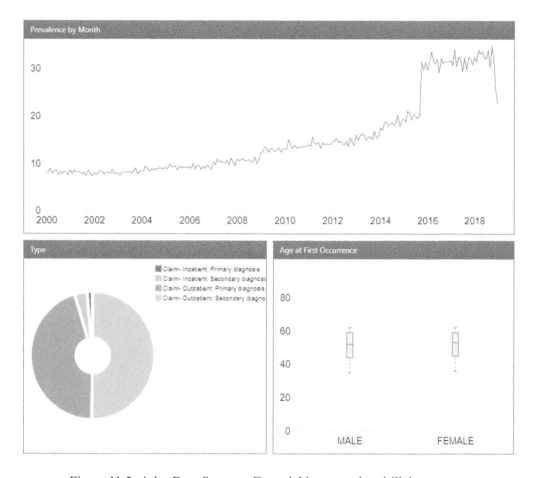

Figure 11.5: Atlas Data Sources: Essential hypertension drill down report

we will select "essential hypertension" to get a breakdown of the trends of the selected condition over time and by gender, the prevalence of the condition by month, the type recorded with the condition and the age at first occurrence of the diagnosis:

Now that we have reviewed the database's characteristics for the presence of hypertension concepts and the trends over time, we can also explore drugs used to treat hypertensive persons. The process to do this follows the same steps except we use the Drug Era report to review characteristics of drugs summarized to their RxNorm Ingredient. Once we have explored the database characteristics to review items of interest, we are ready to move forward with constructing cohorts to identify the hypertensive persons to characterize.

11.7   Cohort Characterization in ATLAS

Here we demonstrate how to use ATLAS to perform large-scale cohort characterization for several cohorts. Click on the [📈 Characterizations] in the left bar of ATLAS and create a new characterization analysis. Give the analysis a name a save using the [💾] button.

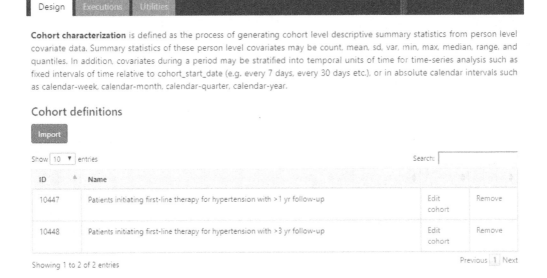

Figure 11.6: Characterization design tab - cohort definition selection

11.7.1   Design

A characterization analysis requires at least one cohort and at least one feature to characterize. For this example, we will use two cohorts. The first cohort will define persons initiating a treatment for hypertension as their index date with at least one diagnosis of hypertension in the year prior. We will also require that persons in this cohort have at least one year of observation after initiating the hypertensive drug (Appendix B.6). The second cohort is identical to the first cohort described with a requirement having at least three years of observation instead of one (Appendix B.7).

Cohort Definitions

We assume the cohorts have already been created in ATLAS as described in Chapter 10. Click on ░Import░ and select the cohorts as shown in figure 11.6. Next, we'll define the features to use for characterizing these two cohorts.

Feature Selection

ATLAS comes with nearly 100 preset feature analyses that are used to perform characterization across the clinical domains modeled in the OMOP CDM. Each of these preset feature analyses perform aggregation and summarization functions on clinical observations for the selected target cohorts. These calculations provide potentially thousands of features to describe the cohorts baseline and post-index characteristics. Under the hood, ATLAS is utilizing the OHDSI FeatureExtraction R package to perform the characterization for each cohort.

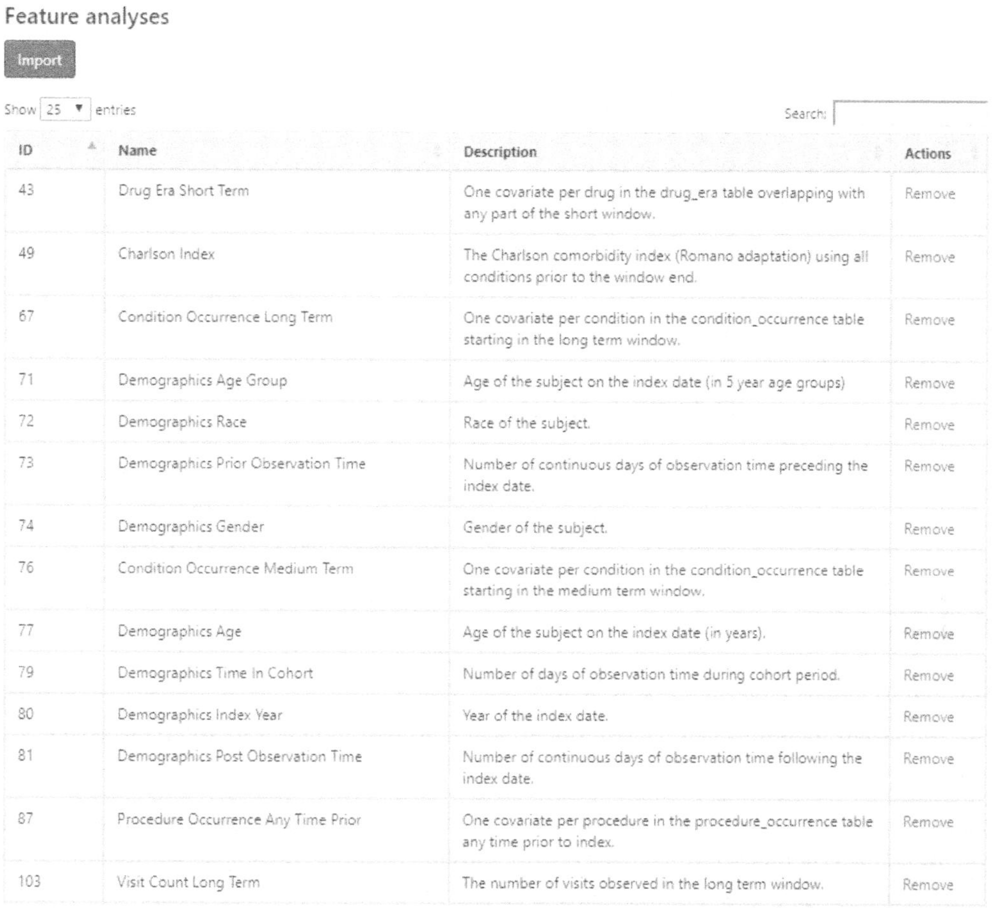

Feature analyses

Import

Show 25 ▼ entries   Search:

ID ▲	Name	Description	Actions
43	Drug Era Short Term	One covariate per drug in the drug_era table overlapping with any part of the short window.	Remove
49	Charlson Index	The Charlson comorbidity index (Romano adaptation) using all conditions prior to the window end.	Remove
67	Condition Occurrence Long Term	One covariate per condition in the condition_occurrence table starting in the long term window.	Remove
71	Demographics Age Group	Age of the subject on the index date (in 5 year age groups)	Remove
72	Demographics Race	Race of the subject.	Remove
73	Demographics Prior Observation Time	Number of continuous days of observation time preceding the index date.	Remove
74	Demographics Gender	Gender of the subject.	Remove
76	Condition Occurrence Medium Term	One covariate per condition in the condition_occurrence table starting in the medium term window.	Remove
77	Demographics Age	Age of the subject on the index date (in years).	Remove
79	Demographics Time In Cohort	Number of days of observation time during cohort period.	Remove
80	Demographics Index Year	Year of the index date.	Remove
81	Demographics Post Observation Time	Number of continuous days of observation time following the index date.	Remove
87	Procedure Occurrence Any Time Prior	One covariate per procedure in the procedure_occurrence table any time prior to index.	Remove
103	Visit Count Long Term	The number of visits observed in the long term window.	Remove

Figure 11.7: Characterization design tab - feature selection.

We will cover the use of FeatureExtraction and R in more detail in the next section.

Click on ▆Import▆ to select the feature to characterize. Below is a list of features we will use to characterize these cohorts:

The figure above shows the list of features selected along with a description of what each feature will characterize for each cohort. The features that start with the name "Demographics" will calculate the demographic information for each person at the cohort start date. For the features that start with a domain name (i.e. Visit, Procedure, Condition, Drug, etc), these will characterize all recorded observations in that domain. Each domain feature has four options of time window preceding the cohort star, namely:

- **Any time prior**: uses all available time prior to cohort start that fall into the person's observation period
- **Long term**: 365 days prior up to and including the cohort start date.
- **Medium term**: 180 days prior up to and including the cohort start date.
- **Short term**: 30 days prior up to and including the cohort start date.

Subgroup analyses

New subgroup

Female

☐ Calculate subgroup analyses only

Female   🗑

having | all   ▼ | of the following criteria: **+ Add criteria to group...▼**

with the following event criteria:

+ Add attribute...▼   Delete Criteria

✖ with a gender of: ✖ FEMALE   Add   Import

Figure 11.8: Characterization design with female sub group analysis.

Subgroup Analysis

What if we were interested in creating different characteristics based on gender? We can use the "subgroup analyses" section to define new subgroups of interest to use in our characterization.

To create a subgroup, click on and add your criteria for subgroup membership. This step is similar to the criteria used to identify cohort enrollment. In this example, we'll define a set of criteria to identify females amongst our cohorts:

 Subgroup analyses in ATLAS are not the same as strata. Strata are mutually exclusive while subgroups may include the same persons based on the criteria chosen.

11.7.2   Executions

Once we have our characterization designed, we can execute this design against one or more databases in our environment. Navigate to the Executions tab and click on the Generate button to start the analysis on a database:

Once the analysis is complete, we can view reports by clicking on the "All Executions" button and from the list of executions, select "View Reports". Alternatively, you can click "View latest result" to view the last execution performed.

11.7.3   Results

The results provide a tabular view of the different features for each cohort selected in the design. In figure 11.10, a table provides a summary of all conditions present in the two

Figure 11.9: Characterization design execution - CDM source selection.

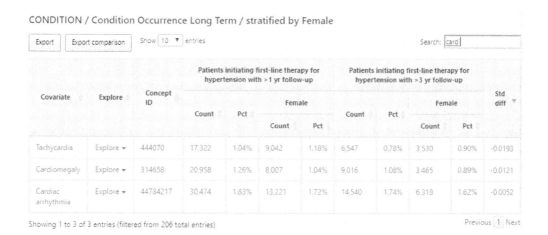

Figure 11.10: Characterization results - condition occurrence long term.

Exploring condition_occurrence during day -365 through 0 days relative to index: Cardiac arrhythmia   ✖

Cohort: Patients initiating first-line therapy for hypertension with >1 yr follow-up

| Export | Show 10 ▼ entries | | | Search: |

Relationship type	Distance ▾	Concept name	All stratas		Female	
			Count	Pct	Count	Pct
Explore Ancestor	4	Disorder by body site	32	0.00%	17	0.00%
Explore Ancestor	4	Finding of trunk structure	991	0.06%	605	0.08%
Explore Ancestor	3	Disorder of trunk	23	0.00%	14	0.00%
Explore Ancestor	3	Disorder of thorax	241	0.01%	104	0.01%
Explore Ancestor	3	Disorder of body system	4,135	0.25%	1,992	0.26%
Explore Ancestor	2	Disorder of cardiovascular system	12,979	0.78%	6,073	0.79%
Explore Ancestor	2	Disorder of mediastinum	138	0.01%	62	0.01%
Explore Ancestor	2	Disorder of body cavity	24	0.00%	10	0.00%
Explore Ancestor	1	Heart disease	4,691	0.28%	1,869	0.24%
Explore Selected	0	Cardiac arrhythmia	30,474	1.83%	13,221	1.72%

Showing 1 to 10 of 62 entries   Previous 1 2 3 4 5 6 7 Next

Figure 11.11: Characterization results - exploring a single concept.

cohorts in the preceding 365 days from the cohort start. Each covariate has a count and percentage for each cohort and the female subgroup we defined within each cohort.

We used the search box to filter the results to see what proportion of persons have a `cardiac arrhythmia` in their history in an effort to understand what cardiovascular-related diagnoses are observed in the populations. We can use the `Explore` link next to the cardiac arrhythmia concept to open a new window with more details about the concept for a single cohort as shown in figure 11.11:

Since we have characterized all condition concepts for our cohorts, the explore option enables a view of all ancestor and descendant concepts for the selected concept, in this case cardiac arrhythmia. This exploration allows us to navigate the hierarchy of concepts to explore other cardiac diseases that may appear for our hypertensive persons. Like in the summary view, the count and percentage are displayed.

We can also use the same characterization results to find conditions that are contraindicated for some anti-hypertensive treatment such as angioedema. To do this, we'll follow the same steps above but this time search for 'edema' as shown in figure 11.12:

Once again, we'll use the explore feature to see the characteristics of Edema in the hypertension population to find the prevalence of angioedema:

Here we find that a portion of this population has a record of angioedema in the year prior to starting an anti-hypertensive medication.

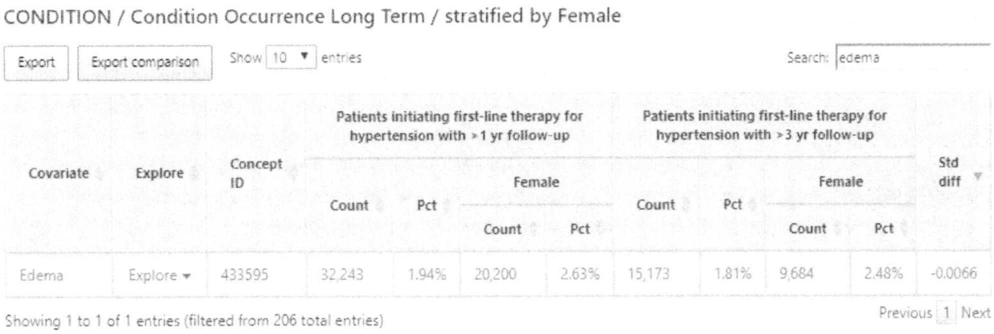

CONDITION / Condition Occurrence Long Term / stratified by Female

Covariate	Explore	Concept ID	Patients initiating first-line therapy for hypertension with >1 yr follow-up				Patients initiating first-line therapy for hypertension with >3 yr follow-up				Std diff
			Count	Pct	Female		Count	Pct	Female		
					Count	Pct			Count	Pct	
Edema	Explore ▼	433595	32,243	1.94%	20,200	2.63%	15,173	1.81%	9,684	2.48%	-0.0066

Showing 1 to 1 of 1 entries (filtered from 206 total entries)   Previous 1 Next

Figure 11.12: Characterization results - exploring a contraindicated condition.

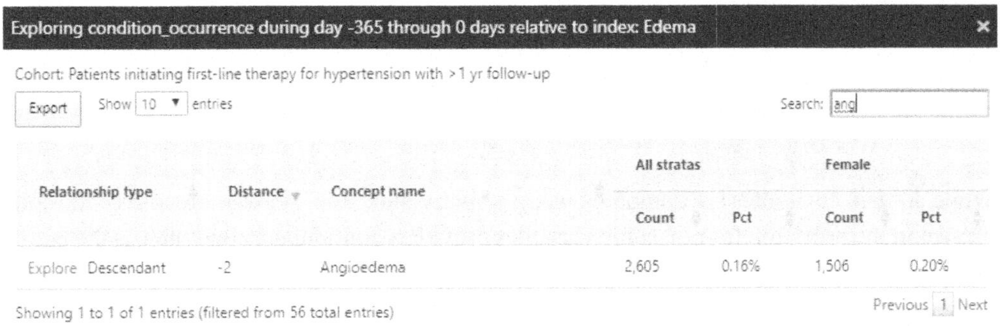

Exploring condition_occurrence during day -365 through 0 days relative to index: Edema ✕

Cohort: Patients initiating first-line therapy for hypertension with >1 yr follow-up

Relationship type	Distance	Concept name	All stratas		Female	
			Count	Pct	Count	Pct
Explore Descendant	-2	Angioedema	2,605	0.16%	1,506	0.20%

Showing 1 to 1 of 1 entries (filtered from 56 total entries)   Previous 1 Next

Figure 11.13: Characterization results - exploring a contraindicated condition details.

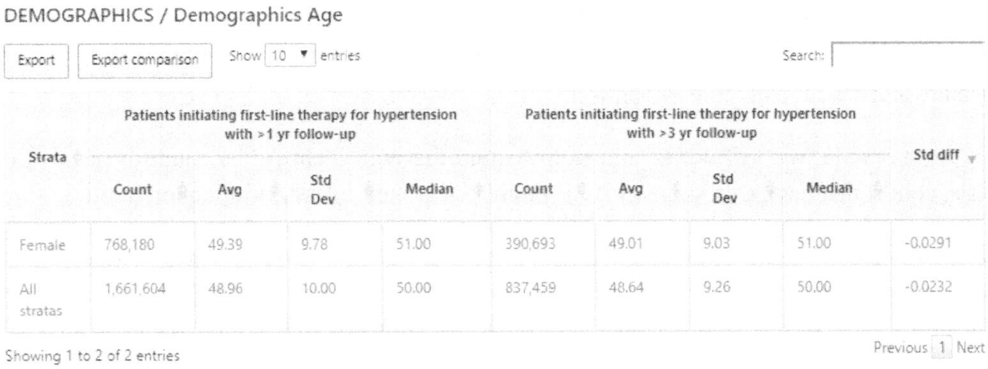

DEMOGRAPHICS / Demographics Age

Strata	Patients initiating first-line therapy for hypertension with >1 yr follow-up				Patients initiating first-line therapy for hypertension with >3 yr follow-up				Std diff
	Count	Avg	Std Dev	Median	Count	Avg	Std Dev	Median	
Female	768,180	49.39	9.78	51.00	390,693	49.01	9.03	51.00	-0.0291
All stratas	1,661,604	48.96	10.00	50.00	837,459	48.64	9.26	50.00	-0.0232

Showing 1 to 2 of 2 entries   Previous 1 Next

Figure 11.14: Characterization results of age for each cohort and sub group.

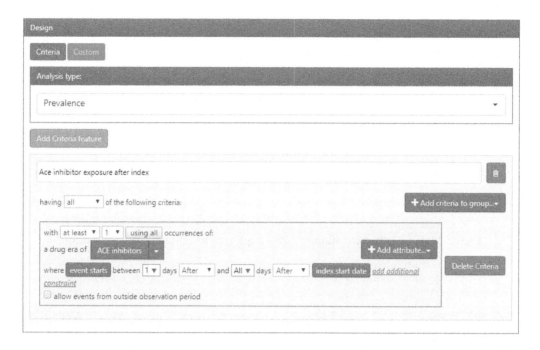

Figure 11.15: Custom feature definition in ATLAS.

While domain covariates are computed using a binary indicator (i.e. was a record of the code present in the prior timeframe), some variables provide a continuous value such as the age of persons at cohort start. In the example above, we show the age for the 2 cohorts characterized expressed with the count of persons, mean age, median age and standard deviation.

11.7.4   Defining Custom Features

In addition to the preset features, ATLAS supports the ability to allow for user-defined custom features. To do this, click the **Characterization** left-hand menu item, then click the **Feature Analysis** tab and click the **New Feature Analysis** button. Provide a name for the custom feature and save it using the ⊟ button.

In this example, we will define a custom feature that will identify the count of persons in each cohort that have a drug era of ACE inhibitors in their history after cohort start:

The criteria defined above assumes that it will be applied to a cohort start date. Once we have defined the criteria and saved it, we can apply it to the characterization design we created in the previous section. To do this, open the characterization design and navigate to the Feature Analysis section. Click the Import button and from the menu select the new custom features. They will now appear in the feature list for the characterization design. As described earlier, we can execute this design against a database to produce the characterization for this custom feature:

Figure 11.16: Custom feature results display.

11.8 Cohort Characterization in R

We may also choose to characterize cohorts using R. Here we'll describe how to use the OHDSI R package FeatureExtraction to generate baseline features (covariates) for our hypertension cohorts. FeatureExtraction provides users with the ability to construct covariates in three ways:

- Choose the default set of covariates
- Choose from a set of pre-specified analyses
- Create a set of custom analyses

FeatureExtraction creates covariates in two distinct ways: person-level features and aggregate features. Person-level features are useful for machine learning applications. In this section, we'll focus on using aggregate features that are useful for generating baseline covariates that describe the cohort of interest. Additionally, we'll focus on the second two ways of constructing covariates: pre-specified and custom analyses and leave using the default set as an exercise for the reader.

11.8.1 Cohort Instantiation

We first need to instantiate the cohort to characterize it. Instantiating cohorts is described in Chapter 10. In this example, we'll use the persons initiating a first-line therapy for hypertension with 1 year follow up (Appendix B.6). We leave characterizing the other cohorts in Appendix B as an exercise for the reader. We will assume the cohort has been instantiated in a table called `scratch.my_cohorts` with cohort definition ID equal to 1.

11.8.2 Data Extraction

We first need to tell R how to connect to the server. FeatureExtraction uses the DatabaseConnector package, which provides a function called `createConnectionDetails`. Type

?createConnectionDetails for the specific settings required for the various database management systems (DBMS). For example, one might connect to a PostgreSQL database using this code:

```
library(FeatureExtraction)
connDetails <- createConnectionDetails(dbms = "postgresql",
                                       server = "localhost/ohdsi",
                                       user = "joe",
                                       password = "supersecret")

cdmDbSchema <- "my_cdm_data"
cohortsDbSchema <- "scratch"
cohortsDbTable <- "my_cohorts"
cdmVersion <- "5"
```

The last four lines define the cdmDbSchema, cohortsDbSchema, and cohortsDbTable variables, as well as the CDM version. We will use these later to tell R where the data in CDM format live, where the cohorts of interest have been created, and what version CDM is used. Note that for Microsoft SQL Server, database schemas need to specify both the database and the schema, so for example cdmDbSchema <- "my_cdm_data.dbo".

11.8.3 Using Prespecified Analyses

The function createCovariateSettings allow the user to choose from a large set of pre-defined covariates. Type ?createCovariateSettings to get an overview of the available options. For example:

```
settings <- createCovariateSettings(
  useDemographicsGender = TRUE,
  useDemographicsAgeGroup = TRUE,
  useConditionOccurrenceAnyTimePrior = TRUE)
```

This will create binary covariates for gender, age (in 5 year age groups), and each concept observed in the condition_occurrence table any time prior to (and including) the cohort start date.

Many of the prespecified analyses refer to a short, medium, or long term time window. By default, these windows are defined as:

- **Long term**: 365 days prior up to and including the cohort start date.
- **Medium term**: 180 days prior up to and including the cohort start date.
- **Short term**: 30 days prior up to and including the cohort start date.

However, the user can change these values. For example:

```
settings <- createCovariateSettings(useConditionEraLongTerm = TRUE,
                                     useConditionEraShortTerm = TRUE,
                                     useDrugEraLongTerm = TRUE,
                                     useDrugEraShortTerm = TRUE,
                                     longTermStartDays = -180,
                                     shortTermStartDays = -14,
                                     endDays = -1)
```

This redefines the long-term window as 180 days prior up to (but not including) the cohort start date, and redefines the short term window as 14 days prior up to (but not including) the cohort start date.

Again, we can also specify which concept IDs should or should not be used to construct covariates:

```
settings <- createCovariateSettings(useConditionEraLongTerm = TRUE,
                                     useConditionEraShortTerm = TRUE,
                                     useDrugEraLongTerm = TRUE,
                                     useDrugEraShortTerm = TRUE,
                                     longTermStartDays = -180,
                                     shortTermStartDays = -14,
                                     endDays = -1,
                                     excludedCovariateConceptIds = 1124300,
                                     addDescendantsToExclude = TRUE,
                                     aggregated = TRUE)
```

The use of `aggregated` = `TRUE` for all of the examples above indicate to Feature-Extraction to provide summary statistics. Excluding this flag will compute covariates for each person in the cohort.

11.8.4   Creating Aggregated Covariates

The following code block will generate aggregated statistics for a cohort:

```
covariateSettings <- createDefaultCovariateSettings()

covariateData2 <- getDbCovariateData(
  connectionDetails = connectionDetails,
  cdmDatabaseSchema = cdmDatabaseSchema,
  cohortDatabaseSchema = resultsDatabaseSchema,
  cohortTable = "cohorts_of_interest",
  cohortId = 1,
  covariateSettings = covariateSettings,
  aggregated = TRUE)
```

```
summary(covariateData2)
```

And the output will look similar to the following:

```
## CovariateData Object Summary
##
## Number of Covariates: 41330
## Number of Non-Zero Covariate Values: 41330
```

11.8.5 Output Format

The two main components of the aggregated `covariateData` object are `covariates` and `covariatesContinuous` for binary and continuous covariates respectively:

```
covariateData2$covariates
covariateData2$covariatesContinuous
```

11.8.6 Custom Covariates

FeatureExtraction also provides the ability to define and utilize custom covariates. These details are an advanced topic and covered in the user documentation: http://ohdsi.github.io/FeatureExtraction/.

11.9 Cohort Pathways in ATLAS

The goal with a pathway analysis is to understand the sequencing of treatments along in one or more cohorts of interest. The methods applied are based on the design reported by Hripcsak et al. (2016). These methods were generalized and codified into a feature called Cohort Pathways in ATLAS.

Cohort pathways aims to provide analytic capabilities to summarize the events following the cohort start date of one or more target cohorts. To do this, we create a set of cohorts to identify the clinical events of interest for the target population called event cohort. Focusing on how this might look for a person in the target cohort:

In figure 11.17, the person is part of the target cohort with a defined start and end date. Then, the numbered line segments represent where that person also is identified in an event cohort for a duration of time. Event cohorts allow us to describe any clinical event of interest that is represented in the CDM such that we are not constrained to creating a pathway for a single domain or concept.

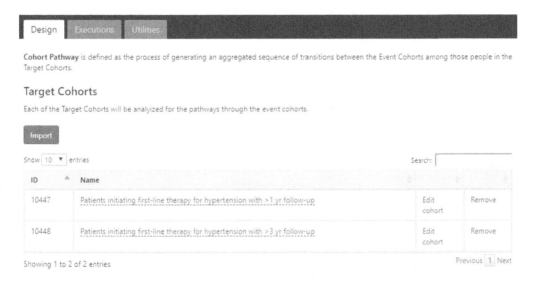

Figure 11.17: Pathways analysis in the context of a single person.

Figure 11.18: Pathways analysis with target cohorts selected.

To start, click on **⚙ Cohort Pathways** in the left bar of ATLAS to create a new cohort pathways study. Provide a descriptive name and press the save button.

11.9.1 Design

To start, we will continue to use the cohorts initiating a first-line therapy for hypertension with 1 and 3 years follow up (Appendix B.6, B.7). Use the button to import the 2 cohorts.

Next we'll define the event cohorts by creating a cohort for each first-line hypertensive drug of interest. For this, we'll start by creating a cohort of ACE inhibitor users and define the cohort end date as the end of continuous exposure. We'll do the same for 8 other hypertensive medications and note that these definitions are found in Appendix B.8-B.16. Once complete use the **Import** button to import these into the Event Cohort section of the pathway design:

When complete, your design should look like the one above. Next, we'll need to decide on a few additional analysis settings:

- **Combination window**: This setting allows you to define a window of time, in days, in

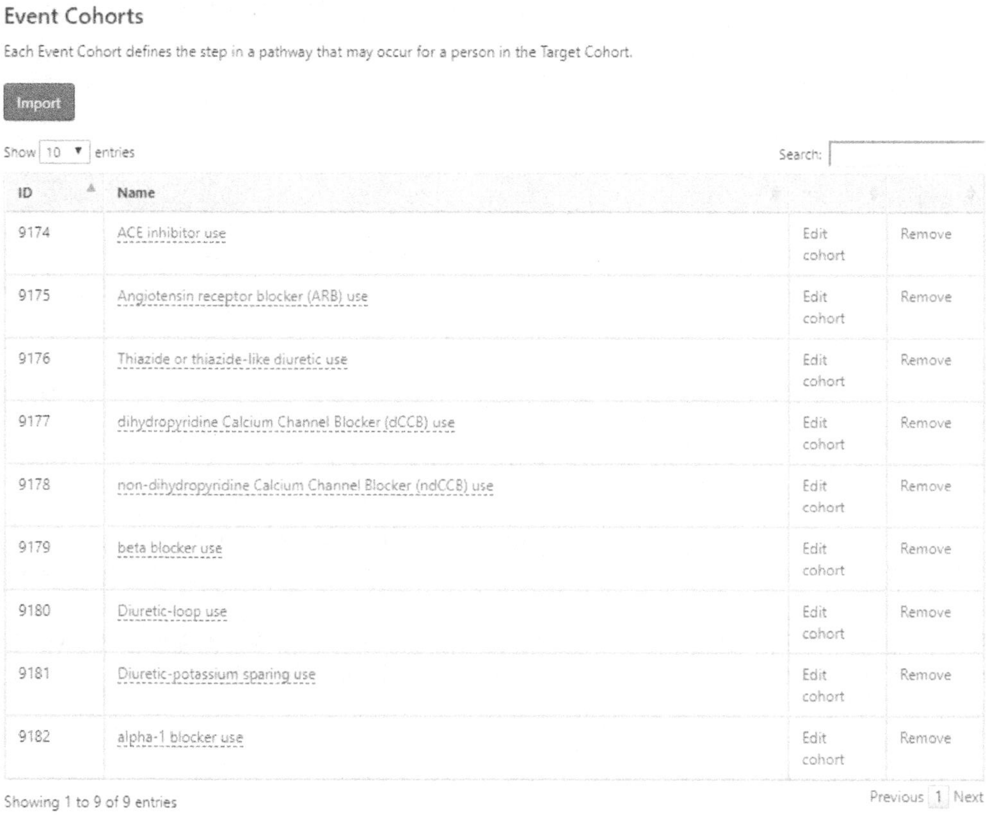

Event Cohorts

Each Event Cohort defines the step in a pathway that may occur for a person in the Target Cohort.

[Import]

Show [10 ▼] entries   Search: [   ]

ID ▲	Name		
9174	ACE inhibitor use	Edit cohort	Remove
9175	Angiotensin receptor blocker (ARB) use	Edit cohort	Remove
9176	Thiazide or thiazide-like diuretic use	Edit cohort	Remove
9177	dihydropyridine Calcium Channel Blocker (dCCB) use	Edit cohort	Remove
9178	non-dihydropyridine Calcium Channel Blocker (ndCCB) use	Edit cohort	Remove
9179	beta blocker use	Edit cohort	Remove
9180	Diuretic-loop use	Edit cohort	Remove
9181	Diuretic-potassium sparing use	Edit cohort	Remove
9182	alpha-1 blocker use	Edit cohort	Remove

Showing 1 to 9 of 9 entries   Previous 1 Next

Figure 11.19: Event cohorts for pathway design for initiating a first-line antihypertensive therapy.

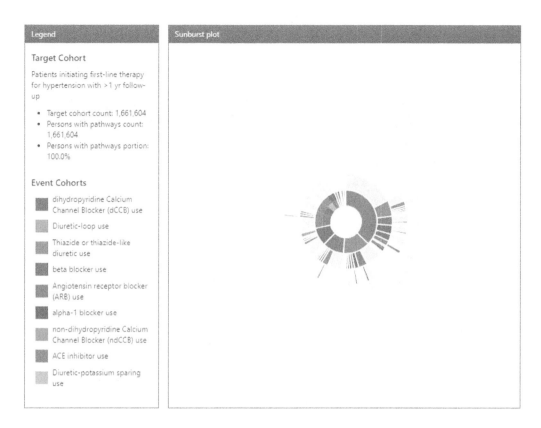

Figure 11.20: Pathways results legend and sunburst visualization.

which overlap between events is considered a combination of events. For example, if two drugs represented by 2 event cohorts (event cohort 1 and event cohort 2) overlap within the combination window the pathways algorithm will combine them into "event cohort 1 + event cohort 2".

- **Minimum cell count**: Event cohorts with less than this number of people will be censored (removed) from the output to protect privacy.
- **Max path length**: This refers to the maximum number of sequential events to consider for the analysis.

11.9.2 Executions

Once we have our pathway analysis designed, we can execute this design against one or more databases in our environment. This works the same way as we described for cohort characterization in ATLAS. Once complete, we can review the results of the analysis.

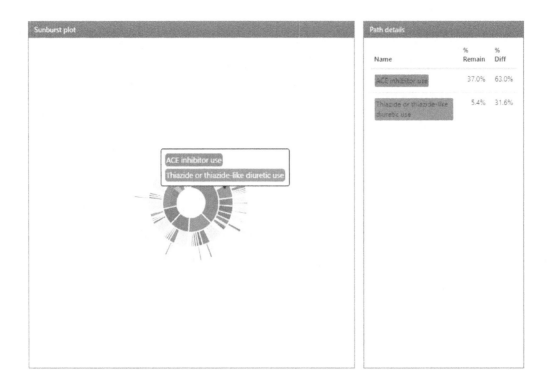

Figure 11.21: Pathways results displaying path details.

11.9.3   Viewing Results

The results of a pathway analysis are broken into 3 sections: The legend section displays the total number of persons in the target cohort along with the number of persons that had 1 or more events in the pathway analysis. Below that summary are the color designations for each of the cohorts that appear in the sunburst plot in the center section.

The sunburst plot is a visualization that represents the various event pathways taken by persons over time. The center of the plot represents the cohort entry and the first color-coded ring shows the proportion of persons in each event cohort. In our example, the center of the circle represents hypertensive persons initiating a first line therapy. Then, the first ring in the sunburst plot shows the proportion of persons that initiated a type of first-line therapy defined by the event cohorts (i.e. ACE inhibitors, Angiotensin receptor blockers, etc). The second set of rings represents the 2nd event cohort for persons. In certain event sequences, a person may never have a 2nd event cohort observed in the data and that proportion is represented by the grey portion of the ring.

Clicking on a section of the sunburst plot will display the path details on the right. Here we can see that the largest proportion of people in our target cohort initiated a first-line therapy with ACE inhibitors and from that group, a smaller proportion started a Thiazide or thiazide diuretics.

Figure 11.22: Incidence Rate target and outcome definition.

11.10 Incidence Analysis in ATLAS

In an incidence calculation, we describe: amongst the persons in the target cohort, who experienced the outcome cohort during the time at risk period. Here we will design an incidence analysis to characterize angioedema and acute myocardial infarction outcomes amongst new users of ACE inhibitors (ACEi) and Thiazides and thiazide-like diuretics (THZ). We will assess these outcomes during the TAR that a person was exposed to the drug. Additionally, we will add an outcome of drug exposure to Angiotensin receptor blockers (ARBs) to measure the incidence of new use of ARBs during exposure to the target cohorts (ACEi and THZ). This outcome definition provides an understanding of how ARBs are utilized amongst the target populations.

To start, click on **Incidence Rates** in the left bar of ATLAS to create a new incidence analysis. Provide a descriptive name and press the save button ⊟.

11.10.1 Design

We assume the cohorts used in this example have already been created in ATLAS as described in Chapter 10. The Appendix provides the full definitions of the target cohorts (Appendix B.2, B.5), and outcomes (Appendix B.4, B.3, B.9) cohorts.

On the definition tab, click to choose the *New users of ACE inhibitors* cohort and the *New users of Thiazide or Thiazide-like diuretics* cohort. Close the dialog to view that these cohorts are added to the design. Next we add our outcome cohorts by clicking on and from the dialog box, select the outcome cohorts of *acute myocardial infarction events*, *angioedema events* and *Angiotensin receptor blocker (ARB) use*. Again, close the window to view that these cohorts are added to the outcome cohorts section of the design.

Next, we will define the time at risk window for the analysis. As shown above, the time at risk window is defined relative to the cohort start and end dates. Here we will define the time at risk start as 1 day after cohort start for our target cohorts. Next, we'll define the time at risk to end at the cohort end date. In this case, the definition of the ACEi and THZ cohorts have a cohort end date when the drug exposure ends.

ATLAS also provides a way to stratify the target cohorts as part of the analysis specification:

Figure 11.23: Incidence Rate target and outcome definition.

Figure 11.24: Incidence Rate strata definition for females.

To do this, click the New Stratify Criteria button and follow the same steps described in Chapter 11. Now that we have completed the design, we can move to executing our design against one or more databases.

11.10.2   Executions

Click the Generation tab and then the [▶ Generate] button to reveal a list of databases to use to execute the analysis:

Select one or more databases and click the Generate button to start the analysis to analyze all combinations of targets and outcomes specified in the design.

11.10.3   Viewing Results

On the Generation tab, the top portion of the screen allows you to select a target and outcome to use when viewing the results. Just below this a summary of the incidence is shown for each database used in the analysis.

Select the target cohort of ACEi users and the Acute Myocardial Infarction (AMI) from the respective dropdown lists. Click the [⊕ Reports] button to reveal the incidence analysis results:

A summary for the database shows the total persons in the cohort that were observed during the TAR along with the total number of cases. The proportion shows the number of cases

Select sources   ✕

Select All   Deselect All

Filter: [   ]

	Name	▲
☐	SYNPUF 1K	
☑	SYNPUF 5%	

Previous 1 Next

Generate

Figure 11.25: Incidence Rate analysis execution.

	Persons	Cases	Proportion [+|-] per 1k persons		Time At Risk (years)	Rate [+|-] per 1k years
Summary Statistics:	816,867	1,703	2.08		623,402	2.73

Stratify Rule	N	Cases	Proportion [+|-] per 1k persons	Time At Risk (years)	Rate [+|-] per 1k years
1. Gender = Female	313,518	416	1.33	230,157	1.81

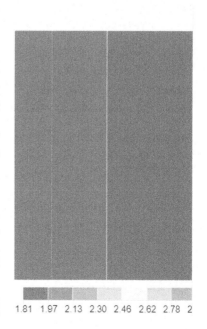

1.81 1.97 2.13 2.30 2.46 2.62 2.78 2

Figure 11.26: Incidence Rate analysis output - New ACEi users with AMI outcome.

	Persons	Cases	Proportion [+|-] per 1k persons	Time At Risk (years)	Rate [+|-] per 1k years
Summary Statistics:	818,520	43,868	53.59	621,094	70.63

Stratify Rule	N	Cases	Proportion [+|-] per 1k persons	Time At Risk (years)	Rate [+|-] per 1k years
1. Gender = Female	313,832	21,049	67.07	228,369	92.17

58.10 61.89 65.67 69.46 73 25 77.03 80.82 8⸱

Figure 11.27: Incidence Rate - New users of ACEi receiving ARBs treatment during ACEi exposure.

per 1000 people. The time at risk, in years, is calculated for the target cohort. The incidence rate is expressed as the number of cases per 1000 person-years.

We can also view the incidence metrics for the strata that we defined in the design. The same metrics mentioned above are calculated for each stratum. Additionally, a treemap visualization provides a representation of the proportion of each stratum represented by the boxed areas. The color represents the incidence rate as shown in the scale along the bottom.

We can gather the same information to see the incidence of new use of ARBs amongst the ACEi population. Using the dropdown at the top, change the outcome to ARBs use and click the button to reveal the details.

As shown, the metrics calculated are the same but the interpretation is different since the input (ARB use) references a drug utilization estimate instead of a health outcome.

11.11   Summary

- OHDSI offers tools to characterize an entire database, or a cohort of interest.
- Cohort characterization describes a cohort of interest during the time preceding the index date (**baseline**) and the time after index (**post-index**).

– ATLAS's characterization module and the OHDSI Methods Library provide the capability to calculate baseline characteristics for multiple time windows.

– ATLAS's pathways and incidence rate modules provide descriptive statistics during the post-index time period.

11.12 Exercises

Prerequisites

For these exercises, access to an ATLAS instance is required. You can use the instance at http://atlas-demo.ohdsi.org, or any other instance you have acces to.

Exercise 11.1. We would like to understand how celecoxib is used in the real world. To start, we would like to understand what data a database has on this drug. Use the ATLAS Data Sources module to find information on celecoxib.

Exercise 11.2. We would like to better understand the disease natural history of celecoxib users. Create a simple cohort of new users of celecoxib using a 365-day washout period (see Chapter 10 for details on how to do this), and use ATLAS to create a characterization of this cohort, showing co-morbid conditions and drug-exposures.

Exercise 11.3. We are interested in understand how often gastrointestinal (GI) bleeds occur any time after people initiate celecoxib treatment. Create a cohort of GI bleed events, simply defined as any occurrence of concept 192671 ("Gastrointestinal hemorrhage") or any of its descendants. Compute the incidence rate of these GI events after celecoxib initiation, using the exposure cohort defined in the previous exercise.

Suggested answers can be found in Appendix E.7.

Chapter 12

Population-Level Estimation

Chapter leads: Martijn Schuemie, David Madigan, Marc Suchard & Patrick Ryan

Observational healthcare data, such as administrative claims and electronic health records, offer opportunities to generate real-world evidence about the effect of treatments that can meaningfully improve the lives of patients. In this chapter we focus on population-level effect estimation, which refers to the estimation of average causal effects of exposures (e.g. medical interventions such as drug exposures or procedures) on specific health outcomes of interest. In what follows, we consider two different estimation tasks:

- **Direct effect estimation**: estimating the effect of an exposure on the risk of an outcome, as compared to no exposure.
- **Comparative effect estimation**: estimating the effect of an exposure (the target exposure) on the risk of an outcome, as compared to another exposure (the comparator exposure).

In both cases, the patient-level causal effect contrasts a factual outcome, i.e., what happened to the exposed patient, with a counterfactual outcome, i.e., what would have happened had the exposure not occurred (direct) or had a different exposure occurred (comparative). Since any one patient reveals only the factual outcome (the fundamental problem of causal inference), the various effect estimation designs employ different analytic devices to shed light on the counterfactual outcomes.

Use-cases for population-level effect estimation include treatment selection, safety surveillance, and comparative effectiveness. Methods can test specific hypotheses one at a time (e.g. 'signal evaluation') or explore multiple-hypotheses-at-once (e.g. 'signal detection'). In all cases, the objective remains the same: to produce a high-quality estimate of the causal effect.

In this chapter we first describe various population-level estimation study designs, all of which are implemented as R packages in the OHDSI Methods Library. We then detail the design of an example estimation study, followed by step-by-step guides of how to implement the design using ATLAS and R. Finally, we review the various outputs generated by the study,

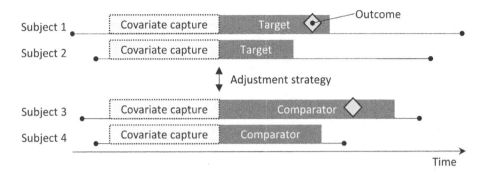

Figure 12.1: The new-user cohort design. Subjects observed to initiate the target treatment are compared to those initiating the comparator treatment. To adjust for differences between the two treatment groups several adjustment strategies can be used, such as stratification, matching, or weighting by the propensity score, or by adding baseline characteristics to the outcome model. The characteristics included in the propensity model or outcome model are captured prior to treatment initiation.

including study diagnostics and effect size estimates.

12.1   The Cohort Method Design

The cohort method attempts to emulate a randomized clinical trial. (Hernan and Robins, 2016) Subjects that are observed to initiate one treatment (the target) are compared to subjects initiating another treatment (the comparator) and are followed for a specific amount of time following treatment initiation, for example the time they stay on the treatment. We can specify the questions we wish to answer in a cohort study by making the five choices highlighted in Table 12.1.

Table 12.1: Main design choices in a comparative cohort design.

Choice	Description
Target cohort	A cohort representing the target treatment
Comparator cohort	A cohort representing the comparator treatment
Outcome cohort	A cohort representing the outcome of interest
Time-at-risk	At what time (often relative to the target and comparator cohort start and end dates) do we consider the risk of the outcome?
Model	The model used to estimate the effect while adjusting for differences between the target and comparator

The choice of model specifies, among others, the type of outcome model. For example, we could use a logistic regression, which evaluates whether or not the outcome has occurred, and produces an odds ratio. A logistic regression assumes the time-at-risk is of the same length for both target and comparator, or is irrelevant. Alternatively, we could choose a Poisson regression which estimates the incidence rate ratio, assuming a constant incidence rate. Often a Cox regression is used which considers time to first outcome to estimate the hazard ratio, assuming proportional hazards between target and comparator.

 The new-user cohort method inherently is a method for comparative effect estimation, comparing one treatment to another. It is difficult to use this method to compare a treatment against no treatment, since it is hard to define a group of unexposed people that is comparable with the exposed group. If one wants to use this design for direct effect estimation, the preferred way is to select a comparator treatment for the same indication as the exposure of interest, where the comparator treatment is believed to have no effect on the outcome. Unfortunately, such a comparator might not always be available.

A key concern is that the patients receiving the target treatment may systematically differ from those receiving the comparator treatment. For example, suppose the target cohort is on average 60 years old, whereas the comparator cohort is on average 40 years old. Comparing target to comparator with respect to any age-related health outcome (e.g. stroke) might then show substantial differences between the cohorts. An uninformed investigator might reach the conclusion there is a causal association between the target treatment and stroke as compared to the comparator. More prosaically or commonplace, the investigator might conclude that there exist target patients that experienced stroke that would not have done so had they received the comparator. This conclusion could well be entirely incorrect! Maybe those target patients disproportionately experienced stroke simply because they are older; maybe the target patients that experienced stroke might well have done so even if they had received the comparator. In this context, age is a "confounder." One mechanism to deal with confounders in observational studies is through propensity scores.

12.1.1 Propensity Scores

In a randomized trial, a (virtual) coin toss assigns patients to their respective groups. Thus, by design, the probability that a patient receives the target treatment as against the comparator treatment does not relate in any way to patient characteristics such as age. The coin has no knowledge of the patient, and, what's more, we know with certainty the exact probability that a patient receives the target exposure. As a consequence, and with increasing confidence as the number of patients in the trial increases, the two groups of patients essentially *cannot* differ systematically with respect to *any* patient characteristic. This guaranteed balance holds true for characteristics that the trial measured (such as age) as well as characteristics that the trial failed to measure, such as patient genetic factors.

For a given patient, the *propensity score* (PS) is the probability that that patient received the target treatment as against the comparator. (Rosenbaum and Rubin, 1983) In a balanced two-arm randomized trial, the propensity score is 0.5 for every patient. In a propensity score-adjusted observational study, we estimate the probability of a patient receiving the target treatment based on what we can observe in the data on and before the time of treatment initiation (irrespective of the treatment they actually received). This is a straightforward predictive modeling application; we fit a model (e.g. a logistic regression) that predicts whether a subject receives the target treatment, and use this model to generate predicted probabilities (the PS) for each subject. Unlike in a standard randomized trial, different patients will have different probabilities of receiving the target treatment. The PS can be used in several ways including matching target subjects to comparator subjects with similar PS, stratifying the study population based on the PS, or weighting subjects using Inverse Probability of Treatment Weighting (IPTW) derived from the PS. When matching we can select just one comparator subject for each target subject, or we can allow more than one comparator subject per target subject, a technique know as variable-ratio matching. (Rassen et al., 2012)

For example, suppose we use one-on-one PS matching, and that Jan has a priori probability of 0.4 of receiving the target treatment and in fact receives the target treatment. If we can find a patient (named Jun) that also had an a priori probability of 0.4 of receiving the target treatment but in fact received the comparator, the comparison of Jan and Jun's outcomes is like a mini-randomized trial, at least with respect to measured confounders. This comparison will yield an estimate of the Jan-Jun causal contrast that is as good as the one randomization would have produced. Estimation then proceeds as follows: for every patient that received the target, find one or more matched patients that received the comparator but had the same prior probability of receiving the target. Compare the outcome for the target patient with the outcomes for the comparator patients within each of these matched groups.

Propensity scoring controls for measured confounders. In fact, if treatment assignment is "strongly ignorable" given measured characteristics, propensity scoring will yield an unbiased estimate of the causal effect. "Strongly ignorable" essentially means that there are no unmeasured confounders, and that the measured confounders are adjusted for appropriately. Unfortunately this is not a testable assumption. See Chapter 18 for further discussion of this issue.

12.1.2 Variable Selection

In the past, PS were computed based on manually selected characteristics, and although the OHDSI tools can support such practices, we prefer using many generic characteristics (i.e. characteristics that are not selected based on the specific exposures and outcomes in the study). (Tian et al., 2018) These characteristics include demographics, as well as all diagnoses, drug exposures, measurement, and medical procedures observed prior to and on the day of treatment initiation. A model typically involves 10,000 to 100,000 unique characteristics, which we fit using large-scale regularized regression (Suchard et al., 2013) implemented in the Cyclops package. In essence, we let the data decide which characteristics are predictive of the treatment assignment and should be included in the model.

 We typically include the day of treatment initiation in the covariate capture window because many relevant data points such as the diagnosis leading to the treatment are recorded on that date. On this day the target and comparator treatment themselves are also recorded, but these should *not* be included in the propensity model, because they are the very thing we are trying to predict. We must therefore explicitly exclude the target and comparator treatment from the set of covariates

Some have argued that a data-driven approach to covariate selection that does not depend on clinical expertise to specify the "right" causal structure runs the risk of erroneously including so-called instrumental variables and colliders, thus increasing variance and potentially introducing bias. (Hernan et al., 2002) However, these concerns are unlikely to have a large impact in real-world scenarios. (Schneeweiss, 2018) Furthermore, in medicine the true causal structure is rarely known, and when different researchers are asked to identify the 'right' covariates to include for a specific research question, each researcher invariably comes up with a different list, thus making the process irreproducible. Most importantly, our diagnostics such as inspection of the propensity model, evaluating balance on all covariates, and including negative controls would identify most problems related to colliders and instrumental variables.

12.1.3 Caliper

Since propensity scores fall on a continuum from 0 to 1, exact matching is rarely possible. Instead, the matching process finds patients that match the propensity score of a target patient(s) within some tolerance known as a "caliper." Following Austin (2011), we use a default caliper of 0.2 standard deviations on the logit scale.

12.1.4 Overlap: Preference Scores

The propensity method requires that matching patients exist! As such, a key diagnostic shows the distribution of the propensity scores in the two groups. To facilitate interpretation, the OHDSI tools plot a transformation of the propensity score called the "preference score". (Walker et al., 2013) The preference score adjusts for the "market share" of the two treatments. For example, if 10% of patients receive the target treatment (and 90% receive the comparator treatment), then patients with a preference score of 0.5 have a 10% probability of receiving the target treatment. Mathematically, the preference score is

$$\ln\left(\frac{F}{1-F}\right) = \ln\left(\frac{S}{1-S}\right) - \ln\left(\frac{P}{1-P}\right)$$

Where F is the preference score, S is the propensity score, and P is the proportion of patients receiving the target treatment.

Walker et al. (2013) discuss the concept of "empirical equipoise." They accept exposure pairs as emerging from empirical equipoise if at least half of the exposures are to patients with a preference score of between 0.3 and 0.7.

Table 12.2: Main design choices in a self-controlled cohort design.

Choice	Description
Target cohort	A cohort representing the treatment
Outcome cohort	A cohort representing the outcome of interest
Time-at-risk	At what time (often relative to the target cohort start and end dates) do we consider the risk of the outcome?
Control time	The time period used as the control time

12.1.5 Balance

Good practice always checks that the PS adjustment succeeds in creating balanced groups of patients. Figure 12.19 shows the standard OHDSI output for checking balance. For each patient characteristic, this plots the standardized difference between means between the two exposure groups before and after PS adjustment. Some guidelines recommend an after-adjustment standardized difference upper bound of 0.1. (Rubin, 2001)

12.2 The Self-Controlled Cohort Design

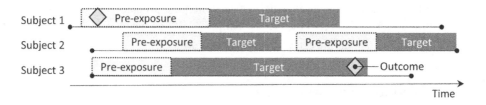

Figure 12.2: The self-controlled cohort design. The rate of outcomes during exposure to the target is compared to the rate of outcomes in the time pre-exposure.

The self-controlled cohort (SCC) design (Ryan et al., 2013a) compares the rate of outcomes during exposure to the rate of outcomes in the time just prior to the exposure. The four choices shown in Table 12.2 define a self-controlled cohort question.

Because the same subject that make up the exposed group are also used as the control group, no adjustment for between-person differences need to be made. However, the method is vulnerable to other differences, such as differences in the baseline risk of the outcome between different time periods.

12.3 The Case-Control Design

Case-control studies (Vandenbroucke and Pearce, 2012) consider the question "are persons with a specific disease outcome exposed more frequently to a specific agent than those with-

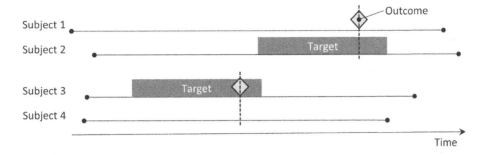

Figure 12.3: The case-control design. Subjects with the outcome ('cases') are compared to subjects without the outcome ('controls') in terms of their exposure status. Often, cases and controls are matched on various characteristics such as age and sex.

Table 12.3: Main design choices in a case-control design.

Choice	Description
Outcome cohort	A cohort representing the cases (the outcome of interest)
Control cohort	A cohort representing the controls. Typically the control cohort is automatically derived from the outcome cohort using some selection logic
Target cohort	A cohort representing the treatment
Nesting cohort	Optionally, a cohort defining the subpopulation from which cases and controls are drawn
Time-at-risk	At what time (often relative to the index date) do we consider exposure status?

out the disease?" Thus, the central idea is to compare "cases," i.e., subjects that experience the outcome of interest, with "controls," i.e., subjects that did not experience the outcome of interest. The choices in Table 12.3 define a case-control question.

Often, one selects controls to match cases based on characteristics such as age and sex to make them more comparable. Another widespread practice is to nest the analysis within a specific subgroup of people, for example people that have all been diagnosed with one of the indications of the exposure of interest.

12.4 The Case-Crossover Design

The case-crossover (Maclure, 1991) design evaluates whether the rate of exposure is different at the time of the outcome than at some predefined number of days prior to the outcome. It is trying to determine whether there is something special about the day the outcome occurred. Table 12.4 shows the choices that define a case-crossover question.

Cases serve as their own controls. As self-controlled designs, they should be robust to confounding due to between-person differences. One concern is that, because the outcome date is

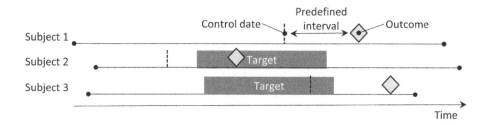

Figure 12.4: The case-crossover design. The time around the outcome is compared to a control date set at a predefined interval prior to the outcome date.

Table 12.4: Main design choices in a case-crossover design.

Choice	Description
Outcome cohort	A cohort representing the cases (the outcome of interest)
Target cohort	A cohort representing the treatment
Time-at-risk	At what time (often relative to the index date) do we consider exposure status?
Control time	The time period used as the control time

always later than the control date, the method will be positively biased if the overall frequency of exposure increases over time (or negatively biased if there is a decrease). To address this, the case-time-control design (Suissa, 1995) was developed, which adds controls, matched for example on age and sex, to the case-crossover design to adjust for exposure trends.

12.5   The Self-Controlled Case Series Design

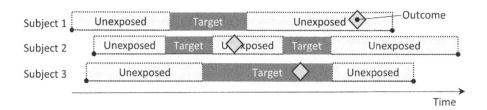

Figure 12.5: The Self-Controlled Case Series design. The rate of outcomes during exposure is compared to the rate of outcomes when not exposed.

The Self-Controlled Case Series (SCCS) design (Farrington, 1995; Whitaker et al., 2006) compares the rate of outcomes during exposure to the rate of outcomes during all unexposed time, including before, between, and after exposures. It is a Poisson regression that is conditioned on the person. Thus, it seeks to answer the question: "Given that a patient has the outcome, is the outcome more likely during exposed time compared to non-exposed time?". The choices in Table 12.5 define an SCCS question.

Table 12.5: Main design choices in a self-controlled case series design.

Choice	Description
Target cohort	A cohort representing the treatment
Outcome cohort	A cohort representing the outcome of interest
Time-at-risk	At what time (often relative to the target cohort start and end dates) do we consider the risk of the outcome?
Model	The model to estimate the effect, including any adjustments for time-varying confounders

Like other self-controlled designs, the SCCS is robust to confounding due to between-person differences, but vulnerable to confounding due to time-varying effects. Several adjustments are possible to attempt to account for these, for example by including age and season. A special variant of the SCCS includes not just the exposure of interest, but all other exposures to drugs recorded in the database (Simpson et al., 2013) potentially adding thousands of additional variables to the model. L1-regularization using cross-validation to select the regularization hyperparameter is applied to the coefficients of all exposures except the exposure of interest.

One important assumption underlying the SCCS is that the observation period end is independent of the date of the outcome. For some outcomes, especially ones that can be fatal such as stroke, this assumption can be violated. An extension to the SCCS has been developed that corrects for any such dependency. (Farrington et al., 2011)

12.6 Designing a Hypertension Study

12.6.1 Problem Definition

ACE inhibitors (ACEi) are widely used in patients with hypertension or ischemic heart disease, especially those with other comorbidities such as congestive heart failure, diabetes mellitus, or chronic kidney disease. (Zaman et al., 2002) Angioedema, a serious and sometimes life-threatening adverse event that usually manifests as swelling of the lips, tongue, mouth, larynx, pharynx, or periorbital region, has been linked to the use of these medications. (Sabroe and Black, 1997) However, limited information is available about the absolute and relative risks for angioedema associated with the use of these medications. Existing evidence is primarily based on investigations of specific cohorts (e.g., predominantly male veterans or Medicaid beneficiaries) whose findings may not be generalizable to other populations, or based on investigations with few events, which provide unstable risk estimates. (Powers et al., 2012) Several observational studies compare ACEi to beta-blockers for the risk of angioedema, (Magid et al., 2010; Toh et al., 2012) but beta-blockers are no longer recommended as first-line treatment of hypertension. (Whelton et al., 2018) A viable alternative treatment could be thiazides or thiazide-like diuretics (THZ), which could be just as effective in managing hypertension and its associated risks such as acute myocardial infarction (AMI), but without increasing the risk of angioedema.

The following will demonstrate how to apply our population-level estimation framework to observational healthcare data to address the following comparative estimation questions:

> What is the risk of angioedema in new users of ACE inhibitors compared to new users of thiazide and thiazide-like diuretics?

> What is the risk of acute myocardial infarction in new users of ACE inhibitors compared to new users of thiazide and thiazide-like diuretics?

Since these are comparative effect estimation questions we will apply the cohort method as described in Section 12.1.

12.6.2 Target and Comparator

We consider patients new-users if their first observed treatment for hypertension was monotherapy with any active ingredient in either the ACEi or THZ class. We define mono therapy as not starting on any other anti-hypertensive drug in the seven days following treatment initiation. We require patients to have at least one year of prior continuous observation in the database before first exposure and a recorded hypertension diagnosis at or in the year preceding treatment initiation.

12.6.3 Outcome

We define angioedema as any occurrence of an angioedema condition concept during an inpatient or emergency room (ER) visit, and require there to be no angioedema diagnosis recorded in the seven days prior. We define AMI as any occurrence of an AMI condition concept during an inpatient or ER visit, and require there to be no AMI diagnosis record in the 180 days prior.

12.6.4 Time-At-Risk

We define time-at-risk to start on the day after treatment initiation, and stop when exposure stops, allowing for a 30-day gap between subsequent drug exposures.

12.6.5 Model

We fit a PS model using the default set of covariates, including demographics, conditions, drugs, procedures, measurements, observations, and several co-morbidity scores. We exclude ACEi and THZ from the covariates. We perform variable-ratio matching and condition the Cox regression on the matched sets.

12.6.6 Study Summary

Table 12.6: Main design choices for our comparative cohort study.

Choice	Value
Target cohort	New users of ACE inhibitors as first-line monotherapy for hypertension.
Comparator cohort	New users of thiazides or thiazide-like diuretics as first-line monotherapy for hypertension.
Outcome cohort	Angioedema or acute myocardial infarction.
Time-at-risk	Starting the day after treatment initiation, stopping when exposure stops.
Model	Cox proportional hazards model using variable-ratio matching.

12.6.7 Control Questions

To evaluate whether our study design produces estimates in line with the truth, we additionally include a set of control questions where the true effect size is known. Control questions can be divided in negative controls, having a hazard ratio of 1, and positive controls, having a known hazard ratio greater than 1. For several reasons we use real negative controls, and synthesize positive controls based on these negative controls. How to define and use control questions is discussed in detail in Chapter 18.

12.7 Implementing the Study Using ATLAS

Here we demonstrate how this study can be implemented using the Estimation function in ATLAS. Click on ⚖️ Estimation in the left bar of ATLAS, and create a new estimation study. Make sure to give the study an easy-to-recognize name. The study design can be saved at any time by clicking the 🖫 button.

In the Estimation design function, there are three sections: Comparisons, Analysis Settings, and Evaluation Settings. We can specify multiple comparisons and multiple analysis settings, and ATLAS will execute all combinations of these as separate analyses. Here we discuss each section:

12.7.1 Comparative Cohort Settings

A study can have one or more comparisons. Click on "Add Comparison," which will open a new dialog. Click on 🗁 to select the target and comparator cohorts. By clicking on "Add Outcome" we can add our two outcome cohorts. We assume the cohorts have already been

Figure 12.6: The comparison dialog

created in ATLAS as described in Chapter 10. The Appendix provides the full definitions of the target (Appendix B.2), comparator (Appendix B.5), and outcome (Appendix B.4 and Appendix B.3) cohorts. When done, the dialog should look like Figure 12.6.

Note that we can select multiple outcomes for a target-comparator pair. Each outcome will be treated independently, and will result in a separate analysis.

Negative Control Outcomes

Negative control outcomes are outcomes that are not believed to be caused by either the target or the comparator, and where therefore the true hazard ratio equals 1. Ideally, we would have proper cohort definitions for each outcome cohort. However, typically, we only have a concept set, with one concept per negative control outcome, and some standard logic to turn these into outcome cohorts. Here we assume the concept set has already been created as described in Chapter 18 and can simply be selected. The negative control concept set should contain a concept per negative control, and not include descendants. Figure 12.7 shows the negative control concept set used for this study.

Concepts to Include

When selecting concept to include, we can specify which covariates we would like to generate, for example to use in a propensity model. When specifying covariates here, all other covariates (aside from those you specified) are left out. We usually want to include all baseline covariates, letting the regularized regression build a model that balances all covariates. The

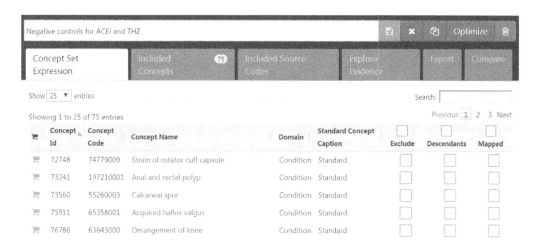

Figure 12.7: Negative Control concept set.

only reason we might want to specify particular covariates is to replicate an existing study that manually picked covariates. These inclusions can be specified in this comparison section or in the analysis section, because sometimes they pertain to a specific comparison (e.g. known confounders in a comparison), or sometimes they pertain to an analysis (e.g. when evaluating a particular covariate selection strategy).

Concepts to Exclude

Rather than specifying which concepts to include, we can instead specify concepts to *exclude*. When we submit a concept set in this field, we use every covariate except for those that we submitted. When using the default set of covariates, which includes all drugs and procedures occurring on the day of treatment initiation, we must exclude the target and comparator treatment, as well as any concepts that are directly related to these. For example, if the target exposure is an injectable, we should not only exclude the drug, but also the injection procedure from the propensity model. In this example, the covariates we want to exclude are ACEi and THZ. Figure 12.8 shows we select a concept set that includes all these concepts, including their descendants.

After selecting the negative controls and covariates to exclude, the lower half of the comparisons dialog should look like Figure 12.9.

12.7.2 Effect Estimation Analysis Settings

After closing the comparisons dialog we can click on "Add Analysis Settings." In the box labeled "Analysis Name," we can give the analysis a unique name that is easy to remember and locate in the future. For example, we could set the name to "Propensity score matching."

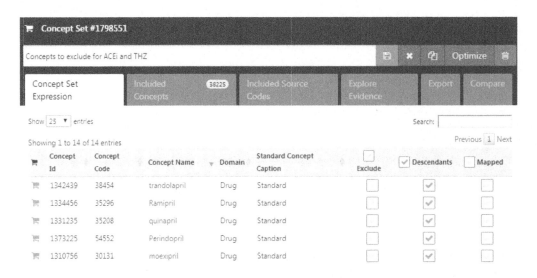

Figure 12.8: The concept set defining the concepts to exclude.

Figure 12.9: The comparison window showing concept sets for negative controls and concepts to exclude.

Study Population

There are a wide range of options to specify the study population, which is the set of subjects that will enter the analysis. Many of these overlap with options available when designing the target and comparator cohorts in the cohort definition tool. One reason for using the options in Estimation instead of in the cohort definition is re-usability; we can define the target, comparator, and outcome cohorts completely independently, and add dependencies between these at a later point in time. For example, if we wish to remove people who had the outcome before treatment initiation, we could do so in the definitions of the target and comparator cohort, but then we would need to create separate cohorts for every outcome! Instead, we can choose to have people with prior outcomes be removed in the analysis settings, and now we can reuse our target and comparator cohorts for our two outcomes of interest (as well as our negative control outcomes).

The **study start and end dates** can be used to limit the analyses to a specific period. The study end date also truncates risk windows, meaning no outcomes beyond the study end date will be considered. One reason for selecting a study start date might be that one of the drugs being studied is new and did not exist in an earlier time. Automatically adjusting for this can be done by answering "yes" to the question "**Restrict the analysis to the period when both exposures are present in the data?**". Another reason to adjust study start and end dates might be that medical practice changed over time (e.g., due to a drug warning) and we are only interested in the time where medicine was practiced a specific way.

The option "**Should only the first exposure per subject be included?**" can be used to restrict to the first exposure per patient. Often this is already done in the cohort definition, as is the case in this example. Similarly, the option "**The minimum required continuous observation time prior to index date for a person to be included in the cohort**" is often already set in the cohort definition, and can therefore be left at 0 here. Having observed time (as defined in the OBSERVATION_PERIOD table) before the index date ensures that there is sufficient information about the patient to calculate a propensity score, and is also often used to ensure the patient is truly a new user, and therefore was not exposed before.

"**Remove subjects that are in both the target and comparator cohort?**" defines, together with the option "**If a subject is in multiple cohorts, should time-at-risk be censored when the new time-at-risk starts to prevent overlap?**" what happens when a subject is in both target and comparator cohorts. The first setting has three choices:

- "**Keep All**" indicating to keep the subjects in both cohorts. With this option it might be possible to double-count subjects and outcomes.
- "**Keep First**" indicating to keep the subject in the first cohort that occurred.
- "**Remove All**" indicating to remove the subject from both cohorts.

If the options "keep all" or "keep first" are selected, we may wish to censor the time when a person is in both cohorts. This is illustrated in Figure 12.10. By default, the time-at-risk is defined relative to the cohort start and end date. In this example, the time-at-risk starts one day after cohort entry, and stops at cohort end. Without censoring the time-at-risk for the two cohorts might overlap. This is especially problematic if we choose to keep all, because any

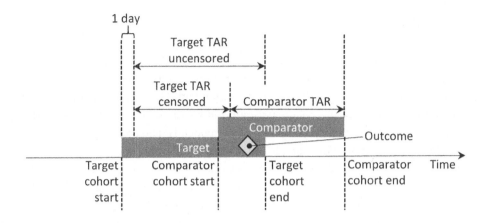

Figure 12.10: Time-at-risk (TAR) for subjects who are in both cohorts, assuming time-at-risk starts the day after treatment initiation, and stops at exposure end.

outcome that occurs during this overlap (as shown) will be counted twice. If we choose to censor, the first cohort's time-at-risk ends when the second cohort's time-at-risk starts.

We can choose to **remove subjects that have the outcome prior to the risk window start**, because often a second outcome occurrence is the continuation of the first one. For instance, when someone develops heart failure, a second occurrence is likely, which means the heart failure probably never fully resolved in between. On the other hand, some outcomes are episodic, and it would be expected for patients to have more than one independent occurrence, like an upper respiratory infection. If we choose to remove people that had the outcome before, we can select **how many days we should look back when identifying prior outcomes**.

Our choices for our example study are shown in Figure 12.11. Because our target and comparator cohort definitions already restrict to the first exposure and require observation time prior to treatment initiation, we do not apply these criteria here.

Covariate Settings

Here we specify the covariates to construct. These covariates are typically used in the propensity model, but can also be included in the outcome model (the Cox proportional hazards model in this case). If we **click to view details** of our covariate settings, we can select which sets of covariates to construct. However, the recommendation is to use the default set, which constructs covariates for demographics, all conditions, drugs, procedures, measurements, etc.

We can modify the set of covariates by specifying concepts to **include** and/or **exclude**. These settings are the same as the ones found in Section 12.7.1 on comparison settings. The reason why they can be found in two places is because sometimes these settings are related to a specific comparison, as is the case here because we wish to exclude the drugs we are comparing, and sometimes the settings are related to a specific analysis. When executing an analysis for

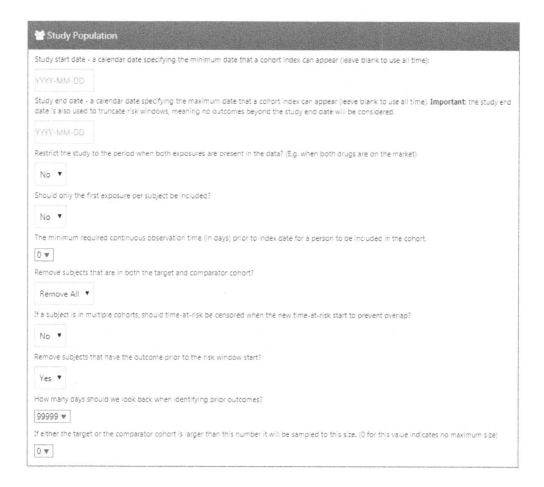

Figure 12.11: Study population settings.

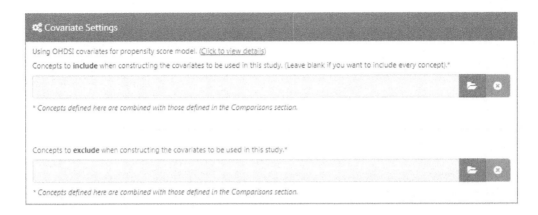

Figure 12.12: Covariate settings.

a specific comparison using specific analysis settings, the OHDSI tools will take the union of these sets.

Figure 12.12 shows our choices for this study. Note that we have selected to add descendants to the concept to exclude, which we defined in the comparison settings in Figure 12.9.

Time At Risk

Time-at-risk is defined relative to the start and end dates of our target and comparator cohorts. In our example, we had set the cohort start date to start on treatment initiation, and cohort end date when exposure stops (for at least 30 days). We set the start of time-at-risk to one day after cohort start, so one day after treatment initiation. A reason to set the time-at-risk start to be later than the cohort start is because we may want to exclude outcome events that occur on the day of treatment initiation if we do not believe it biologically plausible they can be caused by the drug.

We set the end of the time-at-risk to the cohort end, so when exposure stops. We could choose to set the end date later if for example we believe events closely following treatment end may still be attributable to the exposure. In the extreme we could set the time-at-risk end to a large number of days (e.g. 99999) after the cohort end date, meaning we will effectively follow up subjects until observation end. Such a design is sometimes referred to as an *intent-to-treat* design.

A patient with zero days at risk adds no information, so the **minimum days at risk** is normally set at one day. If there is a known latency for the side effect, then this may be increased to get a more informative proportion. It can also be used to create a cohort more similar to that of a randomized trial it is being compared to (e.g., all the patients in the randomized trial were observed for at least N days).

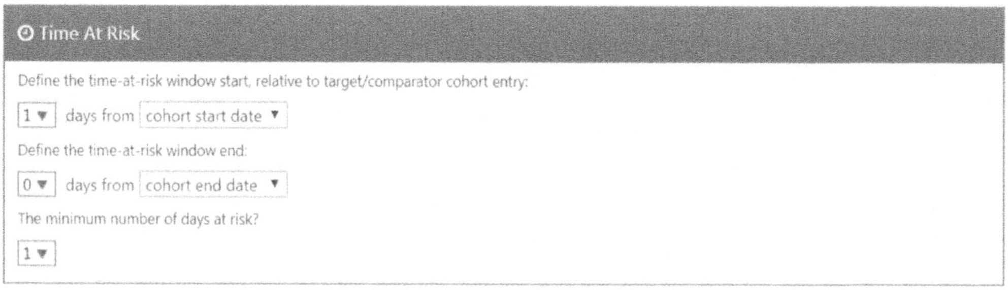

⊘ Time At Risk

Define the time-at-risk window start, relative to target/comparator cohort entry:

[1 ▼] days from [cohort start date ▼]

Define the time-at-risk window end:

[0 ▼] days from [cohort end date ▼]

The minimum number of days at risk?

[1 ▼]

Figure 12.13: Time-at-risk settings.

A golden rule in designing a cohort study is to never use information that falls after the cohort start date to define the study population, as this may introduce bias. For example, if we require everyone to have at least a year of time-at-risk, we will likely have limited our analyses to those who tolerate the treatment well. This setting should therefore be used with extreme care.

Propensity Score Adjustment

We can opt to **trim** the study population, removing people with extreme PS values. We can choose to remove the top and bottom percentage, or we can remove subjects whose preference score falls outside the range we specify. Trimming the cohorts is generally not recommended because it requires discarding observations, which reduces statistical power. It may be desirable to trim in some cases, for example when using IPTW.

In addition to, or instead of trimming, we can choose to **stratify** or **match** on the propensity score. When stratifying we need to specify the **number of strata** and whether to select the strata based on the target, comparator, or entire study population. When matching we need to specify the **maximum number of people from the comparator group to match to each person in the target group**. Typical values are 1 for one-on-one matching, or a large number (e.g. 100) for variable-ratio matching. We also need to specify the **caliper**: the maximum allowed difference between propensity scores to allow a match. The caliper can be defined on difference **caliper scales**:

- **The propensity score scale**: the PS itself
- **The standardized scale**: in standard deviations of the PS distributions
- **The standardized logit scale**: in standard deviations of the PS distributions after the logit transformation to make the PS more normally distributed.

In case of doubt, we suggest using the default values, or consult the work on this topic by Austin (2011).

Fitting large-scale propensity models can be computationally expensive, so we may want to restrict the data used to fit the model to just a sample of the data. By default the maximum

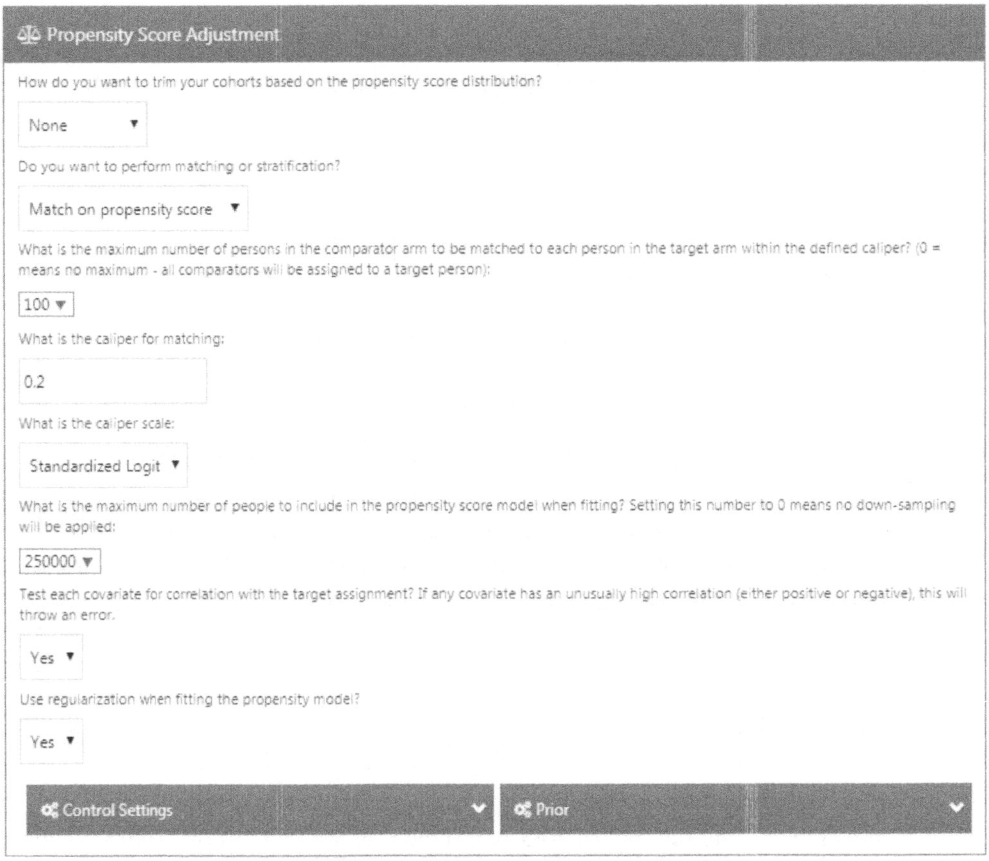

Figure 12.14: Propensity score adjustment settings.

size of the target and comparator cohort is set to 250,000. In most studies this limit will not be reached. It is also unlikely that more data will lead to a better model. Note that although a sample of the data may be used to fit the model, the model will be used to compute PS for the entire population.

Test each covariate for correlation with the target assignment? If any covariate has an unusually high correlation (either positive or negative), this will throw an error. This avoids lengthy calculation of a propensity model only to discover complete separation. Finding very high univariate correlation allows you to review the covariate to determine why it has high correlation and whether it should be dropped.

Use regularization when fitting the model? The standard procedure is to include many covariates (typically more than 10,000) in the propensity model. In order to fit such models some regularization is required. If only a few hand-picked covariates are included, it is also possible to fit the model without regularization.

Figure 12.14 shows our choices for this study. Note that we select variable-ratio matching by setting the maximum number of people to match to 100.

Outcome Model Settings

First, we need to **specify the statistical model we will use to estimate the relative risk of the outcome between target and comparator cohorts**. We can choose between Cox, Poisson, and logistic regression, as discussed briefly in Section 12.1. For our example we choose a Cox proportional hazards model, which considers time to first event with possible censoring. Next, we need to specify **whether the regression should be conditioned on the strata**. One way to understand conditioning is to imagine a separate estimate is produced in each stratum, and then combined across strata. For one-to-one matching this is likely unnecessary and would just lose power. For stratification or variable-ratio matching it is required.

We can also choose to **add the covariates to the outcome model** to adjust the analysis. This can be done in addition or instead of using a propensity model. However, whereas there usually is ample data to fit a propensity model, with many people in both treatment groups, there is typically very little data to fit the outcome model, with only few people having the outcome. We therefore recommend keeping the outcome model as simple as possible and not include additional covariates.

Instead of stratifying or matching on the propensity score we can also choose to **use inverse probability of treatment weighting** (IPTW).

If we choose to include all covariates in the outcome model, it may make sense to use regularization when fitting the model if there are many covariates. Note that no regularization will be applied to the treatment variable to allow for unbiased estimation.

Figure 12.15 shows our choices for this study. Because we use variable-ratio matching, we must condition the regression on the strata (i.e. the matched sets).

12.7.3 Evaluation Settings

As described in Chapter 18, negative and positive controls should be included in our study to evaluate the operating characteristics, and perform empirical calibration.

Negative Control Outcome Cohort Definition

In Section 12.7.1 we selected a concept set representing the negative control outcomes. However, we need logic to convert concepts to cohorts to be used as outcomes in our analysis. ATLAS provides standard logic with three choices. The first choice is whether to **use all occurrences** or just the **first occurrence** of the concept. The second choice determines **whether occurrences of descendant concepts should be considered**. For example, occurrences of the descendant "ingrown nail of foot" can also be counted as an occurrence of the ancestor "ingrown nail." The third choice specifies which domains should be considered when looking for the concepts.

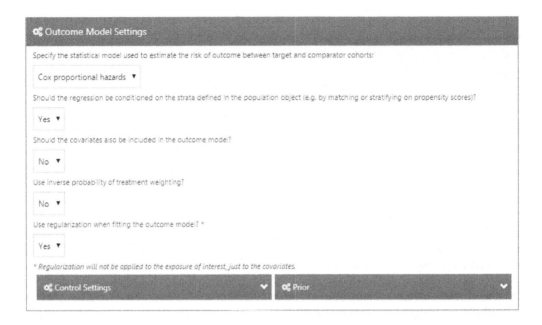

Figure 12.15: Outcome model settings.

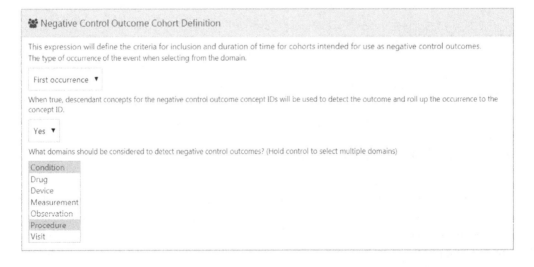

Figure 12.16: Negative control outcome cohort definition settings.

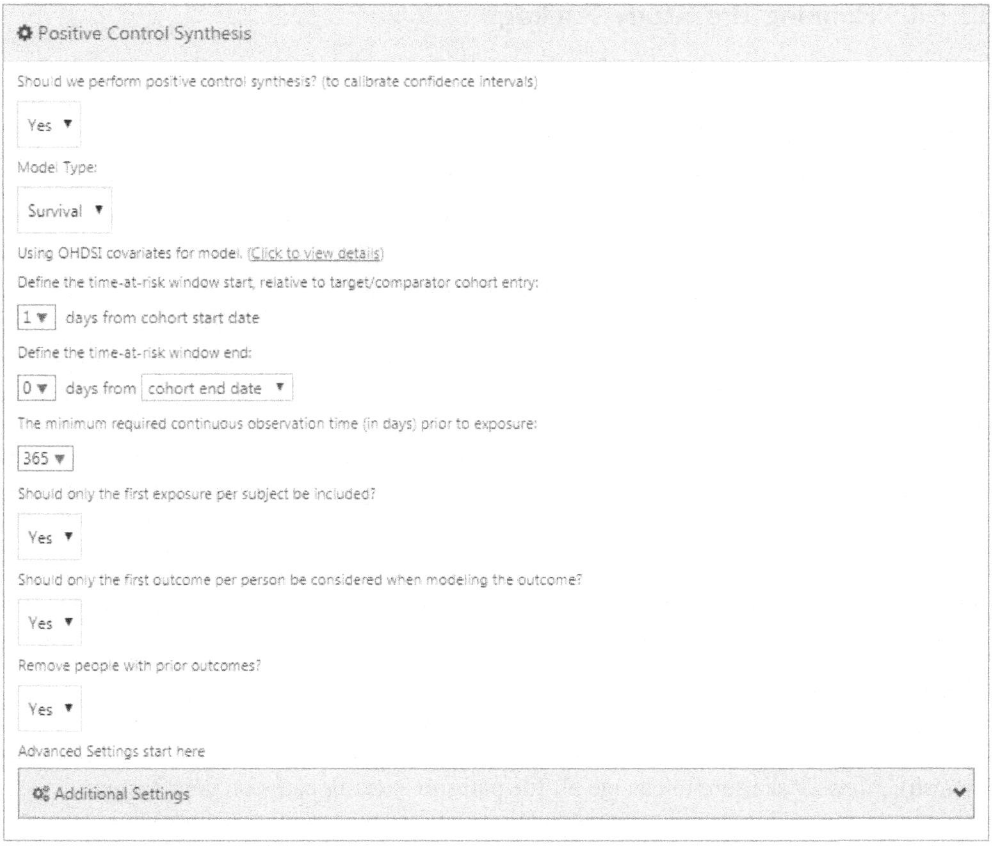

Figure 12.17: Negative control outcome cohort definition settings.

Positive Control Synthesis

In addition to negative controls we can also include positive controls, which are exposure-outcome pairs where a causal effect is believed to exist with known effect size. For various reasons real positive controls are problematic, so instead we rely on synthetic positive controls, derived from negative controls as described in Chapter 18. We can choose to **perform positive control synthesis**. If "yes", we must choose the **model type**, currently being "Poisson" and "survival". Since we use a survival (Cox) model in our estimation study, we should choose "survival". We define the time-at-risk model for the positive control synthesis to be the same as in our estimation settings, and similarly mimic the choices for the **minimum required continuous observation prior to exposure**, **should only the first exposure be included**, **should only the first outcome be included**, as well as **remove people with prior outcomes**. Figure 12.15 shows the settings for the positive control synthesis.

12.7.4   Running the Study Package

Now that we have fully defined our study, we can export it as an executable R package. This package contains everything that is needed to execute the study at a site that has data in CDM. This includes the cohort definitions that can be used to instantiate the target, comparator and outcome cohorts, the negative control concept set and logic to create the negative control outcome cohorts, as well as the R code to execute the analysis. Before generating the package make sure to save your study, then click on the **Utilities** tab. Here we can review the set of analyses that will be performed. As mentioned before, every combination of a comparison and an analysis setting will result in a separate analysis. In our example we have specified two analyses: ACEi versus THZ for AMI, and ACEi versus THZ for angioedema, both using propensity score matching.

We must provide a name for our package, after which we can click on "Download" to download the zip file. The zip file contains an R package, with the usual required folder structure for R packages. (Wickham, 2015) To use this package we recommend using R Studio. If you are running R Studio locally, unzip the file, and double click the .Rproj file to open it in R Studio. If you are running R Studio on an R studio server, click ⬆ Upload to upload and unzip the file, then click on the .Rproj file to open the project.

Once you have opened the project in R Studio, you can open the README file, and follow the instructions. Make sure to change all file paths to existing paths on your system.

A common error message that may appear when running the study is "High correlation between covariate(s) and treatment detected." This indicates that when fitting the propensity model, some covariates were observed to be highly correlated with the exposure. Please review the covariates mentioned in the error message, and exclude them from the set of covariates if appropriate (see Section 12.1.2).

12.8   Implementing the Study Using R

Instead of using ATLAS to write the R code that executes the study, we can also write the R code ourselves. One reason we might want to do this is because R offers far greater flexibility than is exposed in ATLAS. If we for example wish to use custom covariates, or a linear outcome model, we will need to write some custom R code, and combine it with the functionality provided by the OHDSI R packages.

For our example study we will rely on the CohortMethod package to execute our study. CohortMethod extracts the necessary data from a database in the CDM and can use a large set of covariates for the propensity model. In the following example we first only consider angioedema as outcome. In Section 12.8.6 we then describe how this can be extended to include AMI and the negative control outcomes.

12.8.1 Cohort Instantiation

We first need to instantiate the target and outcome cohorts. Instantiating cohorts is described in Chapter 10. The Appendix provides the full definitions of the target (Appendix B.2), comparator (Appendix B.5), and outcome (Appendix B.4) cohorts. We will assume the ACEi, THZ, and angioedema cohorts have been instantiated in a table called `scratch.my_cohorts` with cohort definition IDs 1, 2, and 3 respectively.

12.8.2 Data Extraction

We first need to tell R how to connect to the server. CohortMethod uses the DatabaseConnector package, which provides a function called `createConnectionDetails`. Type `?createConnectionDetails` for the specific settings required for the various database management systems (DBMS). For example, one might connect to a PostgreSQL database using this code:

```
library(CohortMethod)
connDetails <- createConnectionDetails(dbms = "postgresql",
                                       server = "localhost/ohdsi",
                                       user = "joe",
                                       password = "supersecret")

cdmDbSchema <- "my_cdm_data"
cohortDbSchema <- "scratch"
cohortTable <- "my_cohorts"
cdmVersion <- "5"
```

The last four lines define the `cdmDbSchema`, `cohortDbSchema`, and `cohortTable` variables, as well as the CDM version. We will use these later to tell R where the data in CDM format live, where the cohorts of interest have been created, and what version CDM is used. Note that for Microsoft SQL Server, database schemas need to specify both the database and the schema, so for example `cdmDbSchema <- "my_cdm_data.dbo"`.

Now we can tell CohortMethod to extract the cohorts, construct covariates, and extract all necessary data for our analysis:

```
# target and comparator ingredient concepts:
aceI <- c(1335471,1340128,1341927,1363749,1308216,1310756,1373225,
          1331235,1334456,1342439)
thz <- c(1395058,974166,978555,907013)

# Define which types of covariates must be constructed:
cs <- createDefaultCovariateSettings(excludedCovariateConceptIds = c(aceI,
                                                                     thz),
                                     addDescendantsToExclude = TRUE)
```

```
#Load data:
cmData <- getDbCohortMethodData(connectionDetails = connectionDetails,
                                cdmDatabaseSchema = cdmDatabaseSchema,
                                oracleTempSchema = NULL,
                                targetId = 1,
                                comparatorId = 2,
                                outcomeIds = 3,
                                studyStartDate = "",
                                studyEndDate = "",
                                exposureDatabaseSchema = cohortDbSchema,
                                exposureTable = cohortTable,
                                outcomeDatabaseSchema = cohortDbSchema,
                                outcomeTable = cohortTable,
                                cdmVersion = cdmVersion,
                                firstExposureOnly = FALSE,
                                removeDuplicateSubjects = FALSE,
                                restrictToCommonPeriod = FALSE,
                                washoutPeriod = 0,
                                covariateSettings = cs)
cmData
```

```
## CohortMethodData object
##
## Treatment concept ID: 1
## Comparator concept ID: 2
## Outcome concept ID(s): 3
```

There are many parameters, but they are all documented in the CohortMethod manual. The `createDefaultCovariateSettings` function is described in the FeatureExtraction package. In short, we are pointing the function to the table containing our cohorts and specify which cohort definition IDs in that table identify the target, comparator and outcome. We instruct that the default set of covariates should be constructed, including covariates for all conditions, drug exposures, and procedures that were found on or before the index date. As mentioned in Section 12.1 we must exclude the target and comparator treatments from the set of covariates, and here we achieve this by listing all ingredients in the two classes, and tell FeatureExtraction to also exclude all descendants, thus excluding all drugs that contain these ingredients.

All data about the cohorts, outcomes, and covariates are extracted from the server and stored in the `cohortMethodData` object. This object uses the package `ff` to store information in a way that ensures R does not run out of memory, even when the data are large, as mentioned in Section 8.4.2.

We can use the generic `summary()` function to view some more information of the data we extracted:

```
summary(cmData)
```

```
## CohortMethodData object summary
##
## Treatment concept ID: 1
## Comparator concept ID: 2
## Outcome concept ID(s): 3
##
## Treated persons: 67166
## Comparator persons: 35333
##
## Outcome counts:
##          Event count Person count
## 3              980          891
##
## Covariates:
## Number of covariates: 58349
## Number of non-zero covariate values: 24484665
```

Creating the `cohortMethodData` file can take considerable computing time, and it is probably a good idea to save it for future sessions. Because `cohortMethodData` uses `ff`, we cannot use R's regular save function. Instead, we'll have to use the `saveCohortMethodData()` function:

```
saveCohortMethodData(cmData, "AceiVsThzForAngioedema")
```

We can use the `loadCohortMethodData()` function to load the data in a future session.

Defining New Users

Typically, a new user is defined as first time use of a drug (either target or comparator), and typically a washout period (a minimum number of days prior to first use) is used to increase the probability that it is truly first use. When using the CohortMethod package, you can enforce the necessary requirements for new use in three ways:

1. When defining the cohorts.
2. When loading the cohorts using the `getDbCohortMethodData` function, you can use the `firstExposureOnly`, `removeDuplicateSubjects`, `restrictToCommonPeriod`, and `washoutPeriod` arguments.
3. When defining the study population using the `createStudyPopulation` function (see below).

The advantage of option 1 is that the input cohorts are already fully defined outside of the CohortMethod package, and external cohort characterization tools can be used on the same cohorts used in this analysis. The advantage of options 2 and 3 is that they save you the trouble of limiting to first use yourself, for example allowing you to directly use the DRUG_ERA table in the CDM. Option 2 is more efficient than 3, since only data for first use will be fetched, while option 3 is less efficient but allows you to compare the original cohorts to the study population.

12.8.3 Defining the Study Population

Typically, the exposure cohorts and outcome cohorts will be defined independently of each other. When we want to produce an effect size estimate, we need to further restrict these cohorts and put them together, for example by removing exposed subjects that had the outcome prior to exposure, and only keeping outcomes that fall within a defined risk window. For this we can use the `createStudyPopulation` function:

```
studyPop <- createStudyPopulation(cohortMethodData = cmData,
                                  outcomeId = 3,
                                  firstExposureOnly = FALSE,
                                  restrictToCommonPeriod = FALSE,
                                  washoutPeriod = 0,
                                  removeDuplicateSubjects = "remove all",
                                  removeSubjectsWithPriorOutcome = TRUE,
                                  minDaysAtRisk = 1,
                                  riskWindowStart = 1,
                                  startAnchor = "cohort start",
                                  riskWindowEnd = 0,
                                  endAnchor = "cohort end")
```

Note that we've set `firstExposureOnly` and `removeDuplicateSubjects` to FALSE, and `washoutPeriod` to 0 because we already applied those criteria in the cohort definitions. We specify the outcome ID we will use, and that people with outcomes prior to the risk window start date will be removed. The risk window is defined as starting on the day after the cohort start date (`riskWindowStart = 1` and `startAnchor = "cohort start"`), and the risk windows ends when the cohort exposure ends (`riskWindowEnd = 0` and `endAnchor = "cohort end"`), which was defined as the end of exposure in the cohort definition. Note that the risk windows are automatically truncated at the end of observation or the study end date. We also remove subjects who have no time at risk. To see how many people are left in the study population we can always use the `getAttritionTable` function:

```
getAttritionTable(studyPop)
```

```
##                        description targetPersons comparatorPersons ...
## 1           Original cohorts             67212             35379 ...
## 2 Removed subs in both cohorts         67166             35333 ...
```

```
## 3                No prior outcome         67061          35238 ...
## 4 Have at least 1 days at risk         66780          35086 ...
```

12.8.4 Propensity Scores

We can fit a propensity model using the covariates constructed by getDbcohortMethodData(), and compute a PS for each person:

```
ps <- createPs(cohortMethodData = cmData, population = studyPop)
```

The createPs function uses the Cyclops package to fit a large-scale regularized logistic regression. To fit the propensity model, Cyclops needs to know the hyperparameter value which specifies the variance of the prior. By default Cyclops will use cross-validation to estimate the optimal hyperparameter. However, be aware that this can take a really long time. You can use the prior and control parameters of the createPs function to specify Cyclops' behavior, including using multiple CPUs to speed-up the cross-validation.

Here we use the PS to perform variable-ratio matching:

```
matchedPop <- matchOnPs(population = ps, caliper = 0.2,
                        caliperScale = "standardized logit", maxRatio = 100)
```

Alternatively, we could have used the PS in the trimByPs, trimByPsToEquipoise, or stratifyByPs functions.

12.8.5 Outcome Models

The outcome model is a model describing which variables are associated with the outcome. Under strict assumptions, the coefficient for the treatment variable can be interpreted as the causal effect. In this case we fit a Cox proportional hazards model, conditioned (stratified) on the matched sets:

```
outcomeModel <- fitOutcomeModel(population = matchedPop,
                                modelType = "cox",
                                stratified = TRUE)
outcomeModel
```

```
## Model type: cox
## Stratified: TRUE
## Use covariates: FALSE
## Use inverse probability of treatment weighting: FALSE
## Status: OK
##
```

```
##              Estimate lower .95 upper .95    logRr seLogRr
## treatment    4.3203     2.4531    8.0771 1.4633   0.304
```

12.8.6   Running Multiple Analyses

Often we want to perform more than one analysis, for example for multiple outcomes including negative controls. The CohortMethod offers functions for performing such studies
efficiently. This is described in detail in the package vignette on running multiple analyses.
Briefly, assuming the outcome of interest and negative control cohorts have already been
created, we can specify all target-comparator-outcome combinations we wish to analyze:

```
# Outcomes of interest:
ois <- c(3, 4) # Angioedema, AMI

# Negative controls:
ncs <- c(434165,436409,199192,4088290,4092879,44783954,75911,137951,77965,
         376707,4103640,73241,133655,73560,434327,4213540,140842,81378,
         432303,4201390,46269889,134438,78619,201606,76786,4115402,
         45757370,433111,433527,4170770,4092896,259995,40481632,4166231,
         433577,4231770,440329,4012570,4012934,441788,4201717,374375,
         4344500,139099,444132,196168,432593,434203,438329,195873,4083487,
         4103703,4209423,377572,40480893,136368,140648,438130,4091513,
         4202045,373478,46286594,439790,81634,380706,141932,36713918,
         443172,81151,72748,378427,437264,194083,140641,440193,4115367)

tcos <- createTargetComparatorOutcomes(targetId = 1,
                                       comparatorId = 2,
                                       outcomeIds = c(ois, ncs))

tcosList <- list(tcos)
```

Next, we specify what arguments should be used when calling the various functions described
previously in our example with one outcome:

```
aceI <- c(1335471,1340128,1341927,1363749,1308216,1310756,1373225,
          1331235,1334456,1342439)
thz <- c(1395058,974166,978555,907013)

cs <- createDefaultCovariateSettings(excludedCovariateConceptIds = c(aceI,
                                                                     thz),
                                     addDescendantsToExclude = TRUE)

cmdArgs <- createGetDbCohortMethodDataArgs(
  studyStartDate = "",
  studyEndDate = "",
  firstExposureOnly = FALSE,
```

```
  removeDuplicateSubjects = FALSE,
  restrictToCommonPeriod = FALSE,
  washoutPeriod = 0,
  covariateSettings = cs)

spArgs <- createCreateStudyPopulationArgs(
  firstExposureOnly = FALSE,
  restrictToCommonPeriod = FALSE,
  washoutPeriod = 0,
  removeDuplicateSubjects = "remove all",
  removeSubjectsWithPriorOutcome = TRUE,
  minDaysAtRisk = 1,
  startAnchor = "cohort start",
  addExposureDaysToStart = FALSE,
  endAnchor = "cohort end",
  addExposureDaysToEnd = TRUE)

psArgs <- createCreatePsArgs()

matchArgs <- createMatchOnPsArgs(
  caliper = 0.2,
  caliperScale = "standardized logit",
  maxRatio = 100)

fomArgs <- createFitOutcomeModelArgs(
  modelType = "cox",
  stratified = TRUE)
```

We then combine these into a single analysis settings object, which we provide a unique analysis ID and some description. We can combine one or more analysis settings objects into a list:

```
cmAnalysis <- createCmAnalysis(
  analysisId = 1,
  description = "Propensity score matching",
  getDbCohortMethodDataArgs = cmdArgs,
  createStudyPopArgs = spArgs,
  createPs = TRUE,
  createPsArgs = psArgs,
  matchOnPs = TRUE,
  matchOnPsArgs = matchArgs
  fitOutcomeModel = TRUE,
  fitOutcomeModelArgs = fomArgs)

cmAnalysisList <- list(cmAnalysis)
```

We can now run the study including all comparisons and analysis settings:

```
result <- runCmAnalyses(connectionDetails = connectionDetails,
                        cdmDatabaseSchema = cdmDatabaseSchema,
                        exposureDatabaseSchema = cohortDbSchema,
                        exposureTable = cohortTable,
                        outcomeDatabaseSchema = cohortDbSchema,
                        outcomeTable = cohortTable,
                        cdmVersion = cdmVersion,
                        outputFolder = outputFolder,
                        cmAnalysisList = cmAnalysisList,
                        targetComparatorOutcomesList = tcosList)
```

The `result` object contains references to all the artifacts that were created. For example, we can retrieve the outcome model for AMI:

```
omFile <- result$outcomeModelFile[result$targetId == 1 &
                                  result$comparatorId == 2 &
                                  result$outcomeId == 4 &
                                  result$analysisId == 1]
outcomeModel <- readRDS(file.path(outputFolder, omFile))
outcomeModel
```

```
## Model type: cox
## Stratified: TRUE
## Use covariates: FALSE
## Use inverse probability of treatment weighting: FALSE
## Status: OK
##
##            Estimate lower .95 upper .95   logRr seLogRr
## treatment    1.1338    0.5921    2.1765 0.1256   0.332
```

We can also retrieve the effect size estimates for all outcomes with one command:

```
summ <- summarizeAnalyses(result, outputFolder = outputFolder)
head(summ)
```

```
##   analysisId targetId comparatorId outcomeId        rr ...
## 1          1        1            2     72748 0.9734698 ...
## 2          1        1            2     73241 0.7067981 ...
## 3          1        1            2     73560 1.0623951 ...
## 4          1        1            2     75911 0.9952184 ...
## 5          1        1            2     76786 1.0861746 ...
## 6          1        1            2     77965 1.1439772 ...
```

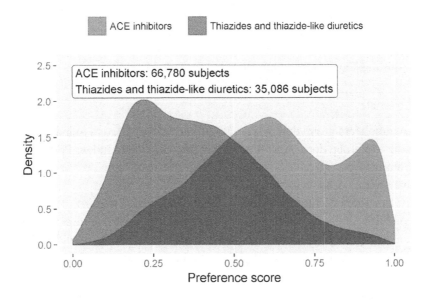

Figure 12.18: Preference score distribution.

12.9 Study Outputs

Our estimates are only valid if several assumptions have been met. We use a wide set of diagnostics to evaluate whether this is the case. These are available in the results produced by the R package generated by ATLAS, or can be generated on the fly using specific R functions.

12.9.1 Propensity Scores and Model

We first need to evaluate whether the target and comparator cohort are to some extent comparable. For this we can compute the Area Under the Receiver Operator Curve (AUC) statistic for the propensity model. An AUC of 1 indicates the treatment assignment was completely predictable based on baseline covariates, and that the two groups are therefore incomparable. We can use the `computePsAuc` function to compute the AUC, which in our example is 0.79. Using the `plotPs` function, we can also generate the preference score distribution as shown in Figure 12.18. Here we see that for many people the treatment they received was predictable, but there is also a large amount of overlap, indicating that adjustment can be used to select comparable groups.

In general it is a good idea to also inspect the propensity model itself, and especially so if the model is very predictive. That way we may discover which variables are most predictive. Table 12.7 shows the top predictors in our propensity model. Note that if a variable is too predictive, the CohortMethod package will throw an informative error rather than attempt to fit a model that is already known to be perfectly predictive.

Table 12.7: Top 10 predictors in the propensity model for ACEi and THZ. Positive values mean subjects with the covariate are more likely to receive the target treatment. "(Intercept)" indicates the intercept of this logistic regression model.

Beta	Covariate
-1.42	condition_era group during day -30 through 0 days relative to index: Edema
-1.11	drug_era group during day 0 through 0 days relative to index: Potassium Chloride
0.68	age group: 05-09
0.64	measurement during day -365 through 0 days relative to index: Renin
0.63	condition_era group during day -30 through 0 days relative to index: Urticaria
0.57	condition_era group during day -30 through 0 days relative to index: Proteinuria
0.55	drug_era group during day -365 through 0 days relative to index: INSULINS AND ANALOGUES
-0.54	race = Black or African American
0.52	(Intercept)
0.50	gender = MALE

If a variable is found to be highly predictive, there are two possible conclusions: Either we find that the variable is clearly part of the exposure itself and should be removed before fitting the model, or else we must conclude that the two populations are truly incomparable, and the analysis must be stopped.

12.9.2   Covariate Balance

The goal of using PS is to make the two groups comparable (or at least to select comparable groups). We must verify whether this is achieved, for example by checking whether the baseline covariates are indeed balanced after adjustment. We can use the `computeCovariateBalance` and `plotCovariateBalanceScatterPlot` functions to generate Figure 12.19. One rule-of-thumb to use is that no covariate may have an absolute standardized difference of means greater than 0.1 after propensity score adjustment. Here we see that although there was substantial imbalance before matching, after matching we meet this criterion.

12.9.3   Follow Up and Power

Before fitting an outcome model, we might be interested to know whether we have sufficient power to detect a particular effect size. It makes sense to perform these power calculations once the study population has been fully defined, so taking into account loss to

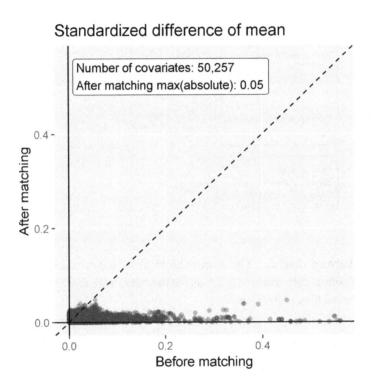

Figure 12.19: Covariate balance, showing the absolute standardized difference of mean before and after propensity score matching. Each dot represents a covariate.

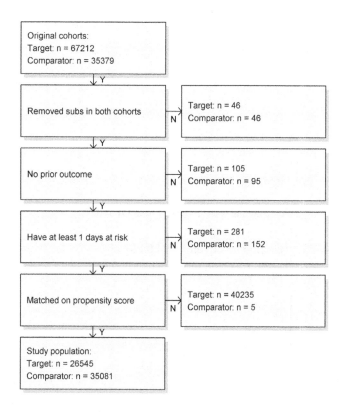

Figure 12.20: Attrition diagram. The counts shown at the top are those that meet our target and comparator cohort definitions. The counts at the bottom are those that enter our outcome model, in this case a Cox regression.

the various inclusion and exclusion criteria (such as no prior outcomes), and loss due to matching and/or trimming. We can view the attrition of subjects in our study using the `drawAttritionDiagram` function as shown in Figure 12.20.

Since the sample size is fixed in retrospective studies (the data has already been collected), and the true effect size is unknown, it is therefore less meaningful to compute the power given an expected effect size. Instead, the CohortMethod package provides the `computeMdrr` function to compute the minimum detectable relative risk (MDRR). In our example study the MDRR is 1.69.

To gain a better understanding of the amount of follow-up available we can also inspect the distribution of follow-up time. We defined follow-up time as time at risk, so not censored by the occurrence of the outcome. The `getFollowUpDistribution` can provide a simple overview as shown in Figure 12.21, which suggests the follow-up time for both cohorts is comparable.

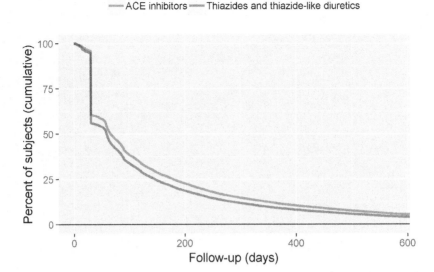

Figure 12.21: Distribution of follow-up time for the target and comparator cohorts.

12.9.4 Kaplan-Meier

One last check is to review the Kaplan-Meier plot, showing the survival over time in both cohorts. Using the `plotKaplanMeier` function we can create 12.22, which we can check for example if our assumption of proportionality of hazards holds. The Kaplan-Meier plot automatically adjusts for stratification or weighting by PS. In this case, because variable-ratio matching is used, the survival curve for the comparator groups is adjusted to mimic what the curve had looked like for the target group had they been exposed to the comparator instead.

12.9.5 Effect Size Estimate

We observe a hazard ratio of 4.32 (95% confidence interval: 2.45 - 8.08) for angioedema, which tells us that ACEi appears to increase the risk of angioedema compared to THZ. Similarly, we observe a hazard ratio of 1.13 (95% confidence interval: 0.59 - 2.18) for AMI, suggesting little or no effect for AMI. Our diagnostics, as reviewed earlier, give no reason for doubt. However, ultimately the quality of this evidence, and whether we choose to trust it, depends on many factors that are not covered by the study diagnostics as described in Chapter 14.

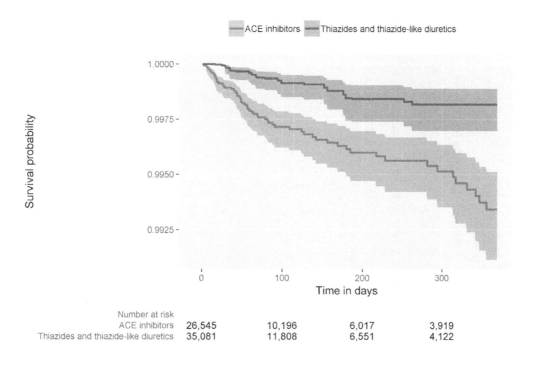

Figure 12.22: Kaplan-Meier plot.

12.10   Summary

- Population-level estimation aims to infer causal effects from observational data.

- The **counterfactual**, what would have happened if the subject had received an alternative exposure or no exposure, cannot be observed.

- Different designs aim to construct the counterfactual in different ways.

- The various designs as implemented in the OHDSI Methods Library provide diagnostics to evaluate whether the assumptions for creating an appropriate counterfactual have been met.

12.11   Exercises

Prerequisites

For these exercises we assume R, R-Studio and Java have been installed as described in Section 8.4.5. Also required are the SqlRender, DatabaseConnector, Eunomia and Cohort-

Method packages, which can be installed using:

```
install.packages(c("SqlRender", "DatabaseConnector", "devtools"))
devtools::install_github("ohdsi/Eunomia", ref = "v1.0.0")
devtools::install_github("ohdsi/CohortMethod")
```

The Eunomia package provides a simulated dataset in the CDM that will run inside your local R session. The connection details can be obtained using:

```
connectionDetails <- Eunomia::getEunomiaConnectionDetails()
```

The CDM database schema is "main". These exercises also make use of several cohorts. The `createCohorts` function in the Eunomia package will create these in the COHORT table:

```
Eunomia::createCohorts(connectionDetails)
```

Problem Definition

> What is the risk of gastrointestinal (GI) bleed in new users of celecoxib compared to new users of diclofenac?

The celecoxib new-user cohort has COHORT_DEFINITION_ID = 1. The diclofenac new-user cohort has COHORT_DEFINITION_ID = 2. The GI bleed cohort has CO-HORT_DEFINITION_ID = 3. The ingredient concept IDs for celecoxib and diclofenac are 1118084 and 1124300, respectively. Time-at-risk starts on day of treatment initiation, and stops at the end of observation (a so-called intent-to-treat analysis).

Exercise 12.1. Using the CohortMethod R package, use the default set of covariates and extract the CohortMethodData from the CDM. Create the summary of the CohortMethodData.

Exercise 12.2. Create a study population using the `createStudyPopulation` function, requiring a 180-day washout period, excluding people who had a prior outcome, and removing people that appear in both cohorts. Did we lose people?

Exercise 12.3. Fit a Cox proportional hazards model without using any adjustments. What could go wrong if you do this?

Exercise 12.4. Fit a propensity model. Are the two groups comparable?

Exercise 12.5. Perform PS stratification using 5 strata. Is covariate balance achieved?

Exercise 12.6. Fit a Cox proportional hazards model using the PS strata. Why is the result different from the unadjusted model?

Suggested answers can be found in Appendix E.8.

Chapter 13

Patient Level Prediction

Chapter leads: Peter Rijnbeek & Jenna Reps

Clinical decision making is a complicated task in which the clinician has to infer a diagnosis or treatment pathway based on the available medical history of the patient and the current clinical guidelines. Clinical prediction models have been developed to support this decision-making process and are used in clinical practice in a wide spectrum of specialties. These models predict a diagnostic or prognostic outcome based on a combination of patient characteristics, e.g. demographic information, disease history, and treatment history.

The number of publications describing clinical prediction models has increased strongly over the last 10 years. Most currently-used models are estimated using small datasets and consider only a small set of patient characteristics. This low sample size, and thus low statistical power, forces the data analyst to make strong modelling assumptions. The selection of the limited set of patient characteristics is strongly guided by the expert knowledge at hand. This contrasts sharply with the reality of modern medicine wherein patients generate a rich digital trail, which is well beyond the power of any medical practitioner to fully assimilate. Presently, health care is generating a huge amount of patient-specific information stored in Electronic Health Records (EHRs). This includes structured data in the form of diagnosis, medication, laboratory test results, and unstructured data contained in clinical narratives. It is unknown how much predictive accuracy can be gained by leveraging the large amount of data originating from the complete EHR of a patient.

Advances in machine learning for large dataset analysis have led to increased interest in applying patient-level prediction on this type of data. However, many published efforts in patient-level prediction do not follow the model development guidelines, fail to perform extensive external validation, or provide insufficient model details which limits the ability of independent researchers to reproduce the models and perform external validation. This makes it hard to fairly evaluate the predictive performance of the models and reduces the likelihood of the model being used appropriately in clinical practice. To improve standards, several papers have been written detailing guidelines for best practices in developing and reporting prediction models. For example, the Transparent Reporting of a multivariable pre-

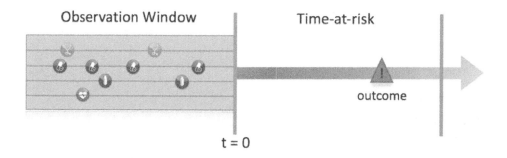

Figure 13.1: The prediction problem.

diction model for Individual Prognosis Or Diagnosis (TRIPOD) statement[1] provides clear recommendations for reporting prediction model development and validation and addresses some of the concerns related to transparency.

Massive-scale, patient-specific predictive modeling has become reality due to OHDSI, where the common data model (CDM) allows for uniform and transparent analysis at an unprecedented scale. The growing network of databases standardized to the CDM enables external validation of models in different healthcare settings on a global scale. We believe this provides immediate opportunity to serve large communities of patients who are in most need of improved quality of care. Such models can inform truly personalized medical care, leading hopefully to sharply improved patient outcomes.

In this chapter we describe OHDSI's standardized framework for patient-level prediction, (Reps et al., 2018) and discuss the PatientLevelPrediction R package that implements established best practices for development and validation. We start with providing the necessary theory behind the development and evaluation of patient-level prediction and provide a high-level overview of the implemented machine learning algorithms. We then discuss an example prediction problem and provide step-by-step guidance on its definition and implementation using ATLAS or custom R code. Finally, we discuss the use of Shiny applications for the dissemination of study results.

13.1   The Prediction Problem

Figure 13.1 illustrates the prediction problem we address. Among a population at risk, we aim to predict which patients at a defined moment in time (t = 0) will experience some outcome during a time-at-risk. Prediction is done using only information about the patients in an observation window prior to that moment in time.

As shown in Table 13.1, to define a prediction problem we have to define t=0 by a target cohort, the outcome we like to predict by an outcome cohort, and the time-at-risk. We define

---
[1]https://www.equator-network.org/reporting-guidelines/tripod-statement/

the standard prediction question as:

> Among *[target cohort definition]*, who will go on to have *[outcome cohort definition]* within *[time-at-risk period]*?

Furthermore, we have to make design choices for the model we like to develop, and determine the observational datasets to perform internal and external validation.

Table 13.1: Main design choices in a prediction design.

Choice	Description
Target cohort	How do we define the cohort of persons for whom we wish to predict?
Outcome cohort	How do we define the outcome we want to predict?
Time-at-risk	In which time window relative to t=0 do we want to make the prediction?
Model	What algorithms do we want to use, and which potential predictor variables do we include?

This conceptual framework works for all types of prediction problems, for example:

- Disease onset and progression
  - **Structure**: Among patients who are newly diagnosed with *[a disease]*, who will go on to have *[another disease or complication]* within *[time horizon from diagnosis]*?
  - **Example**: Among newly diagnosed atrial fibrillation patients, who will go on to have ischemic stroke in the next three years?
- Treatment choice
  - **Structure**: Among patients with *[indicated disease]* who are treated with either *[treatment 1]* or *[treatment 2]*, which patients were treated with *[treatment 1]*?
  - **Example**: Among patients with atrial fibrillation who took either warfarin or rivaroxaban, which patients get warfarin? (e.g. for a propensity model)
- Treatment response
  - **Structure**: Among new users of *[a treatment]*, who will experience *[some effect]* in *[time window]*?
  - **Example**: Which patients with diabetes who start on metformin stay on metformin for three years?
- Treatment safety
  - **Structure**: Among new users of *[a treatment]*, who will experience *[adverse event]* in *[time window]*?
  - **Example**: Among new users of warfarin, who will have a gastrointestinal bleed in one year?
- Treatment adherence
  - **Structure**: Among new users of *[a treatment]*, who will achieve *[adherence metric]* at *[time window]*?

 – **Example**: Which patients with diabetes who start on metformin achieve >=80% proportion of days covered at one year?

13.2   Data Extraction

When creating a predictive model we use a process known as supervised learning — a form of machine learning — that infers the relationship between the covariates and the outcome status based on a labelled set of examples. Therefore, we need methods to extract the covariates from the CDM for the persons in the target cohort and we need to obtain their outcome labels.

The **covariates** (also referred to as "predictors", "features" or "independent variables") describe the characteristics of the patients. Covariates can include age, gender, presence of specific conditions and exposure codes in a patient's record, etc. Covariates are typically constructed using the FeatureExtraction package, described in more detail in Chapter 11. For prediction we can only use data prior to (and on) the date the person enters the target cohort. This date we will call the index date.

We also need to obtain the **outcome status** (also referred to as the "labels" or "classes") of all the patients during the time-at-risk. If the outcome occurs within the time-at-risk, the outcome status is defined as "positive."

13.2.1   Data Extraction Example

Table 13.2 shows an example COHORT table with two cohorts. The cohort with cohort definition ID 1 is the target cohort (e.g. "people recently diagnosed with atrial fibrillation"). Cohort definition ID 2 defines the outcome cohort (e.g. "stroke").

Table 13.2: Example COHORT table.   For simplicity the COHORT_END_DATE has been omitted.

COHORT_DEFINITION_ID	SUBJECT_ID	COHORT_START_DATE
1	1	2000-06-01
1	2	2001-06-01
2	2	2001-07-01

Table 13.3 provides an example CONDITION_OCCURRENCE table. Concept ID 320128 refers to "Essential hypertension."

Table 13.3: Example CONDITION_OCCURRENCE table. For simplicity only three columns are shown.

PERSON_ID	CONDITION_CONCEPT_ID	CONDITION_START_DATE
1	320128	2000-10-01

PERSON_ID	CONDITION_CONCEPT_ID	CONDITION_START_DATE
2	320128	2001-05-01

Based on this example data, and assuming the time at risk is the year following the index date (the target cohort start date), we can construct the covariates and the outcome status. A covariate indicating "Essential hypertension in the year prior" will have the value 0 (not present) for person ID 1 (the condition occurred *after* the index date), and the value 1 (present) for person ID 2. Similarly, the outcome status will be 0 for person ID 1 (this person had no entry in the outcome cohort), and 1 for person ID 2 (the outcome occurred within a year following the index date).

13.2.2 Missingness

Observational healthcare data rarely reflects whether data is missing. In the prior example, we simply observed the person with ID 1 had no essential hypertension occurrence prior to the index date. This could be because the condition was not present at that time, or because it was not recorded. It is important to realize that the machine learning algorithm cannot distinguish between the two scenarios and will simply assess the predictive value in the available data.

13.3 Fitting the Model

When fitting a prediction model we are trying to learn the relationship between the covariates and the observed outcome status from labelled examples. Suppose we only have two covariates, systolic and diastolic blood pressure, then we can represent each patient as a plot in two dimensional space as shown in Figure 13.2. In this figure the shape of the data point corresponds to the patient's outcome status (e.g. stroke).

A supervised learning model will try to find a decision boundary that optimally separates the two outcome classes. Different supervised learning techniques lead to different decision boundaries and there are often hyper-parameters that can impact the complexity of the decision boundary.

In Figure 13.2 we can see three different decision boundaries. The boundaries are used to infer the outcome status of any new data point. If a new data point falls into the shaded area then the model will predict "has outcome", otherwise it will predict "no outcome". Ideally a decision boundary should perfectly partition the two classes. However, there is a risk that too complex models "overfit" to the data. This can negatively impact the generalizability of the model to unseen data. For example, if the data contains noise, with mislabeled or incorrectly positioned data points, we would not want to fit our model to that noise. We therefore may prefer to define a decision boundary that does not perfectly discriminate in our training data but captures the "real" complexity. Techniques such as regularization aim to maximize model performance while minimizing complexity.

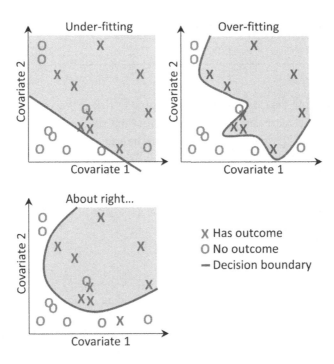

Figure 13.2: Decision boundary.

Each supervised learning algorithm has a different way to learn the decision boundary and it is not straightforward which algorithm will work best on your data. As the No Free Lunch theorem states not one algorithm is always going to outperform the others on all prediction problems. Therefore, we recommend trying multiple supervised learning algorithms with various hyper-parameter settings when developing patient-level prediction models.

The following algorithms are available in the PatientLevelPrediction package:

13.3.1 Regularized Logistic Regression

LASSO (least absolute shrinkage and selection operator) logistic regression belongs to the family of generalized linear models, where a linear combination of the variables is learned and finally a logistic function maps the linear combination to a value between 0 and 1. The LASSO regularization adds a cost based on model complexity to the objective function when training the model. This cost is the sum of the absolute values of the linear combination of the coefficients. The model automatically performs feature selection by minimizing this cost. We use the Cyclops (Cyclic coordinate descent for logistic, Poisson and survival analysis) package to perform large-scale regularized logistic regression.

Table 13.4: Hyper-parameters for the regularized logistic regression.

Parameter	Description	Typical values
Starting variance	The starting variance of the prior distribution.	0.1

Note that the variance is optimized by maximizing the out-of-sample likelihood in a cross-validation, so the starting variance has little impact on the performance of the resulting model. However, picking a starting variance that is too far from the optimal value may lead to long fitting time.

13.3.2   Gradient Boosting Machines

Gradient boosting machines is a boosting ensemble technique and in our framework it combines multiple decision trees. Boosting works by iteratively adding decision trees but adds more weight to the data-points that are misclassified by prior decision trees in the cost function when training the next tree. We use Extreme Gradient Boosting, which is an efficient implementation of the gradient boosting framework implemented in the xgboost R package available from CRAN.

Table 13.5: Hyper-parameters for gradient boosting machines.

Parameter	Description	Typical values
earlyStopRound	Stopping after rounds without improvement	25
learningRate	The boosting learn rate	0.005,0.01,0.1
maxDepth	Max levels in a tree	4,6,17
minRows	Min data points in a node	2
ntrees	Number of trees	100,1000

13.3.3   Random Forest

Random forest is a bagging ensemble technique that combines multiple decision trees. The idea behind bagging is to reduce the likelihood of overfitting by using weak classifiers and combining them into a strong classifier. Random forest accomplishes this by training multiple decision trees but only using a subset of the variables in each tree and the subset of variables differ between trees. Our package uses the sklearn implementation of Random Forest in Python.

Table 13.6: Hyper-parameters for random forests.

Parameter	Description	Typical values
maxDepth	Max levels in a tree	4,10,17

Parameter	Description	Typical values
mtries	Number of features in each tree	-1 = square root of total features,5,20
ntrees	Number of trees	500

13.3.4 K-Nearest Neighbors

K-nearest neighbors (KNN) is an algorithm that uses some distance metric to find the K closest labelled data-points to a new unlabeled data-point. The prediction of the new data-points is then the most prevalent class of the K-nearest labelled data-points. There is a sharing limitation of KNN, as the model requires labelled data to perform the prediction on new data, and it is often not possible to share this data across data sites. We included the BigKnn package developed in OHDSI which is a large scale KNN classifier.

Table 13.7: Hyper-parameters for K-nearest neighbors.

Parameter	Description	Typical values
k	Number of neighbors	1000

13.3.5 Naive Bayes

The Naive Bayes algorithm applies the Bayes theorem with the naive assumption of conditional independence between every pair of features given the value of the class variable. Based on the likelihood the data belongs to a class and the prior distribution of the class, a posterior distribution is obtained. Naive Bayes has no hyper-parameters.

13.3.6 AdaBoost

AdaBoost is a boosting ensemble technique. Boosting works by iteratively adding classifiers but adds more weight to the data-points that are misclassified by prior classifiers in the cost function when training the next classifier. We use the sklearn AdaboostClassifier implementation in Python.

Table 13.8: Hyper-parameters for AdaBoost.

Parameter	Description	Typical values
nEstimators	The maximum number of estimators at which boosting is terminated	4

Parameter	Description	Typical values
learningRate	Learning rate shrinks the contribution of each classifier by learning_rate. There is a trade-off between learningRate and nEstimators	1

13.3.7 Decision Tree

A decision tree is a classifier that partitions the variable space using individual tests selected using a greedy approach. It aims to find partitions that have the highest information gain to separate the classes. The decision tree can easily overfit by enabling a large number of partitions (tree depth) and often needs some regularization (e.g., pruning or specifying hyper-parameters that limit the complexity of the model). We use the sklearn DecisionTreeClassifier implementation in Python.

Table: Hyper-parameters for decision trees.

Parameter| Description | Typical values |

|:——— |:——— |:——— |
| classWeight | "Balance" or "None" | None | | maxDepth | The maximum depth of the tree | 10 | | minImpuritySplit | Threshold for early stopping in tree growth. A node will split if its impurity is above the threshold, otherwise it is a leaf | 10^{-7}| | minSamplesLeaf | The minimum number of samples per leaf | 10 | | minSamplesSplit | The minimum samples per split | 2 |

13.3.8 Multilayer Perceptron

Multilayer perceptrons are neural networks that contain multiple layers of nodes that weight their inputs using a non-linear function. The first layer is the input layer, the last layer is the output layer, and in between are the hidden layers. Neural networks are generally trained using back-propagation, meaning the training input is propagated forward through the network to produce an output, the error between the output and the outcome status is computed, and this error is propagated backwards through the network to update the linear function weights.

Table 13.9: Hyper-parameters for Multilayer Perceptrons.

Parameter	Description	Typical values
alpha	The l2 regularization	0.00001
size	The number of hidden nodes	4

13.3.9   Deep Learning

Deep learning such as deep nets, convolutional neural networks or recurrent neural networks are similar to Multilayer Perceptrons but have multiple hidden layers that aim to learn latent representations useful for prediction. In a separate vignette in the PatientLevelPrediction package we describe these models and hyper-parameters in more detail.

13.3.10   Other Algorithms

Other algorithms can be added to the patient-level prediction framework. This is out-of-scope for this chapter. Details can be found in the "Adding Custom Patient-Level Prediction Algorithms" vignette in the PatientLevelPrediction package.

13.4   Evaluating Prediction Models

13.4.1   Evaluation Types

We can evaluate a prediction model by measuring the agreement between the model's prediction and observed outcome status, which means we need data where the outcome status is known.

 For evaluation we must use a different dataset than was used to develop the model, or else we run the risk of favoring models that are over-fitted (see Section 13.3) and may not perform well for new patients.

We distinguish between

- **Internal validation**: Using different sets of data extracted from the same database to develop and evaluate the model.
- **External validation**: Developing the model in one database, and evaluating in another database.

There are two ways to perform internal validation:

- A **holdout set** approach splits the labelled data into two independent sets: a train set and a test set (the hold out set). The train set is used to learn the model and the test set is used to evaluate it. We can simply divide our patients randomly into a train and test set, or we may choose to:
  - Split the data based on time (temporal validation), for example training on data before a specific date, and evaluating on data after that date. This may inform us on whether our model generalizes to different time periods.
  - Split the data based on geographic location (spatial validation).

- **Cross validation** is useful when the data are limited. The data is split into n equally-sized sets, where n needs to be prespecified (e.g. $n = 10$). For each of these sets a model is trained on all data except the data in that set and used to generate predictions for the hold-out set. In this way, all data is used once to evaluate the model-building algorithm. In the patient-level prediction framework we use cross validation to pick the optimal hyper-parameters.

External validation aims to assess model performance on data from another database, i.e. outside of the settings it was developed in. This measure of model transportability is important because we want to apply our models not only on the database it was trained on. Different databases may represent different patient populations, different healthcare systems and different data-capture processes. We believe that the external validation of prediction models on a large set of databases is a crucial step in model acceptance and implementation in clinical practice.

13.4.2 Performance Metrics

Threshold Measures

A prediction model assigns a value between 0 and 1 for each patient corresponding to the risk of the patient having the outcome during the time at risk. A value of 0 means 0% risk, a value of 0.5 means 50% risk and a value of 1 means 100% risk. Common metrics such as accuracy, sensitivity, specificity, positive predictive value can be calculated by first specifying a threshold that is used to classify patients as having the outcome or not during the time at risk. For example, given Table 13.10, if we set the threshold as 0.5, patients 1, 3, 7 and 10 have a predicted risk greater than or equal to the threshold of 0.5 so they would be predicted to have the outcome. All other patients had a predicted risk less than 0.5, so they would be predicted to not have the outcome.

Table 13.10: Example of using a threshold on the predicted probability.

Patient ID	Predicted risk	Predicted class at 0.5 threshold	Has outcome during time-at-risk	Type
1	0.8	1	1	TP
2	0.1	0	0	TN
3	0.7	1	0	FP
4	0	0	0	TN
5	0.05	0	0	TN
6	0.1	0	0	TN
7	0.9	1	1	TP
8	0.2	0	1	FN
9	0.3	0	0	TN

Patient ID	Predicted risk	Predicted class at 0.5 threshold	Has outcome during time-at-risk	Type
10	0.5	1	0	FP

If a patient is predicted to have the outcome and has the outcome (during the time-at-risk) then this is called a true positive (TP). If a patient is predicted to have the outcome but does not have the outcome then this is called a false positive (FP). If a patient is predicted to not have the outcome and does not have the outcome then this is called a true negative (TN). Finally, if a patient is predicted to not have the outcome but does have the outcome then this is called a false negative (FN).

The following threshold-based metrics can be calculated:

- accuracy: $(TP + TN)/(TP + TN + FP + FN)$
- sensitivity: $TP/(TP + FN)$
- specificity: $TN/(TN + FP)$
- positive predictive value: $TP/(TP + FP)$

Note that these values can either decrease or increase if the threshold is lowered. Lowering the threshold of a classifier may increase the denominator by increasing the number of results returned. If the threshold was previously set too high, the new results may all be true positives, which will increase positive predictive value. If the previous threshold was about right or too low, further lowering the threshold will introduce false positives, decreasing positive predictive value. For sensitivity the denominator does not depend on the classifier threshold ($TP + FN$ is a constant). This means that lowering the classifier threshold may increase sensitivity by increasing the number of true positive results. It is also possible that lowering the threshold may leave sensitivity unchanged, while the positive predictive value fluctuates.

Discrimination

Discrimination is the ability to assign a higher risk to patients who will experience the outcome during the time at risk. The Receiver Operating Characteristics (ROC) curve is created by plotting 1 – specificity on the x-axis and sensitivity on the y-axis at all possible thresholds. An example ROC plot is presented later in this chapter in Figure 13.17. The area under the receiver operating characteristic curve (AUC) gives an overall measure of discrimination where a value of 0.5 corresponds to randomly assigning the risk and a value of 1 means perfect discrimination. Most published prediction models obtain AUCs between 0.6-0.8.

The AUC provides a way to determine how different the predicted risk distributions are between the patients who experience the outcome during the time at risk and those who do not. If the AUC is high, then the distributions will be mostly disjointed, whereas when there is a lot of overlap, the AUC will be closer to 0.5, as shown in Figure 13.3.

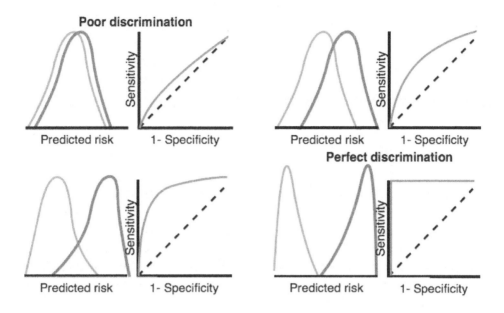

Figure 13.3: How the ROC plots are linked to discrimination. If the two classes have similar distributions of predicted risk, the ROC will be close to the diagonal, with AUC close to 0.5.

For rare outcomes even a model with a high AUC may not be practical, because for every positive above a given threshold there could also be many negatives (i.e. the positive predictive value will be low). Depending on the severity of the outcome and cost (health risk and/or monetary) of some intervention, a high false positive rate may be unwanted. When the outcome is rare another measure known as the area under the precision-recall curve (AUPRC) is therefore recommended. The AUPRC is the area under the line generated by plotting the sensitivity on the x-axis (also known as the recall) and the positive predictive value (also known as the precision) on the y-axis.

Calibration

Calibration is the ability of the model to assign the correct risk. For example, if the model assigned one hundred patients a risk of 10% then ten of the patients should experience the outcome during the time at risk. If the model assigned 100 patients a risk of 80% then eighty of the patients should experience the outcome during the time at risk. The calibration is generally calculated by partitioning the patients into deciles based on the predicted risk and in each group calculating the mean predicted risk and the fraction of the patients who experienced the outcome during the time at risk. We then plot these ten points (predicted risk on the y-axis and observed risk on the x-axis) and see whether they fall on the x = y line, indicating the model is well calibrated. An example calibration plot is presented later in this chapter in Figure 13.18. We also fit a linear model using the points to calculate the intercept (which should be close to zero) and the gradient (which should be close to one). If the gradient is greater than one then the model is assigning a higher risk than the true risk and if the gradient is less than one the model is assigning a lower risk than the true risk. Note that we also implemented Smooth Calibration Curves in our R-package to better capture the non-linear relationship between predicted and observed risk.

13.5   Designing a Patient-Level Prediction Study

In this section we will demonstrate how to design a prediction study. The first step is to clearly define the prediction problem. Interestingly, in many published papers the prediction problem is poorly defined, for example it is unclear how the index date (start of the target cohort) is defined. A poorly defined prediction problem does not allow for external validation by others, let alone implementation in clinical practice. In the patient-level prediction framework we enforce proper specification of the prediction problem by requiring the key choices defined in Table 13.1 to be explicitly defined. Here we will walk through this process using a "treatment safety" type prediction problem as an example.

13.5.1   Problem Definition

Angioedema is a well-known side-effect of ACE inhibitors, and the incidence of angioedema reported in the labeling for ACE inhibitors is in the range of 0.1% to 0.7%. (Byrd et al., 2006) Monitoring patients for this adverse effect is important, because although angioedema is rare, it may be life-threatening, leading to respiratory arrest and death. (Norman et al., 2013) Further, if angioedema is not initially recognized, it may lead to extensive and expensive workups before it is identified as a cause. (Norman et al., 2013; Thompson and Frable, 1993) Other than the higher risk among African-American patients, there are no known predisposing factors for the development of ACE inhibitor related angioedema. (Byrd et al., 2006) Most reactions occur within the first week or month of initial therapy and often within hours of the initial dose. (Cicardi et al., 2004) However, some cases may occur years after therapy has begun. (O'Mara and O'Mara, 1996) No diagnostic test is available that specifically identifies those at risk. If we could identify those at risk, doctors could act, for example by discontinuing the ACE inhibitor in favor of another hypertension drug.

We will apply the patient-level prediction framework to observational healthcare data to address the following patient-level prediction question:

> Among patients who have just started on an ACE inhibitor for the first time, who will experience angioedema in the following year?

13.5.2   Study Population Definition

The final study population in which we will develop our model is often a subset of the target cohort, because we may for example apply criteria that are dependent on the outcome, or we want to perform sensitivity analyses with sub-populations of the target cohort. For this we have to answer the following questions:

- *What is the minimum amount of observation time we require before the start of the target cohort?* This choice could depend on the available patient time in the training data, but also on the time we expect to be available in the data sources we want to apply the model on in the future. The longer the minimum observation time, the more baseline history time is available for each person to use for feature extraction, but the fewer patients will qualify for analysis. Moreover, there could be clinical reasons to choose a short or longer look-back period. For our example, we will use a 365-day prior history as look-back period (washout period).

- *Can patients enter the target cohort multiple times?* In the target cohort definition, a person may qualify for the cohort multiple times during different spans of time, for example if they had different episodes of a disease or separate periods of exposure to a medical product. The cohort definition does not necessarily apply a restriction to only let the patients enter once, but in the context of a particular patient-level prediction problem we may want to restrict the cohort to the first qualifying episode. In our example, a person can only enter the target cohort once since our criteria was based on first use of an ACE inhibitor.

- *Do we allow persons to enter the cohort if they experienced the outcome before?* Do we allow persons to enter the target cohort if they experienced the outcome before qualifying for the target cohort? Depending on the particular patient-level prediction problem, there may be a desire to predict incident first occurrence of an outcome, in which case patients who have previously experienced the outcome are not at risk for having a first occurrence and therefore should be excluded from the target cohort. In other circumstances, there may be a desire to predict prevalent episodes, whereby patients with prior outcomes can be included in the analysis and the prior outcome itself can be a predictor of future outcomes. For our prediction example, we will choose not to include those with prior angioedema.

- *How do we define the period in which we will predict our outcome relative to the target cohort start?* We have to make two decisions to answer this question. First, does the time-at-risk window start at the date of the start of the target cohort or later? Arguments to make it start later could be that we want to avoid outcomes that were entered late in the record that actually occurred before the start of the target cohort or we want to leave a gap where interventions to prevent the outcome could theoretically be implemented. Second, we need to define the time-at-risk by setting the risk window end, as some specification of days offset relative to the target cohort start or end dates. For our problem we will predict in a time-at-risk window starting 1 day after the start of the target cohort up to 365 days later.

- *Do we require a minimum amount of time-at-risk?* We have to decide if we want to include patients that did not experience the outcome but did leave the database earlier than the end of our time-at-risk period. These patients may experience the outcome when we no longer observe them. For our prediction problem we decide to answer this question with "yes," requiring a minimum time-at-risk for that reason. Furthermore, we have to decide if this constraint also applies to persons who experienced the outcome or we will include all persons with the outcome irrespective of their total time at risk. For example, if the outcome is death, then persons with the outcome are likely censored before the full time-at-risk period is complete.

13.5.3 Model Development Settings

To develop the prediction model we have to decide which algorithm(s) we like to train. We see the selection of the best algorithm for a certain prediction problem as an empirical question, i.e. we prefer to let the data speak for itself and try different approaches to find the best one. In our framework we have therefore implemented many algorithms as described in Section 13.3, and allow others to be added. In this example, to keep things simple, we select just one algorithm: Gradient Boosting Machines.

Furthermore, we have to decide on the covariates that we will use to train our model. In our example, we like to add gender, age, all conditions, drugs and drug groups, and visit counts. We will look for these clinical events in the year before and any time prior to the index date.

13.5.4 Model Evaluation

Finally, we have to define how we will evaluate our model. For simplicity, we here choose internal validation. We have to decide how we divide our dataset in a training and test dataset and how we assign patients to these two sets. Here we will use a typical 75% - 25% split. Note that for very large datasets we could use more data for training.

13.5.5 Study Summary

We have now completely defined our study as shown in Table 13.11.

Table 13.11: Main design choices for our study.

Choice	Value
Target cohort	Patients who have just started on an ACE inhibitor for the first time. Patients are excluded if they have less than 365 days of prior observation time or have prior angioedema.
Outcome cohort	Angioedema.
Time-at-risk	1 day until 365 days from cohort start. We will require at least 364 days at risk.

Choice	Value
Model	Gradient Boosting Machine with hyper-parameters ntree: 5000, max depth: 4 or 7 or 10 and learning rate: 0.001 or 0.01 or 0.1 or 0.9. Covariates will include gender, age, conditions, drugs, drug groups, and visit count. Data split: 75% train - 25% test, randomly assigned by person.

13.6 Implementing the Study in ATLAS

The interface for designing a prediction study can be opened by clicking on the ❤ Prediction button in the left hand side ATLAS menu. Create a new prediction study. Make sure to give the study an easy-to-recognize name. The study design can be saved at any time by clicking the 💾 button.

In the Prediction design function, there are four sections: Prediction Problem Settings, Analysis Settings, Execution Settings, and Training Settings. Here we discuss each section:

13.6.1 Prediction Problem Settings

Here we select the target population cohorts and outcome cohorts for the analysis. A prediction model will be developed for all combinations of the target population cohorts and the outcome cohorts. For example, if we specify two target populations and two outcomes, we have specified four prediction problems.

To select a target population cohort we need to have previously defined it in ATLAS. Instantiating cohorts is described in Chapter 10. The Appendix provides the full definitions of the target (Appendix B.1) and outcome (Appendix B.4) cohorts used in this example. To add a target population to the cohort, click on the "Add Target Cohort" button. Adding outcome cohorts similarly works by clicking the "Add Outcome Cohort" button. When done, the dialog should look like Figure 13.4.

13.6.2 Analysis Settings

The analysis settings enable selection of the supervised learning algorithm, the covariates and population settings.

Model Settings

We can pick one or more supervised learning algorithms for model development. To add a supervised learning algorithm click on the "Add Model Settings" button. A dropdown

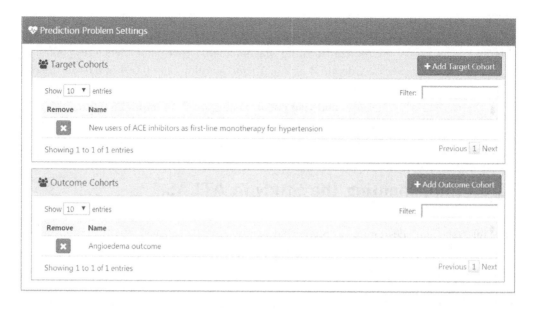

Figure 13.4: Prediction problem settings.

containing all the models currently supported in the ATLAS interface will appear. We can select the supervised learning model we want to include in the study by clicking on the name in the dropdown menu. This will then show a view for that specific model, allowing the selection of the hyper-parameter values. If multiple values are provided, a grid search is performed across all possible combinations of values to select the optimal combination using cross-validation.

For our example we select gradient boosting machines, and set the hyper-parameters as specified in Figure 13.5.

Covariate Settings

We have defined a set of standard covariates that can be extracted from the observational data in the CDM format. In the covariate settings view, it is possible to select which of the standard covariates to include. We can define different types of covariate settings, and each model will be created separately with each specified covariate setting.

To add a covariate setting into the study, click on the "Add Covariate Settings". This will open the covariate setting view.

The first part of the covariate settings view is the exclude/include option. Covariates are generally constructed for any concept. However, we may want to include or exclude specific concepts, for example if a concept is linked to the target cohort definition. To only include certain concepts, create a concept set in ATLAS and then under the "**What concepts do you want to include in baseline covariates in the patient-level prediction model? (Leave blank if you want to include everything)**" select the concept set by clicking on ▣. We can auto-

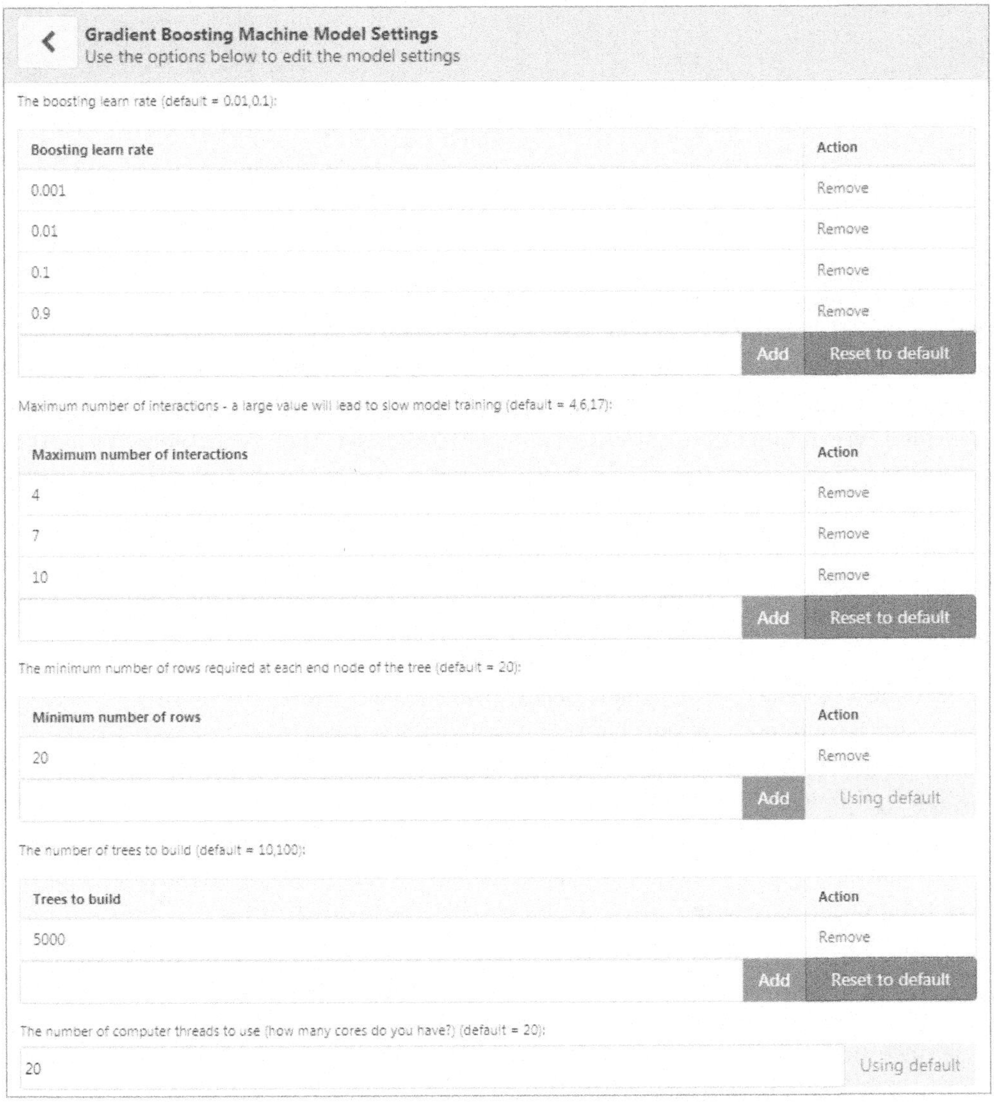

Figure 13.5: Gradient boosting machine settings

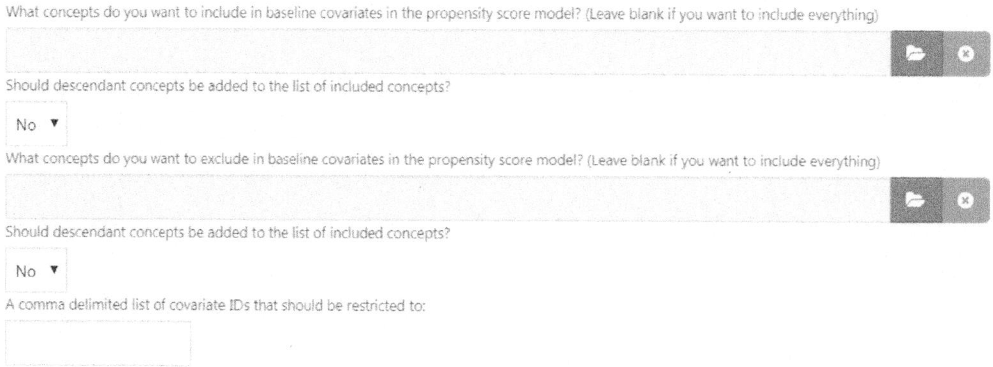

What concepts do you want to include in baseline covariates in the propensity score model? (Leave blank if you want to include everything)

Should descendant concepts be added to the list of included concepts?

No ▼

What concepts do you want to exclude in baseline covariates in the propensity score model? (Leave blank if you want to include everything)

Should descendant concepts be added to the list of included concepts?

No ▼

A comma delimited list of covariate IDs that should be restricted to:

Figure 13.6: Covariate inclusion and exclusion settings.

matically add all descendant concepts to the concepts in the concept set by answering "yes" to the question "**Should descendant concepts be added to the list of included concepts?**" The same process can be repeated for the question "**What concepts do you want to exclude in baseline covariates in the patient-level prediction model? (Leave blank if you want to include everything)**", allowing covariates corresponding to the selected concepts to be removed. The final option "**A comma delimited list of covariate IDs that should be restricted to**" enables us to add a set of covariate IDs (rather than concept IDs) comma separated that will only be included in the model. This option is for advanced users only. Once done, the inclusion and exclusion settings should look like Figure 13.6.

The next section enables the selection of non-time bound variables.

- Gender: a binary variable indicating male or female gender
- Age: a continuous variable corresponding to age in years
- Age group: binary variables for every 5 years of age (0-4, 5-9, 10-14, ..., 95+)
- Race: a binary variable for each race, 1 means the patient has that race recorded, 0 otherwise
- Ethnicity: a binary variable for each ethnicity, 1 means the patient has that ethnicity recorded, 0 otherwise
- Index year: a binary variable for each cohort start date year, 1 means that was the patients cohort start date year, 0 otherwise. **It often does not make sense to include index year, since we would like to apply our model to the future**.
- Index month - a binary variable for each cohort start date month, 1 means that was the patient's cohort start date month, 0 otherwise
- Prior observation time: [Not recommended for prediction] a continuous variable corresponding to how long in days the patient was in the database prior to the cohort start date
- Post observation time: [Not recommended for prediction] a continuous variable corresponding to how long in days the patient was in the database post cohort start date
- Time in cohort: a continuous variable corresponding to how long in days the patient was in the cohort (cohort end date minus cohort start date)
- Index year and month: [Not recommended for prediction] a binary variable for each

Select Covariates

	Gender	Age	Age Groups	Race	Ethnicity	Index Year	Index Month	Prior Observation Time	Post Observation Time	Time In Cohort	Index Year & Month
Demographics	✔	☐	✔	✔	✔	☐	✔	☐	☐	☐	☐

Figure 13.7: Select covariates.

Time bound covariates

Set the time windows for the time bound covariates in days relative to the cohort index

	Any Time Prior	Long Term	Medium Term	Short Term	End Days
Time Windows	All Time	-365	-180	-30	0

Figure 13.8: Time bound covariates.

cohort start date year and month combination, 1 means that was the patients cohort start date year and month, 0 otherwise

Once done, this section should look like Figure 13.7.

The standard covariates enable three flexible time intervals for the covariates:

- end days: when to end the time intervals relative to the cohort start date [default is 0]
- long term [default -365 days to end days prior to cohort start date]
- medium term [default -180 days to end days prior to cohort start date]
- short term [default -30 days to end days prior to cohort start date]

Once done, this section should look like Figure 13.8.

The next option is the covariates extracted from the era tables:

- Condition: Construct covariates for each condition concept ID and time interval selected and if a patient has the concept ID with an era (i.e., the condition starts or ends during the time interval or starts before and ends after the time interval) during the specified time interval prior to the cohort start date in the condition era table, the covariate value is 1, otherwise 0.
- Condition group: Construct covariates for each condition concept ID and time interval selected and if a patient has the concept ID **or any descendant concept ID** with an era during the specified time interval prior to the cohort start date in the condition era table, the covariate value is 1, otherwise 0.
- Drug: Construct covariates for each drug concept ID and time interval selected and if a patient has the concept ID with an era during the specified time interval prior to the cohort start date in the drug era table, the covariate value is 1, otherwise 0.
- Drug group: Construct covariates for each drug concept ID and time interval selected and if a patient has the concept ID **or any descendant concept ID** with an era during the specified time interval prior to the cohort start date in the drug era table, the covariate

Set the time bound era covariates

Domain	Any Time Prior	Long Term (-365 days)	Medium Term (-180 days)	Short Term (-30 days)	Overlapping	Era Start		
						Long Term (-365 days)	Medium Term (-180 days)	Short Term (-30 days)
Condition	☐	☐	☑	☐	☐	☐	☐	☐
Condition Group	☐	☑	☐	☑	☐	☐	☐	☐
Drug	☐	☐	☐	☐	☐	☐	☐	☐
Drug Group	☐	☑	☐	☑	☐	☐	☐	☐

Figure 13.9: Time bound era covariates.

value is 1, otherwise 0.

Overlapping time interval setting means that the drug or condition era should start prior to the cohort start date and end after the cohort start date, so it overlaps with the cohort start date. The **era start** option restricts to finding condition or drug eras that start during the time interval selected.

Once done, this section should look like Figure 13.9.

The next option selects covariates corresponding to concept IDs in each domain for the various time intervals:

- Condition: Construct covariates for each condition concept ID and time interval selected and if a patient has the concept ID recorded during the specified time interval prior to the cohort start date in the condition occurrence table, the covariate value is 1, otherwise 0.
- Condition Primary Inpatient: One binary covariate per condition observed as a primary diagnosis in an inpatient setting in the condition_occurrence table.
- Drug: Construct covariates for each drug concept ID and time interval selected and if a patient has the concept ID recorded during the specified time interval prior to the cohort start date in the drug exposure table, the covariate value is 1, otherwise 0.
- Procedure: Construct covariates for each procedure concept ID and time interval selected and if a patient has the concept ID recorded during the specified time interval prior to the cohort start date in the procedure occurrence table, the covariate value is 1, otherwise 0.
- Measurement: Construct covariates for each measurement concept ID and time interval selected and if a patient has the concept ID recorded during the specified time interval prior to the cohort start date in the measurement table, the covariate value is 1, otherwise 0.
- Measurement Value: Construct covariates for each measurement concept ID with a value and time interval selected and if a patient has the concept ID recorded during the specified time interval prior to the cohort start date in the measurement table, the covariate value is the measurement value, otherwise 0.
- Measurement range group: Binary covariates indicating whether measurements are below, within, or above normal range.
- Observation: Construct covariates for each observation concept ID and time interval

Set the time bound covariates

Domain	Any Time Prior	Long Term (-365 days)	Medium Term (-180 days)	Short Term (-30 days)	Distinct Count — Long Term (-365 days)	Medium Term (-180 days)	Short Term (-30 days)
Condition	☐	☐	☐	☐	☐	☐	☐
Condition - Primary Inpatient	☐	☐	☐	☐			
Drug	☐	☐	☐	☐	☐	☐	☐
Procedure	☐	☑	☐	☐	☐	☐	☐
Measurement	☐	☑	☐	☐	☐	☐	☐
Measurement - Value	☐	☐	☐	☐			
Measurement - Range Group	☐	☑	☐	☐			
Observation	☐	☑	☐	☐	☐	☐	☐
Device	☐	☑	☐	☐			
Visit - Count		☑	☐	☐			
Visit - Concept Count		☐	☐	☐			

Figure 13.10: Time bound covariates.

Set the index score covariates

Index Score Type	
CHADS$_2$	☐
CHA$_2$DS$_2$VASc	☑
DCSI	☑
Charlson	☑

Figure 13.11: Risk score covariate settings.

selected and if a patient has the concept ID recorded during the specified time interval prior to the cohort start date in the observation table, the covariate value is 1, otherwise 0.

- Device: Construct covariates for each device concept ID and time interval selected and if a patient has the concept ID recorded during the specified time interval prior to the cohort start date in the device table, the covariate value is 1, otherwise 0.
- Visit Count: Construct covariates for each visit and time interval selected and count the number of visits recorded during the time interval as the covariate value.
- Visit Concept Count: Construct covariates for each visit, domain and time interval selected and count the number of records per domain recorded during the visit type and time interval as the covariate value.

The distinct count option counts the number of distinct concept IDs per domain and time interval.

Once done, this section should look like Figure 13.10.

The final option is whether to include commonly used risk scores as covariates. Once done, the risk score settings should look like Figure 13.11.

Population Settings

The population settings is where addition inclusion criteria can be applied to the target population and is also where the time-at-risk is defined. To add a population setting into the study, click on the "Add Population Settings" button. This will open up the population setting view.

The first set of options enable the user to specify the time-at-risk period. This is the time interval where we look to see whether the outcome of interest occurs. If a patient has the outcome during the time-at-risk period then we will classify them as "Has outcome", otherwise they are classified as "No outcome". **"Define the time-at-risk window start, relative to target cohort entry:"** defines the start of the time-at-risk, relative to the target cohort start or end date. Similarly, **"Define the time-at-risk window end:"** defines the end of the time-at-risk.

"Minimum lookback period applied to target cohort" specifies the minimum baseline period, the minimum number of days prior to the cohort start date that a patient is continuously observed. The default is 365 days. Expanding the minimum look-back will give a more complete picture of a patient (as they must have been observed for longer) but will filter patients who do not have the minimum number of days prior observation.

If **"Should subjects without time at risk be removed?"** is set to yes, then a value for **"Minimum time at risk:"** is also required. This allows removing people who are lost to follow-up (i.e. that have left the database during the time-at-risk period). For example, if the time-at-risk period was 1 day from cohort start until 365 days from cohort start, then the full time-at-risk interval is 364 days (365-1). If we only want to include patients who are observed the whole interval, then we set the minimum time at risk to be 364. If we are happy as long as people are in the time-at-risk for the first 100 days, then we select minimum time at risk to be 100. In this case as the time-at-risk start is 1 day from the cohort start, a patient will be included if they remain in the database for at least 101 days from the cohort start date. If we set "Should subjects without time at risk be removed?" to 'No', then this will keep all patients, even those who drop out from the database during the time-at-risk.

The option **"Include people with outcomes who are not observed for the whole at risk period?"** is related to the previous option. If set to "yes", then people who experience the outcome during the time-at-risk are always kept, even if they are not observed for the specified minimum amount of time.

The option **"Should only the first exposure per subject be included?"** is only useful if our target cohort contains patients multiple times with different cohort start dates. In this situation, picking "yes" will result in only keeping the earliest target cohort date per patient in the analysis. Otherwise a patient can be in the dataset multiple times.

Setting **"Remove patients who have observed the outcome prior to cohort entry?"** to "yes" will remove patients who have the outcome prior to the time-at-risk start date, so the model is for patients who have never experienced the outcome before. If "no" is selected, then patients could have had the outcome prior. Often, having the outcome prior is very predictive of having the outcome during the time-at-risk.

Once done, the population settings dialog should look like Figure 13.12.

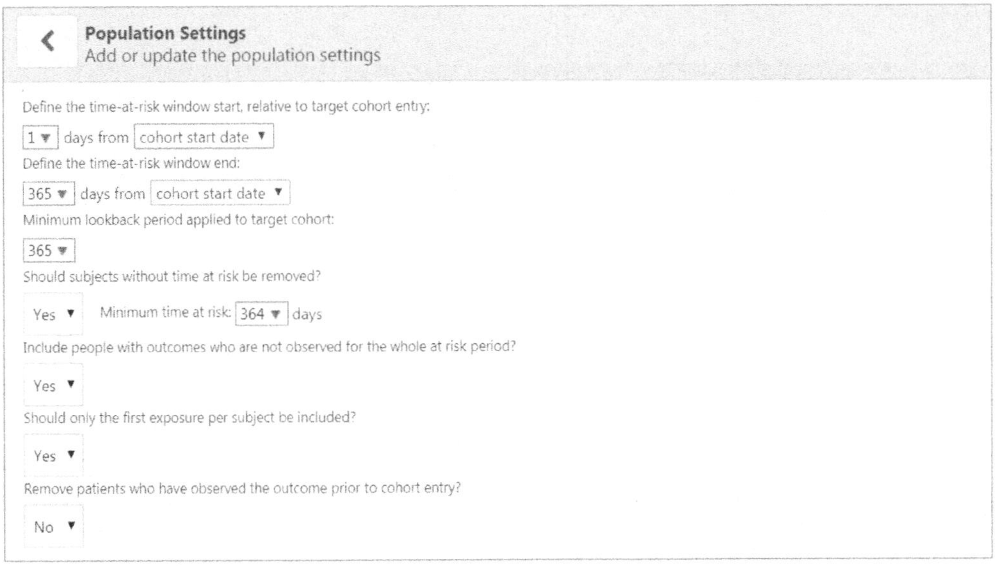

Figure 13.12: Population settings.

Now that we are finished with the Analysis Settings, the entire dialog should look like Figure 13.13.

13.6.3 Execution Settings

There are three options:

- "**Perform sampling**": here we choose whether to perform sampling (default = "no"). If set to "yes", another option will appear: "**How many patients to use for a subset?**", where the sample size can be specified. Sampling can be an efficient means to determine if a model for a large population (e.g. 10 million patients) will be predictive by creating and testing the model with a sample of patients. For example, if the AUC is close to 0.5 in the sample, we might abandon the model.
- "**Minimum covariate occurrence: If a covariate occurs in a fraction of the target population less than this value, it will be removed:**": here we choose the minimum covariate occurrence (default = 0.001). A minimum threshold value for covariate occurrence is necessary to remove rare events that are not representative of the overall population.
- "**Normalize covariate**": here we choose whether to normalize covariates (default = "yes"). Normalization of the covariates is usually necessary for successful implementation of a LASSO model.

For our example we make the choices shown in Figure 13.14.

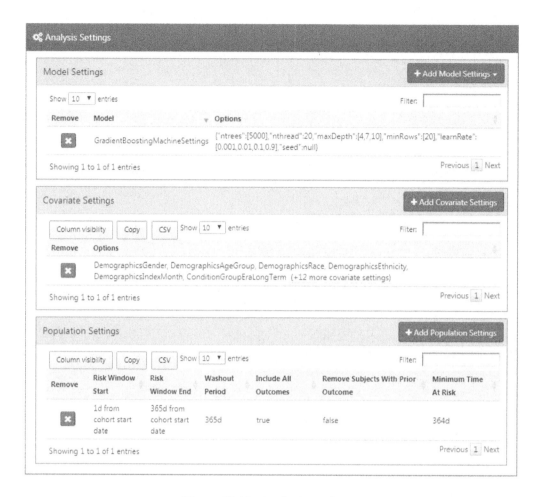

Figure 13.13: Analysis settings.

Figure 13.14: Execution settings.

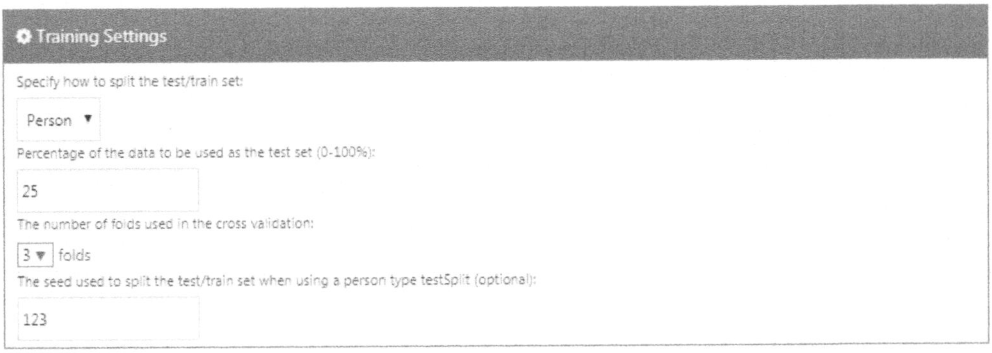

Figure 13.15: Training settings.

13.6.4 Training Settings

There are four options:

- **"Specify how to split the test/train set:"** Select whether to differentiate the train/test data by person (stratified by outcome) or by time (older data to train the model, later data to evaluate the model).
- **"Percentage of the data to be used as the test set (0-100%)"**: Select the percentage of data to be used as test data (default = 25%).
- **"The number of folds used in the cross validation"**: Select the number of folds for cross-validation used to select the optimal hyper-parameter (default = 3).
- **"The seed used to split the test/train set when using a person type testSplit (optional):"**: Select the random seed used to split the train/test set when using a person type test split.

For our example we make the choices shown in Figure 13.15.

13.6.5 Importing and Exporting a Study

To export a study, click on the "Export" tab under "Utilities." ATLAS will produce JSON that can be directly copied and pasted into a file that contains all of the data, such as the study name, cohort definitions, models selected, covariates, settings, needed to run the study.

To import a study, click on the "Import" tab under "Utilities." Paste the contents of a patient-level prediction study JSON into this window, then click on the Import button below the other tab buttons. Note that this will overwrite all previous settings for that study, so this is typically done using a new, empty study design.

13.6.6 Downloading the Study Package

Click on the "Review & Download" tab under "Utilities." In the "Download Study Package" section, enter a descriptive name for the R package, noting that any illegal characters in R will automatically be removed from the file name by ATLAS. Click on ![Download] to download the R package to a local folder.

13.6.7 Running the Study

To run the R package requires having R, RStudio, and Java installed as described in Section 8.4.5. Also required is the PatientLevelPrediction package, which can be installed in R using:

```
install.packages("drat")
drat::addRepo("OHDSI")
install.packages("PatientLevelPrediction")
```

Some of the machine learning algorithms require additional software to be installed. For a full description of how to install the PatientLevelPrediction package, see the "Patient-Level Prediction Installation Guide" vignette.

To use the study R package we recommend using R Studio. If you are running R Studio locally, unzip the file generated by ATLAS, and double click the .Rproj file to open it in R Studio. If you are running R Studio on an R studio server, click ![Upload] to upload and unzip the file, then click on the .Rproj file to open the project.

Once you have opened the project in R Studio, you can open the README file, and follow the instructions. Make sure to change all file paths to existing paths on your system.

13.7 Implementing the Study in R

An alternative to implementing our study design using ATLAS is to write the study code ourselves in R. We can make use of the functions provided in the PatientLevelPrediction package. The package enables data extraction, model building, and model evaluation using data from databases that are translated into the OMOP CDM.

13.7.1 Cohort Instantiation

We first need to instantiate the target and outcome cohorts. Instantiating cohorts is described in Chapter 10. The Appendix provides the full definitions of the target (Appendix B.1) and outcome (Appendix B.4) cohorts. In this example we will assume the ACE inhibitors cohort has ID 1, and the angioedema cohort has ID 2.

13.7.2 Data Extraction

We first need to tell R how to connect to the server. PatientLevelPrediction uses the DatabaseConnector package, which provides a function called createConnectionDetails.

Type `?createConnectionDetails` for the specific settings required for the various database management systems (DBMS). For example, one might connect to a PostgreSQL database using this code:

```
library(PatientLevelPrediction)
connDetails <- createConnectionDetails(dbms = "postgresql",
                                       server = "localhost/ohdsi",
                                       user = "joe",
                                       password = "supersecret")

cdmDbSchema <- "my_cdm_data"
cohortsDbSchema <- "scratch"
cohortsDbTable <- "my_cohorts"
cdmVersion <- "5"
```

The last four lines define the `cdmDbSchema`, `cohortsDbSchema`, and `cohortsDbTable` variables, as well as the CDM version. We will use these later to tell R where the data in CDM format live, where the cohorts of interest have been created, and what version CDM is used. Note that for Microsoft SQL Server, database schemas need to specify both the database and the schema, so for example `cdmDbSchema <- "my_cdm_data.dbo"`.

First it makes sense to verify that the cohort creation has succeeded by counting the number of cohort entries:

```
sql <- paste("SELECT cohort_definition_id, COUNT(*) AS count",
"FROM @cohortsDbSchema.cohortsDbTable",
"GROUP BY cohort_definition_id")
conn <- connect(connDetails)
renderTranslateQuerySql(connection = conn,
                        sql = sql,
                        cohortsDbSchema = cohortsDbSchema,
                        cohortsDbTable = cohortsDbTable)
```

```
##    cohort_definition_id   count
## 1                     1 527616
## 2                     2   3201
```

Now we can tell PatientLevelPrediction to extract all necessary data for our analysis. Covariates are extracted using the `FeatureExtraction` package. For more detailed information on the FeatureExtraction package see its vignettes. For our example study we decided to use these settings:

```
covariateSettings <- createCovariateSettings(
useDemographicsGender = TRUE,
                        useDemographicsAge = TRUE,
                        useConditionGroupEraLongTerm = TRUE,
                        useConditionGroupEraAnyTimePrior = TRUE,
```

```
                    useDrugGroupEraLongTerm = TRUE,
                    useDrugGroupEraAnyTimePrior = TRUE,
                    useVisitConceptCountLongTerm = TRUE,
                    longTermStartDays = -365,
                    endDays = -1)
```

The final step for extracting the data is to run the `getPlpData` function and input the connection details, the database schema where the cohorts are stored, the cohort definition IDs
for the cohort and outcome, and the washout period which is the minimum number of days
prior to cohort index date that the person must have been observed to be included into the
data, and finally input the previously constructed covariate settings.

```
plpData <- getPlpData(connectionDetails = connDetails,
                      cdmDatabaseSchema = cdmDbSchema,
                      cohortDatabaseSchema = cohortsDbSchema,
                      cohortTable = cohortsDbSchema,
                      cohortId = 1,
                      covariateSettings = covariateSettings,
                      outcomeDatabaseSchema = cohortsDbSchema,
                      outcomeTable = cohortsDbSchema,
                      outcomeIds = 2,
                      sampleSize = 10000
)
```

There are many additional parameters for the `getPlpData` function which are all documented in the PatientLevelPrediction manual. The resulting `plpData` object uses the package `ff` to store information in a way that ensures R does not run out of memory, even when
the data are large.

Creating the `plpData` object can take considerable computing time, and it is probably a good
idea to save it for future sessions. Because `plpData` uses `ff`, we cannot use R's regular save
function. Instead, we'll have to use the `savePlpData` function:

```
savePlpData(plpData, "angio_in_ace_data")
```

We can use the `loadPlpData()` function to load the data in a future session.

13.7.3 Additional Inclusion Criteria

The final study population is obtained by applying additional constraints on the two earlier
defined cohorts, e.g., a minimum time at risk can be enforced (`requireTimeAtRisk`,
`minTimeAtRisk`) and we can specify if this also applies to patients with the outcome
(`includeAllOutcomes`). Here we also specify the start and end of the risk window
relative to target cohort start. For example, if we like the risk window to start 30 days

after the at-risk cohort start and end a year later we can set `riskWindowStart` = 30 and `riskWindowEnd` = 365. In some cases the risk window needs to start at the cohort end date. This can be achieved by setting `addExposureToStart` = TRUE which adds the cohort (exposure) time to the start date.

In the example below all the settings we defined for our study are imposed:

```
population <- createStudyPopulation(plpData = plpData,
                                    outcomeId = 2,
                                    washoutPeriod = 364,
                                    firstExposureOnly = FALSE,
                                    removeSubjectsWithPriorOutcome = TRUE,
                                    priorOutcomeLookback = 9999,
                                    riskWindowStart = 1,
                                    riskWindowEnd = 365,
                                    addExposureDaysToStart = FALSE,
                                    addExposureDaysToEnd = FALSE,
                                    minTimeAtRisk = 364,
                                    requireTimeAtRisk = TRUE,
                                    includeAllOutcomes = TRUE,
                                    verbosity = "DEBUG"
)
```

13.7.4 Model Development

In the set function of an algorithm the user can specify a list of eligible values for each hyper-parameter. All possible combinations of the hyper-parameters are included in a so-called grid search using cross-validation on the training set. If a user does not specify any value then the default value is used instead.

For example, if we use the following settings for the gradient boosting machine: `ntrees` = `c(100,200)`, `maxDepth` = 4 the grid search will apply the gradient boosting machine algorithm with `ntrees` = 100 and `maxDepth` = 4 plus the default settings for other hyper-parameters and `ntrees` = 200 and `maxDepth` = 4 plus the default settings for other hyper-parameters. The hyper-parameters that lead to the best cross-validation performance will then be chosen for the final model. For our problem we choose to build a gradient boosting machine with several hyper-parameter values:

```
gbmModel <- setGradientBoostingMachine(ntrees = 5000,
                                       maxDepth = c(4,7,10),
                                       learnRate = c(0.001,0.01,0.1,0.9))
```

The `runPlP` function uses the population, `plpData`, and model settings to train and evaluate the model. We can use the `testSplit` (person/time) and `testFraction` parameters to split the data in a 75%-25% split and run the patient-level prediction pipeline:

```
gbmResults <- runPlp(population = population,
                     plpData = plpData,
                     modelSettings = gbmModel,
                     testSplit = 'person',
                     testFraction = 0.25,
                     nfold = 2,
                     splitSeed = 1234)
```

Under the hood the package will now use the R xgboost package to fit a a gradient boosting machine model using 75% of the data and will evaluate the model on the remaining 25%. A results data structure is returned containing information about the model, its performance, etc.

In the `runPlp` function there are several parameters to save the `plpData`, `plpResults`, `plpPlots`, `evaluation`, etc. objects which are all set to TRUE by default.

We can save the model using:

```
savePlpModel(gbmResults$model, dirPath = "model")
```

We can load the model using:

```
plpModel <- loadPlpModel("model")
```

You can also save the full results structure using:

```
savePlpResult(gbmResults, location = "gbmResults")
```

To load the full results structure use:

```
gbmResults <- loadPlpResult("gbmResults")
```

13.7.5 Internal Validation

Once we execute the study, the `runPlp` function returns the trained model and the evaluation of the model on the train/test sets. You can interactively view the results by running: `viewPlp(runPlp = gbmResults)`. This will open a Shiny App in which we can view all performance measures created by the framework, including interactive plots (see Figure 13.16 in the section on the Shiny Application).

To generate and save all the evaluation plots to a folder run the following code:

```
plotPlp(gbmResults, "plots")
```

The plots are described in more detail in Section 13.4.2.

13.7.6   External Validation

We recommend to always perform external validation, i.e. apply the final model on as much new datasets as feasible and evaluate its performance. Here we assume the data extraction has already been performed on a second database and stored in the `newData` folder. We load the model we previously fitted from the `model` folder:

```
# load the trained model
plpModel <- loadPlpModel("model")

#load the new plpData and create the population
plpData <- loadPlpData("newData")

population <- createStudyPopulation(plpData = plpData,
                                    outcomeId = 2,
                                    washoutPeriod = 364,
                                    firstExposureOnly = FALSE,
                                    removeSubjectsWithPriorOutcome = TRUE,
                                    priorOutcomeLookback = 9999,
                                    riskWindowStart = 1,
                                    riskWindowEnd = 365,
                                    addExposureDaysToStart = FALSE,
                                    addExposureDaysToEnd = FALSE,
                                    minTimeAtRisk = 364,
                                    requireTimeAtRisk = TRUE,
                                    includeAllOutcomes = TRUE
)

# apply the trained model on the new data
validationResults <- applyModel(population, plpData, plpModel)
```

To make things easier we also provide the `externalValidatePlp` function for performing external validation that also extracts the required data. Assuming we ran `result <- runPlp(...)` then we can extract the data required for the model and evaluate it on new data. Assuming the validation cohorts are in the table `mainschema.dob.cohort` with IDs 1 and 2 and the CDM data is in the schema `cdmschema.dob`:

```
valResult <- externalValidatePlp(
    plpResult = result,
    connectionDetails = connectionDetails,
    validationSchemaTarget = 'mainschema.dob',
```

```
    validationSchemaOutcome = 'mainschema.dob',
    validationSchemaCdm = 'cdmschema.dbo',
    databaseNames = 'new database',
    validationTableTarget = 'cohort',
    validationTableOutcome = 'cohort',
    validationIdTarget = 1,
    validationIdOutcome = 2
)
```

If we have multiple databases to validate the model on then we can run:

```
valResults <- externalValidatePlp(
    plpResult = result,
    connectionDetails = connectionDetails,
    validationSchemaTarget = list('mainschema.dob',
                                  'difschema.dob',
                                  'anotherschema.dob'),
    validationSchemaOutcome = list('mainschema.dob',
                                   'difschema.dob',
                                   'anotherschema.dob'),
    validationSchemaCdm = list('cdms1chema.dbo',
                               'cdm2schema.dbo',
                               'cdm3schema.dbo'),
    databaseNames = list('new database 1',
                         'new database 2',
                         'new database 3'),
    validationTableTarget = list('cohort1',
                                 'cohort2',
                                 'cohort3'),
    validationTableOutcome = list('cohort1',
                                  'cohort2',
                                  'cohort3'),
    validationIdTarget = list(1,3,5),
    validationIdOutcome = list(2,4,6)
)
```

13.8   Results Dissemination

13.8.1   Model Performance

Exploring the performance of a prediction model is easiest with the `viewPlp` function. This requires a results object as the input. If developing models in R we can use the result of `runPLp` as the input. If using the ATLAS-generated study package, then we need to load one of the models (in this example we will load Analysis_1):

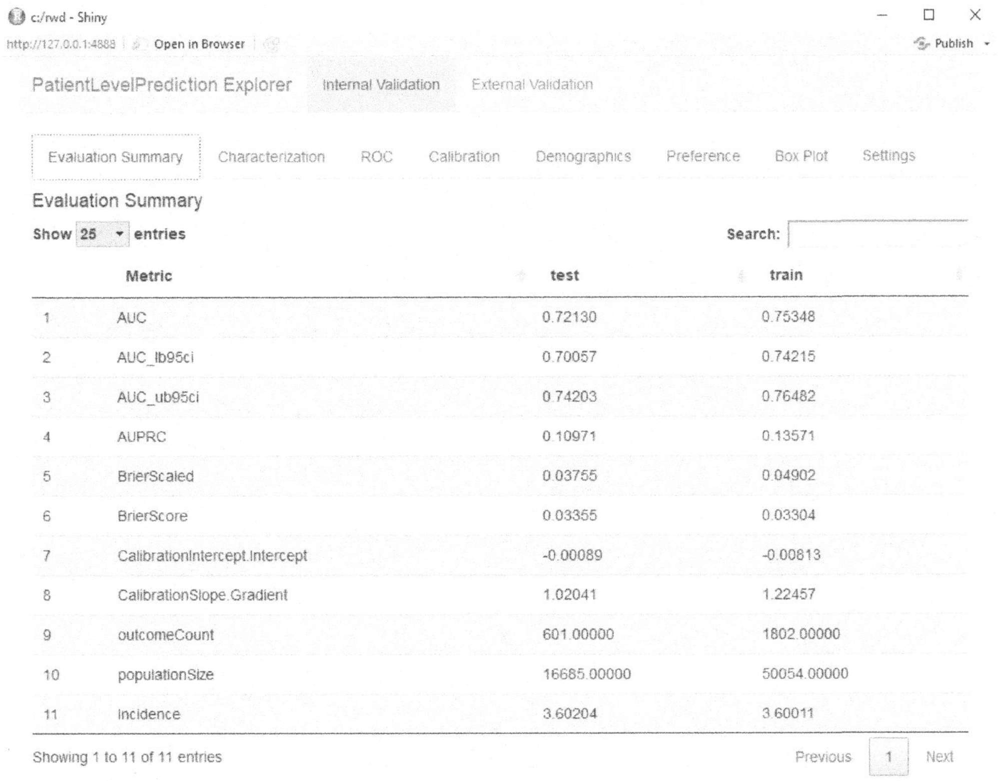

	Metric	test	train
1	AUC	0.72130	0.75348
2	AUC_lb95ci	0.70057	0.74215
3	AUC_ub95ci	0.74203	0.76482
4	AUPRC	0.10971	0.13571
5	BrierScaled	0.03755	0.04902
6	BrierScore	0.03355	0.03304
7	CalibrationIntercept.Intercept	-0.00089	-0.00813
8	CalibrationSlope.Gradient	1.02041	1.22457
9	outcomeCount	601.00000	1802.00000
10	populationSize	16685.00000	50054.00000
11	incidence	3.60204	3.60011

Figure 13.16: Summary evaluation statistics in the Shiny app.

```
plpResult <- loadPlpResult(file.path(outputFolder,
                                     'Analysis_1',
                                     'plpResult'))
```

Here "Analysis_1" corresponds to the analysis we specified earlier.

We can then launch the Shiny app by running:

```
viewPlp(plpResult)
```

The Shiny app opens with a summary of the performance metrics on the test and train sets (see Figure 13.16). The results show that the AUC on the train set was 0.78 and this dropped to 0.74 on the test set. The test set AUC is the more accurate measure. Overall, the model appears to be able to discriminate those who will develop the outcome in new users of ACE inhibitors but it slightly overfit as the performance on the train set is higher than the test set. The ROC plot is presented in Figure 13.17.

The calibration plot in Figure 13.18 shows that generally the observed risk matches the pre-

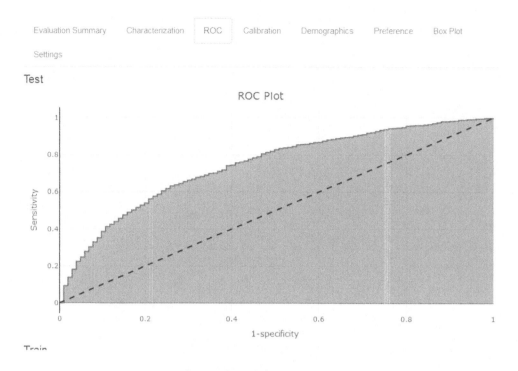

Figure 13.17: The ROC plot.

dicted risk as the dots are around the diagonal line. The demographic calibration plot in Figure 13.19 however shows that the model is not well calibrated for the younger patients, as the curved line (the predicted risk) differs from the red line (the observed risk) for those aged below 40. This may indicate we need to remove the under 40s from the target population (as the observed risk for the younger patients is nearly zero).

Finally, the attrition plot shows the loss of patients from the labelled data based on inclusion/exclusion criteria (see Figure 13.20). The plot shows that we lost a large portion of the target population due to them not being observed for the whole time at risk (1 year follow up). Interestingly, not as many patients with the outcome lacked the complete time at risk.

13.8.2   Comparing Models

The study package as generated by ATLAS allows generating and evaluating many different prediction models for different prediction problems. Therefore, specifically for the output generated by the study package an additional Shiny app has been developed for viewing multiple models. To start this app, run `viewMultiplePlp(outputFolder)` where `outputFolder` is the path containing the analysis results as specified when running the `execute` command (and should for example contain a sub-folder named "Analysis_1").

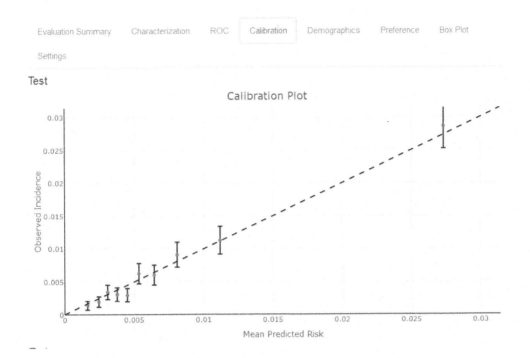

Figure 13.18: The calibration of the model

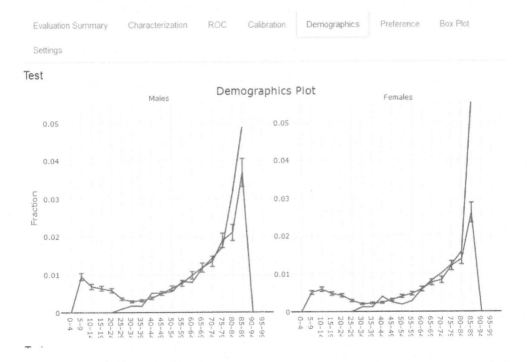

Figure 13.19: The demographic calibration of the model

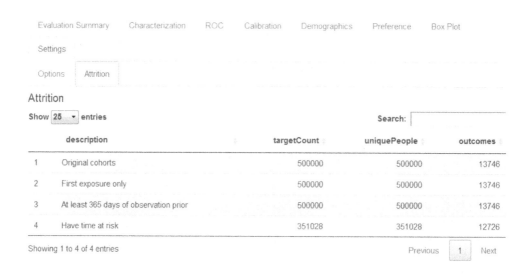

Figure 13.20: The attrition plot for the prediction problem

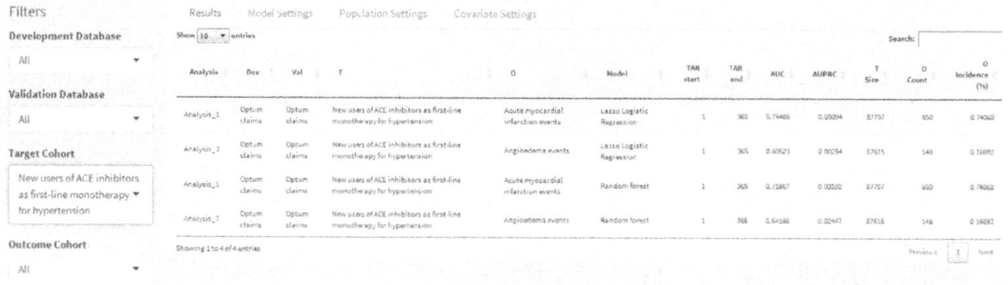

Figure 13.21: The shiny summary page containing key hold out set performance metrics for
each model trained

Viewing the Model Summary and Settings

The interactive Shiny app will start at the summary page as shown in Figure 13.21.

This summary page table contains:

- basic information about the model (e.g., database information, classifier type, time-at-risk settings, target population and outcome names)
- hold out target population count and incidence of outcome
- discrimination metrics: AUC, AUPRC

To the left of the table is the filter option, where we can specify the development/validation
databases to focus on, the type of model, the time at risk settings of interest and/or the cohorts
of interest. For example, to pick the models corresponding to the target population "New
users of ACE inhibitors as first line mono-therapy for hypertension", select this in the *Target
Cohort* option.

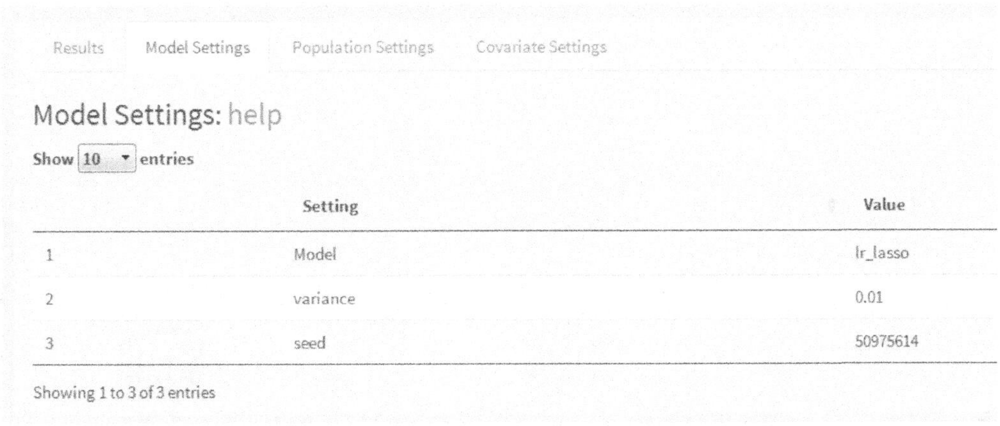

Results   Model Settings   Population Settings   Covariate Settings

Model Settings: help

Show 10 ▾ entries

	Setting	Value
1	Model	lr_lasso
2	variance	0.01
3	seed	50975614

Showing 1 to 3 of 3 entries

Figure 13.22: To view the model settings used when developing the model.

To explore a model click on the corresponding row, a selected row will be highlighted. With a row selected, we can now explore the model settings used when developing the model by clicking on the *Model Settings* tab:

Similarly, we can explore the population and covariate settings used to generate the model in the other tabs.

Viewing Model Performance

Once a model row has been selected we can also view the model performance. Click on ▙ Performance to open the threshold performance summary shown in Figure 13.23.

This summary view shows the selected prediction question in the standard format, a threshold selector and a dashboard containing key threshold-based metrics such as positive predictive value (PPV), negative predictive value (NPV), sensitivity and specificity (see Section 13.4.2). In Figure 13.23 we see that at a threshold of 0.00482 the sensitivity is 83.4% (83.4% of patients with the outcome in the following year have a risk greater than or equal to 0.00482) and the PPV is 1.2% (1.2% of patients with a risk greater than or equal to 0.00482 have the outcome in the following year). As the incidence of the outcome within the year is 0.741%, identifying patients with a risk greater than or equal to 0.00482 would find a subgroup of patients that have nearly double the risk of the population average risk. We can adjust the threshold using the slider to view the performance at other values.

To look at the overall discrimination of the model click on the "Discrimination" tab to view the ROC plot, precision-recall plot, and distribution plots. The line on the plots corresponds to the selected threshold point. Figure 13.24 show the ROC and precision-recall plots. The ROC plot shows the model was able to discriminate between those who will have the outcome within the year and those who will not. However, the performance looks less impressive when we see the precision-recall plot, as the low incidence of the outcome means there is a high false positive rate.

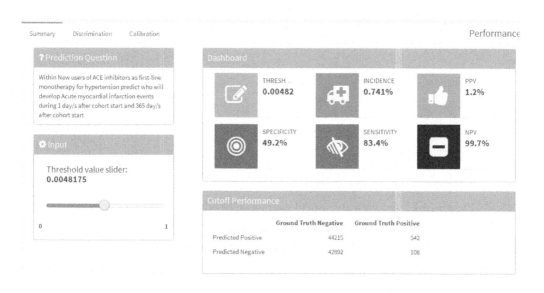

Figure 13.23: The summary performance measures at a set threshold.

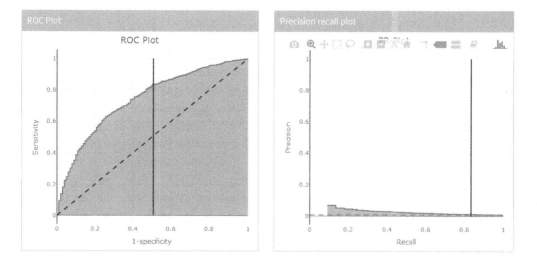

Figure 13.24: The ROC and precision-recall plots used to access the overal discrimination ability of the model.

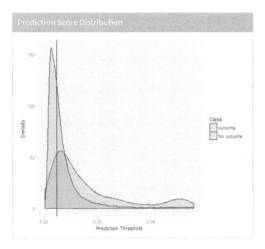
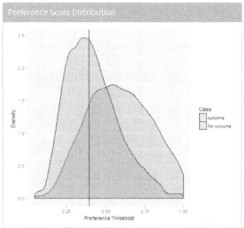

Figure 13.25: The predicted risk distribution for those with and without the outcome. The more these overlap the worse the discrimination

Figure 13.25 shows the prediction and preference score distributions.

Finally, we can also inspect the calibration of the model by clicking on the "Calibration" tab. This displays the calibration plot and the demographic calibration shown in Figure 13.26.

We see that the average predicted risk appears to match the observed fraction who experienced the outcome within a year, so the model is well calibrated. Interestingly, the demographic calibration shows that the expected line is higher than the observed line for young patients, so we are predicting a higher risk for young age groups. Conversely, for the patients above 80 the model is predicting a lower risk than the observed risk. This may prompt us to develop separate models for the younger or older patients.

Viewing the Model

To inspect the final model, select the [Model] option from the left hand menu. This will open a view containing plots for each variable in the model, shown in Figure 13.27, and a table summarizing all the candidate covariates, shown in Figure 13.28. The variable plots are separated into binary variables and continuous variables. The x-axis is the prevalence/mean in patients without the outcome and the y-axis is the prevalence/mean in patients with the outcome. Therefore, any variable's dot falling above the diagonal is more common in patients with the outcome and any variable's dot falling below the diagonal is less common in patients with the outcome.

The table in Figure 13.28 displays the name, value (coefficient if using a general linear model, or variable importance otherwise) for all the candidate covariates, outcome mean (the mean value for those who have the outcome) and non-outcome mean (the mean value for those who do not have the outcome).

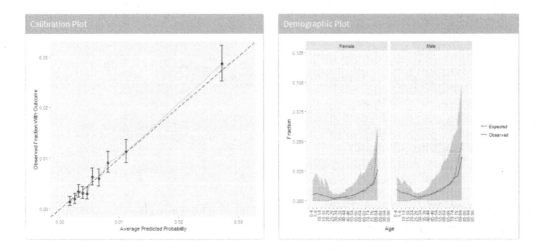

Figure 13.26: The risk stratified calibration and demographic calibration

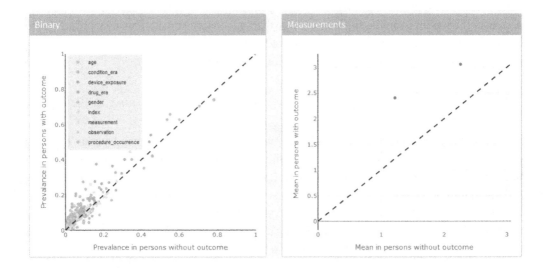

Figure 13.27: Model summary plots. Each dot corresponds to a variable included in the model.

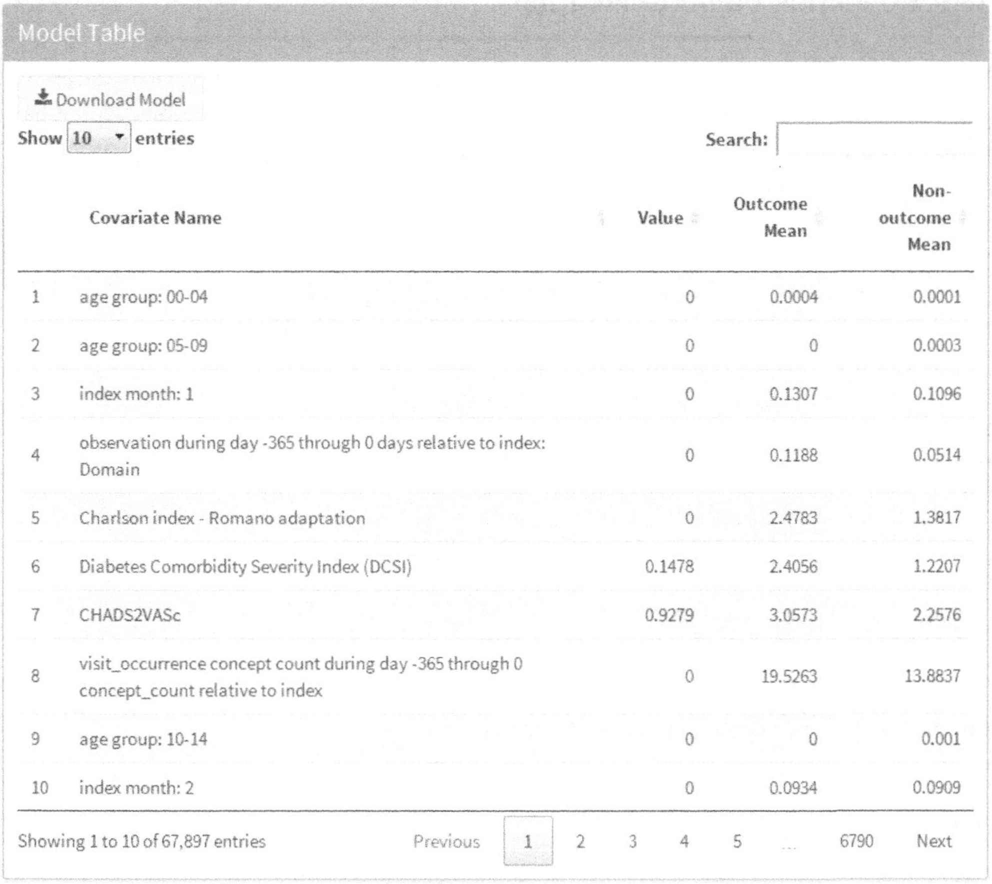

	Covariate Name	Value	Outcome Mean	Non-outcome Mean
1	age group: 00-04	0	0.0004	0.0001
2	age group: 05-09	0	0	0.0003
3	index month: 1	0	0.1307	0.1096
4	observation during day -365 through 0 days relative to index: Domain	0	0.1188	0.0514
5	Charlson index - Romano adaptation	0	2.4783	1.3817
6	Diabetes Comorbidity Severity Index (DCSI)	0.1478	2.4056	1.2207
7	CHADS2VASc	0.9279	3.0573	2.2576
8	visit_occurrence concept count during day -365 through 0 concept_count relative to index	0	19.5263	13.8837
9	age group: 10-14	0	0	0.001
10	index month: 2	0	0.0934	0.0909

Model Table

⬇ Download Model

Show 10 ▾ entries   Search:

Showing 1 to 10 of 67,897 entries   Previous 1 2 3 4 5 ... 6790 Next

Figure 13.28: Model details table.

Predictive models are not causal models, and predictors should not be mistaken for causes. There is no guarantee that modifying any of the variables in Figure 13.28 will have an effect on the risk of the outcome.

13.9   Additional Patient-Level Prediction Features

13.9.1   Journal Paper Generation

We have added functionality to automatically generate a word document we can use as start of a journal paper. It contains many of the generated study details and results. If we have performed external validation these results will can be added as well. Optionally, we can add a "Table 1" that contains data on many covariates for the target population. We can create the draft journal paper by running this function:

```
createPlpJournalDocument(plpResult = <your plp results>,
          plpValidation = <your validation results>,
          plpData = <your plp data>,
          targetName = "<target population>",
          outcomeName = "<outcome>",
          table1 = F,
          connectionDetails = NULL,
          includeTrain = FALSE,
          includeTest = TRUE,
          includePredictionPicture = TRUE,
          includeAttritionPlot = TRUE,
          outputLocation = "<your location>")
```

For more details see the help page of the function.

13.10   Summary

- Patient-level prediction aims to develop a model that predicts future events using data from the past.

- The selection of the best machine algorithm for model development is an empirical question, i.e. it should be driven by the problem and data at hand.

- The PatientLevelPrediction Package implements best practices for the development and validation of prediction models using data stored in the OMOP-CDM.

- The dissemination of the model and its performance measures is implemented through interactive dashboards.

– OHDSI's prediction framework enables large-scale external validation of prediction models which is a pre-requisite for clinical adoption.

13.11   Exercises

Prerequisites

For these exercises we assume R, R-Studio and Java have been installed as described in Section 8.4.5. Also required are the SqlRender, DatabaseConnector, Eunomia and PatientLevelPrediction packages, which can be installed using:

```
install.packages(c("SqlRender", "DatabaseConnector", "devtools"))
devtools::install_github("ohdsi/Eunomia", ref = "v1.0.0")
devtools::install_github("ohdsi/PatientLevelPrediction")
```

The Eunomia package provides a simulated dataset in the CDM that will run inside your local R session. The connection details can be obtained using:

```
connectionDetails <- Eunomia::getEunomiaConnectionDetails()
```

The CDM database schema is "main". These exercises also make use of several cohorts. The `createCohorts` function in the Eunomia package will create these in the COHORT table:

```
Eunomia::createCohorts(connectionDetails)
```

Problem Definition

In patients that started using NSAIDs for the first time, predict who will develop a gastrointestinal (GI) bleed in the next year.

The NSAID new-user cohort has COHORT_DEFINITION_ID = 4. The GI bleed cohort has COHORT_DEFINITION_ID = 3.

Exercise 13.1. Using the PatientLevelPrediction R package, define the covariates you want to use for the prediction and extract the PLP data from the CDM. Create the summary of the PLP data.

Exercise 13.2. Revisit the design choices you have to make to define the final target population and specify these using the `createStudyPopulation` function. What will the effect of your choices be on the final size of the target population?

Exercise 13.3. Build a prediction model using LASSO and evaluate its performance using the Shiny application. How well is your model performing?

Suggested answers can be found in Appendix E.9.

Part IV

Evidence Quality

Chapter 14

Evidence Quality

Chapter leads: Patrick Ryan & Jon Duke

14.1 Attributes of Reliable Evidence

Before embarking on any journey, it can be helpful to envision what the ideal destination might look like. To support our journey from data to evidence, we highlight desired attributes that can underlie what makes evidence quality reliable.

Reliable evidence should be **repeatable**, meaning that researchers should expect to produce identical results when applying the same analysis to the same data for any given question. Implicit in this minimum requirement is the notion that evidence is the result of the execution of a defined process with a specified input, and should be free of manual intervention of post-hoc decision-making along the way. More ideally, reliable evidence should be **reproducible** such that a different researcher should be able to perform the same task of executing a given analysis on a given database and expect to produce an identical result as the first researcher.

Desired attribute	Question	Researcher	Data	Analysis		Result
Repeatable	Identical	Identical	Identical	Identical	=	Identical
Reproducible	Identical	Different	Identical	Identical	=	Identical
Replicable	Identical	Same or different	Similar	Identical	=	Similar
Generalizable	Identical	Same or different	Different	Identical	=	Similar
Robust	Identical	Same or different	Same or different	Different	=	Similar
Calibrated	Similar (controls)	Identical	Identical	Identical	=	Statistically consistent

Figure 14.1: Desired attributes of reliable evidence

Reproducibility requires that the process is fully-specified, generally in both human-readable and computer-executable form such that no study decisions are left to the discretion of the investigator. The most efficient solution to achieve repeatability and reproducibility is to use standardized analytics routines that have defined inputs and outputs, and apply these procedures against version-controlled databases.

We are more likely to be confident that our evidence is reliable if it can be shown to be **replicable**, such that the same question addressed using the identical analysis against similar data yield similar results. For example, evidence generated from an analysis against an administative claims database from one large private insurer may be strengthened if replicated on claims data from a different insurer. In the context of population-level effect estimation, this attribute aligns well with Sir Austin Bradford Hill's causal viewpoint on consistency, "Has it been repeatedly observed by different persons, in different places, circumstances and times?...whether chance is the explanation or wehther a true hazard has been revealed may sometimes be answered only by a repetition of the circumstances and the observations." (Hill, 1965) In the context of patient-level prediction, replicability highlights the value of external validation and the ability to evaluate performance of a model that was trained on one database by observing its discriminative accuracy and calibration when applied to a different database. In circumstances where identical analyses are performed against different databases and still show consistently similar results, we have further gain confidence that our evidence is **generalizable**. A key value of the OHDSI research network is the diversity represented by different populations, geographies and data capture processes. Madigan et al. (2013b) showed that effect estimates can be sensitive to choice of data. Recognizing that each data source carries with it inherent limitations and unique biases that limit our confidence in singular findings, there is tremendous power in observing similar patterns across heterogeneous datasets because it greatly diminishes the likelihood that source-specific biases alone can explain the findings. When network studies show consistent population-level effect estimates across multiple claims and EHR databases across US, Europe and Asia, they should be recognized as stronger evidence about the medical intervention that can have a broader scope to impact medical decision-making.

Reliable evidence should be **robust**, meaning that the findings should not be overly sensitive to the subjective choices that can be made within an analysis. If there are alternative statistical methods that can be considered potentially reasonable for a given study, then it can provide reassurance to see that the different methods yield similar results, or conversely can give caution if discordant results are uncovered. (Madigan et al., 2013a) For population-level effect estimation, sensitivity analyses can include high-level study design choice, such as whether to apply a comparative cohort or self-controlled case series design, or can focus on analytical considerations embedded within a design, such as whether to perform propensity score matching, stratfication or weighting as a confounding adjustment strategy within the comparative cohort framework.

Last, but potentially most important, evidence should be **calibrated**. It is not sufficient to have an evidence generating system that produces answers to unknown questions if the performance of that system cannot be verified. A closed system should be expected to have known operating characteristics, which should be able to measured and communicated as context for interpreting any results that the system produces. Statistical artifacts should be able to be empirically demonstrated to have well-defined properties, such as a 95% confidence interval having 95% coverage probability or a cohort with a predicted probability of 10% having a observed proportion of events in 10% of the population. An observational study should always be accompanied by study diagnostics that test assumptions around the design, methods, and data. These diagnostics should be centered on evaluating the primary threats to study validity: selection bias, confounding, and measurement error. Negative controls have been shown to be a powerful tool for identifying and mitigating systematic error in observational studies. (Schuemie et al., 2016, 2018a,b)

14.2 Understanding Evidence Quality

But how do we know if the results of a study are reliable enough? Can they be trusted for use in clinical settings? What about in regulatory decision-making? Can they serve as a foundation for future research? Each time a new study is published or disseminated, readers must consider these questions, regardless of whether the work was a randomized controlled trial, an observational study, or another type of analysis.

One of the concerns that is often raised around observational studies and the use of "real world data" is the topic of data quality. (Botsis et al., 2010; Hersh et al., 2013; Sherman et al., 2016) Commonly noted is that data used in observational research were not originally gathered for research purposes and thus may suffer from incomplete or inaccurate data capture as well as inherent biases. These concerns have given rise to a growing body of research around how to measure, characterize, and ideally improve data quality. (Kahn et al., 2012; Liaw et al., 2013; Weiskopf and Weng, 2013) The OHDSI community is a strong advocate of such research and community members have led and participated in many studies looking at data quality in the OMOP CDM and the OHDSI network. (Huser et al., 2016; Kahn et al., 2015; Callahan et al., 2017; Yoon et al., 2016)

Given the findings of the past decade in this area, it has become apparent that data quality is not perfect and never will be. This notion is nicely reflected in this quote from Dr. Clem McDonald, a pioneer in the field of medical informatics:

> Loss of fidelity begins with the movement of data from the doctor's brain to the medical record.

Thus, as a community we must ask the question – *given imperfect data, how can we achieve reliable evidence?*

The answer rests in looking holistically at "evidence quality": examining the entire journey from data to evidence, identifying each of the components that make up the evidence generation process, determining how to build confidence in the quality of each component, and transparently communicating what has been learned each step along the way. Evidence quality considers not only the quality of observational data but also the validity of the methods, software, and clinical definitions used in our observational analyses.

In the following chapters, we will explore four components of evidence quality listed in Table 14.1.

Table 14.1: The four components of evidence quality.

Component of Evidence Quality	What it Measures
Data Quality	Are the data completely captured with plausible values in a manner that is conformant to agreed-upon structure and conventions?
Clinical Validity	To what extent does the analysis conducted match the clinical intention?
Software Validity	Can we trust that the process transforming and analyzing the data does what it is supposed to do?
Method Validity	Is the methodology appropriate for the question, given the strengths and weaknesses of the data?

14.3   Communicating Evidence Quality

An important aspect of evidence quality is the ability to express the uncertainty that arises along the journey from data to evidence. The overarching goal of OHDSI's work around evidence quality is to produce confidence in health care decision-makers that the evidence generated by OHDSI – while undoubtedly imperfect in many ways – has been consistently measured for its weaknesses and strengths and that this information has been communicated in a rigorous and open manner.

14.4   Summary

- The evidence we generate should be **repeatable**, **reproducible**, **replicable**, **generalizable**, **robust**, and **calibrated**.

- Evidence quality considers more than just data quality when answering whether evidence is reliable:

  * Data Quality
  * Clinical Validity
  * Software Validity
  * Method Validity

- When communicating evidence, we should express the uncertainty arising from the various challenges to evidence quality.

Chapter 15

Data Quality

Chapter leads: Martijn Schuemie, Vojtech Huser & Clair Blacketer

Most of the data used for observational healthcare research were not collected for research purposes. For example, electronic health records (EHRs) aim to capture the information needed to support the care of patients, and administrative claims are collected to provide a grounds for allocating costs to payers. Many have questioned whether it is appropriate to use such data for clinical research, with van der Lei (1991) even stating that "Data shall be used only for the purpose for which they were collected." The concern is that because the data were not collected for the research that we would like to do, it is not guaranteed to have sufficient quality. If the quality of the data is poor (garbage in), then the quality of the result of research using that data must be poor as well (garbage out). An important aspect of observational healthcare research therefore deals with assessing data quality, aiming to answer the question:

> Are the data of sufficient quality for our research purposes?

We can define data quality (DQ) as (Roebuck, 2012):

> The state of completeness, validity, consistency, timeliness and accuracy that makes data appropriate for a specific use.

Note that it is unlikely that our data are perfect, but they may be good enough for our purposes.

DQ cannot be observed directly, but methodology has been developed to assess it. Two types of DQ assessments can be distinguished (Weiskopf and Weng, 2013): assessments to evaluate DQ in general, and assessments to evaluate DQ in the context of a specific study.

In this chapter we will first review possible sources of DQ problems, after which we'll discuss the theory of general and study-specific DQ assessments, followed by a step-by-step description of how these assessments can be performed using the OHDSI tools.

15.1   Sources of Data Quality Problems

There are many threats to the quality of the data, starting as noted in Chapter 14 when the doctor records her or his thoughts. Dasu and Johnson (2003) distinguish the following steps in the life cycle of data, recommending DQ be integrated in each step. They refer to this as the DQ continuum:

1. **Data gathering and integration**. Possible problems include fallible manual entry, biases (e.g. upcoding in claims), erroneous joining of tables in an EHR, and replacing missing values with default ones.
2. **Data storage and knowledge sharing**. Potential problems are lack of documentation of the data model, and lack of meta-data.
3. **Data analysis**. Problems can include incorrect data transformations, incorrect data interpretation, and use of inappropriate methodology.
4. **Data publishing**. When publishing data for downstream use.

Often the data we use has already been collected and integrated, so there is little we can do to improve step 1. We do have ways to check the DQ produced by this step as will be discussed in subsequent sections in this chapter.

Similarly, we often receive the data in a specific form, so we have little influence over part of step 2. However, in OHDSI we convert all our observational data to the Common Data Model (CDM), and we do have ownership over this process. Some have expressed concerns that this specific step can degrade DQ. But because we control this process, we can build stringent safeguards to preserve DQ as discussed later in Section 15.2.2. Several investigations (Defalco et al., 2013; Makadia and Ryan, 2014; Matcho et al., 2014; Voss et al., 2015a,b; Hripcsak et al., 2018) have shown that when properly executed, little to no error is introduced when converting to the CDM. In fact, having a well-documented data model that is shared by a large community facilitates data storage in an unambiguous and clear manner.

Step 3 (data analysis) also falls under our control. In OHDSI, we tend to not use the term DQ for the quality issues during this step, but rather the terms *clinical validity*, *software validity* and *method validity*, which are discussed at length in Chapters 16, 17, and 18, respectively.

15.2   Data Quality in General

We can ask the question whether our data are fit for the general purpose of observational research. Kahn et al. (2016) define such generic DQ as consisting of three components:

1. **Conformance**: Do data values adhere to specified standards and formats? Three subtypes are identified:
   - **Value**: Are recorded data elements in agreement with the specified formats? For example, are all provider medical specialties valid specialties?
   - **Relational**: Is the recorded data in agreement with specified relational constraints? For example, does the PROVIDER_ID in a DRUG_EXPOSURE data

have a corresponding record in the PROVIDER table?

- **Computation**: Do computations on the data yield the intended results? For example, is BMI computed from height and weight equal to the verbatim BMI recorded in the data?

2. **Completeness**: Refers to whether a particular variable is present (e.g. is weight as measured in the doctor's office recorded?) as well as whether variables contain all recorded values (e.g. do all persons have a known gender?)

3. **Plausibility**: Are data values believable? Three sub-types are defined:
   - **Uniqueness**: For example, does each PERSON_ID occur only once in the PERSON table?
   - **Atemporal**: Do values, distributions, or densities agree with expected values? For example, is the prevalence of diabetes implied by the data in line with the known prevalence?
   - **Temporal**: Are changes in values in line with expectations? For example, are immunization sequences in line with recommendations?

Each component can be evaluated in two ways:

- **Verification** focuses on model and metadata data constraints, system assumptions, and local knowledge. It does not rely on an external reference. The key feature with verification is the ability to determine expected values and distributions using resources within the local environment.
- **Validation** focuses on the alignment of data values with respect to relevant external benchmarks. One possible source of an external benchmark can be to combine results across multiple data sites.

15.2.1 Data Quality Checks

Kahn introduces the term *data quality check* (sometimes referred to as a *data quality rule*) that tests whether data conform to a given requirement (e.g., flagging an implausible age of 141 of a patient, potentially due to incorrect birth year or missing death event). We can implement such checks in software by creating automated DQ tools. One such tool is ACHILLES (Automated Characterization of Health Information at Large-scale Longitudinal Evidence Systems). (Huser et al., 2018) ACHILLES is a software tool that provides characterization and visualization of a database conforming to the CDM. As such, it can be used to evaluate DQ in a network of databases. (Huser et al., 2016) ACHILLES is available as a stand-alone tool, and it is also integrated into ATLAS as the "Data Sources" function.

ACHILLES pre-computes over 170 data characterization analyses, with each analysis having an analysis ID and a short description of the analysis; two such examples are "715: Distribution of DAYS_SUPPLY by DRUG_CONCEPT_ID" and "506: Distribution of age at death by gender." The results of these analyses are stored in a database and can be accessed by a web viewer or by ATLAS.

Another tool created by the community to assess DQ is the Data Quality Dashboard (DQD). Where ACHILLES runs characterization analyses to provide an overall visual understanding of a CDM instance, the DQD goes table by table and field by field to quantify the number of records in a CDM that do not conform to the given specifications. In all, over 1,500 checks are performed, each one organized into the Kahn framework. For each check the result is compared to a threshold whereby a FAIL is considered to be any percentage of violating rows falling above that value. Table 15.1 shows some example checks.

Table 15.1: Example data quality rules in the Data Quality Dashboard.

Fraction violated rows	Check description	Threshold	Status
0.34	A yes or no value indicating if the provider_id in the VISIT_OCCURRENCE is the expected data type based on the specification.	0.05	FAIL
0.99	The number and percent of distinct source values in the measurement_source_value field of the MEASUREMENT table mapped to 0.	0.30	FAIL
0.09	The number and percent of records that have a value in the drug_concept_id field in the DRUG_ERA table that do not conform to the ingredient class.	0.10	PASS
0.02	The number and percent of records with a value in the verbatim_end_date field of the DRUG_EXPOSURE that occurs prior to the date in the DRUG_EXPOSURE_START_DATE field of the DRUG_EXPOSURE table.	0.05	PASS
0.00	The number and percent of records that have a duplicate value in the procedure_occurrence_id field of the PROCEDURE_OCCURRENCE.	0.00	PASS

Within the tool the checks are organized in multiple ways, one being into table, field, and concept level checks. Table checks are those done at a high-level within the CDM, for example determining if all required tables are present. The field level checks are carried out in such a way to evaluate every field within every table for conformance to CDM specifications. These include making sure all primary keys are truly unique and all standard concept fields contain concepts ids in the proper domain, among many others. Concept level checks go a little deeper to examine individual concept ids. Many of these fall into the plausibility category of the Kahn framework such as ensuring that gender-specific concepts are not attributed to persons of incorrect gender (i.e. prostate cancer in a female patient).

 ACHILLES and DQD are executed against the data in the CDM. DQ issues identified this way may be due to the conversion to the CDM, but may also reflect DQ issues already present in the source data. If the conversion is at fault, it is usually within our control to remedy the problem, but if the underlying data are at fault the only course of action may be to delete the offending records.

15.2.2   ETL Unit Tests

In addition to high level data quality checks, individual level data checks should be performed. The ETL (Extract-Transform-Load) process by which data are converted to the CDM is often quite complex, and with that complexity comes the danger of making mistakes that may go unnoticed. Moreover, as time goes by the source data model may change, or the CDM may be updated, making it necessary to modify the ETL process. Changes to a process as complicated as an ETL can have unintended consequences, requiring all aspects of the ETL to be reconsidered and reviewed.

To make sure the ETL does what it is supposed to do, and continues to do so, it is highly recommended to construct a set of unit tests. A unit test is a small piece of code that automatically checks a single aspect. The Rabbit-in-a-Hat tool described in Chapter 6 can create a unit test framework that makes writing such unit tests easier. This framework is a collection of R functions created specifically for the source database and target CDM version of the ETL. Some of these functions are for creating fake data entries that adhere to the source data schema, while other functions can be used to specify expectations on the data in the CDM format. Here is an example unit test:

```
source("Framework.R")
declareTest(101, "Person gender mappings")
add_enrollment(member_id = "M000000102", gender_of_member = "male")
add_enrollment(member_id = "M000000103", gender_of_member = "female")
expect_person(PERSON_ID = 102, GENDER_CONCEPT_ID = 8507)
expect_person(PERSON_ID = 103, GENDER_CONCEPT_ID = 8532)
```

In this example, the framework generated by Rabbit-in-a-Hat is sourced, loading the functions that are used in the remainder of the code. We then declare we will start testing person gender mappings. The source schema has an ENROLLMENT table, and we use the add_enrollment function created by Rabbit-in-a-Hat to create two entries with different values for the MEMBER_ID and GENDER_OF_MEMBER fields. Finally, we specify the expectation that after the ETL two entries should exist in the PERSON table with various expected values.

Note that the ENROLLMENT table has many other fields, but we do not care much about what values these other fields have in the context of this test. However, leaving those values (e.g. date of birth) empty might cause the ETL to discard the record or throw an error. To overcome this problem while keeping the test code easy to read, the add_enrollment function will assign default values (the most prevalent values as observed in the White Rabbit scan report) to field values that are not explicitly specified by the user.

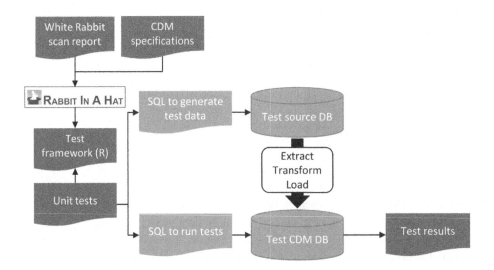

Figure 15.1: Unit testing an ETL (Extract-Transform-Load) process using the Rabbit-in-a-Hat testing framework.

Similar unit tests can be created for all other logic in an ETL, typically resulting in hundreds of tests. When we are done defining the test, we can use the framework to generate two sets of SQL statements, one to create the fake source data, and one to create the tests on the ETL-ed data:

```
insertSql <- generateInsertSql(databaseSchema = "source_schema")
testSql <- generateTestSql(databaseSchema = "cdm_test_schema")
```

The overall process is depicted in Figure 15.1.

The test SQL returns a table that will look like Table 15.2. In this table we see that we passed the two tests we defined earlier.

Table 15.2: Example ETL unit test results.

ID	Description	Status
101	Person gender mappings	PASS
101	Person gender mappings	PASS

The power of these unit tests is that we can easily rerun them any time the ETL process is changed.

15.3   Study-Specific Checks

The chapter has so far focused on general DQ checks. Such checks should be executed prior to using the data for research. Since these checks are done regardless of the research questions we recommend performing study-specific DQ assessments.

Some of these assessments can take the form of DQ rules that are specifically relevant for the study. For example, we may want to impose a rule that at least 90% of the records for our exposure of interest specify the length of exposure.

A standard assessment is to review the concepts that are most relevant for the study in ACHILLES, for example those specified in the study cohort definitions. Sudden changes over time in the rate with which a code is observed may hint at DQ problems. Some examples will be discussed later in this chapter.

Another assessment is to review the prevalence and changes in prevalence over time of the resulting cohorts generated using the cohort definitions developed for the study, and see whether these agree with expectations based on external clinical knowledge. For example, exposure of a new drug should be absent before introduction to the market, and will likely increase over time after introduction. Similarly, the prevalence of outcomes should be in line with what is known of the prevalence of the condition in the population. If a study is executed across a network of databases, we can compare the prevalence of cohorts across databases. If a cohort is highly prevalent in one database, but is missing in another database, there might be a DQ issue. Note that such an assessment overlaps with the notion of *clinical validity*, as discussed in Chapter 16; we may find unexpected prevalence in some databases not because of DQ issues, but because our cohort definition is not truly capturing the health states we are interested in, or because these health state rightly vary over databases that capture different patient populations.

15.3.1   Checking Mappings

One possible source of error that firmly falls under our control is the mapping of source codes to Standard Concepts. The mappings in the Vocabulary are meticulously crafted, and errors in the mapping that are noted by members of the community are reported in the Vocabulary issue tracker[1] and fixed in future releases. Nevertheless, it is impossible to completely check all mappings by hand, and errors likely still exist. When performing a study, we therefore recommend reviewing the mappings for those concepts most relevant to the study. Fortunately, this can be achieved quite easily because in the CDM we store not only the Standard Concepts, but also the source codes. We can review both the source codes that map to the concepts used in the study, as well as those that don't.

One way to review the source codes that map is to use the `checkCohortSourceCodes` function in the MethodEvaluation R package. This function uses a cohort definition as created by ATLAS as input, and for each concept set used in the cohort definition it checks which source

---

[1] https://github.com/OHDSI/Vocabulary-v5.0/issues

‰ per month	Max monthly ‰	Person count	Description
~~⌐	26.81	92,019,885	**Depressive Disorder**
___⌐	6.64	15,969,198	**Depressive disorder** 440383
___⌐	6.64	15,686,275	311 (ICD9CM) Depressive disorder, not elsewhere classified
∧	0.46	188,230	F328 (ICD10CM) Other depressive episodes
∫	0.38	94,693	F3289 (ICD10CM) Other specified depressive episodes
~~⌐	3.10	12,010,783	**Adjustment disorder with mixed emotional features** 433454
~~⌐	3.07	9,839,712	30928 (ICD9CM) Adjustment disorder with mixed anxiety and depressed mood
⌐	3.03	2,049,618	F4323 (ICD10CM) Adjustment disorder with mixed anxiety and depressed mood
~~⌐	0.04	121,453	3091 (ICD9CM) Prolonged depressive reaction
~~⌐	3.17	9,237,192	**Dysthymia** 433440

Figure 15.2: Example output of the checkCohortSourceCodes function.

codes map to the concepts in the set. It also computes the prevalence of these codes over time to help identify temporal issues associated with specific source codes. The example output in Figure 15.2 shows a (partial) breakdown of a concept set called "Depressive disorder." The most prevalent concept in this concept set in the database of interest is concept 440383 ("Depressive disorder"). We see that three source codes in the database map to this concept: ICD-9 code 3.11, and ICD-10 codes F32.8 and F32.89. On the left we see that the concept as a whole first shows a gradual increase over time, but then shows a sharp drop. If we look at the individual codes, we see that this drop can be explained by the fact that the ICD-9 code stops being used at the time of the drop. Even though this is the same time the ICD-10 codes start being used, the combined prevalence of the ICD-10 codes is much smaller than that of the ICD-9 code. This specific example was due to the fact that the ICD-10 code F32.9 ("Major depressive disorder, single episode, unspecified") should have also mapped to the concept. This problem has since been resolved in the Vocabulary.

Even though the previous example demonstrates a chance finding of a source code that was not mapped, in general identifying missing mappings is more difficult than checking mappings that are present. It requires knowing which source codes should map but don't. A semi-automated way to perform this assessment is to use the findOrphanSourceCodes function in the MethodEvaluation R package. This function allows one to search the vocabulary for source codes using a simple text search, and it checks whether these source codes map to a specific concept or to one of the descendants of that concept. The resulting set of source codes is subsequently restricted to only those that appear in the CDM database at hand. For example, in a study the concept "Gangrenous disorder" (439928) and all of its descendants was used to find all occurrences of gangrene. To evaluate whether this truly includes all source codes indicating gangrene, several terms (e.g. "gangrene") were used to search the descriptions in the CONCEPT and SOURCE_TO_CONCEPT_MAP tables to identify source codes. An automated search is then used to evaluate whether each gangrene source

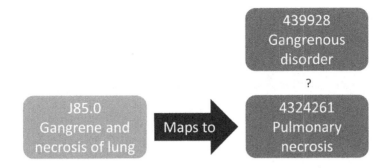

Figure 15.3: Example orphan source code.

code appearing in the data indeed directly or indirectly (through ancestry) maps to the concept "Gangrenous disorder." The result of this evaluation is shown in Figure 15.3, revealing that the ICD-10 code J85.0 ("Gangrene and necrosis of lung") was only mapped to concept 4324261 ("Pulmonary necrosis"), which is not a descendant of "Gangrenous disorder."

15.4 ACHILLES in Practice

Here we will demonstrate how to run ACHILLES against a database in the CDM format.

We first need to tell R how to connect to the server. ACHILLES uses the DatabaseConnector package, which provides a function called `createConnectionDetails`. Type `?createConnectionDetails` for the specific settings required for the various database management systems (DBMS). For example, one might connect to a PostgreSQL database using this code:

```
library(Achilles)
connDetails <- createConnectionDetails(dbms = "postgresql",
                                       server = "localhost/ohdsi",
                                       user = "joe",
                                       password = "supersecret")

cdmDbSchema <- "my_cdm_data"
cdmVersion <- "5.3.0"
```

The last two lines define the `cdmDbSchema` variable, as well as the CDM version. We will use these later to tell R where the data in the CDM format live, and what version CDM is used. Note that for Microsoft SQL Server, database schemas need to specify both the database and the schema, so for example `cdmDbSchema <- "my_cdm_data.dbo"`.

Next, we run ACHILLES:

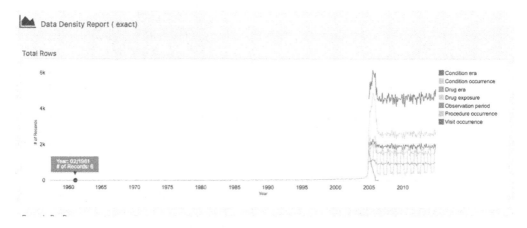

Figure 15.4: The data density plot in the ACHILLES web viewer.

```
result <- achilles(connectionDetails,
                   cdmDatabaseSchema = cdmDbSchema,
                   resultsDatabaseSchema = cdmDbSchema,
                   sourceName = "My database",
                   cdmVersion = cdmVersion)
```

This function will create several tables in the `resultsDatabaseSchema`, which we've set here to the same database schema as the CDM data.

We can view the ACHILLES database characterization. This can be done by pointing ATLAS to the ACHILLES results databases, or by exporting the ACHILLES results to a set of JSON files:

```
exportToJson(connectionDetails,
             cdmDatabaseSchema = cdmDatabaseSchema,
             resultsDatabaseSchema = cdmDatabaseSchema,
             outputPath = "achillesOut")
```

The JSON files will be written to the achillesOut sub-folder, and can be used together with the AchillesWeb web application to explore the results. For example, Figure 15.4 shows the ACHILLES data density plot. This plot shows that the bulk of the data starts in 2005. However, there also appear to be a few records from around 1961, which is likely an error in the data.

Another example is shown in Figure 15.5, revealing a sudden change in the prevalence of a diabetes diagnosis code. This change coincides with changes in the reimbursement rules in this specific country, leading to more diagnoses but probably not a true increase in prevalence in the underlying population.

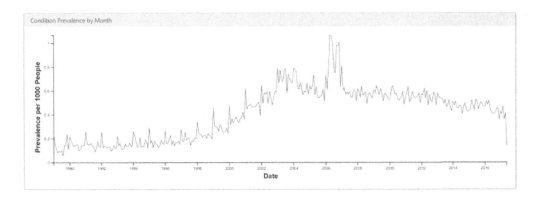

Figure 15.5: Monthly rate of diabetes coded in the ACHILLES web viewer.

15.5   Data Quality Dashboard in Practice

Here we will demonstrate how to run the Data Quality Dashboard against a database in the CDM format. We do this by executing a large set of checks against the CDM connection described in Section 15.4. For now the DQD supports only CDM v5.3.1 so before connecting be sure your database is in the correct version. As with ACHILLES we need to create the variable cdmDbSchema to tell R where to look for the data.

```
cdmDbSchema <- "my_cdm_data.dbo"
```

Next, we run the Dashboard...

```
DataQualityDashboard::executeDqChecks(connectionDetails = connectionDetails,
                                      cdmDatabaseSchema = cdmDbSchema,
                                      resultsDatabaseSchema = cdmDbSchema,
                                      cdmSourceName = "My database",
                                      outputFolder = "My output")
```

The above function will execute all available data quality checks on the schema specified. It will then write a table to the resultsDatabaseSchema which we have here set to the same schema as the CDM. This table will include all information about each check run including the CDM table, CDM field, check name, check description, Kahn category and subcategory, number of violating rows, the threshold level, and whether the check passes or fails, among others. In addition to a table this function also writes a JSON file to the location specified as the outputFolder. Using this JSON file we can launch a web viewer to inspect the results.

```
viewDqDashboard(jsonPath)
```

The variable jsonPath should be the path to the JSON file containing the results of the Dashboard, located in the outputFolder specified when calling the executeDqChecks

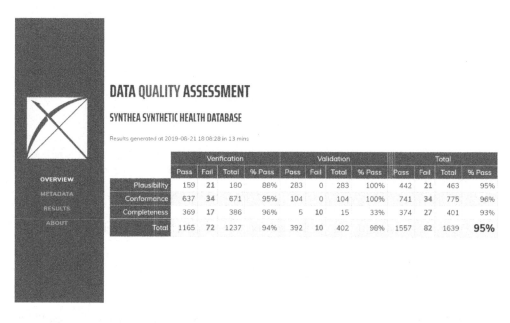

DATA QUALITY ASSESSMENT

SYNTHEA SYNTHETIC HEALTH DATABASE

Results generated at 2019-06-21 18:08:28 in 13 mins

	Verification				Validation				Total			
	Pass	Fail	Total	% Pass	Pass	Fail	Total	% Pass	Pass	Fail	Total	% Pass
Plausibility	159	21	180	88%	283	0	283	100%	442	21	463	95%
Conformance	637	34	671	95%	104	0	104	100%	741	34	775	96%
Completeness	369	17	386	96%	5	10	15	33%	374	27	401	93%
Total	1165	72	1237	94%	392	10	402	98%	1557	82	1639	**95%**

OVERVIEW
METADATA
RESULTS
ABOUT

Figure 15.6: Overview of Data Quality Checks in the Data Quality Dashboard.

function above.

When you first open the Dashboard you will be presented with the overview table, as seen in Figure 15.6. This will show you the total number of checks run in each Kahn category broken out by context, the number and percent that pass in each, as well as the overall pass rate.

Clicking on *Results* in the left-hand menu will take you to the drilldown results for each check that was run (Figure 15.7). In this example, the table showing a check run to determine the completeness of individual CDM tables, or, the number and percent of persons in the CDM that have at least one record in the specified table. In this case the five tables listed are all empty which the Dashboard counts as a fail. Clicking on the ⊞ icon will open a window that displays the exact query that was run on your data to produce the results listed. This allows for easy identification of the rows that were considered failures by the Dashboard.

15.6   Study-Specific Checks in Practice

Next, we will execute several checks specifically for the angioedema cohort definition provided in Appendix B.4. We will assume the connection details have been set as described in Section 15.4, and that the cohort definition JSON and SQL of the cohort definition have been saved in the files "cohort.json" and "cohort.sql", respectively. The JSON and SQL can be obtained from the Export tab in the ATLAS cohort definition function.

RESULTS

SYNTHEA SYNTHETIC HEALTH DATABASE

Results generated at 2019-08-22 14:15:06 in 29 mins

				Column visibility			CSV

Show 5 ▾ entries Search:

	STATUS	CONTEXT	CATEGORY	SUBCATEGORY	LEVEL	DESCRIPTION	% RECORDS
	▾	▾	▾	▾	FIELD ▾		▾
⊞	FAIL	Verification	Plausibility	Atemporal	FIELD	The number and percent of records with a value in the gap_days field of the DRUG_ERA table less than 0. (Threshold=0%)	24.07%
⊞	FAIL	Verification	Completeness	None	FIELD	The number and percent of records with a value of 0 in the standard concept field race_concept_id in the PERSON table. (Threshold=0%)	16.74%
⊞	FAIL	Verification	Conformance	Relational	FIELD	The number and percent of records that have a value in the ethnicity_concept_id field in the PERSON table that does not exist in the CONCEPT table. (Threshold=0%)	16.15%
⊞	PASS	Verification	Completeness	None	FIELD	The number and percent of records with a NULL value in the condition_end_date of the CONDITION_OCCURRENCE (Threshold=100%)	13.24%
⊞	PASS	Verification	Completeness	None	FIELD	The number and percent of records with a NULL value in the condition_end_datetime of the CONDITION_OCCURRENCE (Threshold=100%)	13.24%

Showing 71 to 75 of 1,327 entries (filtered from 1,639 total entries)   Previous 1 .. 14 **15** 16 .. 266 Next

Figure 15.7: Drilldown into Data Quality Checks in the Data Quality Dashboard.

```
library(MethodEvaluation)
json <- readChar("cohort.json", file.info("cohort.json")$size)
sql <- readChar("cohort.sql", file.info("cohort.sql")$size)
checkCohortSourceCodes(connectionDetails,
                       cdmDatabaseSchema = cdmDbSchema,
                       cohortJson = json,
                       cohortSql = sql,
                       outputFile = "output.html")
```

We can open the output file in a web browser as shown in Figure 15.8. Here we see that the angioedema cohort definition has two concept sets: "Inpatient or ER visit", and "Angioedema". In this example database the visits were found through database-specific source codes "ER" and "IP", that are not in the Vocabulary, although they were mapped during the ETL to standard concepts. We also see that angioedema is found through one ICD-9 and two ICD-10 codes. We clearly see the point in time of the cut-over between the two coding systems when we look at the spark-lines for the individual codes, but for the concept set as a whole there is no discontinuity at that time.

Next, we can search for orphan source codes, which are source codes that do not map to standard concept codes. Here we look for the Standard Concept "Angioedema," and then we look for any codes and concepts that have "Angioedema" or any of the synonyms we provide as part of their name:

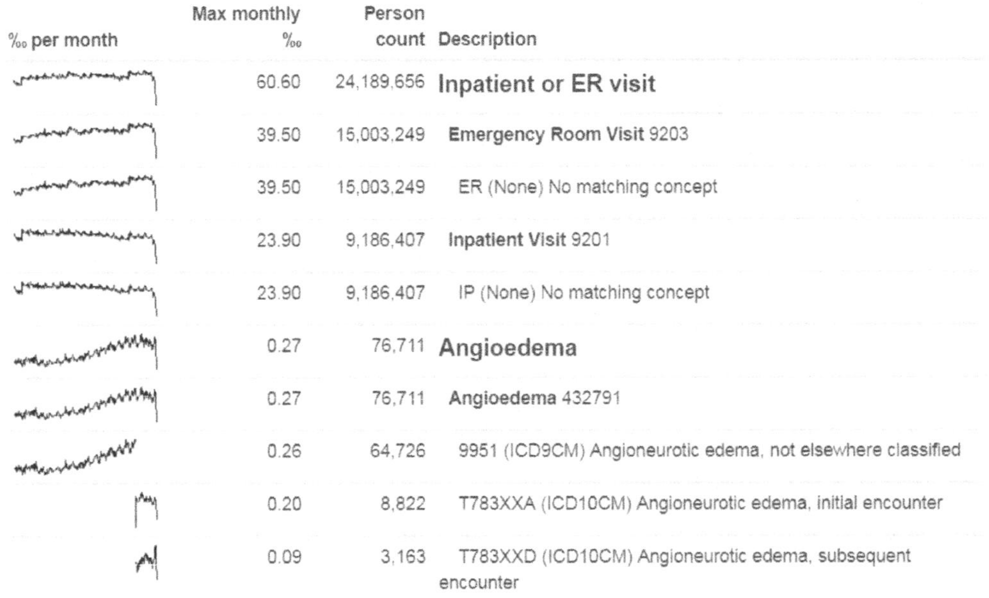

	Max monthly ‰	Person count	Description
‰ per month			
	60.60	24,189,656	**Inpatient or ER visit**
	39.50	15,003,249	**Emergency Room Visit 9203**
	39.50	15,003,249	ER (None) No matching concept
	23.90	9,186,407	**Inpatient Visit 9201**
	23.90	9,186,407	IP (None) No matching concept
	0.27	76,711	**Angioedema**
	0.27	76,711	Angioedema 432791
	0.26	64,726	9951 (ICD9CM) Angioneurotic edema, not elsewhere classified
	0.20	8,822	T783XXA (ICD10CM) Angioneurotic edema, initial encounter
	0.09	3,163	T783XXD (ICD10CM) Angioneurotic edema, subsequent encounter

Figure 15.8: Source codes used in the angioedema cohort definition.

```
orphans <- findOrphanSourceCodes(connectionDetails,
                        cdmDatabaseSchema = cdmDbSchema,
                        conceptName = "Angioedema",
                        conceptSynonyms = c("Angioneurotic edema",
                                            "Giant hives",
                                            "Giant urticaria",
                                            "Periodic edema"))
View(orphans)
```

code	description	vocabularyId	overallCount
T78.3XXS	Angioneurotic edema, sequela	ICD10CM	508
10002425	Angioedemas	MedDRA	0
148774	Angioneurotic Edema of Larynx	CIEL	0
402383003	Idiopathic urticaria and/or angioedema	SNOMED	0
232437009	Angioneurotic edema of larynx	SNOMED	0
10002472	Angioneurotic edema, not elsewhere classified	MedDRA	0

The only potential orphan found that is actually used in the data is "Angioneurotic edema, sequela", which should not be mapped to angioedema. This analysis therefore did not reveal any missing codes.

15.7 Summary

- Most observational healthcare data were not collected for research.

- Data quality checks are an integral part of research. Data quality must be assessed to determine whether the data are of sufficient quality for research purposes.

- We should assess data quality for the purpose of research in general, and critically in the context of a specific study.

- Some aspects of data quality can be assessed automatically through large sets of predefined rules, for example those in the Data Quality Dashboard.

- Other tools exist to evaluate the mapping of codes relevant for a particular study.

15.8 Exercises

Prerequisites

For these exercises we assume R, R-Studio and Java have been installed as described in Section 8.4.5. Also required are the SqlRender, DatabaseConnector, ACHILLES, and Eunomia packages, which can be installed using:

```
install.packages(c("SqlRender", "DatabaseConnector", "devtools"))
devtools::install_github("ohdsi/Achilles")
devtools:install_github("ohdsi/DataQualityDashboard")
devtools::install_github("ohdsi/Eunomia", ref = "v1.0.0")
```

The Eunomia package provides a simulated dataset in the CDM that will run inside your local R session. The connection details can be obtained using:

```
connectionDetails <- Eunomia::getEunomiaConnectionDetails()
```

The CDM database schema is "main".

Exercise 15.1. Execute ACHILLES against the Eunomia database.

Exercise 15.2. Execute the DataQualityDashboard against the Eunomia database.

Exercise 15.3. Extract the DQD list of checks.

Suggested answers can be found in Appendix E.10.

Chapter 16

Clinical Validity

Chapter leads: Joel Swerdel, Seng Chan You, Ray Chen & Patrick Ryan

> The likelihood of transforming matter into energy is something akin to shooting
> birds in the dark in a country where there are only a few birds. *Einstein, 1935*

The vision of OHDSI is "A world in which observational research produces a comprehensive understanding of health and disease." Retrospective designs provide a vehicle for research using existing data but can be riddled with threats to various aspects of validity as discussed in Chapter 14. It is not easy to isolate clinical validity from quality of data and statistical methodology, but here we will focus on three aspects in terms of clinical validity: Characteristics of health care databases, Cohort validation, and Generalizability of the evidence. Let's go back to the example of population-level estimation (Chapter 12). We tried to answer the question "Do ACE inhibitors cause angioedema compared to thiazide or thiazide-like diuretics?" In that example, we demonstrated that ACE inhibitors caused more angioedema than thiazide or thiazide-like diuretics. This chapter is dedicated to answer the question: "To what extent does the analysis conducted match the clinical intention?"

16.1 Characteristics of Health Care Databases

It is possible that what we found is the relationship between **prescription** of ACE inhibitor and angioedema rather than the relationship between **use** of ACE inhibitor and angioedema. We've already discussed data quality in the previous chapter (15). The quality of the converted database into the Common Data Model (CDM) cannot exceed the original database. Here we are addressing the characteristics of most healthcare utilization databases. Many databases used in OHDSI originated from administrative claims or electronic health records (EHR). Claims and EHR have different data capture processes, neither of which has research as a primary intention. Data elements from claims records are captured for the purpose of reimbursement, financial transactions between clinicians and payers whereby services provided to patients by providers are sufficiently justified to enable agreement on payments by the responsible parties. Data elements in EHR records are captured to support clinical care and administrative operations, and they commonly only reflect the information that providers within a given health system feel are necessary to document the current service and provide necessary context for anticipated follow-up care within their health system. They may not represent a patient's complete medical history and may not integrate data from across health systems.

To generate reliable evidence from observational data, it is useful for a researcher to understand the journey that the data undergoes from the moment that a patient seeks care through the moment that the data reflecting that care are used in an analysis. As an example, "drug exposure" can be inferred from various sources of observational data, including prescriptions written by clinicians, pharmacy dispensing records, hospital procedural administrations, or patient self-reported medication history. The source of data can impact our level of confidence in the inference we draw about which patients did or did not use the drug, as well as when and for how long. The data capture process can result in under-estimation of exposure, such as if free samples or over-the counter drugs are not recorded, or over-estimation of exposure, such as if a patient doesn't fill the prescription written or doesn't adherently consume the prescription dispensed. Understanding the potential biases in exposure and outcome ascertainment, and more ideally quantifying and adjusting for these measurement errors, can improve our confidence in the validity of the evidence we draw from the data we have available.

16.2 Cohort Validation

Hripcsak and Albers (2017) described that "a phenotype is a specification of an observable, potentially changing state of an organism, as distinguished from the genotype, which is derived from an organism's genetic makeup. The term phenotype can be applied to patient characteristics inferred from electronic health record (EHR) data. Researchers have been carrying out EHR phenotyping since the beginning of informatics, from both structured data and narrative data. The goal is to draw conclusions about a target concept based on raw EHR data, claims data, or other clinically relevant data. Phenotype algorithms – i.e., algorithms that identify or characterize phenotypes – may be generated by domain exerts and knowledge engineers, including recent research in knowledge engineering or through diverse forms of machine learning...to generate novel representations of the data."

This description highlights several attributes useful to reinforce when considering clinical validity: 1) it makes it clear that we are talking about something that is observable (and therefore possible to be captured in our observational data); 2) it includes the notion of time in the phenotype specification (since a state of a person can change); 3) it draws a distinction between the phenotype as the desired intent vs. the phenotype algorithm, which is the implementation of the desired intent.

OHDSI has adopted the term "cohort" to define the set of persons satisfying one or more inclusion criteria for a duration of time. A "cohort definition" represents the logic necessary to instantiate a cohort against an observational database. In this regard, the cohort definition (or phenotype algorithm) is used to produce a cohort, which is intended to represent the phenotype, being the persons who belong to the observable clinical state of interest.

Most types of observational analyses, including clinical characterization, population-level effect estimation, and patient-level prediction, require one or more cohorts to be established as part of the study process. To evaluate the validity of the evidence produced by these analyses, one must consider this question for each cohort: to what extent do the persons identified in the cohort based on the cohort definition and the available observational data accurately reflect the persons who truly belong to the phenotype?

To return to the population-level estimation example (Chapter 12) "Do ACE inhibitors cause angioedema compared to thiazide or thiazide-like diuretics?", we must define three cohorts: a target cohort of persons who are new users of ACE inhibitors, a comparator cohort of persons who are new users of thiazide diuretics, and an outcome cohort of persons who develop angioedema. How confident are we that all use of ACE inhibitors or thiazide diuretics is completely captured, such that "new users" can be identified by the first observed exposure, without concern of prior (but unobserved) use? Can we comfortably infer that persons who have a drug exposure record for ACE inhibitors were in fact exposed to the drug, and those without a drug exposure were indeed unexposed? Is there uncertainty in defining the duration of time that a person is classified in the state of "ACE inhibitor use," either when inferring cohort entry at the time the drug was started or cohort exit when the drug was discontinued? Have persons with a condition occurrence record of "Angioedema" actually experienced rapid swelling beneath the skin, differentiated from other types of dermatologic allergic reactions? What proportion of patients who developed angioedema received medical attention that would give rise to the observational data used to identify these clinical cases based on the cohort definition? How well can the angioedema events which are potentially drug-induced be disambiguated from the events known to be caused by other agents, such as food allergy or viral infection? Is disease onset sufficiently well captured that we have confidence in drawing a temporal association between exposure status and outcome incidence? Answering these types of questions is at the heart of clinical validity.

In this chapter, we will discuss the methods for validating cohort definitions. We first describe the metrics used to measure the validity of a cohort definition. Next, we describe two methods to estimate these metrics: 1) clinical adjudication through source record verification, and 2) PheValuator, a semi-automated method using diagnostic predictive modeling.

16.2.1 Cohort Evaluation Metrics

Once the cohort definition for the study has been determined, the validity of the definition can be evaluated. A common approach to assess validity is by comparing some or all persons in a defined cohort to a reference 'gold standard' and expressing the results in a confusion matrix, a two-by-two contingency table that stratifies persons according to their gold standard classification and qualification within the cohort definition. Figure 16.1 shows the elements of the confusion matrix.

The true and false results from the cohort definition are determined by applying the definition

Gold Standard

		True	False
Cohort Definition	True	True Positive	False Negative
	False	False Negative	True Negative

Figure 16.1: Confusion matrix.

to a group of persons. Those included in the definition are considered positive for the health condition and are labeled "True." Those persons not included in the cohort definition are considered negative for the health condition and are labeled "False". While the absolute truth of a person's heath state considered in the cohort definition is very difficult to determine, there are multiple methods to establish a reference gold standard, two of which will be described later in the chapter. Regardless of the method used, the labeling of these persons is the same as described for the cohort definition.

In addition to errors in the binary indication of phenotype designation, the timing of the health condition may also be incorrect. For example, while the cohort definition may correctly label a person as belonging to a phenotype, the definition may incorrectly specify the date and time when a person without the condition became a person with the condition. This error would add bias to studies using survival analysis results, e.g., hazard ratios, as an effect measure.

The next step in the process is to assess the concordance of the gold standard with the cohort definition. Those persons that are labeled by both the gold standard method and the cohort definition as "True" are called "True Positives." Those persons that are labeled by the gold standard method as "False" and by the cohort definition as "True" are called "False Positives," i.e., the cohort definition misclassified these persons as having the condition when they do not. Those persons that are labeled by both the gold standard method and the cohort definition as "False" are called "True Negatives." Those persons that are labeled by the gold standard method as "True" and by the cohort definition as "False" are called "False Negatives," i.e., the cohort definition incorrectly classified these persons as not having the condition, when it fact they do belong to the phenotype. Using the counts from the four cells in the confusion matrix, we can quantify the accuracy of the cohort definition in classifying phenotype status in a group of persons. There are standard performance metrics for measuring cohort definition performance:

1. **Sensitivity of the cohort definition** – what proportion of the persons who truly belong to the phenotype in the population were correctly identified to have the health outcome based on the cohort definition? This is determined by the following formula:

   Sensitivity = True Positives / (True Positives + False Negatives)

2. **Specificity of the cohort definition** – what proportion of the persons who do not belong to the phenotype in the population were correctly identified to not have the health outcome based on the cohort definition? This is determined by the following formula:

   Specificity = True Negatives / (True Negatives + False Positives)

3. **Positive predictive value (PPV) of the cohort definition** – what proportion of the persons identified by the cohort definition to have the health condition actually belong to the phenotype? This is determined by the following formula:

PPV = True Positives / (True Positives + False Positives)

4. **Negative predictive value (NPV) of the cohort definition** – what proportion of the persons identified by the cohort definition to not have the health condition actually did not belong to the phenotype? This is determined by the following formula:

NPV = True Negatives / (True Negatives + False Negatives)

Perfect scores for these measures are 100%. Due to the nature of observational data, perfect scores are usually far from the norm. Rubbo et al. (2015) reviewed studies validating cohort definitions for myocardial infarction. Of the 33 studies they examined, only one cohort definition in one dataset obtained a perfect score for PPV. Overall, 31 of the 33 studies reported PPVs $\geq$ 70%. They also found, however, that of the 33 studies only 11 reported sensitivity and 5 reported specificity. PPV is a function of sensitivity, specificity, and prevalence. Datasets with different values for prevalence will produce different values for PPV with sensitivity and specificity held constant. Without sensitivity and specificity, correcting for bias due to imperfect cohort definitions is not possible. Additionally, the misclassification of the health condition may be differential, meaning the cohort definition performs differently on one group of persons relative to the comparison group, or non-differentially, when the cohort definition performs similarly on both comparison groups. Prior cohort definition validation studies have not tested for potential differential misclassification, even though it can lead to strong bias in effect estimates.

Once the performance metrics have been established for the cohort definition, these may be used to adjust the results for studies using these definitions. In theory, adjusting study results for these measurement error estimates has been well established. In practice, though, because of the difficulty in obtaining the performance characteristics, these adjustments are rarely considered. The methods used to determine the gold standard are described in the remainder of this section.

16.3 Source Record Verification

A common method used to validate cohort definitions has been clinical adjudication through source record verification: a thorough examination of a person's records by one or more domain experts with sufficient knowledge to competently classify the clinical condition or characteristic of interest. Chart review generally follows the following steps:

1. Obtain permission from local institutional review board (IRB) and/or persons as needed to conduct study including chart review.
2. Generate cohort using cohort definition to be evaluated. Sample a subset of the persons to manually review if there are insufficient resources to adjudicate the entire cohort.
3. Identify one or more persons with sufficient clinical expertise to review person records.

4. Determine guidelines for adjudicating whether a person is positive or negative for the desired clinical condition or characteristic.

5. Clinical experts review and adjudicate all available data for the persons within the sample to classify each person as to whether they belong to the phenotype or not.

6. Tabulate persons according to the cohort definition classification and clinical adjudication classification into a confusion matrix, and calculate the performance characteristics possible from the data collected.

Results from a chart review are typically limited to the evaluation of one performance characteristic, positive predictive value (PPV). This is because the cohort definition under evaluation only generates persons that are believed to have the desired condition or characteristics. Therefore, each person in the sample of the cohort is classified as either a true positive or false positive based on the clinical adjudication. Without knowledge of all persons in the phenotype in the entire population (including those not identified by the cohort definition), it is not possible to identify the false negatives, and thereby fill in the remainder of the confusion matrix to generate the remaining performance characteristics. Potential methods of identifying all persons in the phenotype across the population include chart review of the entire database, which is generally not feasible unless the overall population is small, or the utilization of comprehensive clinical registries in which all true cases have already been flagged and adjudicated, such as tumor registries (see example below). Alternatively, one can sample persons who do not qualify for the cohort definition to produce a subset of predicted negatives, and then repeating steps 3-6 of the chart review above to check whether these patients are truly lacking the clinical condition or characteristic of interest can identify true negatives or false negatives. This would allow the estimation of negative predictive value (NPV), and if an appropriate estimate of the phenotype prevalence is available, then sensitivity and specificity can be estimated.

There are a number of limitations to clinical adjudication through source record verification. As alluded to earlier, chart review can be a very time-consuming and resource-intensive process, even just for the evaluation of a single metric such as PPV. This limitation significantly impedes the practicality of evaluating an entire population to fill out a complete confusion matrix. In addition, multiple steps in the above process have the potential to bias the results of the study. For example, if records are not equally accessible in the EHR, if there is no EHR, or if individual patient consent is required, then the subset under evaluation may not be truly random and could introduce sampling or selection bias. In addition, manual adjudication is susceptible to human error or misclassification and thereby may not represent a perfectly accurate metric. There can often be disagreement between clinical adjudicators due to the data in the person's record being vague, subjective, or of low quality. In many studies, the process involves a majority-rules decision for consensus which yields a binary classification for persons that does not reflect the inter-rater discordance.

16.3.1   Example of Source Record Verification

An example of the process to conduct a cohort definition validation using chart review is provided from a study by the Columbia University Irving Medical Center (CUIMC), which validated a cohort definition for multiple cancers as part of a feasibility study for the National Cancer Institute (NCI). The steps used to conduct the validation for the example of one of these cancers—prostate cancer—are as follows:

1. Submitted proposal and obtained IRB consent for OHDSI cancer phenotyping study.
2. Developed a cohort definition for prostate cancer: Using ATHENA and ATLAS to explore the vocabulary, we created a cohort definition to include all patients with a condition occurrence for Malignant Tumor of Prostate (concept ID 4163261), excluding Secondary Neoplasm of Prostate (concept ID 4314337) or Non-Hodgkin's Lymphoma of Prostate (concept ID 4048666).
3. Generated cohort using ATLAS and randomly selected 100 patients for manual review, mapping each PERSON_ID back to patient MRN using mapping tables. 100 patients were selected in order to achieve our desired level of statistical precision for the performance metric of PPV.
4. Manually reviewed records in the various EHRs—both inpatient and outpatient—in order to determine whether each person in the random subset was a true or false positive.
5. Manual review and clinical adjudication were performed by one physician (although ideally in future more rigorous validation studies would be done by a higher number of reviewers to assess for consensus and inter-rater reliability).
6. Determination of a reference standard was based on clinical documentation, pathology reports, labs, medications and procedures as documented in the entirety of the available electronic patient record.
7. Patients were labeled as 1) prostate cancer 2) no prostate cancer or 3) unable to determine.
8. A conservative estimate of PPV was calculated using the following: prostate cancer/ (no prostate cancer + unable to determine).
9. Then, using the tumor registry as an additional gold standard to identify a reference standard across the entire CUIMC population, we counted the number of persons in the tumor registry which were and were not accurately identified by the cohort definition, which allowed us to estimate sensitivity using these values as true positives and false negatives.
10. Using the estimated sensitivity, PPV, and prevalence, we could then estimate specificity for this cohort definition. As noted previously, this process was time-consuming and labor-intensive, as each cohort definition had to be individually evaluated through manual chart review as well as correlated with the CUIMC tumor registry in order to identify all performance metrics. The IRB approval process itself took weeks despite an expedited review while obtaining access to the tumor registry, and the process of manual chart review itself took a few weeks longer.

A review of validation efforts for myocardial infarction (MI) cohort definitions by Rubbo et al. (2015) found that there was significant heterogeneity in the cohort definitions used in the studies as well as in the validation methods and the results reported. The authors concluded that for acute myocardial infarction there is no gold standard cohort definition available. They noted that the process was both costly and time-consuming. Due to that limitation, most studies had small sample sizes in their validation leading to wide variations in the estimates for the performance characteristics. They also noted that in the 33 studies, while all the studies reported positive predictive value, only 11 studies reported sensitivity and only five studies reported specificity. As mentioned previously, without estimates of sensitivity and specificity, statistical correction for misclassification bias cannot be performed.

16.4   PheValuator

The OHDSI community has developed a different approach to constructing a gold standard by using diagnostic predictive models. (Swerdel et al., 2019) The general idea is to emulate the ascertainment of the health outcome similar to the way clinicians would in a source record validation, but in an automated way that can be applied at scale. The tool has been developed as an open-source R package called PheValuator.[1] PheValuator uses functions from the Patient Level Prediction package.

The process is as follows:

1. Create an extremely specific ("**xSpec**") cohort: Determine a set of persons with a very high likelihood of having the outcome of interest to be used as noisy positive labels when training a diagnostic predictive model.
2. Create an extremely sensitive ("**xSens**") cohort: Determine a set of persons that should include anyone who could possible have the outcome. This cohort will be used to identify its inverse: the set of people we are confident do not have the outcome, to be used as noisy negative labels when training a diagnostic predictive model.
3. Fit a predictive model using the xSpec and xSens cohort: As described in Chapter 13, we fit a model using a wide array of patient features as predictors, and aim to predict whether a person belongs to the xSpec cohort (those we believe have the outcome) or the inverse of the xSens cohort (those we believe do not have the outcome).
4. Apply the fitted model to estimate the probability of the outcome for a hold-out set of persons who will be used to evaluate cohort definition performance: The set of predictors from the model can be applied to a person's data to estimate the predicted probability that the person belongs to the phenotype. We use these predictions as a **probabilistic gold standard**.
5. Evaluate the performance characteristics of the cohort definitions: We compare the predicted probability to the binary classification of a cohort definition (the test conditions for the confusion matrix). Using the test conditions and the estimates for the true conditions, we can fully populate the confusion matrix and estimate the entire set of performance characteristics, i.e., sensitivity, specificity, and predictive values.

The primary limitation to using this approach is that the estimation of the probability of a person having the health outcome is limited by the data in the database. Depending on the database, important information, such as clinician notes, may not be available.

---

[1] https://github.com/OHDSI/PheValuator

In diagnostic predictive modeling we create a model that discriminates between those with the disease and those without the disease. As described in the Patient-Level Prediction chapter (Chapter 13), prediction models are developed using a *target cohort* and an *outcome cohort*. The target cohort includes persons with and without the health outcome; the outcome cohort identifies those persons in the target cohort with the health outcome. For the PheValuator process, we use an extremely specific cohort definition, the "xSpec" cohort, to determine the outcome cohort for the prediction model. The xSpec cohort uses a definition to find those with a very high probability of having the disease of interest. The xSpec cohort may be defined as those persons who have multiple condition occurrence records for the health outcome of interest. For example, for atrial fibrillation, we may have persons who have 10 or more records with the atrial fibrillation diagnosis code. For MI, an acute outcome, we may use 5 occurrences of MI and include the requirement of having at least two occurrences from an inpatient setting. The target cohort for the predictive model is constructed from the union of persons with a low likelihood of having the health outcome of interest and those persons in the xSpec cohort. To determine those persons with a low likelihood of having the health outcome of interest, we sample from the entire database and exclude persons who have some evidence suggestive of belonging to the phenotype, typically by removing persons with any records containing the concepts used to define the xSpec cohort. There are limitations to this method. It is possible that these xSpec cohort persons may have different characteristics than others with the disease. It may also be that these persons had longer observation time after initial diagnosis than the average patient. We use LASSO logistic regression to create the prediction model used to generate the probabilistic gold standard. (Suchard et al., 2013) This algorithm produces a parsimonious model and typically removes many of the collinear covariates which may be present across the dataset. In the current version of the PheValuator software, outcome status (yes/no) is evaluated based on all data for a person (all observation time), and does not evaluate the accuracy of the cohort start date.

16.4.1 Example Validation By PheValuator

We may use PheValuator to assess the complete performance characteristics for a cohort definition to be used in a study where it is necessary to determine those persons who have had an acute myocardial infarction.

The following are the steps for testing cohort definitions for MI using PheValuator:

Step 1: Define the xSpec Cohort

Determine those with MI with a high probability. We required a condition occurrence record with a concept for myocardial infarction or any of its descendants, with one or more occurrences of MI recorded from a hospital in-patient visit within 5 days, and 4 or more occurrences of MI in the patient record within 365 days. Figure 16.2 illustrates this cohort definition for MI in ATLAS.

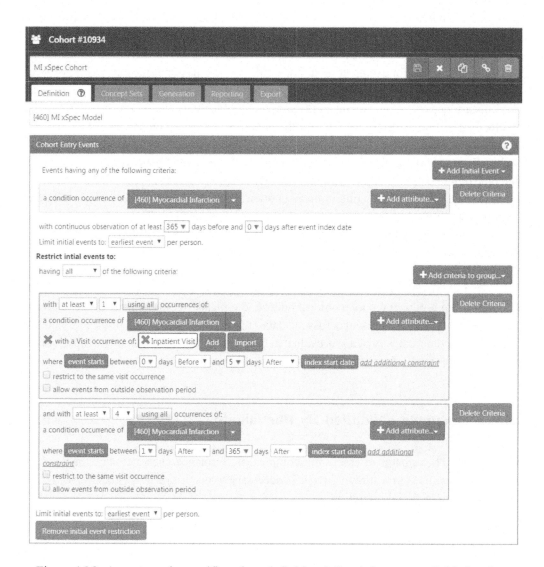

Figure 16.2: An extremely specific cohort definition (xSpec) for myocardial infarction.

Figure 16.3: An extremely sensitive cohort definition (xSens) for myocardial infarction.

Step 2: Define the xSens Cohort

We then develop an extremely sensitive cohort (xSens). This cohort may be defined for MI as those persons with at least one condition occurrence record containing a myocardial infarction concept at any time in their medical history. Figure 16.3 illustrates the xSens cohort definition for MI in ATLAS.

Step 3: Fit the Predictive Model

The function `createPhenoModel` develops the diagnostic predictive model for assessing the probability of having the health outcome of interest in the evaluation cohort. To use this function, we utilize the xSpec and xSens cohorts developed in Steps 1 and 2. The xSpec cohort will be entered as the `xSpecCohort` parameter in the function. The xSens cohort will be entered as the `exclCohort` parameter in the function to indicate that those in the xSens cohort should be excluded from the target cohort used in the modeling process. Using this exclusion method, we can determine persons with a low likelihood of having the health outcome. We may think of this group as "noisy negative" persons, i.e., a group of persons likely negative for the health outcome but allowing for a small possibility of including some persons positive for the health outcome. We may also use the xSens cohort as the `prevCohort` parameter in the function. This parameter is used in the process to determine an approximate prevalence of the health outcome in the population. Normally, a large random sample of persons from a database should produce a population of persons where the persons with the outcome of interest are about in proportion to the prevalence of the outcome in the database. Using the method we described, we no longer have a random sample of persons and need to re-calibrate the predictive model based on resetting the proportion of persons with the outcome to those without the outcome.

All concepts used to define the xSpec cohort must be excluded from the modeling process. To do this we set the `excludedConcepts` parameter to the list of concepts used in the xSpec definition. For example, for MI we created a concept set in ATLAS using the concept for Myocardial infarction plus all its descendants. For this example, we would set the excludedConcepts parameter to 4329847, the concept Id for Myocardial infarction, and we would also set the addDescendantsToExclude parameter to TRUE, indicating that any descendants of the excluded concepts should also be excluded.

There are several parameters that may be used to specify the characteristics of the persons included in the modeling process. We can set the ages of the persons included in the modeling process by setting the `lowerAgeLimit` to the lower bounds of age desired in the model and the `upperAgeLimit` to the upper bounds. We may wish to do this if the cohort definitions for a planned study will be created for a certain age group. For example, if the cohort definition to be used in a study is for Type 1 diabetes mellitus in children, you may want to limit the ages used to develop the diagnostic predictive model to ages 5 to 17 years old for example. In doing so, we will produce a model with features that are likely more closely related to the persons selected by the cohort definitions to be tested. We can also specify which sex is included in the model by setting the `gender` parameter to the concept ID for either male or female. By default, the parameter is set to include both males and females. This feature may be useful in sex-specific health outcomes such as prostate cancer. We can set the time frame for person inclusion based on the first visit in the person's record by setting the `startDate` and `endDate` parameters to the lower and upper bounds of the date range, respectively. Finally, the `mainPopnCohort` parameter may be used to specify a large population cohort from which all persons in the target and outcome cohorts will be selected. In most instances this will be set to 0, indicating no limitation on selecting persons for the target and outcome cohorts. There may be times, however, when this parameter is useful for building a better model, possibly in cases where the prevalence of the health outcome is extremely low, perhaps 0.01% or lower. For example:

```
setwd("c:/temp")
library(PheValuator)
connectionDetails <- createConnectionDetails(
  dbms = "postgresql",
  server = "localhost/ohdsi",
  user = "joe",
  password = "supersecret")


phenoTest <- createPhenoModel(
  connectionDetails = connectionDetails,
  xSpecCohort = 10934,
  cdmDatabaseSchema = "my_cdm_data",
  cohortDatabaseSchema = "my_results",
  cohortDatabaseTable = "cohort",
  outDatabaseSchema = "scratch.dbo", #should have write access
  trainOutFile = "5XMI_train",
  exclCohort = 1770120, #the xSens cohort
```

```
prevCohort = 1770119, #the cohort for prevalence determination
modelAnalysisId = "20181206V1",
excludedConcepts = c(312327, 314666),
addDescendantsToExclude = TRUE,
cdmShortName = "myCDM",
mainPopnCohort = 0, #use the entire person population
lowerAgeLimit = 18,
upperAgeLimit = 90,
gender = c(8507, 8532),
startDate = "20100101",
endDate = "20171231")
```

In this example, we used the cohorts defined in the "my_results" database, specifying the location of the cohort table (cohortDatabaseSchema, cohortDatabaseTable - "my_results.cohort") and where the model will find the conditions, drug exposures, etc. to inform the model (cdm-DatabaseSchema - "my_cdm_data"). The persons included in the model will be those whose first visit in the CDM is between January 1, 2010 and December 31, 2017. We are also specifically excluding the concept IDs 312327, 314666, and their descendants which were used to create the xSpec cohort. Their ages at the time of first visit will be between 18 and 90. With the parameters above, the name of the predictive model output from this step will be: "c:/temp/lr_results_5XMI_train_myCDM_ePPV0.75_20181206V1.rds"

Step 4: Creating the Evaluation Cohort

The function `createEvalCohort` uses the PatientLevelPrediction package function `applyModel` to produce a large cohort of persons, each with a predicted probability for the health outcome of interest. The function requires specifying the xSpec cohort (by setting the `xSpecCohort` parameter to the xSpec cohort ID). We may also specify the characteristics of the persons included in the evaluation cohort as we did in the previous step. This could include specifying the lower and upper ages limits (by setting, as ages, the `lowerAgeLimit` and `upperAgeLimit` arguments, respectively), the sex (by setting the `gender` parameter to the concept IDs for male and/or female), the starting and ending dates (by setting, as dates, the `startDate` and `endDate` arguments, respectively), and designating a large population from which to select the persons by setting the `mainPopnCohort` to the cohort Id for the population to use.

For example:

```
setwd("c:/temp")
connectionDetails <- createConnectionDetails(
  dbms = "postgresql",
  server = "localhost/ohdsi",
  user = "joe",
  password = "supersecret")
```

```
evalCohort <- createEvalCohort(
  connectionDetails = connectionDetails,
  xSpecCohort = 10934,
  cdmDatabaseSchema = "my_cdm_data",
  cohortDatabaseSchema = "my_results",
  cohortDatabaseTable = "cohort",
  outDatabaseSchema = "scratch.dbo",
  testOutFile = "5XMI_eval",
  trainOutFile = "5XMI_train",
  modelAnalysisId = "20181206V1",
  evalAnalysisId = "20181206V1",
  cdmShortName = "myCDM",
  mainPopnCohort = 0,
  lowerAgeLimit = 18,
  upperAgeLimit = 90,
  gender = c(8507, 8532),
  startDate = "20100101",
  endDate = "20171231")
```

In this example, the parameters specify that the function should use the model file: "c:/temp/lr_results_5XMI_train_myCDM_ePPV0.75_20181206V1.rds" to produce the evaluation cohort file: "c:/temp/lr_results_5XMI_eval_myCDM_ePPV0.75_20181206V1.rds" The model and the evaluation cohort files created in this step will be used in the evaluation of the cohort definitions provided in the next step.

Step 5: Creating and Testing Cohort Definitions

The next step is to create and test the cohort definitions to be evaluated. The desired performance characteristics may depend on the intended use of the cohort to address the research question of interest. For certain questions, a very sensitive algorithm may be required; others may require a more specific algorithm. The process for determining the performance characteristics for a cohort definition using PheValuator is shown in Figure 16.4.

In part A of Figure 16.4, we examined the persons from the cohort definition to be tested and found those persons from the evaluation cohort (created in the previous step) who were included in the cohort definition (Person IDs 016, 019, 022, 023, and 025) and those from the evaluation cohort who were not included (Person Ids 017, 018, 020, 021, and 024). For each of these included/excluded persons, we had previously determined the probability of the health outcome using the predictive model (p(O)).

We estimated the values for True Positives, True Negatives, False Positives, and False Negatives as follows (Part B of Figure 16.4):

1. If the cohort definition included a person from the evaluation cohort, i.e., the cohort definition considered the person a "positive." The predicted probability for the health outcome indicated the expected value of the number of counts contributed by that

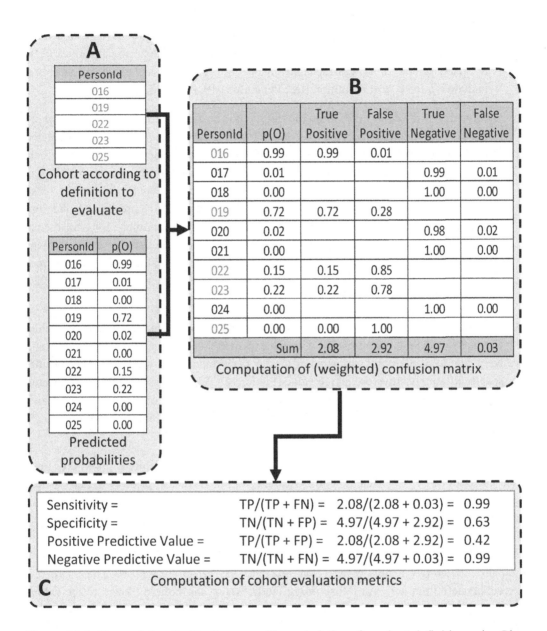

Figure 16.4: Determining the Performance Characteristics of a cohort definition using Phe-Valuator. p(O) = Probability of outcome; TP = True Positive; FN = False Negative; TN = True Negative; FP = False Positive.

person to the True Positives, and one minus the probability indicated the expected value of the number of counts contributed by that person to the False Positives for that person. We added all the expected values of counts across persons to get the total expected value. For example, PersonId 016 had a predicted probability of 99% for the presence of the health outcome, 0.99 was added to the True Positives (expected value of counts added 0.99) and 1.00–0.99 = 0.01 was added to the False Positives (0.01 expected value). This was repeated for all the persons from the evaluation cohort included in the cohort definition (i.e., PersonIds 019, 022, 023, and 025).

2. Similarly, if the cohort definition did not include a person from the evaluation cohort, i.e. the cohort definition considered the person a "negative," one minus the predicted probability for the phenotype for that person was the expected value of counts contributed to True Negatives and was added to it, and, in parallel, the predicted probability for the phenotype was the expected value of counts contributed to the False Negatives and was added to it. For example, PersonId 017 had a predicted probability of 1% for the presence of the health outcome (and, correspondingly, 99% for the absence of the health outcome) and 1.00 − 0.01 = 0.99 was added to the True Negatives and 0.01 was added to the False Negatives. This was repeated for all the persons from the evaluation cohort not included in the cohort definition (i.e., PersonIds 018, 020, 021, and 024).

After adding these values over the full set of persons in the evaluation cohort, we filled the four cells of the confusion matrix with the expected values of counts for each cell, and we were able to create point estimates of the PA performance characteristics like sensitivity, specificity, and positive predictive value (Figure 1C). We emphasize that these expected cell counts cannot be used to assess the variance of the estimates, only the point estimates. In the example, the sensitivity, specificity, PPV, and NPV were 0.99, 0.63, 0.42, and 0.99, respectively.

Determining the performance characteristics of the cohort definition uses the function `testPhenotype`. This function uses the output from the prior two steps where we created the model and evaluation cohorts. We would set the modelFileName parameter to the RDS file output from createPhenoModel function, in this example, "c:/temp/lr_results_5XMI_train_myCDM_ePPV0.75_20181206V1.rds". We would set the resultsFileName parameter to the RDS file output from createEvalCohort function, in this example, "c:/temp/lr_results_5XMI_eval_myCDM_ePPV0.75_20181206V1.rds". To test the cohort definition we wish to use in our study, we set the `cohortPheno` to the cohort ID for that cohort definition. We can set the `phenText` parameter to some human readable description for the cohort definition, such as "MI Occurrence, Hospital In-Patient Setting". We will set the `testText` parameter to some human readable description for the xSpec definition, such as "5 X MI." The output from this step is a data frame that contains the performance characteristics for the cohort definition tested. The settings for the `cutPoints` parameter is a list of values that will be used to develop the performance characteristics results. The performance characteristics are usually calculated using the "expected values" as described in Figure 1. To retrieve the performance characteristics based on the expected values, we include "EV" in the list for the `cutPoints` parameter. We may also want to see the performance characteristics based on specific predicted probabilities, i.e., cut points. For example, if we wanted to see the performance characteristics of all those at or above a predicted probability of 0.5 were considered positive for the health outcome and all those under a predicted probability of 0.5 were considered negative, we would add "0.5" to the `cutPoints` parameter list. For example:

```
setwd("c:/temp")
connectionDetails <- createConnectionDetails(
  dbms = "postgresql",
  server = "localhost/ohdsi",
  user = "joe",
  password = "supersecret")

phenoResult <- testPhenotype(
  connectionDetails = connectionDetails,
  cutPoints = c(0.1, 0.2, 0.3, 0.4, 0.5, "EV", 0.6, 0.7, 0.8, 0.9),
  resultsFileName =
    "c:/temp/lr_results_5XMI_eval_myCDM_ePPV0.75_20181206V1.rds",
  modelFileName =
    "c:/temp/lr_results_5XMI_train_myCDM_ePPV0.75_20181206V1.rds",
  cohortPheno = 1769702,
  phenText = "All MI by Phenotype 1 X In-patient, 1st Position",
  order = 1,
  testText = "MI xSpec Model - 5 X MI",
  cohortDatabaseSchema = "my_results",
  cohortTable = "cohort",
  cdmShortName = "myCDM")
```

In this example, a wide range of prediction thresholds are provided (cutPoints) including the expected value ("EV"). Given that parameter setting, the output from this step will provide performance characteristics (i.e, sensitivity, specificity, etc.) at each prediction threshold as well as those using the expected value calculations. The evaluation uses the prediction information for the evaluation cohort developed in the prior step. The data frames produced from this step may be saved to a csv file for detailed examination.

Using this process, Table 16.1 displays the performance characteristics for four cohort definitions for MI across five datasets. For a cohort definition similar to the one evaluated by Cutrona and colleagues, ">=1 X HOI, In-Patient", we found a mean PPV of 67% (range: 59%-74%).

Table 16.1: Performance characteristics of four cohort definitions using diagnostic condition codes to determine myocardial infarction on multiple datasets using pheValuator. Sens – Sensitivity ; PPV – Positive Predictive Value ; Spec – Specificity; NPV – Negative Predictive Value; Dx Code – Diagnosis code for the cohort.

Phenotype Algorithm	Database	Sens	PPV	Spec	NPV
>=1 X HOI	CCAE	0.761	0.598	0.997	0.999
	Optum1862	0.723	0.530	0.995	0.998
	OptumGE66	0.643	0.534	0.973	0.982
	MDCD	0.676	0.468	0.990	0.996
	MDCR	0.665	0.553	0.977	0.985
>= 2 X HOI	CCAE	0.585	0.769	0.999	0.998
	Optum1862	0.495	0.693	0.998	0.996
	OptumGE66	0.382	0.644	0.990	0.971
	MDCD	0.454	0.628	0.996	0.993
	MDCR	0.418	0.674	0.991	0.975
>=1 X HOI, In-Patient	CCAE	0.674	0.737	0.999	0.998
	Optum1862	0.623	0.693	0.998	0.997
	OptumGE66	0.521	0.655	0.987	0.977
	MDCD	0.573	0.593	0.995	0.994
	MDCR	0.544	0.649	0.987	0.980
1 X HOI, In-Patient, 1st Position	CCAE	0.633	0.788	0.999	0.998
	Optum1862	0.581	0.754	0.999	0.997
	OptumGE66	0.445	0.711	0.991	0.974
	MDCD	0.499	0.666	0.997	0.993
	MDCR	0.445	0.711	0.991	0.974

16.5   Generalizability of the Evidence

While a cohort can be well-defined and fully evaluated within the context of a given observational database, the clinical validity is limited by the extent to which the results are considered generalizable to the target population of interest. Multiple observational studies on the same topic can yield different results, which can be caused by not only by their designs and analytic methods, but also bt their choice of data source. Madigan et al. (2013b) demonstrated that choice of database affects the result of observational study. They systematically investigated heterogeneity in the results for 53 drug-outcome pairs and two study designs (cohort studies and self-controlled case series) across the 10 observational databases. Even though they held study design constant, substantial heterogeneity in effect estimates was observed.

Across the OHDSI network, observational databases vary considerably in the populations they represent (e.g. pediatric vs. elderly, privately-insured employees vs. publicly-insured unemployed), the care settings where data are captured (e.g. inpatient vs. outpatient, primary vs. secondary/specialty care), the data capture processes (e.g. administrative claims, EHRs, clinical registries), and the national and regional health system from which care is based. These differences can manifest as heterogeneity observed when studying disease and the effects of medical interventions and can also influence the confidence we have in the quality of each data source that may contribute evidence within a network study. While all databases within the OHDSI network are standardized to the CDM, it is important to reinforce that standardization does not reduce the true inherent heterogeneity that is present across populations, but simply provides a consistent framework to investigate and better understand the heterogeneity across the network. The OHDSI research network provides the environment to apply the same analytic process on various databases across the world, so that researchers can interpret results across multiple data sources while holding other methodological aspects constant. OHDSI's collaborative approach to open science in network research, where researchers across participating data partners work together alongside those with clinical domain knowledge and methodologists with analytical expertise, is one way of reaching a collective level of understanding of the clinical validity of data across a network that should serve as a foundation for building confidence in the evidence generated using these data.

16.6 Summary

– Clinical validity can be established by understanding the characteristics of the underlying data source, evaluating the performance characteristics of the cohorts within an analysis, and assessing the generalizability of the study to the target population of interest.
– A cohort definition can be evaluated on the extent to which persons identified in the cohort based on the cohort definition and the available observational data accurately reflect the persons who truly belong to the phenotype.
– Cohort definition validation requires estimating multiple performance characteristics, including sensitivity, specificity, and positive predictive value, to fully summarize and enable adjustment for measurement error.
– Clinical adjudication through source record verification and PheValuator represent two alternative approaches to estimating cohort definition validation.
– OHDSI network studies provide a mechanism to examine data source heterogeneity and expand the generalizability of findings to improve clinical validity of real-world evidence.

Chapter 17

Software Validity

Chapter lead: Martijn Schuemie

The central question of software validity is

> Does the software do what it is expected to do?

Software validity is an essential component of evidence quality: only if our analysis software does what it is expected to do can we produce reliable evidence. As described in Section 17.1.1, it is essential to view every study as a software development exercise, creating an automated script that executes the entire analysis, from data in the Common Data Model (CDM) to the results such as estimates, figures as tables. It is this script, and any software used in this script, that must be validated. As described in Section 8.1, we can write the entire analysis as custom code, or we can use the functionality available in the OHDSI Methods Library. The advantage of using the Methods Library is that great care has already been taken to ensure its validity, so establishing the validity of the entire analysis becomes less burdensome.

In this chapter we first describe best practices for writing valid analysis code. After this we discuss how the Methods library is validated through its software development process and testing.

17.1 Study Code Validity

17.1.1 Automation As a Requirement for Reproducibility

Traditionally, observational studies are often viewed as a journey rather than a process: a database expert may extract a data set from the database and hand this over to the data analyst, who may open it in a spreadsheet editor or other interactive tool, and start working on the analysis. In the end, a result is produced, but little is preserved of how it came about. The destination of the journey was reached, but it is not possible to retrace the exact steps taken to get there. This practice is entirely unacceptable, both because it is not reproducible, but also because it lacks transparency; we do not know exactly what was done to produce the result, so we also cannot verify that no mistakes were made.

Every analysis generating evidence must therefore be fully automated. By automated we mean the analysis should be implemented as a single script, and we should be able to redo the entire analysis from database in CDM format to results, including tables and figures, with a single command. The analysis can be of arbitrary complexity, perhaps producing just a single count, or generating empirically calibrated estimates for millions of research questions, but the same principle applies. The script can invoke other scripts, which in turn can invoke even lower-level analysis processes.

The analysis script can be implemented in any computer language, although in OHDSI the preferred language is R. Thanks to the DatabaseConnector R package, we can connect directly to the data in CDM format, and many advanced analytics are available through the other R packages in the OHDSI Methods Library.

17.1.2   Programming Best Practices

Observational analyses can become very complex, with many steps needed to produce the final results. This complexity can make it harder to maintain the analysis code and increase the likelihood of making errors, as well as making it harder to notice errors. Luckily, computer programmers have over many years developed best practices for writing code that can deal with complexity, which are easy to read, reuse, adapt, and verify. (Martin, 2008) A full discussion of these best practices could fill many books. Here, we highlight these four important principles:

- **Abstraction**: Rather than write a single large script that does everything, leading to so-called "spaghetti code" where dependencies between lines of code can go from anywhere to anywhere (e.g. a value set on line 10 is used in line 1,000), we can organize our code in units called "functions." A function should have a clear goal, for example "take random sample," and once created we can then use this function in our larger script without having to think of the minutiae of what the function does; we can abstract the function to a simple-to-understand concept.
- **Encapsulation**: For abstraction to work, we should make sure that dependencies of a function are minimized and clearly defined. Our example sampling function should have a few arguments (e.g. a dataset and a sample size), and one output (e.g. the sample). Nothing else should influence what the function does. So-called "global variables", variables that are set outside a function, are not arguments of a function, but are nevertheless used in the function, should be avoided.
- **Clear naming**: Variables and functions should have clear names, making code read almost like natural language. For example, instead of x <- spl(y, 100), we can write code that reads sampledPatients <- takeSample(patients, sampleSize = 100). Try to resist the urge to abbreviate. Modern languages have no limits on the length of variable and function names.

- **Reuse**: One advantage of writing clear, well encapsulated functions is that they can often be reused. This not only saves time, it also means there will be less code, so less complexity and fewer opportunities for errors.

17.1.3 Code Validation

Several approaches exist to verify the validity of software code, but two are especially relevant for code implementing an observational study:

- **Code review**: One person writes the code, and another person reviews the code.
- **Double coding**: Two persons both independently write the analysis code, and afterwards the results of the two scripts are compared.

Code review has the advantage that it is usually less work, but the disadvantage is that the reviewer might miss some errors. Double coding on the other hand is usually very labor intensive, but it is less likely, although not impossible, that errors are missed. Another disadvantage of double coding is that two separate implementations *almost always* produce different results, due to the many minor arbitrary choices that need to made (e.g. should "until exposure end" be interpreted as including the exposure end date, or not?). As a consequence, the two supposedly independent programmers often need to work together to align their analyses, thus breaking their independence.

Other software validation practices such as unit testing are less relevant here because a study is typically a one-time activity with highly complex relationships between input (the data in CDM) and outputs (the study results), making these practices less usable. Note that these practices are applied in the Methods Library.

17.1.4 Using the Methods Library

The OHDSI Methods Library provides a large set of functions, allowing most observational studies to be implemented using only a few lines of code. Using the Methods Library therefore shifts most of the burden of establishing the validity of one's study code to the Library. Validity of the Methods Library is ensured by its software development process and by extensive testing.

17.2 Methods Library Software Development Process

The OHDSI Methods Library is developed by the OHDSI community. Proposed changes to the Library are discussed in two venues: The GitHub issue trackers (for example the CohortMethod issue tracker[1]) and the OHDSI Forums.[2] Both are open to the public. Any

---

[1]https://github.com/OHDSI/CohortMethod/issues

[2]http://forums.ohdsi.org/

member of the community can contribute software code to the Library, however, final approval of any changes incorporated in the released versions of the software is performed by the OHDSI Population-Level Estimation Workgroup leadership (Drs. Marc Suchard and Martijn Schuemie) and OHDSI Patient-Level Prediction Workgroup leadership (Drs. Peter Rijnbeek and Jenna Reps) only.

Users can install the Methods Library in R directly from the master branches in the GitHub repositories, or through a system known as "drat" that is always up-to-date with the master branches. A number of the Methods Library packages are available through R's Comprehensive R Archive Network (CRAN), and this number is expected to increase over time.

Reasonable software development and testing methodologies are employed by OHDSI to maximize the accuracy, reliability and consistency of the Methods Library performance. Importantly, as the Methods Library is released under the terms of the Apache License V2, all source code underlying the Methods Library, whether it be in R, C++, SQL, or Java is available for peer review by all members of the OHDSI community, and the public in general. Thus, all the functionality embodied within the Methods Library is subject to continuous critique and improvement relative to its accuracy, reliability and consistency.

17.2.1 Source Code Management

All of the Methods Library's source code is managed in the source code version control system "git" publicly accessible via GitHub. The OHDSI Methods Library repositories are access-controlled. Anyone in the world can view the source code, and any member of the OHDSI community can submit changes through so-called pull requests. Only the OHDSI Population-Level Estimation Workgroup and Patient-Level Prediction Workgroup leadership can approve such requests, make changes to the master branches, and release new versions. Continuous logs of code changes are maintained within the GitHub repositories and reflect all aspects of changes in code and documentation. These commit logs are available for public review.

New versions are released by the OHDSI Population-Level Estimation Workgroup and Patient-Level Prediction Workgroup leadership as needed. A new release starts by pushing changes to a master branch with a package version number (as defined in the DESCRIPTION file inside the package) that is greater than the version number of the previous release. This automatically triggers checking and testing of the package. If all tests are passed, the new version is automatically tagged in the version control system and the package is automatically uploaded to the OHDSI drat repository. New versions are numbered using three-component version number:

- New **micro versions** (e.g. from 4.3.2 to 4.3.3) indicate bug fixes only. No new functionality, and forward and backward compatibility are guaranteed
- New **minor versions** (e.g. from 4.3.3 to 4.4.0) indicate added functionality. Only backward compatibility is guaranteed
- New **major versions** (e.g. from 4.4.0 to 5.0.0) indicate major revisions. No guarantees are made in terms of compatibility

17.2.2 Documentation

All packages in the Methods Library are documented through R's internal documentation framework. Each package has a package manual that describes every function available in the package. To promote alignment between the function documentation and the function implementation, the roxygen2 software is used to combine a function's documentation and source code in a single file. The package manual is available on demand through R's command line interface, as a PDF in the package repositories, and as a web page. In addition, many packages also have vignettes that highlight specific use cases of a package. All documentation can be viewed though the Methods Library website.[3]

All Method Library source code is available to end users. Feedback from the community is facilitated using GitHub's issue tracking system and the OHDSI forums.

17.2.3 Availability of Current and Historical Archive Versions

Current and historical versions of the Methods Library packages are available in two locations. First, the GitHub version control system contains the full development history of each package, and the state of a package at each point in time can be reconstructed and retrieved. Most importantly, each released version is tagged in GitHub. Second, the released R source packages are stored in the OHDSI GitHub drat repository.

17.2.4 Maintenance, Support and Retirement

Each current version of the Methods Library is actively supported by OHDSI with respect to bug reporting, fixes and patches. Issues can be reported through GitHub's issue tracking system, and through the OHDSI forums. Each package has a package manual, and zero, one or several vignettes. Online video tutorials are available, and in-person tutorials are provided from time to time.

17.2.5 Qualified Personnel

Members of the OHDSI community represent multiple statistical disciplines and are based at academic, not-for-profit and industry-affiliated institutions on multiple continents.

All leaders of the OHDSI Population-Level Estimation Workgroup and OHDSI Patient-Level Prediction Workgroup hold PhDs from accredited academic institutions and have published extensively in peer reviewed journals.

---

[3] https://ohdsi.github.io/MethodsLibrary/

17.2.6   Physical and Logical Security

The OHDSI Methods Library is hosted on the GitHub[4] system. GitHub's security measures are described at https://github.com/security. Usernames and passwords are required by all members of the OHDSI community to contribute modifications to the Methods Library, and only the Population-Level Estimation Workgroup and Patient-Level Prediction Workgroup leadership can make changes to the master branches. User accounts are limited in access based upon standard security policies and functional requirements.

17.2.7   Disaster Recovery

The OHDSI Methods Library is hosted on the GitHub system. GitHub's disaster recovery facilities are described at https://github.com/security.

17.3   Methods Library Testing

We distinguish between two types of tests performed on the Methods Library: Tests for individual functions in the packages (so-called "unit tests"), and tests for more complex functionality using simulations.

17.3.1   Unit Test

A large set of automated validation tests is maintained and upgraded by OHDSI to enable the testing of source code against known data and known results. Each test begins with specifying some simple input data, then executes a function in one of the packages on this input, and evaluates whether the output is exactly what would be expected. For simple functions, the expected result is often obvious (for example when performing propensity score matching on example data containing only a few subjects); for more complicated functions the expected result may be generated using combinations of other functions available in R (for example, Cyclops, our large-scale regression engine, is tested among others by comparing results on simple problems with other regression routines in R). We aim for these tests in total to cover 100% of the lines of executable source code.

These tests are automatically performed when changes are made to a package (specifically, when changes are pushed to the package repository). Any errors noted during testing automatically trigger emails to the leadership of the Workgroups, and must be resolved prior to release of a new version of a package. The source code and expected results for these tests are available for review and use in other applications as may be appropriate. These tests are also available to end users and/or system administrators and can be run as part of their installation process to provide further documentation and objective evidence as to the accuracy, reliability and consistency of their installation of the Methods Library.

---

[4]https://github.com/

17.3.2   Simulation

For more complex functionality it is not always obvious what the expected output should be given the input. In these cases simulations are sometimes used, generating input given a specific statistical model, and establishing whether the functionality produces results in line with this known model. For example, in the SelfControlledCaseSeries package simulations are used to verify that the method is able to detect and appropriately model temporal trends in simulated data.

17.4   Summary

- An observational study should be implemented as an automated script that executes the entire analysis, from data in the CDM to the results, to ensure reproducibility and transparency.

- Custom study code should adhere to best programming practices, including abstraction, encapsulation, clear naming, and code reuse.

- Custom study code can be validated using code review or double coding.

- The Methods Library provides validated functionality that can be used in observational studies.

- The Methods Library is validated by using a software development process aimed at creating valid software, and by testing.

Chapter 18

Method Validity

Chapter lead: Martijn Schuemie

When considering method validity we aim to answer the question

> Is this method valid for answering this question?

"Method" includes not only the study design, but also the data and the implementation of the design. Method validity is therefore somewhat of a catch-all; it is often not possible to observe good method validity without good data quality, clinical validity, and software validity. Those aspects of evidence quality should have already been addressed separately before we consider method validity.

The core activity when establishing method validity is evaluating whether important assumptions in the analysis have been met. For example, we assume that propensity-score matching makes two populations comparable, but we need to evaluate whether this is the case. Where possible, empirical tests should be performed to verify these assumptions. We can for example generate diagnostics to show that our two populations are indeed comparable on a wide range of characteristics after matching. In OHDSI we have developed many standardized diagnostics that should be generated and evaluated whenever an analysis is performed.

In this chapter we will focus on the validity of methods use in population-level estimation. We will first briefly highlight some study design-specific diagnostics, and will then discuss diagnostics that are applicable to most if not all population-level estimation studies. Following this is a step-by-step description of how to execute these diagnostics using the OHDSI tools. We close this chapter with an advanced topic, reviewing the OHDSI Methods Benchmark and its application to the OHDSI Methods Library.

18.1 Design-Specific Diagnostics

For each study design there are diagnostics specific to such a design. Many of these diagnostics are implemented and readily available in the R packages of the OHDSI Methods Library.

For example, Section 12.9 lists a wide range of diagnostics generated by the CohortMethod package, including:

- **Propensity score distribution** to asses initial comparability of cohorts.
- **Propensity model** to identify potential variables that should be excluded from the model.
- **Covariate balance** to evaluate whether propensity score adjustment has made the cohorts comparable (as measured through baseline covariates).
- **Attrition** to observe how many subjects were excluded in the various analysis steps, which may inform on the generalizability of the results to the initial cohorts of interest.
- **Power** to assess whether enough data is available to answer the question.
- **Kaplan Meier curve** to asses typical time to onset, and whether the proportionality assumption underlying Cox models is met.

Other study designs require different diagnostics to test the different assumptions in those designs. For example, for the self-controlled case series (SCCS) design we may check the necessary assumption that the end of observation is independent of the outcome. This assumption is often violated in the case of serious, potentially lethal, events such as myocardial infarction. We can evaluate whether the assumption holds by generating the plot shown in Figure 18.1, which shows histograms of the time to observation period end for those that are censored, and those that are uncensored. In our data we consider those whose observation period ends at the end date of data capture (the date when observation stopped for the entire data base, for example the date of extraction, or the study end date) to be uncensored, and all others to be censored. In Figure 18.1 we see only minor differences between the two distributions, suggesting our assumptions holds.

18.2   Diagnostics for All Estimation

Next to the design-specific diagnostics, there are also several diagnostics that are applicable across all causal effect estimation methods. Many of these rely on the use of control hypotheses, research questions where the answer is already known. Using control hypotheses we can then evaluate whether our design produces results in line with the truth. Controls can be divided into negative controls and positive controls.

18.2.1   Negative Controls

Negative controls are exposure-outcome pairs where one believes no causal effect exists, and it includes negative controls or "falsification endpoints" (Prasad and Jena, 2013) that have been recommended as a means to detect confounding, (Lipsitch et al., 2010) selection bias, and measurement error. (Arnold et al., 2016) For example, in one study (Zaadstra et al., 2008) investigating the relationship between childhood diseases and later multiple sclerosis (MS), the authors include three negative controls that are not believed to cause MS: a broken arm,

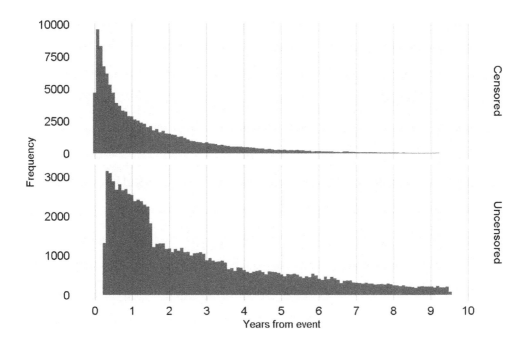

Figure 18.1: Time to observation end for those that are censored, and those that are uncensored.

concussion, and tonsillectomy. Two of these three controls produce statistically significant associations with MS, suggesting that the study may be biased.

We should select negative controls that are comparable to our hypothesis of interest, which means we typically select exposure-outcome pairs that either have the same exposure as the hypothesis of interest (so-called "outcome controls") or the same outcome ("exposure controls"). Our negative controls should further meet these criteria:

- The exposure **should not cause** the outcome. One way to think of causation is to think of the counterfactual: could the outcome be caused (or prevented) if a patient was not exposed, compared to if the patient had been exposed? Sometimes this is clear, for example ACEi are known to cause angioedema. Other times this is far less obvious. For example, a drug that may cause hypertension can therefore indirectly cause cardiovascular diseases that are a consequence of the hypertension.

- The exposure should also **not prevent or treat** the outcome. This is just another causal relationship that should be absent if we are to believe the true effect size (e.g. the hazard ratio) is 1.

- The negative control should **exist in the data**, ideally with sufficient numbers. We try to achieve this by prioritizing candidate negative controls based on prevalence.

- Negative controls should ideally be **independent**. For example, we should avoid having negative controls that are either ancestors of each other (e.g. "ingrown nail" and "ingrown nail of foot") or siblings (e.g. "fracture of left femur" and "fracture of right femur").

- Negative controls should ideally have **some potential for bias**. For example, the last digit of someone's social security number is basically a random number, and is unlikely to show confounding. It should therefore not be used as a negative control.

Some argue that negative controls should also have the same confounding structure as the exposure-outcome pair of interest. (Lipsitch et al., 2010) However, we believe this confounding structure is unknowable; the relationships between variables found in reality is often far more complex than people imagine. Also, even if the confounder structure was known, it is unlikely that a negative control exists having that exact same confounding structure, but lacking the direct causal effect. For this reason in OHDSI we rely on a large number of negative controls, assuming that such a set represents many different types of bias, including the ones present in the hypothesis of interest.

The absence of a causal relationship between an exposure and an outcome is rarely documented. Instead, we often make the assumption that a lack of evidence of a relationship implies the lack of a relationship. This assumption is more likely to hold if the exposure and outcome have both been studied extensively, so a relationship could have been detected. For example, the lack of evidence for a completely novel drug likely implies a lack of knowledge, not the lack of a relationship. With this principle in mind we have developed a semi-automated procedure for selecting negative controls. (Voss et al., 2016) In brief, information from literature, product labels, and spontaneous reporting is automatically extracted and synthesized to produce a candidate list of negative controls. This list must then undergo manual review, not only to verify that the automated extraction was accurate, but also to impose additional criteria such as biological plausibility.

18.2.2   Positive Controls

To understand the behavior of a method when the true relative risk is smaller or greater than one requires the use of positive controls where the null is believed to not be true. Unfortunately, real positive controls for observational research tend to be problematic for three reasons. First, in most research contexts, for example when comparing the effect of two treatments, there is a paucity of positive controls relevant for that specific context. Second, even if positive controls are available, the magnitude of the effect size may not be known with great accuracy, and often depends on the population in which one measures it. Third, when treatments are widely known to cause a particular outcome, this shapes the behavior of physicians prescribing the treatment, for example by taking actions to mitigate the risk of unwanted outcomes, thereby rendering the positive controls useless as a means for evaluation. (Noren et al., 2014)

In OHDSI we therefore use synthetic positive controls, (Schuemie et al., 2018a) created by modifying a negative control through injection of additional, simulated occurrences of the outcome during the time at risk of the exposure. For example, assume that, during exposure to ACEi, n occurrences of our negative control outcome "ingrowing nail" were observed. If we now add an additional n simulated occurrences during exposure, we have doubled the risk. Since this was a negative control, the relative risk compared to the counterfactual was one, but after injection, it becomes two.

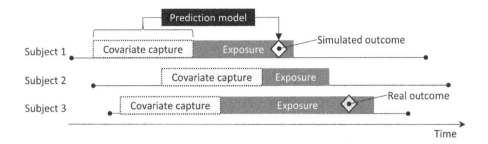

Figure 18.2: Synthesizing positive controls from negative controls.

One issue that stands important is the preservation of confounding. The negative controls may show strong confounding, but if we inject additional outcomes randomly, these new outcomes will not be confounded, and we may therefore be optimistic in our evaluation of our capacity to deal with confounding for positive controls. To preserve confounding, we want the new outcomes to show similar associations with baseline subject-specific covariates as the original outcomes. To achieve this, for each outcome we train a model to predict the survival rate with respect to the outcome during exposure using covariates captured prior to exposure. These covariates include demographics, as well as all recorded diagnoses, drug exposures, measurements, and medical procedures. An L1-regularized Poisson regression (Suchard et al., 2013) using 10-fold cross-validation to select the regularization hyperparameter fits the prediction model. We then use the predicted rates to sample simulated outcomes during exposure to increase the true effect size to the desired magnitude. The resulting positive control thus contains both real and simulated outcomes.

Figure 18.2 depicts this process. Note that although this procedure simulates several important sources of bias, it does not capture all. For example, some effects of measurement error are not present. The synthetic positive controls imply constant positive predictive value and sensitivity, which may not be true in reality.

Although we refer to a single true "effect size" for each control, different methods estimate different statistics of the treatment effect. For negative controls, where we believe no causal effect exists, all such statistics, including the relative risk, hazard ratio, odds ratio, incidence rate ratio, both conditional and marginal, as well as the average treatment effect in the treated (ATT) and the overall average treatment effect (ATE) will be identical to 1. Our process for creating positive controls synthesizes outcomes with a constant incidence rate ratio over time and between patients, using a model conditioned on the patient where this ratio is held constant, up to the point where the marginal effect is achieved. The true effect size is thus guaranteed to hold as the marginal incidence rate ratio in the treated. Under the assumption that our outcome model used during synthesis is correct, this also holds for the conditional effect size and the ATE. Since all outcomes are rare, odds ratios are all but identical to the relative risk.

18.2.3 Empirical Evaluation

Based on the estimates of a particular method for the negative and positive controls, we can then understand the operating characteristics by computing a range of metrics, for example:

- **Area Under the receiver operator Curve (AUC)**: the ability to discriminate between positive and negative controls.
- **Coverage**: how often the true effect size is within the 95% confidence interval.
- **Mean precision**: precision is computed as $1/(standard\ error)^2$, higher precision means narrower confidence intervals. We use the geometric mean to account for the skewed distribution of the precision.
- **Mean squared error (MSE)**: Mean squared error between the log of the effect size point-estimate and the log of the true effect size.
- **Type 1 error**: For negative controls, how often was the null rejected (at $\alpha = 0.05$). This is equivalent to the false positive rate and $1 - specificity$.
- **Type 2 error**: For positive controls, how often was the null not rejected (at $\alpha = 0.05$). This is equivalent to the false negative rate and $1 - sensitivity$.
- **Non-estimable**: For how many of the controls was the method unable to produce an estimate? There can be various reasons why an estimate cannot be produced, for example because there were no subjects left after propensity score matching, or because no subjects remained having the outcome.

Depending on our use case, we can evaluate whether these operating characteristics are suitable for our goal. For example, if we wish to perform signal detection, we may care about type 1 and type 2 error, or if we are willing to modify our α threshold, we may inspect the AUC instead.

18.2.4 P-Value Calibration

Often the type 1 error (at $\alpha = 0.05$) is larger than 5%. In other words, we are often more likely than 5% to reject the null hypothesis when in fact the null hypothesis is true. The reason is that the p-value only reflects random error, the error due to having a limited sample size. It does not reflect systematic error, for example the error due to confounding. OHDSI has developed a process for calibrating p-values to restore the type 1 error to nominal. (Schuemie et al., 2014) We derive an empirical null distribution from the actual effect estimates for the negative controls. These negative control estimates give us an indication of what can be expected when the null hypothesis is true, and we use them to estimate an empirical null distribution.

Formally, we fit a Gaussian probability distribution to the estimates, taking into account the sampling error of each estimate. Let $\hat{\theta}_i$ denote the estimated log effect estimate (relative risk, odds or incidence rate ratio) from the ith negative control drug–outcome pair, and let $\hat{\tau}_i$ denote the corresponding estimated standard error, $i = 1, \ldots, n$. Let θ_i denote the true log effect size (assumed 0 for negative controls), and let β_i denote the true (but unknown) bias associated with pair i , that is, the difference between the log of the true effect size and the log of the estimate that the study would have returned for control i had it been infinitely large. As in the standard p-value computation, we assume that $\hat{\theta}_i$ is normally distributed with mean $\theta_i + \beta_i$ and standard deviation $\hat{\tau}_i^2$. Note that in traditional p-value calculation, β_i is always assumed to be equal to zero, but that we assume the β_i's, arise from a normal distribution with mean μ and variance σ^2. This represents the null (bias) distribution. We estimate μ and σ^2 via maximum likelihood. In summary, we assume the following:

$$\beta_i \sim N(\mu, \sigma^2) \text{ and } \hat{\theta}_i \sim N(\theta_i + \beta_i, \tau_i^2)$$

where $N(a, b)$ denotes a Gaussian distribution with mean a and variance b, and estimate μ and σ^2 by maximizing the following likelihood:

$$L(\mu, \sigma | \theta, \tau) \propto \prod_{i=1}^{n} \int p(\hat{\theta}_i | \beta_i, \theta_i, \hat{\tau}_i) p(\beta_i | \mu, \sigma) \mathrm{d}\beta_i$$

yielding maximum likelihood estimates $\hat{\mu}$ and $\hat{\sigma}$. We compute a calibrated p-value that uses the empirical null distribution. Let $\hat{\theta}_{n+1}$ denote the log of the effect estimate from a new drug–outcome pair, and let $\hat{\tau}_{n+1}$ denote the corresponding estimated standard error. From the aforementioned assumptions and assuming β_{n+1} arises from the same null distribution, we have the following:

$$\hat{\theta}_{n+1} \sim N(\hat{\mu}, \hat{\sigma} + \hat{\tau}_{n+1})$$

When $\hat{\theta}_{n+1}$ is smaller than $\hat{\mu}$, the one-sided calibrated p-value for the new pair is then

$$\phi\left(\frac{\theta_{n+1} - \hat{\mu}}{\sqrt{\hat{\sigma}^2 + \hat{\tau}_{n+1}^2}}\right)$$

where $\phi(\cdot)$ denotes the cumulative distribution function of the standard normal distribution. When $\hat{\theta}_{n+1}$ is bigger than $\hat{\mu}$, the one-sided calibrated p-value is then

$$1 - \phi\left(\frac{\theta_{n+1} - \hat{\mu}}{\sqrt{\hat{\sigma}^2 + \hat{\tau}_{n+1}^2}}\right)$$

18.2.5 Confidence Interval Calibration

Similarly, we typically observe that the coverage of the 95% confidence interval is less than 95%: the true effect size is inside the 95% confidence interval less than 95% of the time. For confidence interval calibration (Schuemie et al., 2018a) we extend the framework for p-value calibration by also making use of our positive controls. Typically, but not necessarily, the calibrated confidence interval is wider than the nominal confidence interval, reflecting the problems unaccounted for in the standard procedure (such as unmeasured confounding, selection bias and measurement error) but accounted for in the calibration.

Formally, we assume that $beta_i$, the bias associated with pair i, again comes from a Gaussian distribution, but this time using a mean and standard deviation that are linearly related to $theta_i$, the true effect size:

$$\beta_i \sim N(\mu(\theta_i), \sigma^2(\theta_i))$$

where

$$\mu(\theta_i) = a + b \times \theta_i \text{ and } \sigma(\theta_i)^2 = c + d \times \mid \theta_i \mid$$

We estimate a, b, c and d by maximizing the marginalized likelihood in which we integrate out the unobserved β_i:

$$l(a, b, c, d | \theta, \hat{\theta}, \hat{\tau}) \propto \prod_{i=1}^{n} \int p(\hat{\theta}_i | \beta_i, \theta_i, \hat{\tau}_i) p(\beta_i | a, b, c, d, \theta_i) \mathrm{d}\beta_i,$$

yielding maximum likelihood estimates $(\hat{a}, \hat{b}, \hat{c}, \hat{d})$.

We compute a calibrated CI that uses the systematic error model. Let $\hat{\theta}_{n+1}$ again denote the log of the effect estimate for a new outcome of interest, and let $\hat{\tau}_{n+1}$ denote the corresponding estimated standard error. From the assumptions above, and assuming β_{n+1} arises from the same systematic error model, we have:

$$\hat{\theta}_{n+1} \sim N(\theta_{n+1} + \hat{a} + \hat{b} \times \theta_{n+1}, \hat{c} + \hat{d} \times \mid \theta_{n+1} \mid) + \hat{\tau}_{n+1}^2).$$

We find the lower bound of the calibrated 95% CI by solving this equation for θ_{n+1}:

$$\Phi \left(\frac{\theta_{n+1} + \hat{a} + \hat{b} \times \theta_{n+1} - \hat{\theta}_{n+1}}{\sqrt{(\hat{c} + \hat{d} \times \mid \theta_{n+1} \mid) + \hat{\tau}_{n+1}^2}} \right) = 0.025,$$

where $\Phi(\cdot)$ denotes the cumulative distribution function of the standard normal distribution. We find the upper bound similarly for probability 0.975. We define the calibrated point estimate by using probability 0.5.

Both p-value calibration and confidence interval calibration are implemented in the EmpiricalCalibration package.

18.2.6   Replication Across Sites

Another form of method validation comes from executing the study across several different databases that represent different populations, different health care systems, and/or different data capture processes. Prior research has shown that executing the same study design across different databases can produce vastly different effect size estimates, (Madigan et al., 2013b) suggesting that either the effect differs greatly for different populations, or that the design does not adequately address the different biases found in the different databases. In fact, we observe that accounting for residual bias in a database through empirical calibration of confidence intervals can greatly reduce between-study heterogeneity. (Schuemie et al., 2018a)

One way to express between-database heterogeneity is the I^2 score, describing the percentage of total variation across studies that is due to heterogeneity rather than chance. (Higgins et al., 2003) A naive categorization of values for I^2 would not be appropriate for all circumstances, although one could tentatively assign adjectives of low, moderate, and high to I^2 values of 25%, 50%, and 75%. In a study estimating the effects for many depression treatments using a new-user cohort design with large-scale propensity score adjustment, (Schuemie et al., 2018b) observed only 58% of the estimates to have an I^2 below 25%. After empirical calibration this increased to 83%.

 Observing between-database heterogeneity casts doubt on the validity of the estimates. Unfortunately, the inverse is not true. Not observing heterogeneity does not guarantee an unbiased estimate. It is not unlikely that all databases share a similar bias, and that all estimates are therefore consistently wrong.

18.2.7   Sensitivity Analyses

When designing a study there are often design choices that are uncertain. For example, should propensity score matching of stratification be used? If stratification is used, how many strata? What is the appropriate time-at-risk? When faced with such uncertainty, one solution is to evaluate various options, and observe the sensitivity of the results to the design choice. If the estimate remains the same under various options, we can say the study is robust to the uncertainty.

This definition of sensitivity analysis should not be confused with the definitions used by others such as, Rosenbaum (2005) who defines sensitivity analysis to "appraise how the conclusions of a study might be altered by hidden biases of various magnitudes."

18.3   Method Validation in Practice

Here we build on the example in Chapter 12, where we investigate the effect of ACE inhibitors (ACEi) on the risk of angioedema and acute myocardial infarction (AMI), compared

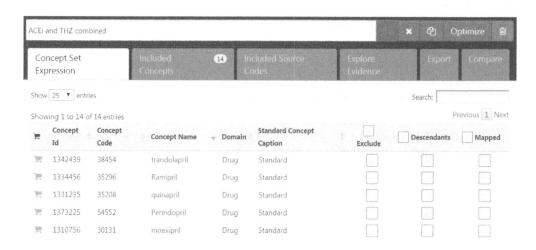

Figure 18.3: A concept set containing the concepts defining the target and comparator exposures.

to thiazides and thiazide-like diuretics (THZ). In that chapter we already explore many of the diagnostics specific to the design we used, the cohort method. Here, we apply additional diagnostics that could also have been applied had other designs been used. If the study is implemented using ATLAS as described in Section 12.7 these diagnostics are available in the Shiny app that is included in the study R package generated by ATLAS. If the study is implemented using R instead, as described in Section 12.8, then R functions available in the various packages should be used, as described in the next sections.

18.3.1   Selecting Negative Controls

We must select negative controls, exposure-outcome pairs where no causal effect is believed to exist. For comparative effect estimation such as our example study, we select negative control outcomes that are believed to be neither caused by the target nor the comparator exposure. We want enough negative controls to make sure we have a diverse mix of biases represented in the controls, and also to allow empirical calibration. As a rule-of-thumb we typically aim to have 50-100 such negative controls. We could come up with these controls completely manually, but fortunately ATLAS provides features to aid the selection of negative controls using data from literature, product labels, and spontaneous reports.

To generate a candidate list of negative controls, we first must create a concept set containing all exposures of interest. In this case we select all ingredients in the ACEi and THZ classes, as shown in Figure 18.3.

Next, we go to the "Explore Evidence" tab, and click on the ▶ Generate button. Generating the evidence overview will take a few minutes, after which you can click on the 👁 View Evidence button. This will open the list of outcomes as shown in Figure 18.4.

This list shows condition concepts, along with an overview of the evidence linking the con-

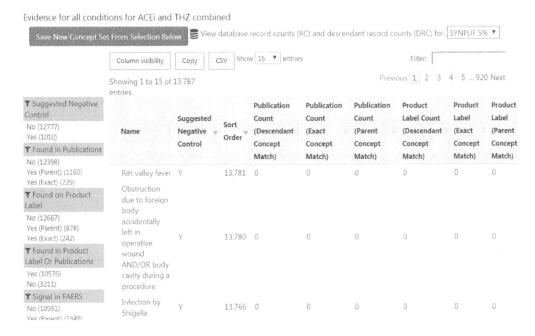

Figure 18.4: Candidate control outcomes with an overview of the evidence found in literature, product labels, and spontaneous reports.

dition to any of the exposures we defined. For example, we see the number of publications that link the exposures to the outcomes found in PubMed using various strategies, the number of product labels of our exposures of interest that list the condition as a possible adverse effect, and the number of spontaneous reports. By default the list is sorted to show candidate negative controls first. It is then sorted by the "Sort Order," which represents the prevalence of the condition in a collection of observational databases. The higher the Sort Order, the higher the prevalence. Although the prevalence in these databases might not correspond with the prevalence in the database we wish to run the study, it is likely a good approximation.

The next step is to manually review the candidate list, typically starting at the top, so with the most prevalent condition, and working our way down until we are satisfied we have enough. One typical way to do this is to export the list to a CSV (comma separated values) file, and have clinicians review these, considering the criteria mentioned in Section 18.2.1.

For our example study we select the 76 negative controls listed in Appendix C.1.

18.3.2 Including Controls

Once we have defined our set of negative controls we must include them in our study. First we must define some logic for turning our negative control condition concepts into outcome cohorts. Section 12.7.3 discusses how ATLAS allows creating such cohorts based on a few choices the user must make. Often we simply choose to create a cohort based on any occurrence of a negative control concept or any of its descendants. If the study is implemented in R, then SQL (Structured Query Language) can be used to construct the negative control cohorts. Chapter 9 describes how cohorts can be created using SQL and R. We leave it as an exercise for the reader to write the appropriate SQL and R.

The OHDSI tools also provide functionality for automatically generating and including positive controls derived from the negative controls. This functionality can be found in the Evaluation Settings section in ATLAS described in Section 12.7.3, and it is implemented in the synthesizePositiveControls function in the MethodEvaluation package. Here we generate three positive controls for each negative control, with true effect sizes of 1.5, 2, and 4, using a survival model:

```
library(MethodEvaluation)
# Create a data frame with all negative control exposure-
# outcome pairs, using only the target exposure (ACEi = 1).
eoPairs <- data.frame(exposureId = 1,
                      outcomeId = ncs)

pcs <- synthesizePositiveControls(
  connectionDetails = connectionDetails,
  cdmDatabaseSchema = cdmDbSchema,
  exposureDatabaseSchema = cohortDbSchema,
  exposureTable = cohortTable,
  outcomeDatabaseSchema = cohortDbSchema,
  outcomeTable = cohortTable,
  outputDatabaseSchema = cohortDbSchema,
  outputTable = cohortTable,
  createOutputTable = FALSE,
  modelType = "survival",
  firstExposureOnly = TRUE,
  firstOutcomeOnly = TRUE,
  removePeopleWithPriorOutcomes = TRUE,
  washoutPeriod = 365,
  riskWindowStart = 1,
  riskWindowEnd = 0,
  endAnchor = "cohort end",
  exposureOutcomePairs = eoPairs,
  effectSizes = c(1.5, 2, 4),
  cdmVersion = cdmVersion,
  workFolder = file.path(outputFolder, "pcSynthesis"))
```

Note that we must mimic the time-at-risk settings used in our estimation study design. The synthesizePositiveControls function will extract information about the exposures and negative control outcomes, fit outcome models per exposure-outcome pair, and synthesize outcomes. The positive control outcome cohorts will be added to the cohort table specified by cohortDbSchema and cohortTable. The resulting pcs data frame contains the information on the synthesized positive controls.

Next we must execute the same study used to estimate the effect of interest to also esti-

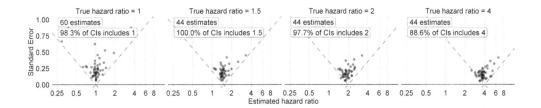

Figure 18.5: Estimates for the negative (true hazard ratio = 1) and positive controls (true hazard ratio > 1). Each dot represents a control. Estimates below the dashed line have a confidence interval that doesn't include the true effect size.

mate effects for the negative and positive controls. Setting the set of negative controls in the comparisons dialog in ATLAS instructs ATLAS to compute estimates for these controls. Similarly, specifying that positive controls be generated in the Evaluation Settings includes these in our analysis. In R, the negative and positive controls should be treated as any other outcome. All estimation packages in the OHDSI Methods Library readily allow estimation of many effects in an efficient manner.

18.3.3 Empirical Performance

Figure 18.5 shows the estimated effect sizes for the negative and positive controls included in our example study, stratified by true effect size. This plot is included in the Shiny app that comes with the study R package generated by ATLAS, and can be generated using the plotControls function in the MethodEvaluation package. Note that the number of controls is often lower than what was defined because there was not enough data to either produce an estimate or to synthesize a positive control.

Based on these estimates we can compute the metrics shown in Table 18.1 using the computeMetrics function in the MethodEvaluation package.

Table 18.1: Method performance metrics derived from the negative and positive control estimates.

Metric	Value
AUC	0.96
Coverage	0.97
Mean Precision	19.33
MSE	2.08
Type 1 error	0.00
Type 2 error	0.18
Non-estimable	0.08

We see that coverage and type 1 error are very close to their nominal values of 95% and 5%, respectively, and that the AUC is very high. This is certainly not always the case.

Note that although in Figure 18.5 not all confidence intervals include one when the true hazard ratio is one, the type 1 error in Table 18.1 is 0%. This is an exceptional situation, caused by the fact that confidence intervals in the Cyclops package are estimated using likelihood profiling, which is more accurate than traditional methods but can result in asymmetric confidence intervals. The p-value instead is computed assuming symmetrical confidence intervals, and this is what was used to compute the type 1 error.

18.3.4   P-Value Calibration

We can use the estimates for our negative controls to calibrate our p-values. This is done automatically in the Shiny app, and can be done manually in R. Assuming we have created the summary object summ as described in Section 12.8.6, we can plot the empirical calibration effect plot:

```
# Estimates for negative controls (ncs) and outcomes of interest (ois):
ncEstimates <- summ[summ$outcomeId %in% ncs, ]
oiEstimates <- summ[summ$outcomeId %in% ois, ]

library(EmpiricalCalibration)
plotCalibrationEffect(logRrNegatives = ncEstimates$logRr,
                      seLogRrNegatives = ncEstimates$seLogRr,
                      logRrPositives = oiEstimates$logRr,
                      seLogRrPositives = oiEstimates$seLogRr,
                      showCis = TRUE)
```

In Figure 18.6 we see that the shaded area almost exactly overlaps with the area denoted by the dashed lines, indicating hardly any bias was observed for the negative controls. One of the outcomes of interest (AMI) is above the dashed line and the shaded area, indicating we cannot reject the null according to both the uncalibrated and calibrated p-value. The other outcome (angioedema) clearly stands out from the negative control, and falls well within the area where both uncalibrated and calibrated p-values are smaller than 0.05.

We can compute the calibrated p-values:

```
null <- fitNull(logRr = ncEstimates$logRr,
                seLogRr = ncEstimates$seLogRr)
calibrateP(null,
           logRr= oiEstimates$logRr,
           seLogRr = oiEstimates$seLogRr)
```

```
## [1]  1.604351e-06  7.159506e-01
```

And contrast these with the uncalibrated p-values:

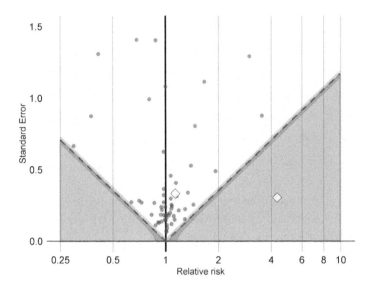

Figure 18.6: P-value calibration: estimates below the dashed line have a conventional p < 0.05. Estimates in the shaded area have calibrated p < 0.05. The narrow band around the edge of the shaded area denotes the 95% credible interval. Dots indicate negative controls. Diamonds indicate outcomes of interest.

```
oiEstimates$p
```

```
## [1] [1] 1.483652e-06 7.052822e-01
```

As expected, because little to no bias was observed, the uncalibrated and calibrated p-values are very similar.

18.3.5 Confidence Interval Calibration

Similarly, we can use the estimates for our negative and positive controls to calibrate the confidence intervals. The Shiny app automatically reports the calibrate confidence intervals. In R we can calibrate intervals using the `fitSystematicErrorModel` and `calibrateConfidenceInterval` functions in the EmpiricalCalibration package, as described in detail in the "Empirical calibration of confidence intervals" vignette.

Before calibration, the estimated hazard ratios (95% confidence interval) are 4.32 (2.45 - 8.08) and 1.13 (0.59 - 2.18), for angioedema and AMI respectively. The calibrated hazard ratios are 4.75 (2.52 - 9.04) and 1.15 (0.58 - 2.30).

Source	Hazard ratio (95% CI)
CCAE	2.22 (1.72-2.88)
MDCD	4.32 (2.45-8.08)
MDCR	2.00 (1.02-4.14)
Optum	2.45 (1.76-3.46)
Panther	3.51 (2.34-5.40)
Summary (I^2 = 0.42)	2.69 (2.11-3.43)

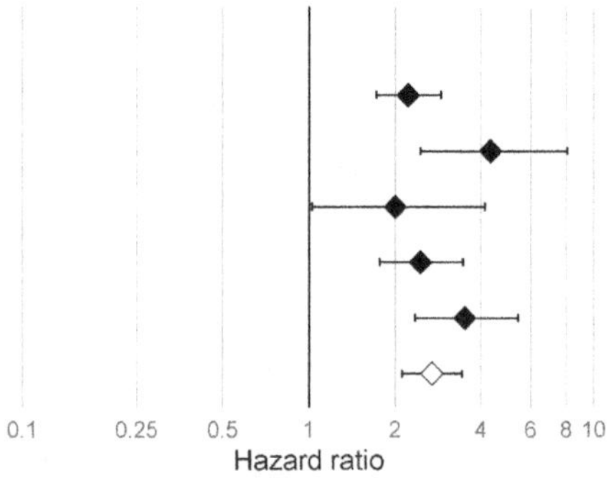

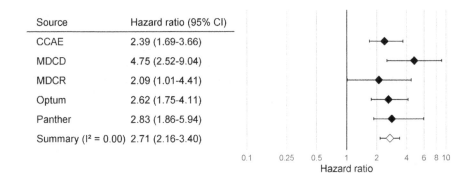

Figure 18.7: Effect size estimates and 95% confidence intervals (CI) from five different databases and a meta-analytic estimate when comparing ACE inhibitors to thiazides and thiazide-like diuretics for the risk of angioedema.

Source	Hazard ratio (95% CI)
CCAE	2.39 (1.69-3.66)
MDCD	4.75 (2.52-9.04)
MDCR	2.09 (1.01-4.41)
Optum	2.62 (1.75-4.11)
Panther	2.83 (1.86-5.94)
Summary (I^2 = 0.00)	2.71 (2.16-3.40)

Figure 18.8: Calibrated Effect size estimates and 95% confidence intervals (CI) from five different databases and a meta-analytic estimate for the hazard ratio of angioedema when comparing ACE inhibitors to thiazides and thiazide-like diuretics.

18.3.6 Between-Database Heterogeneity

Just as we executed our analysis on one database, in this case the IBM MarketScan Medicaid (MDCD) database, we can also run the same analysis code on other databases that adhere to the Common Data Model (CDM). Figure 18.7 shows the forest plot and meta-analytic estimates (assuming random effects) (DerSimonian and Laird, 1986) across a total of five databases for the outcome of angioedema. This figure was generated using the `plotMetaAnalysisForest` function in the EvidenceSynthesis package.

Although all confidence intervals are above one, suggesting agreement on the fact that there is an effect, the I^2 suggests between-database heterogeneity. However, if we compute the I^2 using the calibrated confidence intervals as shown in Figure 18.8, we see that this heterogeneity can be explained by the bias measured in each database through the negative and positive controls. The empirical calibration appears to properly take this bias into account.

18.3.7 Sensitivity Analyses

One of the design choices in our analysis was to use variable-ratio matching on the propensity score. However, we could have also used stratification on the propensity score. Because we are uncertain about this choice, we may decide to use both. Table 18.2 shows the effect size estimates for AMI and angioedema, both calibrated and uncalibrated, when using variable-ratio matching and stratification (with 10 equally-sized strata).

Table 18.2: Uncalibrated and calibrated hazard ratios (95% confidence interval) for the two analysis variants.

Outcome	Adjustment	Uncalibrated	Calibrated
Angioedema	Matching	4.32 (2.45 - 8.08)	4.75 (2.52 - 9.04)
Angioedema	Stratification	4.57 (3.00 - 7.19)	4.52 (2.85 - 7.19)
Acute myocardial infarction	Matching	1.13 (0.59 - 2.18)	1.15 (0.58 - 2.30)
Acute myocardial infarction	Stratification	1.43 (1.02 - 2.06)	1.45 (1.03 - 2.06)

We see that the estimates from the matched and stratified analysis are in strong agreement, with the confidence intervals for stratification falling completely inside of the confidence intervals for matching. This suggests that our uncertainty around this design choice does not impact the validity of our estimates. Stratification does appear to give us more power (narrower confidence intervals), which is not surprising since matching results in loss of data, whereas stratification does not. The price for this could be an increase in bias, due to within-strata residual confounding, although we see no evidence of increased bias reflected in the calibrated confidence intervals.

 Study diagnostics allow us to evaluate design choices even before fully executing a study. It is recommended not to finalize the protocol before generating and reviewing all study diagnostics. To avoid p-hacking (adjusting the design to achieve a desired result), this should be done while blinded to the effect size estimate of interest.

18.4 OHDSI Methods Benchmark

Although the recommended practice is to empirically evaluate a method's performance within the context that it is applied, using negative and positive controls that are in ways similar to the exposures-outcomes pairs of interest (for example using the same exposure or the same outcome) and on the database used in the study, there is also value in evaluating a method's performance in general. This is why the OHDSI Methods Evaluation Benchmark was developed. The benchmark evaluates performance using a wide range of control questions, including those with chronic or acute outcomes, and long-term or short-term exposures. The results on this benchmark can help demonstrate the overall usefulness of a method, and can be used to form a prior belief about the performance of a method when a context-specific empirical evaluation is not (yet) available. The benchmark consists of 200 carefully selected negative controls that can be stratified into eight categories, with the controls in each category either sharing the same exposure or the same outcome. From these 200 negative controls, 600 synthetic positive controls are derived as described in Section 18.2.2. To evaluate a method, it must be used to produce effect size estimates for all controls, after which the metrics described in Section 18.2.3 can be computed. The benchmark is publicly available, and can be deployed as described in the Running the OHDSI Methods Benchmark vignette in the MethodEvaluation package.

We have run all the methods in the OHDSI Methods Library through this benchmark, with various analysis choices per method. For example, the cohort method was evaluated using propensity score matching, stratification, and weighting. This experiment was executed on four large observational healthcare databases. The results, viewable in an online Shiny app[1], show that although several methods show high AUC (the ability to distinguish positive controls from negative controls), most methods in most settings demonstrate high type 1 error and low coverage of the 95% confidence interval, as shown in Figure 18.9.

This emphasizes the need for empirical evaluation and calibration: if no empirical evaluation is performed, which is true for almost all published observational studies, we must assume a prior informed by the results in Figure 18.9, and conclude that it is likely that the true effect size is not contained in the 95% confidence interval!

Our evaluation of the designs in the Methods Library also shows that empirical calibration restores type 1 error and coverage to their nominal values, although often at the cost of increasing type 2 error and decreasing precision.

18.5   Summary

- A method's validity depends on whether the assumptions underlying the method are met.

- Where possible, these assumptions should be empirically tested using study diagnostics.

- Control hypotheses, questions where the answer is known, should be used to evaluate whether a specific study design produces answers in line with the truth.

- Often, p-values and confidence intervals do not demonstrate nominal characteristics as measured using control hypotheses.

- These characteristics can often be restored to nominal using empirical calibration.

---

[1]http://data.ohdsi.org/MethodEvalViewer/

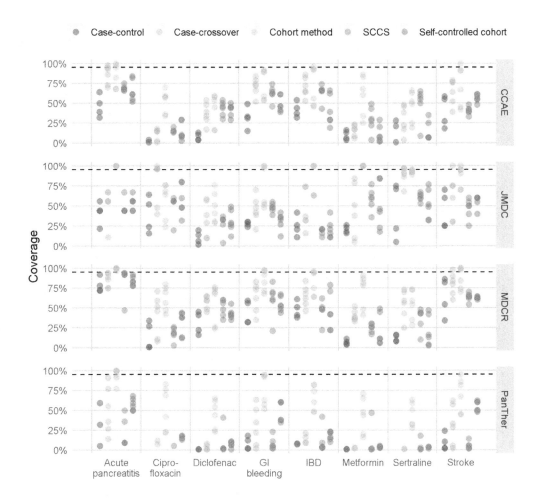

Figure 18.9: Coverage of the 95% confidence interval for the methods in the Methods Library. Each dot represents the performance of a specific set of analysis choices. The dashed line indicates nominal performance (95% coverage). SCCS = Self-Controlled Case Series, GI = Gastrointestinal, IBD = inflammatory bowel disease.

- – Study diagnostics can be used to guide analytic design choices and adapt the protocol, as long as the researcher remains blinded to the effect of interest to avoid p-hacking.

Part V

OHDSI Studies

Chapter 19

Study steps

Chapter leads: Sara Dempster & Martijn Schuemie

Here we aim to provide a general step-by-step guide to the design and implementation of an observational study with the OHDSI tools. We will break out each stage of the study process and then describe steps generically and in some cases discuss specific aspects of the main study types (1) characterization, (2) population level estimation (PLE), and (3) patient level prediction (PLP) described in earlier chapters of the Book of OHDSI. To do so, we will synthesize many elements discussed in the previous chapters in a way that is accessible for the beginner. At the same time, this chapter can stand alone for a reader who wants practical high-level explanations with options to pursue more in-depth materials in other chapters as needed. Finally, we will illustrate throughout with a few key examples.

In addition, we will summarize guidelines and best practices for observational studies as recommended by the OHDSI community. Some principles that we will discuss are generic and shared with best practice recommendations found in many other guidelines for observational research while other recommended processes are more specific to the OHDSI framework. We will therefore highlight where OHDSI-specific approaches are enabled by the OHDSI tool stack.

Throughout the chapter, we assume that an infrastructure of OHDSI tools, R and SQL are available to the reader and therefore we do not discuss any aspects of setting up this infrastructure in this chapter (see Chapters 8 and 9 for guidance). We also assume our reader is interested in running a study primarily on data at their own site using a database in OMOP CDM (for OMOP ETL, see Chapter 6). However, we emphasize that once a study package is prepared as discussed below, it can in principle be distributed and executed at other sites. Additional considerations specific to running OHDSI network studies, including organizational and technical details, are discussed in detail in Chapter 20.

19.1   General Best Practice Guidelines

19.1.1   Observational Study Definition

An observational study is a study where, by definition, patients are simply observed and no attempt is made to intervene in the treatment of specific patients. Sometimes, observational data are collected for a specific purpose as in a registry study, but in many cases, these data are collected for some purpose other than the specific study question at hand. Common examples of the latter type of data are Electronic Health Records (EHRs) or administrative claims data. Observational studies are often referred to as secondary use of data. A fundamental guiding principle for performing any observational study is to explicitly describe one's research question and fully specify the approach in advance of executing a study. In this regard, an observational study should be no different than a clinical trial, except that in a clinical trial, patients are recruited and followed in time for the primary purpose of answering a specific question, usually about the efficacy and/or safety of a therapeutic intervention. There are many ways in which the analysis methods employed in observational studies are different than those used in clinical trials. Most notably, the lack of randomization in PLE observational studies requires approaches to control confounding if the goal is to draw causal inferences (see Chapters 12 and 18 for detailed discussion of OHDSI-supported study designs and methods for PLE such as methods to remove observed confounding by balancing populations across many characteristics).

19.1.2   Pre-Specification of Study Design

Pre-specification of an observational study design and parameters is critical to avoid introducing further bias by subconsciously or consciously evolving one's approach to achieve a desired result, sometimes referred to as p-hacking. The temptation not to fully specify the study details in advance is greater with secondary use of data than primary use because these data, such as EHR and claims, sometimes give the researcher a sense of infinite possibilities, leading to a meandering line of inquiry. The key then is to still impose the rigorous structure of scientific inquiry despite the apparent easy availability of pre-existing data. The principle of pre-specification is especially important in PLE or PLP to ensure rigorous or reproducible results as these findings may ultimately inform clinical practice or regulatory decisions. Even in the case of a characterization study being conducted purely for exploratory reasons, it is still preferable to have a well-specified plan. Otherwise an evolving study design and analysis process will become unwieldy to document, explain and reproduce.

19.1.3   Protocol

An observational study plan should be documented in the form of a protocol created prior to executing a study. At a minimum, a protocol describes the primary study question, the approach, and metrics that will be used to answer the question. The study population should be described to a level of detail such that the study population may be fully reproduced by others. In addition, all methods or statistical procedures and the form of expected study results such as metrics, tables and graphs should be described. Often, a protocol will also describe a set of pre-analyses designed to assess the feasibility or statistical power of the study. Furthermore, protocols may contain descriptions of variations on the primary study question referred to as sensitivity analyses. Sensitivity analyses are designed to evaluate the potential impact of study design choices on the overall study findings and should be described in advance whenever possible. Sometimes unanticipated issues arise that may necessitate a protocol amendment after a protocol is completed. If this becomes necessary, it is critical to document the change and the reasons for the change in the protocol itself. Particularly in the case of PLE or PLP, a completed study protocol will ideally be recorded in an independent platform (such as clinicaltrials.gov or OHDSI's studyProtocols sandbox) where its versions and any amendments can be tracked independently with timestamps. It is also often the case that your institution or the owner of the data source will require the opportunity to review and approve your protocol prior to study execution.

19.1.4 Standardized Analyses

A unique advantage of OHDSI is the ways in which the tools support planning, documentation and reporting by recognizing that there are really a few main classes of questions that are asked repeatedly in observational studies (Chapters 2, 7, 11, 12, 13), thereby streamlining the protocol development and study implementation process through automation of aspects that are repeated. Many of the tools are designed to parameterize a few study designs or metrics that address a majority of use cases that will be encountered. For example, the researchers specify their study populations and a few additional parameters and perform numerous comparative studies iterating over different drugs and/or outcomes. If a researcher's questions fit into the general template, there are ways to automate the generation of many of the basic descriptions of study populations and other parameters required for the protocol. Historically, these approaches were motivated out of the OMOP experiments which sought to evaluate how well observational study designs were able to reproduce known causal links between drugs and adverse events by iterating over many different study designs and parameters.

The OHDSI approach supports the inclusion of feasibility and study diagnostics within the protocol by again enabling these steps to be performed relatively simply within a common framework and tools (see section 19.2.4 below).

19.1.5 Study Packages

Another motivation for standardized templates and designs is that even when a researcher thinks a study is described in complete detail in the form of a protocol, there may be elements that are not actually sufficiently specified to generate the full computer code to execute the study. A related fundamental principle which is enabled by the OHDSI framework is to generate a completely traceable and reproducible process documented in the form of computer code, often referred to as a "study package." OHDSI best practice is to record such a study package in the git environment. This study package contains all parameters and versioning stamps for the code base. As mentioned previously, observational studies are often asking questions with potential to impact public health decisions and policy. Therefore, before acting on any findings, they should ideally be replicated in multiple settings by different researchers. The only way to achieve such a goal is for every detail required to fully reproduce a study to be mapped out explicitly and not left to guesswork or misinterpretation. To support this best practice, the OHDSI tools are designed to aid in the translation from a protocol in the form of a written document into a computer or machine-readable study package. One tradeoff of this framework is that not every use case or customized analysis can easily be addressed with the existing OHDSI tools. As the community grows and evolves, however, more functionality to address a larger array of use cases is being added. Anyone involved in the community may raise suggestions for new functionality driven by a novel use case.

19.1.6   The Data Underlying the CDM

OHDSI studies are premised on observational databases being translated into the OMOP common data model (CDM). All OHDSI tools and downstream analytics steps make an assumption that the data representation conforms to the specifications of the CDM (see Chapter 4). It is therefore also critical that the ETL process (see Chapter 6) for doing so is well-documented for your specific data sources as this process may introduce artifacts or differences between databases at different sites. The purpose of the OMOP CDM is to move in the direction of reducing site specific data representation, but this is far from a perfect process and still remains a challenging area that the community seeks to improve. It therefore remains critical when executing studies to collaborate with individuals at your site, or at external sites when executing network studies, who are intimately familiar with any source data that has been transformed into the OMOP CDM.

In addition to the CDM, the OMOP standardized vocabulary system (Chapter 5) is also a critical component of working with the OHDSI framework to obtain interoperability across diverse data sources. The standardized vocabulary seeks to define a set of standard concepts within each vocabulary domain to which all other source vocabulary systems are mapped. In this way, two different databases which use a different source vocabulary system for drugs, diagnoses or procedures will be comparable when transformed into the CDM. The OMOP vocabularies also contain hierarchies which are useful in identifying the appropriate codes for a particular cohort definition. Again, it is recommended best practice to implement the vocabulary mappings and use the codes of OMOP standardized vocabularies in downstream queries in order to gain the full benefits of ETLing your database into the OMOP CDM and using the OMOP vocabulary.

19.2 Study Steps in Detail

19.2.1 Define Question

The first step is to translate your research interest into a precise question that can be addressed with an observational study. Let's say that you are a clinical diabetes researcher and you want to investigate the quality of care being delivered to patients with type 2 diabetes mellitus (T2DM). You can break this bigger objective down into much more specific questions that fall into one of the three types of questions first described in Chapter 7.

In a characterization study, one could ask, "do prescribing practices conform to what is currently recommended for those with mild T2DM versus those with severe T2DM in a given healthcare environment?" This question does not ask a causal question about the effectiveness of any given treatment relative to another; it is simply characterizing prescribing practices in your database relative to a set of existing clinical guidelines.

Maybe you are also skeptical whether or not the prescribing guidelines for T2DM treatment are best for a particular subset of patients such as those with both a diagnosis of T2DM and heart disease. This line of inquiry can be translated into a PLE study. Specifically, you can ask a question about the comparative effectiveness of 2 different T2DM drug classes in preventing cardiovascular events, such as heart failure. You might design a study to examine the relative risks of hospitalization for heart failure in two separate cohorts of patients taking the different drugs, but where both cohorts have a diagnosis of T2DM and heart disease.

Alternatively, you may want to develop a model to predict which patients will progress from mild T2DM to severe T2DM. This can be framed as a PLP question and could serve to flag patients at greater risk of transitioning to severe T2DM for more vigilant care.

From a purely pragmatic point of view, defining a study question also requires assessing whether the approaches required to answer a question conforms to available functionality within the OHDSI tool set (see Chapter 7 for a detailed discussion of question types that can addressed with current tool). Of course it is always possible to design your own analytic tools or modify those currently available to answer other questions.

19.2.2 Review Data Availability and Quality

Before committing to a particular study question, it is recommended to review the quality of the data (see Chapter 15) and really understand the nature of your particular observational healthcare database in terms of which fields are populated and what care settings the data covers. This can help to quickly identify issues that may make a study question infeasible in a particular database. Below, we point out some common issues that may arise.

Let's return to the example above of developing a predictive model for progression from mild T2DM to severe T2DM. Ideally severity of T2DM might be assessed by examining glycosylated hemoglobin (HbA1c) levels which is a lab measurement that reflects a patient's blood sugar levels averaged over the prior 3 months. These values may or may not be available for all patients. If unavailable for all or even a portion of patients, you will have to consider whether other clinical criteria for severity of T2DM can be identified and used instead. Alternatively, if the HbA1c values are available for only a subset of patients, you will also need to evaluate whether focusing on this subset of patients only would lead to unwanted bias in the study. See Chapter 7 for additional discussion of the issue of missing data.

Another common issue is the lack of information about a particular care setting. In the PLE example described above, the suggested outcome was hospitalization for heart failure. If a given database does not have any inpatient information, one may need to consider a different outcome to evaluate the comparative effectiveness of different T2DM treatment approaches. In other databases, outpatient diagnosis data may not be available and therefore one would need to consider the design of the cohort.

19.2.3   Study Populations

Defining a study population or populations is a fundamental step of any study. In observational research, a group of individuals that is representative of the study population of interest is often referred to as a cohort. The required patient characteristics for selection into a cohort will be determined by the study population that is relevant for the clinical question at hand. An example of a simple cohort would be patients older than 18 years of age AND with a diagnosis code for T2DM in their medical record. This cohort definition has two criteria connected by AND logic. Often cohort definitions contain many more criteria which are connected by more complex, nested boolean logic and additional temporal criteria such as specific study periods or required lengths of time for a patient's baseline period.

A refined set of cohort definitions requires the review of appropriate scientific literature and advice from clinical and technical experts who understand some of the challenges in interpreting your specific database to identify appropriate groups of patients. It's important to keep in mind when working with observational data that these data do not provide a complete picture of a patient's medical history, but rather a snapshot in time whose fidelity is subject to both human error and bias that may have been introduced in recording of the information. A given patient may only be followed for a finite time referred to as their observation period. For a given database or care setting and disease or treatment under study, a clinical researcher may be able to make suggestions to avoid the most common sources of error. To give a straightforward example, a common issue in identifying patients with T2DM is that T1DM patients are sometimes mistakenly coded with a diagnosis of T2DM. Because patients with T1DM are fundamentally a different group, the unintentional inclusion of a group of T1DM patients in a study intended to examine T2DM patients could skew the results. In order to have a robust definition of a T2DM cohort, one may want to eliminate patients who have only ever been prescribed insulin as a diabetes treatment to avoid having patients with T1DM erroneously represented. At the same time, however, there may also be situations where one is simply interested in the characteristics of all patients who have a T2DM diagnosis code in their medical record. In this case, it may not be appropriate to apply further qualifying criteria to attempt to remove erroneously coded T1DM patients.

Once the definition of a study population or populations is described, the OHDSI tool ATLAS is a good starting point to create the relevant cohorts. ATLAS and the cohort generation process are described in detail in Chapters 8 and 10. Briefly, ATLAS provides a user interface (UI) to define and generate cohorts with detailed inclusion criteria. Once cohorts are defined in ATLAS, a user can directly export their detailed definitions in a human-readable format for incorporation in a protocol. If for some reason an ATLAS instance is not connected to an observational health database, ATLAS can still be used to create a cohort definition and directly export the underlying SQL code for incorporation into a study package to be run separately on a SQL database server. Directly using ATLAS is recommended when possible because ATLAS provides some advantages above and beyond the creation of SQL code for the cohort definition (see below). Finally, there may be some rare situations where a cohort definition can not be implemented with the ATLAS UI and requires manual custom SQL code.

The ATLAS UI enables defining cohorts based on numerous selection criteria. Criteria for cohort entry and exit as well as baseline criteria can be defined on the basis of any domains of the OMOP CDM such as conditions, drugs, procedures, etc. where standard codes must be specified for each domain. In addition, logical filters on the basis of these domains, as well as time-based filters to define study periods, and baseline timeframes can be defined within ATLAS. ATLAS can be particularly helpful when selecting codes for each criteria. ATLAS incorporates a vocabulary-browsing feature which can be used to build sets of codes required for your cohort definitions. This feature relies solely on the OMOP standard vocabularies and has options to include all descendants in the vocabulary hierarchy (see Chapter 5). Note therefore that this feature requires that all codes have been appropriately mapped to standard codes during the ETL process (see Chapter 6). If the best codesets to use in your inclusion criteria are not clear, this may be a place where some exploratory analysis may be warranted in cohort definitions. Alternatively a more formal sensitivity analysis could be considered to account for different possible definitions of a cohort using different codesets.

Assuming that ATLAS is configured appropriately to connect to a database, SQL queries to generate the defined cohorts can be run directly within ATLAS. ATLAS will automatically assign each cohort a unique id which can also be used to directly reference the cohort in the backend database for future use. The cohort may be directly used within ATLAS to run an incidence rate study or it may be pointed to directly in the backend database by code in a PLE or PLP study package. For a given cohort, ATLAS saves only the patient ids, index dates and cohort exit dates of the individuals in the cohorts. This information is sufficient to derive all the other attributes or covariates that may be needed for the patients such as patient's baseline covariates for a characterization, PLE or PLP study.

When a cohort is created, summary characteristics of the patient demographics and frequencies of the most frequent drugs and conditions observed can be created and viewed by default directly within ATLAS.

In reality, most studies require specifying multiple cohorts or multiple sets of cohorts which are then compared in various ways to gain new clinical insights. For PLE and PLP, the OHDSI tools provide a structured framework to define these multiple cohorts. For example, in a PLE comparative effectiveness study, you will typically define at least 3 cohorts, a target cohort, a comparator and an outcome cohort (see Chapter 12). In addition, to run a full PLE comparative effectiveness study, you will also need a number of cohorts with negative control outcomes and positive control outcomes. The OHDSI toolset provides ways to help speed and in some cases automate the generation of these negative and positive control cohorts as discussed in detail in Chapter 18.

As a final note, defining cohorts for a study may benefit from ongoing work in the OHDSI community to define a library of robust and validated phenotypes where a phenotype is essentially an exportable cohort definition. If any of these existing cohort definitions are appropriate for your study, the exact definitions can be obtained by import of a json file into your ATLAS instance.

19.2.4   Feasibility and Diagnostics

Once cohorts are defined and generated, a more formal process to examine study feasibility in available data sources can be undertaken and the findings summarized in the finalized protocol. An evaluation of study feasibility can encompass a number of exploratory and sometimes iterative activities. We describe a few common aspects here.

A primary activity at this stage will be to thoroughly review the distributions of characteristics within your cohorts to ensure that the cohort you generated is consistent with the desired clinical characteristics and flag any unexpected characteristics. Returning to our T2DM example above, by characterizing this simple T2DM cohort by reviewing the frequencies of all other diagnoses received, one may be able to flag the issue of also capturing patients with T1DM or other unanticipated issues. It is good practice to build such a step of initially characterizing any new cohort into the study protocol as a quality check of clinical validity of the cohort definition. In terms of implementation, the easiest way to perform a first pass at this will be to examine the cohort demographics and top drugs and conditions that can be generated by default when a cohort is created in ATLAS. If the option to create the cohorts directly within ATLAS is not available, manual SQL or use of the R feature extraction package can be used to characterize a cohort. In practice, in a larger PLE study or PLP study, these steps can be built into the study package with feature extraction steps.

Another common and important step to assess feasibility for a PLE or PLP is an assessment of cohort sizes and the counts of outcomes in the target and comparator cohorts. The incidence rate feature of ATLAS can be used to find these counts which can be used to perform power calculations as described elsewhere.

Another option which is highly recommended for a PLE study is to complete the propensity score (PS) matching steps and relevant diagnostics to ensure that there is sufficient overlap between the populations in the target and comparator groups. These steps are described in detail in Chapter 12. In addition, using these final matched cohorts, the statistical power can then be calculated.

In some cases, work in the OHDSI community examines the statistical power only after a study is run by reporting a minimal detectable relative risk (MDRR) given the available sample sizes. This approach may be more useful when running high throughput, automated studies across a lot of databases and sites. In this scenario, a study's power in any given database is perhaps better explored after the all analyses have been performed rather than pre-filtering.

19.2.5 Finalize Protocol and Study Package

Once the legwork for all the previous steps has been completed, a final protocol should be assembled that includes detailed cohort definitions and study design information ideally exported from ATLAS. In Appendix D, we provide a sample table of contents for a full protocol for a PLE study. This can also be found on the OHDSI github. We provide this sample as a comprehensive guide and checklist, but note some sections may or may not be relevant for your study.

As shown in Figure 19.1, assembling the final study protocol in human-readable form should be performed in parallel with preparing all the machine-readable study code that is incorporated into the final study package. These latter steps are referred to as study implementation in the diagram below. This will include export of the finalized study package from ATLAS and/or development of any custom code that may be required.

The completed study package can then be used to execute only the preliminary diagnostics steps which in turn can be described in the protocol. For example, in the case of a new user cohort PLE study to examine comparative effectiveness of two treatments, the preliminary execution of study diagnostics steps will require cohort creation, propensity score creation, and matching to confirm that the target and comparator populations have sufficient overlap for the study to be feasible. Once this is determined, power calculations can be performed with the matched target and comparator cohorts intersected with the outcome cohort to obtain outcome counts and the results of these calculations can be described in the protocol. On the basis of these diagnostics results, a decision can then be made whether or not to move forward with executing the final outcome model. In the context of a characterization or a PLP study, there may be similar steps that need to be completed at this stage, although we don't attempt to outline all scenarios here.

Importantly, we recommend at this stage to have your finalized protocol reviewed by clinical collaborators and stakeholders.

19.2.6 Execute Study

Once all prior steps have been completed, study execution should ideally be straightforward. Of course, the code or process should be reviewed for fidelity to the methods and parameters outlined in the protocol. It may also be necessary to test and debug a study package to ensure it runs appropriately in your environment.

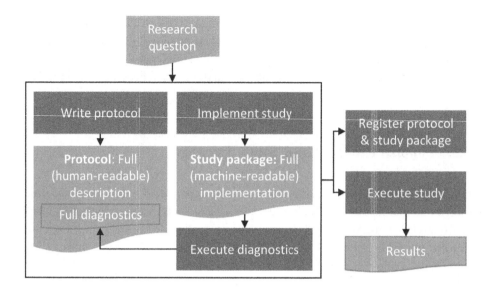

Figure 19.1: Diagram of the study process.

19.2.7   Interpretation and Write-Up

In a well-defined study where sample sizes are sufficient and data quality is reasonable, the interpretation of results will often be straightforward. Similarly, because most of the work of creating a final report other than writing up the final results is done in the planning and creation of the protocol, the final write-up of a report or manuscript for publication will often be straightforward as well.

There are, however, some common situations where interpretation becomes more challenging and should be approached with caution.

1. Sample sizes are borderline for significance and confidence intervals become large
2. Specific for PLE: p-value calibration with negative controls may reveal substantial bias
3. Unanticipated data quality issues come to light during the process of running the study

For any given study, it will be up to the discretion of the study authors to report on any concerns above and temper their interpretation of study results accordingly. As with the protocol development process, we also recommend that the study findings and interpretations be reviewed by clinical experts and stakeholders prior to releasing a final report or submitting a manuscript for publication.

19.3   Summary

- Study should examine a well-defined question.
- Perform appropriate checks of data quality, completeness and relevance in advance.
- Recommend to include source database expert in protocol development process if possible.
- Document proposed study in a protocol ahead of time.
- Generate study package code in parallel with written protocol and perform and describe any feasibility and diagnostics prior to executing the final study.
- Study should be registered and approved (if required) ahead of study execution.
- Finalized report or manuscript should be reviewed by clinical experts and other stakeholders.

Chapter 20

OHDSI Network Research

Chapter leads: Kristin Kostka, Greg Klebanov & Sara Dempster

The mission of OHDSI is to generate high-quality evidence through observational research. A primary way this is accomplished is through collaborative research studies. In prior chapters we discussed how the OHDSI community has authored standards and tools to facilitate high-quality, reproducible research, including OMOP Standardized Vocabularies, the Common Data Model (CDM), analytical methods packages, ATLAS and the study steps (Chapter 19) to run a retrospective database study. OHDSI network studies represent the culmination of a transparent, consistent and reproducible way to conduct research across a large number of geographically dispersed data. In this chapter we will discuss what constitutes an OHDSI network study, how to run a network study and discuss enabling technologies such as the ARACHNE Research Network.

20.1 OHDSI as a Research Network

The OHDSI research network is an international collaboration of researchers seeking to advance observational data research in healthcare. Today, the network consists of over 100 databases standardized to the OMOP common data model, collectively representing over 1 billion patient records. OHDSI is an open network, inviting healthcare institutions across the globe with patient-level data to join the network by converting data to the OMOP CDM and participating in network research studies. As data conversions are complete, collaborators are invited to report site information in the Data Network census maintained by the OHDSI Program Manager. Each OHDSI network site participates voluntarily. There are no hard obligations. Each site opts-in to each respective network study. In each study, data remains at the site behind a firewall. No patient-level data pooling occurs across network sites. **Only aggregate results are shared.**

Benefits of a Data Owner Joining the OHDSI Network

- **Access to free tools:** OHDSI publishes free, open source tools for data characterization and standardized analytics (e.g. browsing the clinical concepts, defining and characterizing cohorts, running Population-Level Estimation and Patient-Level Prediction studies).
- **Participate in a premier research community:** Author and publish network research, collaborate with leaders across various disciplines and stakeholder groups.
- **Opportunity to benchmark care:** Network studies can enable clinical characterizaton and quality improvement benchmarks across data partners.

20.2   OHDSI Network Studies

In the prior chapter (Chapter 19), we discussed general design considerations for running a study using the CDM. In general, a study may be conducted on a single CDM or on multiple CDMs. It can be run within a single institution's CDM data or across many institutions. In this section we will discuss why you may want to expand your analyses across multiple institutions into a network study.

20.2.1   Motivations for Conducting an OHDSI Network Study

A typical use case for observational studies is to examine the comparative effectiveness or safety of a treatment in a "real world" setting. More specifically, you may aim to replicate a clinical trial in a post-market setting to address concerns about generalizability of findings from a clinical trial. In other scenarios, you may want to run a study comparing two treatments that have never been compared in a clinical trial because one treatment is being used off-label. Or you may need to study a rare post-market safety outcome that a clinical trial was underpowered to observe. To address these research questions, it may not be sufficient to run a single observational study in one or even two databases at your site because you are getting an answer that is meaningful in the context of a particular group of patients only.

The results of an observational study can be influenced by many factors that vary by the location of the data source such as adherence, genetic diversity, or environmental factors, overall health status: factors that may not have been possible to vary in the context of a clinical trial even if one exists for your same study question. A typical motivation to run an observational study in a network is therefore to increase the diversity of data sources and potentially study populations to understand how well the results generalize. In other words, can the study findings be replicated across multiple sites or do they differ and if they differ, can any insights be gleaned as to why?

Network studies, therefore, offer the opportunity to investigate the effects of "real world" factors on observational studies' findings by examining a broad array of settings and data sources.

20.2.2 Definition of an OHDSI Network Study

 When is a study considered a *network* study? An OHDSI study becomes an OHDSI network study when it is run across multiple CDMs at different institutions.

The OHDSI approach to network research uses the OMOP CDM and standardized tools and study packages which fully specify all parameters for running a study. OHDSI standardized analytics are designed specifically to reduce artifacts and improve the efficiency and scalability of network studies.

Network studies are an important part of the OHDSI research community. However, there is no mandate that an OHDSI study be packaged and shared across the entire OHDSI network. You may still conduct research using the OMOP CDM and OHDSI methods library within a single institution or limit a research study to only select institutions. These research contributions are equally important to the community. It is at the discretion of each investigator whether a study is designed to run on a single database, conduct a study across a limited set of partners or open the study to full participation the OHDSI network. This chapter intends to speak to the open-to-all network studies that the OHDSI community conducts.

Elements of an *Open* OHDSI Network Study: When conducting an open OHDSI network study, you are committing to fully transparent research. There are a few components that make OHDSI research unique. This includes:

- All documentation, study code and subsequent results are made publicly available on the OHDSI GitHub.
- Investigators must create and publish a public study protocol detailing the scope and intent of the analysis to be performed.
- Investigators must create a study package (typically with R or SQL) with code that is CDM compliant.
- Investigators are encouraged to attend OHDSI Community Calls to promote and recruit collaborators for their OHDSI network study.
- At the end of the analysis, aggregate study results are made available in the OHDSI GitHub.
- Where possible, investigators are encouraged to publish study R Shiny Applications to data.ohdsi.org.

In the next section we will talk about how to create your own network study as well as the unique design and logistical considerations for implementing a network study.

20.2.3   Design Considerations for an OHDSI Network Study

Designing a study to run across the OHDSI network requires a paradigm shift in how you design and assemble your study code. Ordinarily, you may design a study with a target data set in mind. In doing so, you may write code relative to what you know to be true in the data you are utilizing for your analysis. For example, if you were assembling an angioedema cohort you may opt to pick only concept codes for angioedema that are represented in your CDM. This may be problematic if your data are in a specific care setting (e.g. primary care, ambulatory settings) or specific to a region (e.g. US-centric). Your code selections might be biasing your cohort definition.

In an OHDSI network study, you are no longer designing and building a study package just for your data. You are building a study package to be run across multiple sites across the globe. You will never see the underlying data for participating sites outside of your own institution. OHDSI network studies only share results files. Your study package can only collect what data that is available in the domains of the CDM. You will need an exhaustive approach to concept set creation to represent the diversity of care settings that observational health data are captured. OHDSI study packages often use the same cohort definition across all sites. This means that you must think holistically to avoid biasing a cohort definition to only represent a subset of eligible data (e.g. claims-centric data or EHR-specific data) in the network. You are encouraged to write an exhaustive cohort definition that can be ported across multiple CDMs. OHDSI study packages use the same set of parameterized code across all sites – with only minor customizations for connecting into the database layer and storing local results. Later on, we will discuss the implications for interpreting clinical findings from diverse datasets.

In addition to clinical coding variation, you will need to design anticipating variations in the local technical infrastructure. Your study code will no longer be running in a single technical environment. Each OHDSI network site makes its own independent choice of database layer. This means that you cannot hard-code a study package to a specific database dialect. The study code needs to be parameterized to a type of SQL that can be easily modified to the operators in that dialect. Fortunately, the OHDSI Community has solutions such as ATLAS, DatabaseConnector, and SqlRender to help you generalize your study package for CDM compliance across different database dialects. OHDSI investigators are encouraged to solicit help from other network study sites to test and validate the study package can be executed in different environments. When coding errors come up, OHDSI Researchers can utilize the OHDSI Forums to discuss and debug packages.

20.2.4   Logistical Considerations for an OHDSI Network Study

OHDSI is an open science community, and the OHDSI central coordinating center provides a community infrastructure to allow its collaborators to lead and participate in community research. Every OHDSI network study requires a lead investigator, and that can be any collaborator across the OHDSI community. OHDSI network studies require coordination between the lead investigator, collaborating researchers, and participating network data partners. Each site must perform its own due diligence to ensure the study protocol is approved and authorized to be executed on the local CDM. Data analysts may need to enlist assistance from the local IT team to enable appropriate permissions to run the study. The size and scope of the study team at each site will be a function of the size and complexity of the proposed network study as well as the maturity of the site's adoption of the OMOP CDM and OHDSI tool stack. The level of experience that a site has with running an OHDSI network study will also impact the personnel required.

For each study, site start-up activities may include:

- Registering the study with the Institutional Review Board (or equivalent)
- Receiving Institutional Review Board approval to execute the study
- Receiving database level permissions to read/write a schema to the approved CDM
- Ensuring configuration of a functional RStudio environment to execute the study package
- Reviewing the study code for any technical anomalies
- Working with a local IT team to permit and install any dependent R packages needed to execute the package within technical constraints

 Data Quality and Network Studies: As discussed in Chapter 6, quality control is a fundamental and iterative piece of the ETL process. This should be done regularly outside of the network study process. For a network study, a study lead may ask to review participating site's data quality reports or design custom SQL queries to understand potential variation in contributing data sources. For more detail on the data quality efforts going on within OHDSI, please see Chapter 15.

Each site will have a local data analyst who executes the study package. This individual must review the output of the study package to ensure no sensitive information is transmitted. When you are using pre-built OHDSI methods such as Population-Level Effect Estimation (PLE) and Patient Level Prediction (PLP), there are configurable settings for the minimum cell count for a given analysis. The data analyst is required to review these thresholds and ensure it follows local governance policies.

When sharing study results, the data analyst must comply with all local governance policies, inclusive of method of results transmission and adhering to approval processes for external publication of results. **OHDSI network studies do not share patient-level data.** In other words, patient level data from different sites is never pooled in a central environment. Study packages create results files designed to be aggregate results (e.g. summary statistics, point-estimates, diagnostic plots, etc.) and do not share patient-level information. Many organizations do not require data sharing agreements be executed between the participating study team members. However, depending on the institutions involved and the data sources, it may be necessary to have more formal data sharing agreements in place and signed by specific study team members. If you are a data owner interested in participating in network studies, you are encouraged to consult your local governance team to understand what policies are in place and must be fulfilled to join OHDSI community studies.

20.3   Running an OHDSI Network Study

Running an OHDSI Network Study has three general distinct stages:

- Study design and feasibility
- Study execution
- Results dissemination and publication

20.3.1   Study Design and Feasibility

The study feasibility stage *(or the pre-study stage)* defines a study question and describes the process to answer this question via the study protocol. This stage focuses on assessing the feasibility of executing the study protocol across participating sites.

The outcome of the feasibility stage is the generation of a finalized protocol and study package that is published ready for network execution. The formal protocol will detail the study team, including the designated study lead (often the corresponding author for publication purposes), and information on the timeline for the study. The protocol is a critical component for additional network sites to review, approve and execute the full study package on their CDM data. A protocol must include information on study population, the methods being used, how the results will be stored and analyzed as well as how the study results will be disseminated after completion (e.g. a publication, presentation at scientific conference, etc.).

The feasibility stage is not a well-defined process. It is a series of activities that are highly dependent on the type of study proposed. At a minimum, the study lead will spend time identifying relevant network sites that contain the targeted patient population(s) with required drug exposure, procedure information, condition or demographics information. Where possible, the study lead should provisionally use their own CDM to design the target cohorts. However, there is no requirement that a study lead have access to a live OMOP CDM with real patient data to run a network study. The study lead may design their target cohort definition using synthetic data (e.g. CMS Synthetic Public Use Files, SyntheticMass from Mitre or Synthea) and ask collaborators at OHDSI network sites to help with validating the feasibility of this cohort. Feasibility activities may include asking collaborators to create and characterize cohorts using JSON files of cohort definitions from ATLAS or testing study R packages and running initial diagnostics as discussed in Chapter 19. At the same time, the study lead will need to initiate any organization-specific processes to approve an OHDSI study at the organizing institution – such internal Institutional Review Board approval. It is the responsibility of the study lead to complete these organization-specific activities during the feasibility phase.

20.3.2   Study Execution

After completing feasibility exercises, the study advances to the execution phase. This period represents when OHDSI network sites can opt-in to participate in the analysis. This phase is when the design and logistical considerations we discussed become most important.

A study will move to execution when the study lead reaches out to the OHDSI community to formally announce a new OHDSI network study and formally begins recruiting participating sites. The study lead will publish the study protocol to the OHDSI GitHub. The study lead will announce the study on the weekly OHDSI Community Call and OHDSI Forum, inviting participating centers and collaborators. As sites opt-in to participate, a study lead will communicate directly with each site and provide information on the GitHub repository where the study protocol and code are published as well as instructions on how to execute the study package. Ideally, a network study will be performed in parallel by all sites, so the final results are shared concurrently ensuring that no site's team members are biased by knowledge of another team's findings.

At each site, the study team will ensure the study follows institutional procedures for receiving approval to participate in the study, execute the package and share results externally. This will likely include receiving Institutional Review Board (IRB) approval or equivalent for the specified protocol. When the study is approved to run, the site data scientists/statisticians will follow the study lead's instructions to access the OHDSI study package and generate results in the standardized format following OHDSI guidelines. Each participating site will follow internal institutional processes regarding data sharing rules. Sites should not share results unless approval is obtained from IRB or other institutional approval processes.

The study lead will be responsible for communicating how they want to receive results (e.g. via SFTP or a secure Amazon S3 bucket) and the time-frame for turning around results. Sites may specify if the method of transmission is out of compliance with internal protocol and a workaround may be developed accordingly.

During the execution phase, the collective study team (inclusive of the study lead and participating site teams) may iterate on results, if reasonable adjustments are required. If the scope and extent of the protocol evolve beyond what is approved, it is the responsibility of the participating site to communicate this to their organization by working with the study lead to update the protocol then resubmit the protocol for review and re-approval by the local IRB.

It is ultimately the responsibility of the study lead and any supporting data scientist/statistician to perform the aggregation of results across centers and perform meta-analysis, as appropriate. The OHDSI community has validated methodologies to aggregate results files shared from multiple network sites into a single answer. The EvidenceSynthesis package is a freely available R package containing routines for combining evidence and diagnostics across multiple sources, such as multiple data sites in a distributed study. This includes functions for performing meta-analysis and forest plots.

The study lead will need to monitor site participation and help eliminate barriers in executing the package by regularly checking in with participating sites. Study execution is not one-size-fits-all at each site. There may be challenges related to the database layer (e.g. access rights / schema permissions) or analytics tool in their environment (e.g. unable to install required packages, unable to access databases through R, etc.). The participating site will be in the driver's seat and will communicate what barriers exist to executing the study. It is ultimately the discretion of the participating site to enlist appropriate resources to help resolve issues encountered in their local CDM.

While OHDSI studies can be executed rapidly, it is advised to allow for a reasonable amount of time for all participating sites to execute the study and receive appropriate approvals to publish results. Newer OHDSI network sites may find the first network study they participate in to be longer than normal as they work through issues with environment configuration such as database permissions or analytics library updates. Support is available from the OHDSI Community. Issues can be posted to the OHDSI Forum as they are encountered.

A study lead should set study milestones in the protocol and communicate anticipated closure date in advance to assist with managing the overall study timeline. If the timeline is not adhered to, it is the responsibility of the study lead to inform participating sites of updates to the study schedule and manage the overall progress of study execution.

20.3.3   Results Dissemination and Publication

During the results dissemination and publication phase, the study lead will collaborate with other participants on various administrative tasks, such as manuscript development and optimizing data visualizations. Once the study is executed and results are stored centrally for the study lead to further analyze. The study lead is responsible for the creation and dissemination of full study results (e.g. a Shiny Application) for review by participating centers. If the study lead is using an OHDSI study skeleton, either generated by Atlas or manually modified from the GitHub code, the Shiny Application will be automatically created. In the event a study lead is creating custom code, the study lead may use the OHDSI Forum to ask for help to create their own Shiny Application for their study package.

 Not sure where to publish your OHDSI network study? Consult JANE (Journal/Author Name Estimator), a tool which takes your abstract and scans publications for relevance and fit.[1]

As manuscripts are written, each participating collaborator is encouraged to review and ensure the output follows external publication processes. At a minimum, the participating site should designate a publication lead – this individual will ensure that internal processes are adhered to during the manuscript preparation and submission. The choice of which journal to submit a study to is at the discretion of the study lead, though should be the results of collaborative discussion at the onset of a study. All co-authors on OHDSI studies are expected to satisfy ICMJE authorship guidelines.[2] The presentation of results may occur in any forum of their choosing (e.g. an OHDSI Symposium, another academic proceeding or in a journal publication). Researchers are also invited to present OHDSI Network Studies on weekly OHDSI community calls and at OHDSI Symposia across the globe.

---

[2]http://www.icmje.org/recommendations/browse/roles-and-responsibilities/
defining-the-role-of-authors-and-contributors.html

20.4 Forward Looking: Using Network Study Automation

The current network study process is manual – with study team members using various mechanisms (including Wiki, GitHub and email) to collaborate on study design, sharing code and results. This process is not consistent and scalable and to solve that issue, the OHDSI community is actively working to systemize study processes.

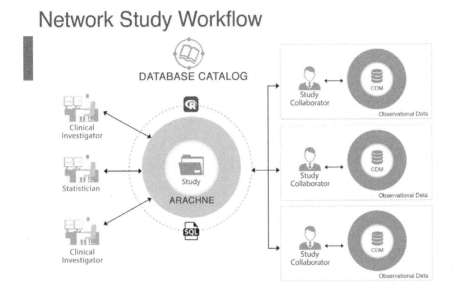

Figure 20.1: The ARACHNE Network Study Process.

ARACHNE is a platform that is designed to streamline and automate the process of conducting network studies. ARACHNE uses OHDSI standards and establishes a consistent, transparent, secure and compliant observational research process across multiple organizations. ARACHNE standardizes the communication protocol to access the data and exchange analysis results, while enabling authentication and authorization for restricted content. It brings participating organizations - data providers, investigators, sponsors and data scientists - into a single collaborative study team and facilitates an end-to-end observational study coordination. The tool enables the creation of a complete, standards-based R, Python and SQL execution environment including approval workflows controlled by the data custodian.

ARACHNE is built to provide a seamless integration with other OHDSI tools, including ACHILLES reports and an ability to import ATLAS design artifacts, create self-contained packages and automatically execute those across multiple sites. The future vision is to eventually enable multiple networks to be linked together for the purpose of conducting research not only between organizations within a single network, but also between organizations across multiple networks.

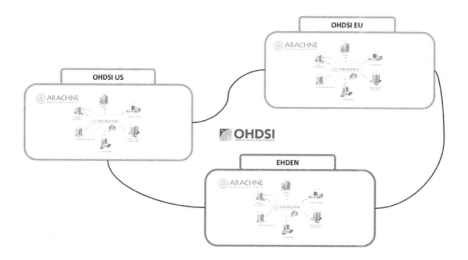

Figure 20.2: The ARACHNE Network of Networks.

20.5   Best Practice for OHDSI Network Studies

As you are conducting a network study, the OHDSI community is available to assist you in ensuring you adhere to best practice for OHDSI Network studies.

Study Design and Feasibility: When running a network study, make sure that you are not biasing your study design to a single type of data. The task of harmonizing the cohort definitions to represent consistent populations across all the sites may be more or less involved depending on the how heterogeneous the data types are and how carefully the study site followed all standardized conventions for converting data to the OMOP CDM. The reason that this is so critical is the need to control differences in data capture, representation and transformation across network sites versus those that are clinically meaningful. In particular, for comparative effectiveness studies, challenges can arise in ensuring concordant exposure cohorts and outcome cohort definitions across the sites. For example, drug exposure information can come from various data sources which may vary in their potential for misclassification. A pharmacy dispensing claim from a health insurance plan may be adjudicated meaning that when there is a claim for a medication, there is a very good chance that the person filled the prescription order. However, a prescription order entered into an EHR may be all that is available, without linkage to other data to determine whether the order was dispensed or consumed. There may be a time gap between the record of a physician writing a prescription order, the time when the pharmacist dispensed the prescription, the time when the patient picked up their medication at the pharmacy, and the time when the patient actually consumed her first pill. This measurement error can potentially bias results across any analytic use case. Thus, it is important to perform study feasibility to evaluate the appropriateness of database participation when developing the study protocol.

Study Execution: Where possible, study leads are encouraged to utilize ATLAS, the OHDSI Methods Library and OHDSI Study Skeletons to create study code that used standardized analytics packages as much as possible. Study code should always be in a CDM compliant, database layer agnostic way using OHDSI packages. Be sure to parameterize all functions and variables (e.g. do not hard database connection, local hard drive path, assume a certain operating system). When recruiting participating sites, a study lead should ensure that each network site is CDM compliant and regularly updates the OMOP standardized vocabularies. A study lead should perform due diligence to ensure with each network site has performed and documented data quality checks on their CDM (e.g. ensuring ETL has followed THEMIS business rules and conventions, correct data was placed into correct CDM tables and fields). Each data analyst is advised to update their local R packages to the latest OHDSI package versions before executing the study package.

Results and dissemination: A study lead should ensure each site follows local governance rules before results are shared. Open, reproducible science means that everything that is designed and executed becomes available. OHDSI Network studies are fully transparent with all documentation and subsequent results published to the OHDSI GitHub repository or the data.ohdsi.org R Shiny server. As you prepare your manuscript, the study lead should review the principles of the OMOP CDM and Standardized Vocabularies to ensure the journal understands how data can vary across OHDSI network sites. For example, if you are performing a network study that uses claims databases and EHRs, you may be asked by journal reviewers to explain how the integrity of the cohort definition was maintained across multiple data types. A reviewer may want to understand how the OMOP observation period (as discussed in Chapter 4 compares to an eligibility file – a file that exists in claims databases to attribute when a person is and is not covered by an insurance provider. This is inherently asking to focus on an artifactual element of the databases themselves and focuses on the ETL of how the CDM transforms the records into observations. In this case, the network study lead may find it helpful to reference how the OMOP CDM OBSERVATION PERIOD is created and describe how observations are created using the encounters in the source system. The manuscript discussion may need to acknowledge the limitations of how EHR data, unlike claims data which reflects all paid encounters for that period of time they are covered, it does not record when a person sees a provider who uses a different EHR of record and thus, breaks in observation periods may occur because of the person seeks care from an out-of-EHR provider. This is an artifact of how data exists in the system it is captured in. It is not a clinically meaningful difference but may confuse those who are unfamiliar with how OMOP derives the observation period table. It is worth explaining in the discussion section to clarify this unfamiliar convention. Similarly, a study lead may find it useful to describe the terminology service provided by the OMOP standard vocabularies enables a clinical concept to be the same across wherever it is captured. There are always decisions made in mapping of source codes to standard concepts however THEMIS conventions and CDM quality checks can help provide information on where information should go and how well a database adhered to that principle.

20.6   Summary

- An OHDSI study becomes an OHDSI Network study when it is run across multiple CDMs at different institutions.
- OHDSI network studies are open to all. Anyone can lead a network study. Anyone with an OMOP compliant database may opt to participate and contribute results.
- Need help running a network study? Consult with the OHDSI Study Nurture Committee to help design and execute your study.
- **Sharing is caring.** All study documentation, code and results are published on the OHDSI GitHub or in an R Shiny application. Study leads are invited to present their research at OHSDSI events.

Chapter A

Glossary

ACHILLES A database-level characterization report.

ARACHNE The OHDSI platform that is being developed to allow the orchestration and execution of federated network studies.

ATLAS A web-based application that is installed on participating sites to support the design and execution of observational analyses to generate real world evidence from patient level clinical data.

Bias The expected value of the error (the difference between the true value and the estimated value).

Boolean Variable that has only two values (true or false).

Care site A uniquely identified institutional (physical or organizational) unit where health-care delivery is practiced (office, ward, hospital, clinic, etc.).

Case control A type of retrospective study design for population-level effect estimation. Case-control studies match "cases" with the target outcome to "controls" without the target outcome. Then they look back in time and compare the odds of exposure in the cases and the controls.

Causal effect What population-level estimation concerns itself with. One definition equates a "causal effect" as the average of the "unit-level causal effects" in a target population. The unit-level causal effect is the contrast between the outcome had an individual been exposed and the outcome had that individual not been exposed (or been exposed to A as against B).

Characterization Descriptive study of a cohort or entire database. See Chapter 11.

Claims data Data generated for the purpose of billing a health insurance company.

Clinical trial Interventional clinical study.

Cohort A set of persons who satisfy one or more inclusion criteria for a duration of time. See Chapter 10.

Concept A term (with a code) defined in a medical terminology (e.g., SNOMED CT). See Chapter 5.

Concept set A concept set is an expression representing a list of concepts that can be used as a reusable component in various analyses. See Chapter 10.

Common Data Model (CDM) A convention for representing healthcare data that allows portability of analysis (the same analysis unmodified can be executed on multiple datasets). See Chapter 4.

Comparative Effectiveness A comparison of the effects of two different exposures on an outcome of interest. See Chapter 12.

Condition A diagnosis, a sign, or a symptom, which is either observed by a provider or reported by the patient.

Confounding Confounding is a distortion (inaccuracy) in the estimated measure of association that occurs when the primary exposure of interest is mixed up with some other factor that is associated with the outcome.

Covariate Data element (e.g., weight) that is used in a statistical model as independent variable.

Data quality The state of completeness, validity, consistency, timeliness and accuracy that makes data appropriate for a specific use.

Device A foreign physical object or instrument which is used for diagnostic or therapeutic purposes through a mechanism beyond chemical action. Devices include implantable objects (e.g. pacemakers, stents, artificial joints), medical equipment and supplies (e.g. bandages, crutches, syringes), other instruments used in medical procedures (e.g. sutures, defibrillators) and material used in clinical care (e.g. adhesives, body material, dental material, surgical material).

Drug A Drug is a biochemical substance formulated in such a way that when administered to a Person it will exert a certain physiological effect. Drugs include prescription and over-the-counter medicines, vaccines, and large-molecule biologic therapies. Radiological devices ingested or applied locally do not count as Drugs.

Domain A Domain defines the set of allowable Concepts for the standardized fields in the CDM tables. For example, the "Condition" Domain contains Concepts that describe a condition of a patient, and these Concepts can only be stored in the condition_concept_id field of the CONDITION_OCCURRENCE and CONDITION_ERA tables.

Electronic Health Record (EHR) Data generated during course of care and recorded in an electronic system.

Epidemiology The study of the distribution, patterns and determinants of health and disease conditions in defined populations.

Evidence-based medicine The use of empirical and scientific evidence in making decisions about the care of individual patients.

ETL (Extract-Transform-Load) The process of converting data from one format to another, for example from a source format to the CDM. See Chapter 6.

Matching Many population-level effect estimation approaches attempt to identify the causal effects of exposures by comparing outcomes in exposed patients to those same outcomes in unexposed patients (or exposed to A versus B). Since these two patient groups might differ in ways other than exposure, "matching" attempts to create exposed and unexposed patient groups that are as similar as possible at least with respect to measured patient characteristics.

Measurement A structured value (numerical or categorical) obtained through systematic and standardized examination or testing of a person or person's sample.

Measurement error Occurs when a recorded measurement (e.g., blood pressure, patient age, duration of treatment) differs from the corresponding true measurement.

Metadata A set of data that describes and gives information about other data and includes descriptive metadata, structural metadata, administrative metadata, reference metadata and statistical metadata.

Methods Library A set of R packages developed by the OHDSI community for performing observational studies.

Model misspecification Many OHDSI methods employ statistical models such as proportional hazards regression or random forests. Insofar as the mechanism that generated the data deviate from the assumed model, the model is "misspecified."

Negative control An exposure-outcome pair where the exposure is believed to not cause or prevent the outcome. Can be used to assess whether effect estimation methods produce results in line with the truth. See Chapter 18.

Observation A clinical fact about a Person obtained in the context of examination, questioning or a procedure.

Observation period The span of time for which a person is at-risk to have clinical events recorded within the source systems, even if no events in fact are recorded (healthy patient with no healthcare interactions).

Observational study A study where the researcher has no control over the intervention.

OHDSI SQL A SQL dialect that can be automatically translated to various other SQL dialects using the SqlRender R package. OHDSI SQL is mostly a subset of SQL Server SQL, but allows for additional parameterization. See Chapter 9.

Open science The movement to make scientific research (including publications, data, physical samples, and software) and its dissemination accessible to all levels of an inquiring society, amateur or professional. See Chapter 3.

Outcome An observation that provides a focal point for an analysis. For example, a patient-level predictive model might predict the outcome "stroke." Or a population-level estimation might estimate the causal effect of a drug on the outcome "headache."

Patient-level prediction Development and application of predictive models to produce patient-specific probabilities for experiencing some future outcome based on baseline characteristics.

Phenotype A description of physical characteristics. This includes visible characteristics like your weight and hair color, but also your overall health, your disease history, and your behavior.

Population-level estimation A study into causal effects. Estimates an average (population-level) effect size.

Positive control An exposure-outcome pair where the exposure is believed to cause or prevent the outcome. Can be used to assess whether effect estimation methods produce results in line with the truth. See Chapter 18.

Procedure Activity or process ordered by, or carried out by, a healthcare provider on the patient to have a diagnostic or therapeutic purpose.

Propensity score (PS) a single metric used in population-level estimation to balance populations in order to mimic randomization between two treatment groups in an observational study. The PS represents the probability of a patient receiving a treatment of interest as a function of a set of observed baseline covariates. It is most often calculated using a logistic regression model where the binary outcome is set to one for the group receiving the target treatment of interest and to zero for the comparator treatment. See Chapter 12.

Protocol A human readable document that fully specifies the design of a study.

Rabbit-in-a-Hat An interactive software tool to help define the ETL from source format to CDM. Uses the database profile generated by White Rabbit as input. See Chapter 7.

Selection bias A bias that occurs when the set of patients in your data deviates from the patients in the population in ways that distort statistical analyses.

Self-controlled designs Study designs that compare outcomes during different exposures within the same patient.

Sensitivity analysis A variant of the main analysis used in a study to asses the impact of an analysis choice over which uncertainty exists.

SNOMED A systematically organized computer processable collection of medical terms providing codes, terms, synonyms and definitions used in clinical documentation and reporting.

Study diagnostics Set of analytical steps where the goal is to determine whether a given analytical approach can be used (is valid) for answering a given research question. See Chapter 18.

Study package A computer-executable program that fully executes the study. See Chapter 17.

Source code A code used in a source database. For example an ICD-10 code.

Standard Concept A concept that is designated as valid concept and allowed to appear in the CDM.

THEMIS OHDSI workgroup that addresses target data format that is of higher granularity and detail with respect to CDM model specifications.

Visit The span of time a person continuously receives medical services from one or more providers at a care site in a given setting within the health care system.

Vocabulary A list of words and often phrases, usually arranged alphabetically and defined or translated. See Chapter 5.

White Rabbit A software tool for profiling a database before defining the ETL to the CDM. See Chapter 6.

Chapter B

Cohort definitions

This Appendix contains cohort definitions used throughout the book.

B.1 ACE Inhibitors

Initial Event Cohort

People having any of the following:

- a drug exposure of *ACE inhibitors* (Table B.1) for the first time in the person's history

with continuous observation of at least 365 days prior and 0 days after event index date, and limit initial events to: all events per person.

Limit qualifying cohort to: all events per person.

End Date Strategy

Custom Drug Era Exit Criteria This strategy creates a drug era from the codes found in the specified concept set. If the index event is found within an era, the cohort end date will use the era's end date. Otherwise, it will use the observation period end date that contains the index event.

Use the era end date of *ACE inhibitors* (Table B.1)

- allowing 30 days between exposures
- adding 0 days after exposure end

Cohort Collapse Strategy

Collapse cohort by era with a gap size of 30 days.

Concept Set Definitions

Table B.1: ACE inhibitors

Concept Id	Concept Name	Excluded	Descendants	Mapped
1308216	Lisinopril	NO	YES	NO
1310756	moexipril	NO	YES	NO
1331235	quinapril	NO	YES	NO
1334456	Ramipril	NO	YES	NO
1335471	benazepril	NO	YES	NO
1340128	Captopril	NO	YES	NO
1341927	Enalapril	NO	YES	NO
1342439	trandolapril	NO	YES	NO
1363749	Fosinopril	NO	YES	NO
1373225	Perindopril	NO	YES	NO

B.2   New Users of ACE Inhibitors Monotherapy

Initial Event Cohort

People having any of the following:

- a drug exposure of *ACE inhibitors* (Table B.2) for the first time in the person's history

with continuous observation of at least 365 days prior and 0 days after event index date, and limit initial events to: earliest event per person.

Inclusion Rules

Inclusion Criteria #1: has hypertension diagnosis in 1 yr prior to treatment

Having all of the following criteria:

- at least 1 occurrences of a condition occurrence of *Hypertensive disorder* (Table B.3) where event starts between 365 days Before and 0 days After index start date

Inclusion Criteria #2: Has no prior antihypertensive drug exposures in medical history

Having all of the following criteria:

- exactly 0 occurrences of a drug exposure of *Hypertension drugs* (Table B.4) where event starts between all days Before and 1 days Before index start date

Inclusion Criteria #3: Is only taking ACE as monotherapy, with no concomitant combination treatments

Having all of the following criteria:

- exactly 1 distinct occurrences of a drug era of *Hypertension drugs* (Table B.4) where event starts between 0 days Before and 7 days After index start date

Limit qualifying cohort to: earliest event per person.

End Date Strategy

Custom Drug Era Exit Criteria. This strategy creates a drug era from the codes found in the specified concept set. If the index event is found within an era, the cohort end date will use the era's end date. Otherwise, it will use the observation period end date that contains the index event.

Use the era end date of *ACE inhibitors* (Table B.2)

- allowing 30 days between exposures
- adding 0 days after exposure end

Cohort Collapse Strategy

Collapse cohort by era with a gap size of 0 days.

Concept Set Definitions

Table B.2: ACE inhibitors

Concept Id	Concept Name	Excluded	Descendants	Mapped
1308216	Lisinopril	NO	YES	NO
1310756	moexipril	NO	YES	NO
1331235	quinapril	NO	YES	NO
1334456	Ramipril	NO	YES	NO
1335471	benazepril	NO	YES	NO
1340128	Captopril	NO	YES	NO
1341927	Enalapril	NO	YES	NO
1342439	trandolapril	NO	YES	NO
1363749	Fosinopril	NO	YES	NO
1373225	Perindopril	NO	YES	NO

Table B.3: Hypertensive disorder

Concept Id	Concept Name	Excluded	Descendants	Mapped
316866	Hypertensive disorder	NO	YES	NO

Table B.4: Hypertension drugs

Concept Id	Concept Name	Excluded	Descendants	Mapped
904542	Triamterene	NO	YES	NO
907013	Metolazone	NO	YES	NO
932745	Bumetanide	NO	YES	NO
942350	torsemide	NO	YES	NO
956874	Furosemide	NO	YES	NO
970250	Spironolactone	NO	YES	NO
974166	Hydrochlorothiazide	NO	YES	NO
978555	Indapamide	NO	YES	NO
991382	Amiloride	NO	YES	NO
1305447	Methyldopa	NO	YES	NO
1307046	Metoprolol	NO	YES	NO
1307863	Verapamil	NO	YES	NO
1308216	Lisinopril	NO	YES	NO
1308842	valsartan	NO	YES	NO
1309068	Minoxidil	NO	YES	NO
1309799	eplerenone	NO	YES	NO
1310756	moexipril	NO	YES	NO
1313200	Nadolol	NO	YES	NO
1314002	Atenolol	NO	YES	NO
1314577	nebivolol	NO	YES	NO
1317640	telmisartan	NO	YES	NO
1317967	aliskiren	NO	YES	NO
1318137	Nicardipine	NO	YES	NO
1318853	Nifedipine	NO	YES	NO
1319880	Nisoldipine	NO	YES	NO
1319998	Acebutolol	NO	YES	NO
1322081	Betaxolol	NO	YES	NO
1326012	Isradipine	NO	YES	NO
1327978	Penbutolol	NO	YES	NO
1328165	Diltiazem	NO	YES	NO
1331235	quinapril	NO	YES	NO
1332418	Amlodipine	NO	YES	NO
1334456	Ramipril	NO	YES	NO
1335471	benazepril	NO	YES	NO
1338005	Bisoprolol	NO	YES	NO

Concept Id	Concept Name	Excluded	Descendants	Mapped
1340128	Captopril	NO	YES	NO
1341238	Terazosin	NO	YES	NO
1341927	Enalapril	NO	YES	NO
1342439	trandolapril	NO	YES	NO
1344965	Guanfacine	NO	YES	NO
1345858	Pindolol	NO	YES	NO
1346686	eprosartan	NO	YES	NO
1346823	carvedilol	NO	YES	NO
1347384	irbesartan	NO	YES	NO
1350489	Prazosin	NO	YES	NO
1351557	candesartan	NO	YES	NO
1353766	Propranolol	NO	YES	NO
1353776	Felodipine	NO	YES	NO
1363053	Doxazosin	NO	YES	NO
1363749	Fosinopril	NO	YES	NO
1367500	Losartan	NO	YES	NO
1373225	Perindopril	NO	YES	NO
1373928	Hydralazine	NO	YES	NO
1386957	Labetalol	NO	YES	NO
1395058	Chlorthalidone	NO	YES	NO
1398937	Clonidine	NO	YES	NO
40226742	olmesartan	NO	YES	NO
40235485	azilsartan	NO	YES	NO

B.3 Acute Myocardial Infarction (AMI)

Initial Event Cohort

People having any of the following:

- a condition occurrence of *Acute myocardial Infarction* (Table B.5)

with continuous observation of at least 0 days prior and 0 days after event index date, and limit initial events to: all events per person.

For people matching the Primary Events, include: Having any of the following criteria:

- at least 1 occurrences of a visit occurrence of *Inpatient or ER visit* (Table B.6) where event starts between all days Before and 0 days After index start date and event ends between 0 days Before and all days After index start date

Limit cohort of initial events to: all events per person.

Limit qualifying cohort to: all events per person.

End Date Strategy

Date Offset Exit Criteria. This cohort definition end date will be the index event's start date plus 7 days

Cohort Collapse Strategy

Collapse cohort by era with a gap size of 180 days.

Concept Set Definitions

Table B.5: Inpatient or ER visit

Concept Id	Concept Name	Excluded	Descendants	Mapped
314666	Old myocardial infarction	YES	YES	NO
4329847	Myocardial infarction	NO	YES	NO

Table B.6: Inpatient or ER visit

Concept Id	Concept Name	Excluded	Descendants	Mapped
262	Emergency Room and Inpatient Visit	NO	YES	NO
9201	Inpatient Visit	NO	YES	NO
9203	Emergency Room Visit	NO	YES	NO

B.4 Angioedema

Initial Event Cohort

People having any of the following:

- a condition occurrence of *Angioedema* (Table B.7)

with continuous observation of at least 0 days prior and 0 days after event index date, and limit initial events to: all events per person.

For people matching the Primary Events, include: Having any of the following criteria:

- at least 1 occurrences of a visit occurrence of *Inpatient or ER visit* (Table B.8) where event starts between all days Before and 0 days After index start date and event ends between 0 days Before and all days After index start date

Limit cohort of initial events to: all events per person.

Limit qualifying cohort to: all events per person.

End Date Strategy

This cohort definition end date will be the index event's start date plus 7 days

Cohort Collapse Strategy

Collapse cohort by era with a gap size of 30 days.

Concept Set Definitions

Table B.7: Angioedema

Concept Id	Concept Name	Excluded	Descendants	Mapped
432791	Angioedema	NO	YES	NO

Table B.8: Inpatient or ER visit

Concept Id	Concept Name	Excluded	Descendants	Mapped
262	Emergency Room and Inpatient Visit	NO	YES	NO
9201	Inpatient Visit	NO	YES	NO
9203	Emergency Room Visit	NO	YES	NO

B.5 New Users of Thiazide-Like Diuretics Monotherapy

Initial Event Cohort

People having any of the following:

- a drug exposure of *Thiazide or thiazide-like diuretic* (Table B.9) for the first time in the person's history

with continuous observation of at least 365 days prior and 0 days after event index date, and limit initial events to: earliest event per person.

Inclusion Rules

Inclusion Criteria #1: has hypertension diagnosis in 1 yr prior to treatment

Having all of the following criteria:

- at least 1 occurrences of a condition occurrence of *Hypertensive disorder* (Table B.10) where event starts between 365 days Before and 0 days After index start date

Inclusion Criteria #2: Has no prior antihypertensive drug exposures in medical history

Having all of the following criteria:

- exactly 0 occurrences of a drug exposure of *Hypertension drugs* (Table B.11) where event starts between all days Before and 1 days Before index start date

Inclusion Criteria #3: Is only taking ACE as monotherapy, with no concomitant combination treatments

Having all of the following criteria:

- exactly 1 distinct occurrences of a drug era of *Hypertension drugs* (Table B.11) where event starts between 0 days Before and 7 days After index start date

Limit qualifying cohort to: earliest event per person.

End Date Strategy

Custom Drug Era Exit Criteria. This strategy creates a drug era from the codes found in the specified concept set. If the index event is found within an era, the cohort end date will use the era's end date. Otherwise, it will use the observation period end date that contains the index event.

Use the era end date of *Thiazide or thiazide-like diuretic* (Table B.9)

- allowing 30 days between exposures
- adding 0 days after exposure end

Cohort Collapse Strategy

Collapse cohort by era with a gap size of 0 days.

Concept Set Definitions

Table B.9: Thiazide or thiazide-like diuretic

Concept Id	Concept Name	Excluded	Descendants	Mapped
907013	Metolazone	NO	YES	NO

Concept Id	Concept Name	Excluded	Descendants	Mapped
974166	Hydrochlorothiazide	NO	YES	NO
978555	Indapamide	NO	YES	NO
1395058	Chlorthalidone	NO	YES	NO

Table B.10: Hypertensive disorder

Concept Id	Concept Name	Excluded	Descendants	Mapped
316866	Hypertensive disorder	NO	YES	NO

Table B.11: Hypertension drugs

Concept Id	Concept Name	Excluded	Descendants	Mapped
904542	Triamterene	NO	YES	NO
907013	Metolazone	NO	YES	NO
932745	Bumetanide	NO	YES	NO
942350	torsemide	NO	YES	NO
956874	Furosemide	NO	YES	NO
970250	Spironolactone	NO	YES	NO
974166	Hydrochlorothiazide	NO	YES	NO
978555	Indapamide	NO	YES	NO
991382	Amiloride	NO	YES	NO
1305447	Methyldopa	NO	YES	NO
1307046	Metoprolol	NO	YES	NO
1307863	Verapamil	NO	YES	NO
1308216	Lisinopril	NO	YES	NO
1308842	valsartan	NO	YES	NO
1309068	Minoxidil	NO	YES	NO
1309799	eplerenone	NO	YES	NO
1310756	moexipril	NO	YES	NO
1313200	Nadolol	NO	YES	NO
1314002	Atenolol	NO	YES	NO
1314577	nebivolol	NO	YES	NO
1317640	telmisartan	NO	YES	NO
1317967	aliskiren	NO	YES	NO
1318137	Nicardipine	NO	YES	NO
1318853	Nifedipine	NO	YES	NO
1319880	Nisoldipine	NO	YES	NO
1319998	Acebutolol	NO	YES	NO
1322081	Betaxolol	NO	YES	NO
1326012	Isradipine	NO	YES	NO

Concept Id	Concept Name	Excluded	Descendants	Mapped
1327978	Penbutolol	NO	YES	NO
1328165	Diltiazem	NO	YES	NO
1331235	quinapril	NO	YES	NO
1332418	Amlodipine	NO	YES	NO
1334456	Ramipril	NO	YES	NO
1335471	benazepril	NO	YES	NO
1338005	Bisoprolol	NO	YES	NO
1340128	Captopril	NO	YES	NO
1341238	Terazosin	NO	YES	NO
1341927	Enalapril	NO	YES	NO
1342439	trandolapril	NO	YES	NO
1344965	Guanfacine	NO	YES	NO
1345858	Pindolol	NO	YES	NO
1346686	eprosartan	NO	YES	NO
1346823	carvedilol	NO	YES	NO
1347384	irbesartan	NO	YES	NO
1350489	Prazosin	NO	YES	NO
1351557	candesartan	NO	YES	NO
1353766	Propranolol	NO	YES	NO
1353776	Felodipine	NO	YES	NO
1363053	Doxazosin	NO	YES	NO
1363749	Fosinopril	NO	YES	NO
1367500	Losartan	NO	YES	NO
1373225	Perindopril	NO	YES	NO
1373928	Hydralazine	NO	YES	NO
1386957	Labetalol	NO	YES	NO
1395058	Chlorthalidone	NO	YES	NO
1398937	Clonidine	NO	YES	NO
40226742	olmesartan	NO	YES	NO
40235485	azilsartan	NO	YES	NO

B.6   Patients Initiating First-Line Therapy for Hypertension

Initial Event Cohort

People having any of the following:

- a drug exposure of *First-line hypertension drugs* (Table B.12) for the first time in the person's history

with continuous observation of at least 365 days prior and 365 days after event index date, and limit initial events to: earliest event per person.

Inclusion Rules

Having all of the following criteria:

- exactly 0 occurrences of a drug exposure of *Hypertension drugs* (Table B.13) where event starts between all days Before and 1 days Before index start date
- and at least 1 occurrences of a condition occurrence of *Hypertensive disorder* (Table B.14) where event starts between 365 days Before and 0 days After index start date

Limit cohort of initial events to: earliest event per person. Limit qualifying cohort to: earliest event per person.

End Date Strategy

No end date strategy selected. By default, the cohort end date will be the end of the observation period that contains the index event.

Cohort Collapse Strategy

Collapse cohort by era with a gap size of 0 days.

Concept Set Definitions

Table B.12: First-line hypertension drugs

Concept Id	Concept Name	Excluded	Descendants	Mapped
907013	Metolazone	NO	YES	NO
974166	Hydrochlorothiazide	NO	YES	NO
978555	Indapamide	NO	YES	NO
1307863	Verapamil	NO	YES	NO
1308216	Lisinopril	NO	YES	NO
1308842	valsartan	NO	YES	NO
1310756	moexipril	NO	YES	NO
1317640	telmisartan	NO	YES	NO
1318137	Nicardipine	NO	YES	NO
1318853	Nifedipine	NO	YES	NO
1319880	Nisoldipine	NO	YES	NO
1326012	Isradipine	NO	YES	NO
1328165	Diltiazem	NO	YES	NO
1331235	quinapril	NO	YES	NO

Concept Id	Concept Name	Excluded	Descendants	Mapped
1332418	Amlodipine	NO	YES	NO
1334456	Ramipril	NO	YES	NO
1335471	benazepril	NO	YES	NO
1340128	Captopril	NO	YES	NO
1341927	Enalapril	NO	YES	NO
1342439	trandolapril	NO	YES	NO
1346686	eprosartan	NO	YES	NO
1347384	irbesartan	NO	YES	NO
1351557	candesartan	NO	YES	NO
1353776	Felodipine	NO	YES	NO
1363749	Fosinopril	NO	YES	NO
1367500	Losartan	NO	YES	NO
1373225	Perindopril	NO	YES	NO
1395058	Chlorthalidone	NO	YES	NO
40226742	olmesartan	NO	YES	NO
40235485	azilsartan	NO	YES	NO

Table B.13: Hypertension drugs

Concept Id	Concept Name	Excluded	Descendants	Mapped
904542	Triamterene	NO	YES	NO
907013	Metolazone	NO	YES	NO
932745	Bumetanide	NO	YES	NO
942350	torsemide	NO	YES	NO
956874	Furosemide	NO	YES	NO
970250	Spironolactone	NO	YES	NO
974166	Hydrochlorothiazide	NO	YES	NO
978555	Indapamide	NO	YES	NO
991382	Amiloride	NO	YES	NO
1305447	Methyldopa	NO	YES	NO
1307046	Metoprolol	NO	YES	NO
1307863	Verapamil	NO	YES	NO
1308216	Lisinopril	NO	YES	NO
1308842	valsartan	NO	YES	NO
1309068	Minoxidil	NO	YES	NO
1309799	eplerenone	NO	YES	NO
1310756	moexipril	NO	YES	NO
1313200	Nadolol	NO	YES	NO
1314002	Atenolol	NO	YES	NO
1314577	nebivolol	NO	YES	NO
1317640	telmisartan	NO	YES	NO
1317967	aliskiren	NO	YES	NO

Concept Id	Concept Name	Excluded	Descendants	Mapped
1318137	Nicardipine	NO	YES	NO
1318853	Nifedipine	NO	YES	NO
1319880	Nisoldipine	NO	YES	NO
1319998	Acebutolol	NO	YES	NO
1322081	Betaxolol	NO	YES	NO
1326012	Isradipine	NO	YES	NO
1327978	Penbutolol	NO	YES	NO
1328165	Diltiazem	NO	YES	NO
1331235	quinapril	NO	YES	NO
1332418	Amlodipine	NO	YES	NO
1334456	Ramipril	NO	YES	NO
1335471	benazepril	NO	YES	NO
1338005	Bisoprolol	NO	YES	NO
1340128	Captopril	NO	YES	NO
1341238	Terazosin	NO	YES	NO
1341927	Enalapril	NO	YES	NO
1342439	trandolapril	NO	YES	NO
1344965	Guanfacine	NO	YES	NO
1345858	Pindolol	NO	YES	NO
1346686	eprosartan	NO	YES	NO
1346823	carvedilol	NO	YES	NO
1347384	irbesartan	NO	YES	NO
1350489	Prazosin	NO	YES	NO
1351557	candesartan	NO	YES	NO
1353766	Propranolol	NO	YES	NO
1353776	Felodipine	NO	YES	NO
1363053	Doxazosin	NO	YES	NO
1363749	Fosinopril	NO	YES	NO
1367500	Losartan	NO	YES	NO
1373225	Perindopril	NO	YES	NO
1373928	Hydralazine	NO	YES	NO
1386957	Labetalol	NO	YES	NO
1395058	Chlorthalidone	NO	YES	NO
1398937	Clonidine	NO	YES	NO
40226742	olmesartan	NO	YES	NO
40235485	azilsartan	NO	YES	NO

Table B.14: Hypertensive disorder

Concept Id	Concept Name	Excluded	Descendants	Mapped
316866	Hypertensive disorder	NO	YES	NO

B.7 Patients Initiating First-Line Therapy for Hypertension With >3 Yr Follow-Up

Same as *cohort definition B.6* but with continuous observation of at least 365 days prior and **1095 days** after event index date

B.8 ACE Inhibitor Use

Initial Event Cohort

People having any of the following:

- a drug exposure of *ACE inhibitors* (Table B.15)

with continuous observation of at least 0 days prior and 0 days after event index date, and limit initial events to: all events per person.

Limit qualifying cohort to: all events per person.

End Date Strategy

This strategy creates a drug era from the codes found in the specified concept set. If the index event is found within an era, the cohort end date will use the era's end date. Otherwise, it will use the observation period end date that contains the index event.

Use the era end date of *ACE inhibitors* (Table B.15)

- allowing 30 days between exposures
- adding 0 days after exposure end

Cohort Collapse Strategy

Collapse cohort by era with a gap size of 30 days.

Concept Set Definitions

Table B.15: ACE inhibitors

Concept Id	Concept Name	Excluded	Descendants	Mapped
1308216	Lisinopril	NO	YES	NO
1310756	moexipril	NO	YES	NO
1331235	quinapril	NO	YES	NO

Concept Id	Concept Name	Excluded	Descendants	Mapped
1334456	Ramipril	NO	YES	NO
1335471	benazepril	NO	YES	NO
1340128	Captopril	NO	YES	NO
1341927	Enalapril	NO	YES	NO
1342439	trandolapril	NO	YES	NO
1363749	Fosinopril	NO	YES	NO
1373225	Perindopril	NO	YES	NO

B.9   Angiotensin Receptor Blocker (ARB) Use

Same as *cohort definition B.8* with *Angiotensin Receptor Blockers (ARBs)* (Table B.16) in place of *ACE inhibitors* (Table B.15).

Concept Set Definitions

Table B.16: Angiotensin Receptor Blockers (ARBs)

Concept Id	Concept Name	Excluded	Descendants	Mapped
1308842	valsartan	NO	YES	NO
1317640	telmisartan	NO	YES	NO
1346686	eprosartan	NO	YES	NO
1347384	irbesartan	NO	YES	NO
1351557	candesartan	NO	YES	NO
1367500	Losartan	NO	YES	NO
40226742	olmesartan	NO	YES	NO
40235485	azilsartan	NO	YES	NO

B.10   Thiazide Or Thiazide-Like Diuretic Use

Same as *cohort definition B.8* with *Thiazide or thiazide-like diuretic* (Table B.17) in place of *ACE inhibitors* (Table B.15).

Concept Set Definitions

Table B.17: Thiazide or thiazide-like diuretic

Concept Id	Concept Name	Excluded	Descendants	Mapped
907013	Metolazone	NO	YES	NO
974166	Hydrochlorothiazide	NO	YES	NO
978555	Indapamide	NO	YES	NO
1395058	Chlorthalidone	NO	YES	NO

B.11 Dihydropyridine Calcium Channel Blocker (dCCB) Use

Same as *cohort definition B.8* with *dihydropyridine Calcium Channel Blocker (dCCB)* (Table B.18) in place of *ACE inhibitors* (Table B.15).

Concept Set Definitions

Table B.18: Dihydropyridine Calcium channel blockers (dCCB)

Concept Id	Concept Name	Excluded	Descendants	Mapped
1318137	Nicardipine	NO	YES	NO
1318853	Nifedipine	NO	YES	NO
1319880	Nisoldipine	NO	YES	NO
1326012	Isradipine	NO	YES	NO
1332418	Amlodipine	NO	YES	NO
1353776	Felodipine	NO	YES	NO

B.12 Non-Dihydropyridine Calcium Channel Blocker (nd-CCB) Use

Same as *cohort definition B.8* with *non-dihydropyridine Calcium channel blockers (ndCCB)* (Table B.19) in place of *ACE inhibitors* (Table B.15).

Concept Set Definitions

Table B.19: non-dihydropyridine Calcium channel blockers (ndCCB)

Concept Id	Concept Name	Excluded	Descendants	Mapped
1307863	Verapamil	NO	YES	NO

Concept Id	Concept Name	Excluded	Descendants	Mapped
1328165	Diltiazem	NO	YES	NO

B.13 Beta-Blocker Use

Same as *cohort definition B.8* with *Beta blockers* (Table B.20) in place of *ACE inhibitors* (Table B.15).

Concept Set Definitions

Table B.20: Beta blockers

Concept Id	Concept Name	Excluded	Descendants	Mapped
1307046	Metoprolol	NO	YES	NO
1313200	Nadolol	NO	YES	NO
1314002	Atenolol	NO	YES	NO
1314577	nebivolol	NO	YES	NO
1319998	Acebutolol	NO	YES	NO
1322081	Betaxolol	NO	YES	NO
1327978	Penbutolol	NO	YES	NO
1338005	Bisoprolol	NO	YES	NO
1345858	Pindolol	NO	YES	NO
1346823	carvedilol	NO	YES	NO
1353766	Propranolol	NO	YES	NO
1386957	Labetalol	NO	YES	NO

B.14 Diuretic-Loop Use

Same as *cohort definition B.8* with *Diuretics - Loop* (Table B.21) in place of *ACE inhibitors* (Table B.15).

Concept Set Definitions

Table B.21: Diuretics - Loop

Concept Id	Concept Name	Excluded	Descendants	Mapped
932745	Bumetanide	NO	YES	NO
942350	torsemide	NO	YES	NO

956874	Furosemide	NO	YES	NO

B.15   Diuretic-Potassium Sparing Use

Same as *cohort definition B.8* with *Diuretics - potassium sparing* (Table B.22) in place of *ACE inhibitors* (Table B.15).

Concept Set Definitions

Table B.22: Diuretics - potassium sparing

Concept Id	Concept Name	Excluded	Descendants	Mapped
904542	Triamterene	NO	YES	NO
991382	Amiloride	NO	YES	NO

B.16   Alpha-1 Blocker Use

Same as *cohort definition B.8* with *Alpha-1 blocker* (Table B.23) in place of *ACE inhibitors* (Table B.15).

Concept Set Definitions

Table B.23: Alpha-1 blocker

Concept Id	Concept Name	Excluded	Descendants	Mapped
1341238	Terazosin	NO	YES	NO
1350489	Prazosin	NO	YES	NO
1363053	Doxazosin	NO	YES	NO

Chapter C

Negative controls

This Appendix contains negative controls used in various chapters of the book.

C.1   ACEi and THZ

Table C.1: Negative control outcomes when comparing ACE inhibitors (ACEi) to thiazides and thiazide-like diuretics (THZ).

Concept ID	Concept Name
434165	Abnormal cervical smear
436409	Abnormal pupil
199192	Abrasion and/or friction burn of trunk without infection
4088290	Absence of breast
4092879	Absent kidney
44783954	Acid reflux
75911	Acquired hallux valgus
137951	Acquired keratoderma
77965	Acquired trigger finger
376707	Acute conjunctivitis
4103640	Amputated foot
73241	Anal and rectal polyp
133655	Burn of forearm
73560	Calcaneal spur
434327	Cannabis abuse
4213540	Cervical somatic dysfunction
140842	Changes in skin texture
81378	Chondromalacia of patella
432303	Cocaine abuse

Concept ID	Concept Name
4201390	Colostomy present
46269889	Complication due to Crohn's disease
134438	Contact dermatitis
78619	Contusion of knee
201606	Crohn's disease
76786	Derangement of knee
4115402	Difficulty sleeping
45757370	Disproportion of reconstructed breast
433111	Effects of hunger
433527	Endometriosis
4170770	Epidermoid cyst
4092896	Feces contents abnormal
259995	Foreign body in orifice
40481632	Ganglion cyst
4166231	Genetic predisposition
433577	Hammer toe
4231770	Hereditary thrombophilia
440329	Herpes zoster without complication
4012570	High risk sexual behavior
4012934	Homocystinuria
441788	Human papilloma virus infection
4201717	Ileostomy present
374375	Impacted cerumen
4344500	Impingement syndrome of shoulder region
139099	Ingrowing nail
444132	Injury of knee
196168	Irregular periods
432593	Kwashiorkor
434203	Late effect of contusion
438329	Late effect of motor vehicle accident
195873	Leukorrhea
4083487	Macular drusen
4103703	Melena
4209423	Nicotine dependence
377572	Noise effects on inner ear
40480893	Nonspecific tuberculin test reaction
136368	Non-toxic multinodular goiter
140648	Onychomycosis due to dermatophyte
438130	Opioid abuse
4091513	Passing flatus
4202045	Postviral fatigue syndrome
373478	Presbyopia
46286594	Problem related to lifestyle

Concept ID	Concept Name
439790	Psychalgia
81634	Ptotic breast
380706	Regular astigmatism
141932	Senile hyperkeratosis
36713918	Somatic dysfunction of lumbar region
443172	Splinter of face, without major open wound
81151	Sprain of ankle
72748	Strain of rotator cuff capsule
378427	Tear film insufficiency
437264	Tobacco dependence syndrome
194083	Vaginitis and vulvovaginitis
140641	Verruca vulgaris
440193	Wristdrop
4115367	Wrist joint pain

Chapter D

Protocol template

1. Table of contents

2. List of abbreviations

3. Abstract
4. Amendments and Updates

5. Milestones

6. Rationale and Background
7. Study Objectives
    - Primary Hypotheses

    - Secondary Hypotheses

    - Primary Objectives

    - Secondary Objectives

8. Research methods
    - Study Design

    - Data Source(s)

    - Study population

    - Exposures
    - Outcomes

- Covariates

9. Data Analysis Plan
   - Calculation of time-at risk

   - Model Specification

   - Pooling effect estimates across databases
   - Analyses to perform

   - Output

   - Evidence Evaluation

10. Study Diagnostics
    - Sample Size and Study Power

    - Cohort Comparability

    - Systematic Error Assessment

11. Strengths and Limitations of the Research Methods

12. Protection of Human Subjects

13. Management and Reporting of Adverse Events and Adverse Reactions

14. Plans for Disseminating and Communicating Study Results
15. Appendix: Negative controls
16. References

Chapter E

Suggested Answers

This Appendix contains suggested answers for the exercises in the book.

E.1 The Common Data Model

Exercise 4.1

Based on the description in the exercise, John's record should look like Table E.1.

Table E.1: The PERSON table.

Column name	Value	Explanation
PERSON_ID	2	A unique integer.
GENDER_CONCEPT_ID	8507	The concept ID for male gender is 8507.
YEAR_OF_BIRTH	1974	
MONTH_OF_BIRTH	8	
DAY_OF_BIRTH	4	
BIRTH_DATETIME	1974-08-04 00:00:00	When the time is not known midnight is used.
DEATH_DATETIME	NULL	
RACE_CONCEPT_ID	8516	The concept ID for black or African American is 8516.
ETHNICITY_ CONCEPT_ID	38003564	38003564 refers to "Not hispanic".
LOCATION_ID		His address is not known.
PROVIDER_ID		His primary care Provider is not known.
CARE_SITE		His primary Care Site is not known.
PERSON_SOURCE_ VALUE	NULL	Not provided.

Column name	Value	Explanation
GENDER_SOURCE_ VALUE	Man	The text used in the description.
GENDER_SOURCE_ CONCEPT_ID	0	
RACE_SOURCE_ VALUE	African American	The text used in the description.
RACE_SOURCE_ CONCEPT_ID	0	
ETHNICITY_SOURCE_ VALUE	NULL	
ETHNICITY_SOURCE_ CONCEPT_ID	0	

Exercise 4.2

Based on the description in the exercise, John's record should look like Table E.2.

Table E.2: The OBSERVATION_PERIOD table.

Column name	Value	Explanation
OBSERVATION_ PERIOD_ID	2	A unique integer.
PERSON_ID	2	This is a foreign key to John's record in the PERSON table.
OBSERVATION_PERIOD_ START_DATE	2015-01-01	The date of enrollment.
OBSERVATION_PERIOD_ END_DATE	2019-07-01	No data can be expected after the data extraction date.
PERIOD_TYPE_ CONCEPT_ID	44814722	44814724 refers to "Period while enrolled in insurance".

Exercise 4.3

Based on the description in the exercise, John's record should look like Table E.3.

Table E.3: The DRUG_EXPOSURE table.

Column name	Value	Explanation
DRUG_EXPOSURE_ID	1001	Some unique integer

Column name	Value	Explanation
PERSON_ID	2	This is a foreign key to John's record in the PERSON table.
DRUG_CONCEPT_ID	19078461	The provided NDC code maps to Standard Concept 19078461.
DRUG_EXPOSURE_ START_DATE	2019-05-01	The start date of the exposure to the drug.
DRUG_EXPOSURE_ START_DATETIME	2019-05-01 00:00:00	Midnight is used as the time is not known.
DRUG_EXPOSURE_ END_DATE	2019-05-31	Based on start date + days supply.
DRUG_EXPOSURE_ END_DATETIME	2019-05-31 00:00:00	Midnight is used as time is unknown.
VERBATIM_END_DATE	NULL	Not provided.
DRUG_TYPE_ CONCEPT_ID	38000177	38000177 indicates "Prescription written".
STOP_REASON	NULL	
REFILLS	NULL	
QUANTITY	NULL	Not provided.
DAYS_SUPPLY	30	As described in the exercise.
SIG	NULL	Not provided.
ROUTE_CONCEPT_ID	4132161	4132161 indicates "Oral".
LOT_NUMBER	NULL	Not provided.
PROVIDER_ID	NULL	Not provided.
VISIT_OCCURRENCE_ ID	NULL	No information on the visit was provided..
VISIT_DETAIL_ID	NULL	
DRUG_SOURCE_ VALUE	76168009520	This is provided NDC code.
DRUG_SOURCE_ CONCEPT_ID	583945	583945 represents the drug source value (NDC code "76168009520").
ROUTE_SOURCE_ VALUE	NULL	

Exercise 4.4

To find the set of records, we can query the CONDITION_OCCURRENCE table:

```
library(DatabaseConnector)
connection <- connect(connectionDetails)
sql <- "SELECT *
FROM @cdm.condition_occurrence
```

```
WHERE condition_concept_id = 192671;"

result <- renderTranslateQuerySql(connection, sql, cdm = "main")
head(result)
```

```
##   CONDITION_OCCURRENCE_ID PERSON_ID CONDITION_CONCEPT_ID ...
## 1                    4657       273               192671 ...
## 2                    1021        61               192671 ...
## 3                    5978       351               192671 ...
## 4                    9798       579               192671 ...
## 5                    9301       549               192671 ...
## 6                    1997       116               192671 ...
```

Exercise 4.5

To find the set of records, we can query the CONDITION_OCCURRENCE table using the CONDITION_SOURCE_VALUE field:

```
sql <- "SELECT *
FROM @cdm.condition_occurrence
WHERE condition_source_value = 'K92.2';"

result <- renderTranslateQuerySql(connection, sql, cdm = "main")
head(result)
```

```
##   CONDITION_OCCURRENCE_ID PERSON_ID CONDITION_CONCEPT_ID ...
## 1                    4657       273               192671 ...
## 2                    1021        61               192671 ...
## 3                    5978       351               192671 ...
## 4                    9798       579               192671 ...
## 5                    9301       549               192671 ...
## 6                    1997       116               192671 ...
```

Exercise 4.6

This information is stored in the OBSERVATION_PERIOD table:

```
library(DatabaseConnector)
connection <- connect(connectionDetails)
sql <- "SELECT *
FROM @cdm.observation_period
WHERE person_id = 61;"
```

```
renderTranslateQuerySql(connection, sql, cdm = "main")
```

```
##   OBSERVATION_PERIOD_ID PERSON_ID OBSERVATION_PERIOD_START_DATE ...
## 1                    61        61                    1968-01-21 ...
```

E.2   Standardized Vocabularies

Exercise 5.1

Concept ID 192671 ("Gastrointestinal hemorrhage")

Exercise 5.2

ICD-10CM codes:

- K29.91 "Gastroduodenitis, unspecified, with bleeding"
- K92.2 "Gastrointestinal hemorrhage, unspecified"

ICD-9CM codes:

- 578 "Gastrointestinal hemorrhage"
- 578.9 "Hemorrhage of gastrointestinal tract, unspecified"

Exercise 5.3

MedDRA preferred terms:

- "Gastrointestinal haemorrhage" (Concept ID 35707864)
- "Intestinal haemorrhage" (Concept ID 35707858)

E.3   Extract Transform Load

Exercise 6.1

- A) Data experts and CDM experts together design the ETL
- B) People with medical knowledge create the code mappings
- C) A technical person implements the ETL
- D) All are involved in quality control

Exercise 6.2

Column	Value	Answer
PERSON_ID	A123B456	This column has a data type of integer so the source record value needs to be translated to a numeric value.
GENDER_CONCEPT_ID	8532	
YEAR_OF_BIRTH	NULL	If we do not know the month or day of birth, we do not guess. A person can exist without a month or day of birth. If a person lacks a birth year that person should be dropped. This person would have to be dropped due to now year of birth.
MONTH_OF_BIRTH	NULL	
DAY_OF_BIRTH	NULL	
RACE_CONCEPT_ID	0	The race is WHITE which should be mapped to 8527.
ETHNICITY_CONCEPT_ID	8527	No ethnicity was provided, this should be mapped to 0.
PERSON_SOURCE_VALUE	A123B456	
GENDER_SOURCE_VALUE	F	
RACE_SOURCE_VALUE	WHITE	
ETHNICITY_SOURCE_VALUE	NONE PROVIDED	

Exercise 6.3

Column	Value
VISIT_OCCURRENCE_ID	1
PERSON_ID	11
VISIT_START_DATE	2004-09-26
VISIT_END_DATE	2004-09-30
VISIT_CONCEPT_ID	9201
VISIT_SOURCE_VALUE	inpatient

E.4   Data Analytics Use Cases

Exercise 7.1

1. Characterization

2. Patient-level prediction

3. Population-level estimation

Exercise 7.2

Probably not. Defining a non-exposure cohort that is comparable to your diclofenac exposure cohort is often impossible, since people take diclofenac for a reason. This precludes a
between-person comparison. It might possible to a within-person comparison, so for each
patient in the diclofenac cohort identifying time when they are not exposed, but a similar
problem occurs here: these times are likely incomparable, because there are reasons when at
one time someone is exposed and at other times not.

E.5   SQL and R

Exercise 9.1

To compute the number of people we can simply query the PERSON table:

```
library(DatabaseConnector)
connection <- connect(connectionDetails)
sql <- "SELECT COUNT(*) AS person_count
FROM @cdm.person;"

renderTranslateQuerySql(connection, sql, cdm = "main")
```

```
##    PERSON_COUNT
## 1         2694
```

Exercise 9.2

To compute the number of people with at least one prescription of celecoxib, we can query
the DRUG_EXPOSURE table. To find all drugs containing the ingredient celecoxib, we join
to the CONCEPT_ANCESTOR and CONCEPT tables:

```
library(DatabaseConnector)
connection <- connect(connectionDetails)
sql <- "SELECT COUNT(DISTINCT(person_id)) AS person_count
FROM @cdm.drug_exposure
INNER JOIN @cdm.concept_ancestor
  ON drug_concept_id = descendant_concept_id
INNER JOIN @cdm.concept ingredient
  ON ancestor_concept_id = ingredient.concept_id
WHERE LOWER(ingredient.concept_name) = 'celecoxib'
  AND ingredient.concept_class_id = 'Ingredient'
  AND ingredient.standard_concept = 'S';"

renderTranslateQuerySql(connection, sql, cdm = "main")
```

```
##    PERSON_COUNT
## 1          1844
```

Note that we use COUNT(DISTINCT(person_id)) to find the number of distinct persons, considering that a person might have more than one prescription. Also note that we use the LOWER function to make our search for "celecoxib" case-insensitive.

Alternatively, we can use the DRUG_ERA table, which is already rolled up to the ingredient level:

```
library(DatabaseConnector)
connection <- connect(connectionDetails)

sql <- "SELECT COUNT(DISTINCT(person_id)) AS person_count
FROM @cdm.drug_era
INNER JOIN @cdm.concept ingredient
  ON drug_concept_id = ingredient.concept_id
WHERE LOWER(ingredient.concept_name) = 'celecoxib'
  AND ingredient.concept_class_id = 'Ingredient'
  AND ingredient.standard_concept = 'S';"

renderTranslateQuerySql(connection, sql, cdm = "main")
```

```
##    PERSON_COUNT
## 1          1844
```

Exercise 9.3

To compute the number of diagnoses during exposure we extend our previous query by joining to the CONDITION_OCCURRENCE table. We join to the CONCEPT_ANCESTOR table to find all condition concepts that imply a gastrointestinal haemorrhage:

```
library(DatabaseConnector)
connection <- connect(connectionDetails)
sql <- "SELECT COUNT(*) AS diagnose_count
FROM @cdm.drug_era
INNER JOIN @cdm.concept ingredient
  ON drug_concept_id = ingredient.concept_id
INNER JOIN @cdm.condition_occurrence
  ON condition_start_date >= drug_era_start_date
    AND condition_start_date <= drug_era_end_date
INNER JOIN @cdm.concept_ancestor
  ON condition_concept_id =descendant_concept_id
WHERE LOWER(ingredient.concept_name) = 'celecoxib'
  AND ingredient.concept_class_id = 'Ingredient'
  AND ingredient.standard_concept = 'S'
  AND ancestor_concept_id = 192671;"

renderTranslateQuerySql(connection, sql, cdm = "main")
```

```
##    DIAGNOSE_COUNT
## 1            41
```

Note that in this case it is essential to use the DRUG_ERA table instead of the DRUG_EXPOSURE table, because drug exposures with the same ingredient can overlap, but drug eras can. This could lead to double counting. For example, imagine a person received two drug drugs containing celecoxib at the same time. This would be recorded as two drug exposures, so any diagnoses occurring during the exposure would be counted twice. The two exposures will be merged into a single non-overlapping drug era.

E.6   Defining Cohorts

Exercise 10.1

We create initial event criteria encoding these requirements:

- New users of diclofenac
- Ages 16 or older
- With at least 365 days of continuous observation prior to exposure

When done, the cohort entry event section should look like Figure E.1.

The concept set expression for diclofenac should look like Figure E.2, including the ingredient 'Diclofenac' and all of its descendant, thus including all drugs containing the ingredient diclofenac.

Next, we require no prior exposure to any NSAID, as shown in Figure E.3.

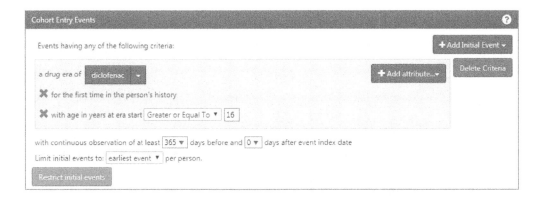

Figure E.1: Cohort entry event settings for new users of diclofenac

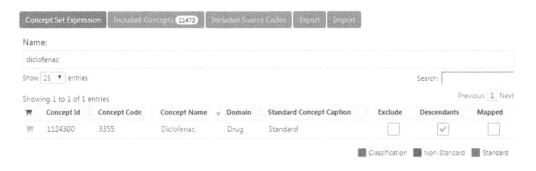

Figure E.2: Concept set expression for diclofenac.

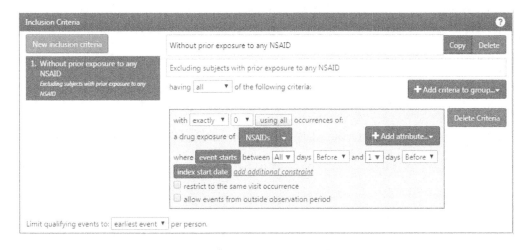

Figure E.3: Requiring no prior exposure to any NSAID.

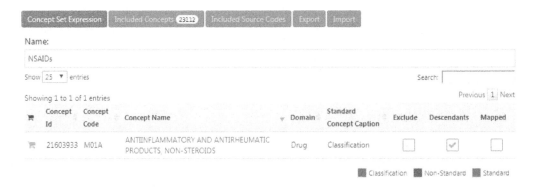

Figure E.4: Concept set expression for NSAIDs

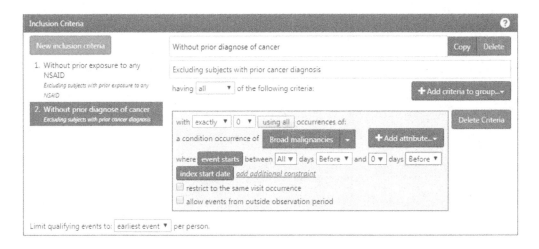

Figure E.5: Requiring no prior cancer diagnosis.

The concept set expression for NSAIDs should look like Figure E.4, including the NSAIDs class and all of its descendant, thus including all drugs containing any NSAID.

Additionally, we require no prior diagnosis of cancer, as shown in Figure E.5.

The concept set expression for "Broad malignancies" should look like Figure E.6, including the high level concept "Malignant neoplastic disease" and all of its descendant.

Finally, we define the cohort exit criteria as discontinuation of exposure (allowing for a 30-day gap), as shown in Figure E.7.

Exercise 10.2

For readability we here split the SQL into two steps. We first find all condition occurrences of myocardial infarction, and store these in a temp table called "#diagnoses":

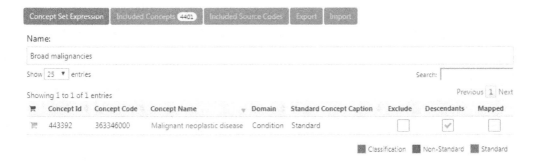

Figure E.6: Concept set expression for broad malignancies

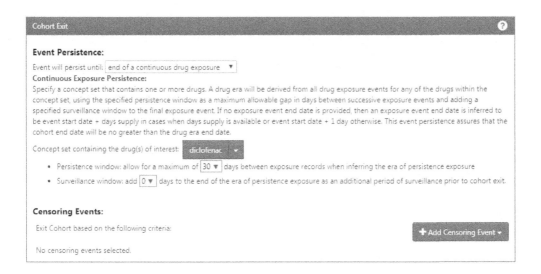

Figure E.7: Setting the cohort exit date.

```
library(DatabaseConnector)
connection <- connect(connectionDetails)
sql <- "SELECT person_id AS subject_id,
  condition_start_date AS cohort_start_date
INTO #diagnoses
FROM @cdm.condition_occurrence
WHERE condition_concept_id IN (
    SELECT descendant_concept_id
    FROM @cdm.concept_ancestor
    WHERE ancestor_concept_id = 4329847 -- Myocardial infarction
)
  AND condition_concept_id NOT IN (
    SELECT descendant_concept_id
    FROM @cdm.concept_ancestor
    WHERE ancestor_concept_id = 314666 -- Old myocardial infarction
);"

renderTranslateExecuteSql(connection, sql, cdm = "main")
```

We then select only those that occur during an inpatient or ER visit, using some unique
COHORT_DEFINITION_ID (we selected '1'):

```
sql <- "INSERT INTO @cdm.cohort (
  subject_id,
  cohort_start_date,
  cohort_definition_id
  )
SELECT subject_id,
  cohort_start_date,
  CAST (1 AS INT) AS cohort_definition_id
FROM #diagnoses
INNER JOIN @cdm.visit_occurrence
  ON subject_id = person_id
    AND cohort_start_date >= visit_start_date
    AND cohort_start_date <= visit_end_date
WHERE visit_concept_id IN (9201, 9203, 262); -- Inpatient or ER;"

renderTranslateExecuteSql(connection, sql, cdm = "main")
```

Note that an alternative approach would have been to join the conditions to the visits based
on the VISIT_OCCURRENCE_ID, instead of requiring the condition date to fall within the
visit start and end date. This would likely be more accurate, as it would guarantee that the
condition was recorded in relation to the inpatient or ER visit. However, many observational
databases do not record the link between visit and diagnose, and we therefore chose to use
the dates instead, likely giving us a higher sensitivity but perhaps lower specificity.

Note also that we ignored the cohort end date. Often, when a cohort is used to define an outcome we are only interested in the cohort start date, and there is no point in creating an (ill-defined) cohort end date.

It is recommended to clean up any temp tables when no longer needed:

```
sql <- "TRUNCATE TABLE #diagnoses;
DROP TABLE #diagnoses;"

renderTranslateExecuteSql(connection, sql)
```

E.7 Characterization

Exercise 11.1

In ATLAS we click on 🗄 Data Sources and select the data source we're interested in. We could select the Drug Exposure report, select the "Table" tab, and search for "celecoxib" as shown in Figure E.8. Here we see that this particular database has exposures to various formulations of celecoxib. We could click on any of these drugs to get a more detailed view, for example showing age and gender distributions for these drugs.

Exercise 11.2

Click on 🎗 Cohort Definitions and then "New cohort" to create a new cohort. Give the cohort a meaningful name (e.g. "Celecoxib new users") and go to the "Concept Sets" tab. Click on "New Concept Set", and give your concept set a meaningful names (e.g. "Celecoxib"). Open the 🔍 Search module, search for "celecoxib", restrict the Class to "Ingredient" and Standard Concept to "Standard", and click the 🛒 to add the concept to your concept set as show in Figure E.9.

Click on the left arrow shown at the top left of Figure E.9 to return to your cohort definition. Click on "+Add Initial Event" and then "Add Drug Era". Select your previously created concept set for the drug era criterion. Click on "Add attribute..." and select "Add First Exposure Criteria." Set the required continuous observation to at least 365 days before the index date. The result should look like Figure E.10. Leave the Inclusion Criteria, Cohort Exit, and Cohort Eras section as they are. Make sure to save the cohort definition by clicking 💾, and close it by clicking ❌.

Now that we have our cohort defined, we can characterize it. Click on 📈 Characterizations and then "New Characterization". Give you characterization a meaningful name (e.g. "Celecoxib new users characterization"). Under Cohort Definitions, click on "Import" and select your recently created cohort definition. Under "Feature Analyses", click on "Import" and select at least one condition analysis and one drug analysis, for example "Drug Group

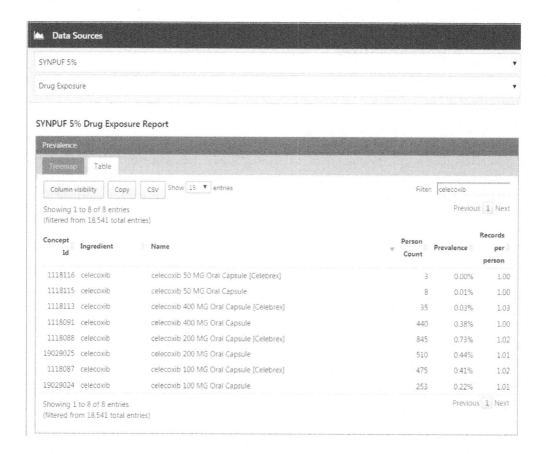

Figure E.8: Data source characterization.

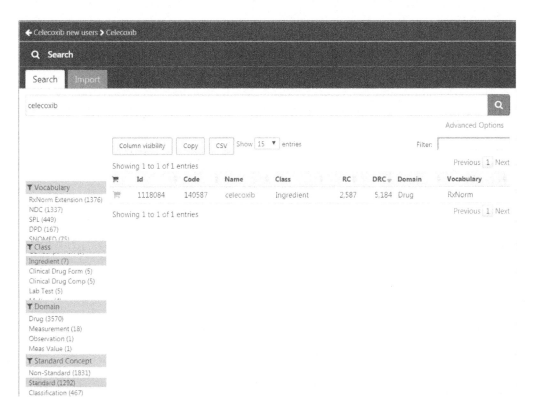

Figure E.9: Selecting the standard concept for the ingredient "celecoxib".

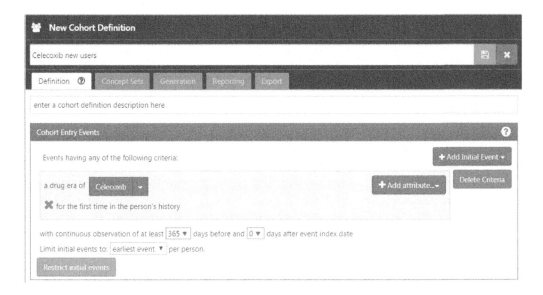

Figure E.10: A simple celecoxib new user cohort definition.

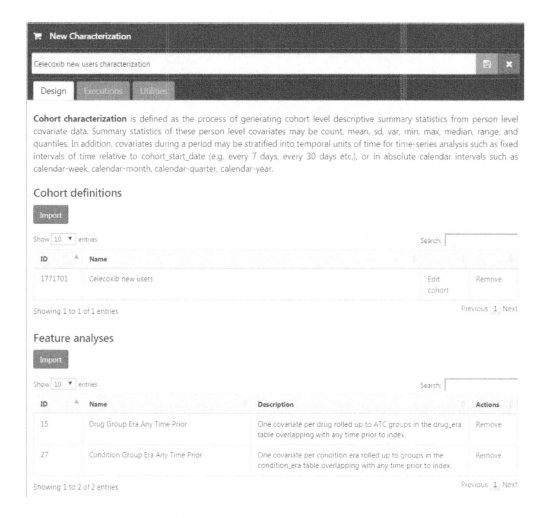

Figure E.11: Characterization settings.

Era Any Time Prior" and "Condition Group Era Any Time Prior". Your characterization definition should now look like Figure E.11. Make sure to save the characterization settings by clicking [image].

Click on the "Exections" tab, and click on "Generate" for one of the data sources. It may take a while for the generation to complete. When done, we can click on "View latest results". The resulting screen will look something like Figure E.12, showing for example that pain and arthropathy are commonly observed, which should not surprise use as these are indications for celecoxib. Lower on the list we may see conditions we were not expecting.

Exercise 11.3

Click on [image] and then "New cohort" to create a new cohort. Give the cohort a meaningful name (e.g. "GI bleed") and go to the "Concept Sets" tab. Click on

Figure E.12: Characterization settings.

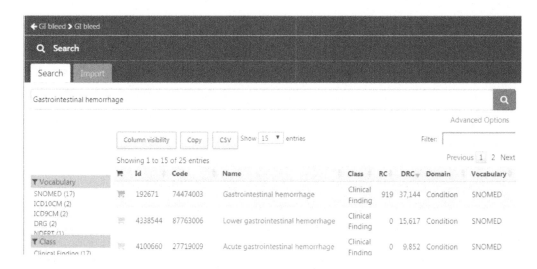

Figure E.13: Selecting the standard concept for "Gastrointestinal hemorrhage".

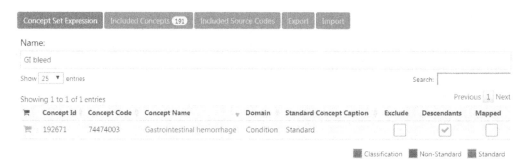

Figure E.14: Adding all descendants to "Gastrointestinal hemorrhage".

"New Concept Set", and give your concept set a meaningful names (e.g. "GI bleed"). Open
the Q Search module, search for "Gastrointestinal hemorrhage", and click the 🛒 next to
the top concept to add the concept to your concept set as show in Figure E.13.

Click on the left arrow shown at the top left of Figure E.13 to return to your cohort definition.
Open the "Concept Sets" tab again, and check "Descendants" next to the GI hemorrhage
concept, as shown in Figure E.14.

Return to the "Definition" tab, click on "+Add Initial Event" and then "Add Condition Occurrence". Select your previously created concept set for the condition occurrence criterion.
The result should look like Figure E.15. Leave the Inclusion Criteria, Cohort Exit, and Cohort Eras section as they are. Make sure to save the cohort definition by clicking 🖫, and
close it by clicking ❌.

Now that we have our cohort defined, we can compute the incidence rate. Click on
⚡ Incidence Rates and then "New Analysis". Give your analysis a meaningful name
(e.g. "Incidence of GI bleed after celecoxib initiation"). Click "Add Target Cohort" and

Figure E.15: A simple gastrointestinal bleed cohort definition.

select our celecoxib new user cohort. Click on "Add Outcome Cohort" and add our new GI bleed cohort. Set the Time At Risk to end 1095 days after the start date. The analysis should now look like Figure E.16. Make sure to save the analysis settings by clicking ⊟.

Click on the "Generation" tab, and click on "Generate". Select one of the data sources and click "Generate". When done, we can see the computed incidence rate and proportion, as shown in Figure E.17.

E.8   Population-Level Estimation

Exercise 12.1

We specify the default set of covariates, but we must exclude the two drugs we're comparing, including all their descendants, because else our propensity model will become perfectly predictive:

```
library(CohortMethod)
nsaids <- c(1118084, 1124300) # celecoxib, diclofenac
covSettings <- createDefaultCovariateSettings(
  excludedCovariateConceptIds = nsaids,
  addDescendantsToExclude = TRUE)

# Load data:
cmData <- getDbCohortMethodData(
  connectionDetails = connectionDetails,
  cdmDatabaseSchema = "main",
```

Figure E.16: A incidence rate analysis.

Figure E.17: Incidence results.

```
  targetId = 1,
  comparatorId = 2,
  outcomeIds = 3,
  exposureDatabaseSchema = "main",
  exposureTable = "cohort",
  outcomeDatabaseSchema = "main",
  outcomeTable = "cohort",
  covariateSettings = covSettings)
summary(cmData)
```

```
## CohortMethodData object summary
##
## Treatment concept ID: 1
## Comparator concept ID: 2
## Outcome concept ID(s): 3
##
## Treated persons: 1800
## Comparator persons: 830
##
## Outcome counts:
##    Event count Person count
## 3          479          479
##
## Covariates:
## Number of covariates: 389
## Number of non-zero covariate values: 26923
```

Exercise 12.2

We create the study population following the specifications, and output the attrition diagram:

```
studyPop <- createStudyPopulation(
  cohortMethodData = cmData,
  outcomeId = 3,
  washoutPeriod = 180,
  removeDuplicateSubjects = "remove all",
  removeSubjectsWithPriorOutcome = TRUE,
  riskWindowStart = 0,
  startAnchor = "cohort start",
  riskWindowEnd = 99999)
drawAttritionDiagram(studyPop)
```

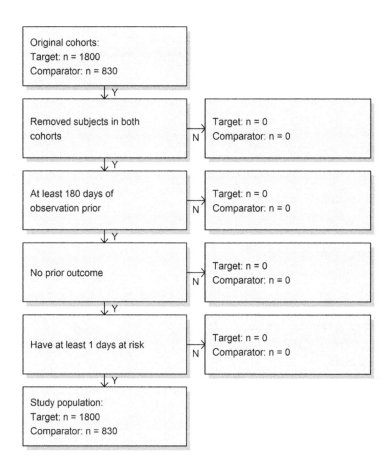

We see that we did not lose any subjects compared to the original cohorts, probably because the restrictions used here were already applied in the cohort definitions.

Exercise 12.3

We fit a simple outcome model using a Cox regression:

```
model <- fitOutcomeModel(population = studyPop,
                         modelType = "cox")
model
```

```
## Model type: cox
## Stratified: FALSE
## Use covariates: FALSE
## Use inverse probability of treatment weighting: FALSE
## Status: OK
##
```

```
##            Estimate lower .95 upper .95   logRr seLogRr
## treatment  1.34612    1.10065    1.65741 0.29723  0.1044
```

It is likely that celecoxib users are not exchangeable with diclofenac users, and that these baseline differences already lead to different risks of the outcome. If we do not adjust for these difference, like in this analysis, we are likely producing biased estimates.

Exercise 12.4

We fit a propensity model on our study population, using all covariates we extracted. We then show the preference score distribution:

```
ps <- createPs(cohortMethodData = cmData,
               population = studyPop)
plotPs(ps, showCountsLabel = TRUE, showAucLabel = TRUE)
```

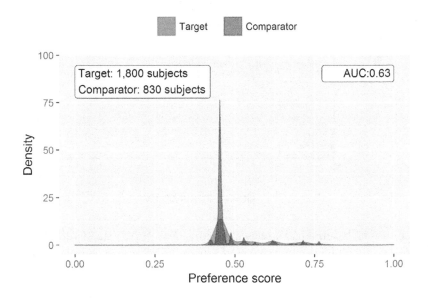

Note that this distribution looks a bit odd, with several spikes. This is because we are using a very small simulated dataset. Real preference score distributions tend to be much smoother.

The propensity model achieves an AUC of 0.63, suggested there are differences between target and comparator cohort. We see quite a lot overlap between the two groups suggesting PS adjustment can make them more comparable.

Exercise 12.5

We stratify the population based on the propensity scores, and compute the covariate balance before and after stratification:

```
strataPop <- stratifyByPs(ps, numberOfStrata = 5)
bal <- computeCovariateBalance(strataPop, cmData)
plotCovariateBalanceScatterPlot(bal,
                                showCovariateCountLabel = TRUE,
                                showMaxLabel = TRUE,
                                beforeLabel = "Before stratification",
                                afterLabel = "After stratification")
```

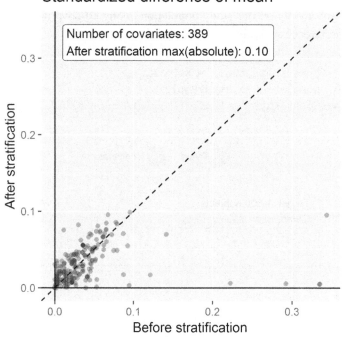

We see that various baseline covariates showed a large (>0.3) standardized difference of means before stratification (x-axis). After stratification, balance is increased, with the maximum standardized difference <= 0.1.

Exercise 12.6

We fit a outcome model using a Cox regression, but stratify it by the PS strata:

```
adjModel <- fitOutcomeModel(population = strataPop,
                            modelType = "cox",
                            stratified = TRUE)
adjModel
```

```
## Model type: cox
## Stratified: TRUE
```

```
## Use covariates: FALSE
## Use inverse probability of treatment weighting: FALSE
## Status: OK
##
##            Estimate lower .95 upper .95   logRr seLogRr
## treatment   1.13211   0.92132   1.40008 0.12409  0.1068
```

We see the adjusted estimate is lower than the unadjusted estimate, and that the 95% confidence interval now includes 1. This is because we are now adjusting for baseline differences between the two exposure groups, thus reducing bias.

E.9   Patient-Level Prediction

Exercise 13.1

We specify a set of covariate settings, and use the `getPlpData` function to extract the data from the database:

```
library(PatientLevelPrediction)
covSettings <- createCovariateSettings(
  useDemographicsGender = TRUE,
  useDemographicsAge = TRUE,
  useConditionGroupEraLongTerm = TRUE,
  useConditionGroupEraAnyTimePrior = TRUE,
  useDrugGroupEraLongTerm = TRUE,
  useDrugGroupEraAnyTimePrior = TRUE,
  useVisitConceptCountLongTerm = TRUE,
  longTermStartDays = -365,
  endDays = -1)


plpData <- getPlpData(connectionDetails = connectionDetails,
                      cdmDatabaseSchema = "main",
                      cohortDatabaseSchema = "main",
                      cohortTable = "cohort",
                      cohortId = 4,
                      covariateSettings = covSettings,
                      outcomeDatabaseSchema = "main",
                      outcomeTable = "cohort",
                      outcomeIds = 3)

summary(plpData)


## plpData object summary
##
## At risk cohort concept ID: -1
## Outcome concept ID(s): 3
```

```
##
## People: 2630
##
## Outcome counts:
##    Event count Person count
## 3          479          479
##
## Covariates:
## Number of covariates: 245
## Number of non-zero covariate values: 54079
```

Exercise 13.2

We create a study population for the outcome of interest (in this case the only outcome for which we extracted data), removing subjects who experienced the outcome before they started the NSAID, and requiring 364 days of time-at-risk:

```
population <- createStudyPopulation(plpData = plpData,
                                    outcomeId = 3,
                                    washoutPeriod = 364,
                                    firstExposureOnly = FALSE,
                                    removeSubjectsWithPriorOutcome = TRUE,
                                    priorOutcomeLookback = 9999,
                                    riskWindowStart = 1,
                                    riskWindowEnd = 365,
                                    addExposureDaysToStart = FALSE,
                                    addExposureDaysToEnd = FALSE,
                                    minTimeAtRisk = 364,
                                    requireTimeAtRisk = TRUE,
                                    includeAllOutcomes = TRUE)
nrow(population)
```

```
## [1] 2578
```

In this case we have lost a few people by removing those that had the outcome prior, and by requiring a time-at-risk of at least 364 days.

Exercise 13.3

We run a LASSO model by first creating a model settings object, and then calling the `runPlp` function. In this case we do a person split, training the model on 75% of the data and evaluating on 25% of the data:

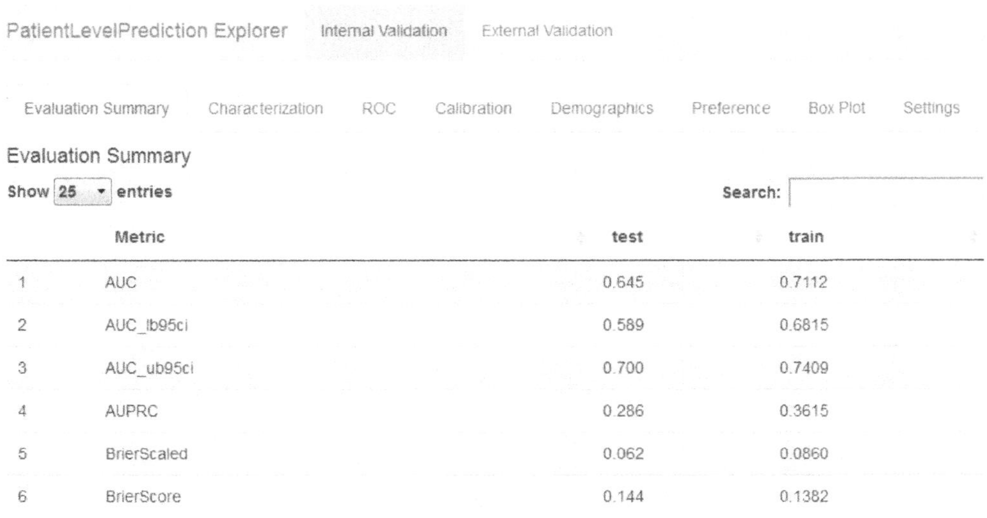

PatientLevelPrediction Explorer   Internal Validation   External Validation

Evaluation Summary   Characterization   ROC   Calibration   Demographics   Preference   Box Plot   Settings

Evaluation Summary

Show 25 ▾ entries   Search:

	Metric	test	train
1	AUC	0.645	0.7112
2	AUC_lb95ci	0.589	0.6815
3	AUC_ub95ci	0.700	0.7409
4	AUPRC	0.286	0.3615
5	BrierScaled	0.062	0.0860
6	BrierScore	0.144	0.1382

Figure E.18: Patient-level prediction Shiny app.

```
lassoModel <- setLassoLogisticRegression(seed = 0)

lassoResults <- runPlp(population = population,
                       plpData = plpData,
                       modelSettings = lassoModel,
                       testSplit = 'person',
                       testFraction = 0.25,
                       nfold = 2,
                       splitSeed = 0)
```

Note that for this example set the random seeds both for the LASSO cross-validation and for the train-test split to make sure the results will be the same on multiple runs.

We can now view the results using the Shiny app:

```
viewPlp(lassoResults)
```

This will launch the app as shown in Figure E.18. Here we see an AUC on the test set of 0.645, which is better than random guessing, but maybe not good enough for clinical pratice.

E.10 Data Quality

Exercise 15.1

To run ACHILLES:

```
library(ACHILLES)
result <- achilles(connectionDetails,
                   cdmDatabaseSchema = "main",
                   resultsDatabaseSchema = "main",
                   sourceName = "Eunomia",
                   cdmVersion = "5.3.0")
```

Exercise 15.2

To run the Data Quality Dashboard:

```
DataQualityDashboard::executeDqChecks(
  connectionDetails,
  cdmDatabaseSchema = "main",
  resultsDatabaseSchema = "main",
  cdmSourceName = "Eunomia",
  outputFolder = "C:/dataQualityExample")
```

Exercise 15.3

To view the list of data quality checks:

```
DataQualityDashboard::viewDqDashboard(
  "C:/dataQualityExample/Eunomia/results_Eunomia.json")
```

Bibliography

Allison, D. B., Brown, A. W., George, B. J., and Kaiser, K. A. (2016). Reproducibility: A tragedy of errors. *Nature*, 530(7588):27–29.

Arnold, B. F., Ercumen, A., Benjamin-Chung, J., and Colford, J. M. (2016). Brief Report: Negative Controls to Detect Selection Bias and Measurement Bias in Epidemiologic Studies. *Epidemiology*, 27(5):637–641.

Austin, P. C. (2011). Optimal caliper widths for propensity-score matching when estimating differences in means and differences in proportions in observational studies. *Pharmaceutical statistics*, 10(2):150–161.

Banda, J. M., Halpern, Y., Sontag, D., and Shah, N. H. (2017). Electronic phenotyping with APHRODITE and the Observational Health Sciences and Informatics (OHDSI) data network. *AMIA Jt Summits Transl Sci Proc*, 2017:48–57.

Boland, M. R., Parhi, P., Li, L., Miotto, R., Carroll, R., Iqbal, U., Nguyen, P. A., Schuemie, M., You, S. C., Smith, D., Mooney, S., Ryan, P., Li, Y. J., Park, R. W., Denny, J., Dudley, J. T., Hripcsak, G., Gentine, P., and Tatonetti, N. P. (2017). Uncovering exposures responsible for birth season - disease effects: a global study. *J Am Med Inform Assoc*.

Botsis, T., Hartvigsen, G., Chen, F., and Weng, C. (2010). Secondary use of ehr: data quality issues and informatics opportunities. *Summit on Translational Bioinformatics*, 2010:1.

Byrd, J. B., Adam, A., and Brown, N. J. (2006). Angiotensin-converting enzyme inhibitor-associated angioedema. *Immunol Allergy Clin North Am*, 26(4):725–737.

Callahan, T. J., Bauck, A. E., Bertoch, D., Brown, J., Khare, R., Ryan, P. B., Staab, J., Zozus, M. N., and Kahn, M. G. (2017). A comparison of data quality assessment checks in six data sharing networks. *eGEMs*, 5(1).

Cepeda, M. S., Reps, J., Fife, D., Blacketer, C., Stang, P., and Ryan, P. (2018). Finding treatment-resistant depression in real-world data: How a data-driven approach compares with expert-based heuristics. *Depress Anxiety*, 35(3):220–228.

Chen, X., Dallmeier-Tiessen, S., Dasler, R., Feger, S., Fokianos, P., Gonzalez, J. B., Hirvonsalo, H., Kousidis, D., Lavasa, A., Mele, S., Rodriguez, D. R., Šimko, T., Smith, T., Trisovic, A., Trzcinska, A., Tsanaktsidis, I., Zimmermann, M., Cranmer, K., Heinrich, L.,

Watts, G., Hildreth, M., Iglesias, L. L., Lassila-Perini, K., and Neubert, S. (2018). Open is not enough. *Nature Physics*, 15(2):113–119.

Cicardi, M., Zingale, L. C., Bergamaschini, L., and Agostoni, A. (2004). Angioedema associated with angiotensin-converting enzyme inhibitor use: outcome after switching to a different treatment. *Arch. Intern. Med.*, 164(8):910–913.

Dasu, T. and Johnson, T. (2003). *Exploratory data mining and data cleaning*, volume 479. John Wiley & Sons.

Defalco, F. J., Ryan, P. B., and Soledad Cepeda, M. (2013). Applying standardized drug terminologies to observational healthcare databases: a case study on opioid exposure. *Health Serv Outcomes Res Methodol*, 13(1):58–67.

DerSimonian, R. and Laird, N. (1986). Meta-analysis in clinical trials. *Control Clin Trials*, 7(3):177–188.

Duke, J. D., Ryan, P. B., Suchard, M. A., Hripcsak, G., Jin, P., Reich, C., Schwalm, M. S., Khoma, Y., Wu, Y., Xu, H., Shah, N. H., Banda, J. M., and Schuemie, M. J. (2017). Risk of angioedema associated with levetiracetam compared with phenytoin: Findings of the observational health data sciences and informatics research network. *Epilepsia*, 58(8):e101–e106.

Farrington, C. P. (1995). Relative incidence estimation from case series for vaccine safety evaluation. *Biometrics*, 51(1):228–235.

Farrington, C. P., Anaya-Izquierdo, K., Whitaker, H. J., Hocine, M. N., Douglas, I., and Smeeth, L. (2011). Self-controlled case series analysis with event-dependent observation periods. *Journal of the American Statistical Association*, 106(494):417–426.

Fuller, W. A. (2009). *Measurement error models*, volume 305. John Wiley & Sons.

Garza, M., Del Fiol, G., Tenenbaum, J., Walden, A., and Zozus, M. N. (2016). Evaluating common data models for use with a longitudinal community registry. *J Biomed Inform*, 64:333–341.

Hernan, M. A., Hernandez-Diaz, S., Werler, M. M., and Mitchell, A. A. (2002). Causal knowledge as a prerequisite for confounding evaluation: an application to birth defects epidemiology. *Am. J. Epidemiol.*, 155(2):176–184.

Hernan, M. A. and Robins, J. M. (2016). Using Big Data to Emulate a Target Trial When a Randomized Trial Is Not Available. *Am. J. Epidemiol.*, 183(8):758–764.

Hersh, W. R., Weiner, M. G., Embi, P. J., Logan, J. R., Payne, P. R., Bernstam, E. V., Lehmann, H. P., Hripcsak, G., Hartzog, T. H., Cimino, J. J., et al. (2013). Caveats for the use of operational electronic health record data in comparative effectiveness research. *Medical care*, 51(8 0 3):S30.

Higgins, J. P., Thompson, S. G., Deeks, J. J., and Altman, D. G. (2003). Measuring inconsistency in meta-analyses. *BMJ*, 327(7414):557–560.

Hill, A. B. (1965). THE ENVIRONMENT AND DISEASE: ASSOCIATION OR CAUSATION? *Proc. R. Soc. Med.*, 58:295–300.

Hripcsak, G. and Albers, D. J. (2017). High-fidelity phenotyping: richness and freedom from bias. *J Am Med Inform Assoc*.

Hripcsak, G., Duke, J. D., Shah, N. H., Reich, C. G., Huser, V., Schuemie, M. J., Suchard, M. A., Park, R. W., Wong, I. C. K., Rijnbeek, P. R., van der Lei, J., Pratt, N., Norén, G. N., Li, Y.-C., Stang, P. E., Madigan, D., and Ryan, P. B. (2015). Observational Health Data Sciences and Informatics (OHDSI): Opportunities for Observational Researchers. *Studies in health technology and informatics*, 216:574–578.

Hripcsak, G., Levine, M. E., Shang, N., and Ryan, P. B. (2018). Effect of vocabulary mapping for conditions on phenotype cohorts. *J Am Med Inform Assoc*, 25(12):1618–1625.

Hripcsak, G., Ryan, P. B., Duke, J. D., Shah, N. H., Park, R. W., Huser, V., Suchard, M. A., Schuemie, M. J., DeFalco, F. J., Perotte, A., Banda, J. M., Reich, C. G., Schilling, L. M., Matheny, M. E., Meeker, D., Pratt, N., and Madigan, D. (2016). Characterizing treatment pathways at scale using the OHDSI network. *Proceedings of the National Academy of Sciences*, 113(27):7329–7336.

Hripcsak, G., Shang, N., Peissig, P. L., Rasmussen, L. V., Liu, C., Benoit, B., Carroll, R. J., Carrell, D. S., Denny, J. C., Dikilitas, O., Gainer, V. S., Marie Howell, K., Klann, J. G., Kullo, I. J., Lingren, T., Mentch, F. D., Murphy, S. N., Natarajan, K., Pacheco, J. A., Wei, W. Q., Wiley, K., and Weng, C. (2019). Facilitating phenotype transfer using a common data model. *J Biomed Inform*, page 103253.

Huser, V., DeFalco, F. J., Schuemie, M., Ryan, P. B., Shang, N., Velez, M., Park, R. W., Boyce, R. D., Duke, J., Khare, R., Utidjian, L., and Bailey, C. (2016). Multisite Evaluation of a Data Quality Tool for Patient-Level Clinical Data Sets. *EGEMS (Washington, DC)*, 4(1):1239.

Huser, V., Kahn, M. G., Brown, J. S., and Gouripeddi, R. (2018). Methods for examining data quality in healthcare integrated data repositories. *Pacific Symposium on Biocomputing. Pacific Symposium on Biocomputing*, 23:628–633.

Johnston, S. S., Morton, J. M., Kalsekar, I., Ammann, E. M., Hsiao, C. W., and Reps, J. (2019). Using Machine Learning Applied to Real-World Healthcare Data for Predictive Analytics: An Applied Example in Bariatric Surgery. *Value Health*, 22(5):580–586.

Kahn, M. G., Brown, J. S., Chun, A. T., Davidson, B. N., Meeker, D., Ryan, P. B., Schilling, L. M., Weiskopf, N. G., Williams, A. E., and Zozus, M. N. (2015). Transparent reporting of data quality in distributed data networks. *EGEMS (Washington, DC)*, 3(1):1052.

Kahn, M. G., Callahan, T. J., Barnard, J., Bauck, A. E., Brown, J., Davidson, B. N., Estiri, H., Goerg, C., Holve, E., Johnson, S. G., Liaw, S.-T., Hamilton-Lopez, M., Meeker, D., Ong, T. C., Ryan, P. B., Shang, N., Weiskopf, N. G., Weng, C., Zozus, M. N., and Schilling, L. (2016). A Harmonized Data Quality Assessment Terminology and Framework for the Secondary Use of Electronic Health Record Data. *EGEMS (Washington, DC)*, 4(1):1244.

Kahn, M. G., Raebel, M. A., Glanz, J. M., Riedlinger, K., and Steiner, J. F. (2012). A pragmatic framework for single-site and multisite data quality assessment in electronic health record-based clinical research. *Medical care*, 50.

Liaw, S.-T., Rahimi, A., Ray, P., Taggart, J., Dennis, S., de Lusignan, S., Jalaludin, B., Yeo, A., and Talaei-Khoei, A. (2013). Towards an ontology for data quality in integrated chronic disease management: a realist review of the literature. *International journal of medical informatics*, 82(1):10–24.

Lipsitch, M., Tchetgen Tchetgen, E., and Cohen, T. (2010). Negative controls: a tool for detecting confounding and bias in observational studies. *Epidemiology*, 21(3):383–388.

Maclure, M. (1991). The case-crossover design: a method for studying transient effects on the risk of acute events. *Am. J. Epidemiol.*, 133(2):144–153.

Madigan, D., Ryan, P. B., and Schuemie, M. (2013a). Does design matter? Systematic evaluation of the impact of analytical choices on effect estimates in observational studies. *Ther Adv Drug Saf*, 4(2):53–62.

Madigan, D., Ryan, P. B., Schuemie, M., Stang, P. E., Overhage, J. M., Hartzema, A. G., Suchard, M. A., DuMouchel, W., and Berlin, J. A. (2013b). Evaluating the impact of database heterogeneity on observational study results. *Am. J. Epidemiol.*, 178(4):645–651.

Magid, D. J., Shetterly, S. M., Margolis, K. L., Tavel, H. M., O'Connor, P. J., Selby, J. V., and Ho, P. M. (2010). Comparative effectiveness of angiotensin-converting enzyme inhibitors versus beta-blockers as second-line therapy for hypertension. *Circ Cardiovasc Qual Outcomes*, 3(5):453–458.

Makadia, R. and Ryan, P. B. (2014). Transforming the Premier Perspective Hospital Database into the Observational Medical Outcomes Partnership (OMOP) Common Data Model. *EGEMS (Wash DC)*, 2(1):1110.

Martin, R. C. (2008). *Clean Code: A Handbook of Agile Software Craftsmanship*. Prentice Hall PTR, Upper Saddle River, NJ, USA, 1 edition.

Matcho, A., Ryan, P., Fife, D., and Reich, C. (2014). Fidelity assessment of a clinical practice research datalink conversion to the OMOP common data model. *Drug Saf*, 37(11):945–959.

Noren, G. N., Caster, O., Juhlin, K., and Lindquist, M. (2014). Zoo or savannah? Choice of training ground for evidence-based pharmacovigilance. *Drug Saf*, 37(9):655–659.

Norman, J. L., Holmes, W. L., Bell, W. A., and Finks, S. W. (2013). Life-threatening ACE inhibitor-induced angioedema after eleven years on lisinopril. *J Pharm Pract*, 26(4):382–388.

Oliveira, J. L., Trifan, A., and Silva, L. A. B. (2019). EMIF catalogue: A collaborative platform for sharing and reusing biomedical data. *International Journal of Medical Informatics*, 126:35–45.

Olsen, L., Aisner, D., McGinnis, J. M., et al. (2007). *The learning healthcare system: workshop summary*. Natl Academy Pr.

O'Mara, N. B. and O'Mara, E. M. (1996). Delayed onset of angioedema with angiotensin-converting enzyme inhibitors: case report and review of the literature. *Pharmacotherapy*, 16(4):675–679.

Overhage, J. M., Ryan, P. B., Reich, C. G., Hartzema, A. G., and Stang, P. E. (2012). Validation of a common data model for active safety surveillance research. *J Am Med Inform Assoc*, 19(1):54–60.

Perkins, N. J., Cole, S. R., Harel, O., Tchetgen Tchetgen, E. J., Sun, B., Mitchell, E. M., and Schisterman, E. F. (2017). Principled approaches to missing data in epidemiologic studies. *American journal of epidemiology*, 187(3):568–575.

Powers, B. J., Coeytaux, R. R., Dolor, R. J., Hasselblad, V., Patel, U. D., Yancy, W. S., Gray, R. N., Irvine, R. J., Kendrick, A. S., and Sanders, G. D. (2012). Updated report on comparative effectiveness of ACE inhibitors, ARBs, and direct renin inhibitors for patients with essential hypertension: much more data, little new information. *J Gen Intern Med*, 27(6):716–729.

Prasad, V. and Jena, A. B. (2013). Prespecified falsification end points: can they validate true observational associations? *JAMA*, 309(3):241–242.

Ramcharran, D., Qiu, H., Schuemie, M. J., and Ryan, P. B. (2017). Atypical Antipsychotics and the Risk of Falls and Fractures Among Older Adults: An Emulation Analysis and an Evaluation of Additional Confounding Control Strategies. *J Clin Psychopharmacol*, 37(2):162–168.

Rassen, J. A., Shelat, A. A., Myers, J., Glynn, R. J., Rothman, K. J., and Schneeweiss, S. (2012). One-to-many propensity score matching in cohort studies. *Pharmacoepidemiol Drug Saf*, 21 Suppl 2:69–80.

Reps, J. M., Rijnbeek, P. R., and Ryan, P. B. (2019). Identifying the DEAD: Development and Validation of a Patient-Level Model to Predict Death Status in Population-Level Claims Data. *Drug Saf*.

Reps, J. M., Schuemie, M. J., Suchard, M. A., Ryan, P. B., and Rijnbeek, P. R. (2018). Design and implementation of a standardized framework to generate and evaluate patient-level prediction models using observational healthcare data. *Journal of the American Medical Informatics Association*, 25(8):969–975.

Roebuck, K. (2012). *Data quality: high-impact strategies-what you need to know: definitions, adoptions, impact, benefits, maturity, vendors*. Emereo Publishing.

Rosenbaum, P. (2005). *Sensitivity Analysis in Observational Studies*. American Cancer Society.

Rosenbaum, P. and Rubin, D. (1983). The central role of the propensity score in observational studies for causal effects. *Biometrika*, 70:41–55.

Rubbo, B., Fitzpatrick, N. K., Denaxas, S., Daskalopoulou, M., Yu, N., Patel, R. S., Hemingway, H., Danesh, J., Allen, N., Atkinson, M., Blaveri, E., Brannan, R., Brayne, C., Brophy, S., Chaturvedi, N., Collins, R., deLusignan, S., Denaxas, S., Desai, P., Eastwood, S., Gallacher, J., Hemingway, H., Hotopf, M., Landray, M., Lyons, R., O'Neil, T., Pringle, M., Sprosen, T., Strachan, D., Sudlow, C., Sullivan, F., Zhang, Q., and Flaig, R. (2015). Use of electronic health records to ascertain, validate and phenotype acute myocardial infarction: A systematic review and recommendations. *Int. J. Cardiol.*, 187:705–711.

Rubin, D. B. (2001). Using propensity scores to help design observational studies: application to the tobacco litigation. *Health Services and Outcomes Research Methodology*, 2(3-4):169–188.

Ryan, P. B., Buse, J. B., Schuemie, M. J., DeFalco, F., Yuan, Z., Stang, P. E., Berlin, J. A., and Rosenthal, N. (2018). Comparative effectiveness of canagliflozin, SGLT2 inhibitors and non-SGLT2 inhibitors on the risk of hospitalization for heart failure and amputation in patients with type 2 diabetes mellitus: A real-world meta-analysis of 4 observational databases (OBSERVE-4D). *Diabetes Obes Metab*, 20(11):2585–2597.

Ryan, P. B., Madigan, D., Stang, P. E., Overhage, J. M., Racoosin, J. A., and Hartzema, A. G. (2012). Empirical assessment of methods for risk identification in healthcare data: results from the experiments of the Observational Medical Outcomes Partnership. *Stat Med*, 31(30):4401–4415.

Ryan, P. B., Schuemie, M. J., and Madigan, D. (2013a). Empirical performance of a self-controlled cohort method: lessons for developing a risk identification and analysis system. *Drug Saf*, 36 Suppl 1:95–106.

Ryan, P. B., Schuemie, M. J., Ramcharran, D., and Stang, P. E. (2017). Atypical Antipsychotics and the Risks of Acute Kidney Injury and Related Outcomes Among Older Adults: A Replication Analysis and an Evaluation of Adapted Confounding Control Strategies. *Drugs Aging*, 34(3):211–219.

Ryan, P. B., Stang, P. E., Overhage, J. M., Suchard, M. A., Hartzema, A. G., DuMouchel, W., Reich, C. G., Schuemie, M. J., and Madigan, D. (2013b). A comparison of the empirical performance of methods for a risk identification system. *Drug Saf*, 36 Suppl 1:S143–158.

Sabroe, R. A. and Black, A. K. (1997). Angiotensin-converting enzyme (ACE) inhibitors and angio-oedema. *Br. J. Dermatol.*, 136(2):153–158.

Schneeweiss, S. (2018). Automated data-adaptive analytics for electronic healthcare data to study causal treatment effects. *Clin Epidemiol*, 10:771–788.

Schuemie, M. J., Hripcsak, G., Ryan, P. B., Madigan, D., and Suchard, M. A. (2016). Robust empirical calibration of p-values using observational data. *Stat Med*, 35(22):3883–3888.

Schuemie, M. J., Hripcsak, G., Ryan, P. B., Madigan, D., and Suchard, M. A. (2018a). Empirical confidence interval calibration for population-level effect estimation studies in observational healthcare data. *Proc. Natl. Acad. Sci. U.S.A.*, 115(11):2571–2577.

Schuemie, M. J., Ryan, P. B., DuMouchel, W., Suchard, M. A., and Madigan, D. (2014). Interpreting observational studies: why empirical calibration is needed to correct p-values. *Stat Med*, 33(2):209–218.

Schuemie, M. J., Ryan, P. B., Hripcsak, G., Madigan, D., and Suchard, M. A. (2018b). Improving reproducibility by using high-throughput observational studies with empirical calibration. *Philos Trans A Math Phys Eng Sci*, 376(2128).

Sherman, R. E., Anderson, S. A., Dal Pan, G. J., Gray, G. W., Gross, T., Hunter, N. L., LaVange, L., Marinac-Dabic, D., Marks, P. W., Robb, M. A., et al. (2016). Real-world evidence—what is it and what can it tell us. *N Engl J Med*, 375(23):2293–2297.

Simpson, S. E., Madigan, D., Zorych, I., Schuemie, M. J., Ryan, P. B., and Suchard, M. A. (2013). Multiple self-controlled case series for large-scale longitudinal observational databases. *Biometrics*, 69(4):893–902.

Slater, E. E., Merrill, D. D., Guess, H. A., Roylance, P. J., Cooper, W. D., Inman, W. H. W., and Ewan, P. W. (1988). Clinical Profile of Angioedema Associated With Angiotensin Converting-Enzyme Inhibition. *JAMA*, 260(7):967–970.

Stang, P. E., Ryan, P. B., Racoosin, J. A., Overhage, J. M., Hartzema, A. G., Reich, C., Welebob, E., Scarnecchia, T., and Woodcock, J. (2010). Advancing the science for active surveillance: rationale and design for the Observational Medical Outcomes Partnership. *Ann. Intern. Med.*, 153(9):600–606.

Suchard, M. A., Simpson, S. E., Zorych, I., Ryan, P. B., and Madigan, D. (2013). Massive parallelization of serial inference algorithms for a complex generalized linear model. *ACM Trans. Model. Comput. Simul.*, 23(1):10:1–10:17.

Suissa, S. (1995). The case-time-control design. *Epidemiology*, 6(3):248–253.

Swerdel, J. N., Hripcsak, G., and Ryan, P. B. (2019). PheValuator: Development and Evaluation of a Phenotype Algorithm Evaluator. *J Biomed Inform*, page 103258.

Thompson, T. and Frable, M. A. (1993). Drug-induced, life-threatening angioedema revisited. *Laryngoscope*, 103(1 Pt 1):10–12.

Tian, Y., Schuemie, M. J., and Suchard, M. A. (2018). Evaluating large-scale propensity score performance through real-world and synthetic data experiments. *Int J Epidemiol*, 47(6):2005–2014.

Toh, S., Reichman, M. E., Houstoun, M., Ross Southworth, M., Ding, X., Hernandez, A. F., Levenson, M., Li, L., McCloskey, C., Shoaibi, A., Wu, E., Zornberg, G., and Hennessy, S. (2012). Comparative risk for angioedema associated with the use of drugs that target the renin-angiotensin-aldosterone system. *Arch. Intern. Med.*, 172(20):1582–1589.

van der Lei, J. (1991). Use and abuse of computer-stored medical records. *Methods of information in medicine*, 30(02):79–80.

Vandenbroucke, J. P. and Pearce, N. (2012). Case-control studies: basic concepts. *Int J Epidemiol*, 41(5):1480–1489.

Vashisht, R., Jung, K., Schuler, A., Banda, J. M., Park, R. W., Jin, S., Li, L., Dudley, J. T., Johnson, K. W., Shervey, M. M., Xu, H., Wu, Y., Natrajan, K., Hripcsak, G., Jin, P., Van Zandt, M., Reckard, A., Reich, C. G., Weaver, J., Schuemie, M. J., Ryan, P. B., Callahan, A., and Shah, N. H. (2018). Association of Hemoglobin A1c Levels With Use of Sulfonylureas, Dipeptidyl Peptidase 4 Inhibitors, and Thiazolidinediones in Patients With Type 2 Diabetes Treated With Metformin: Analysis From the Observational Health Data Sciences and Informatics Initiative. *JAMA Netw Open*, 1(4):e181755.

von Elm, E., Altman, D. G., Egger, M., Pocock, S. J., Gøtzsche, P. C., and Vandenbroucke, J. P. (2008). The strengthening the reporting of observational studies in epidemiology (strobe) statement: guidelines for reporting observational studies. *Journal of Clinical Epidemiology*, 61(4):344 – 349.

Voss, E. A., Boyce, R. D., Ryan, P. B., van der Lei, J., Rijnbeek, P. R., and Schuemie, M. J. (2016). Accuracy of an Automated Knowledge Base for Identifying Drug Adverse Reactions. *J Biomed Inform*.

Voss, E. A., Ma, Q., and Ryan, P. B. (2015a). The impact of standardizing the definition of visits on the consistency of multi-database observational health research. *BMC Med Res Methodol*, 15:13.

Voss, E. A., Makadia, R., Matcho, A., Ma, Q., Knoll, C., Schuemie, M., DeFalco, F. J., Londhe, A., Zhu, V., and Ryan, P. B. (2015b). Feasibility and utility of applications of the common data model to multiple, disparate observational health databases. *J Am Med Inform Assoc*, 22(3):553–564.

Walker, A. M., Patrick, A. R., Lauer, M. S., Hornbrook, M. C., Marin, M. G., Platt, R., Roger, V. L., Stang, P., and Schneeweiss, S. (2013). A tool for assessing the feasibility of comparative effectiveness research. *Comp Eff Res*, 3:11–20.

Wang, Y., Desai, M., Ryan, P. B., DeFalco, F. J., Schuemie, M. J., Stang, P. E., Berlin, J. A., and Yuan, Z. (2017). Incidence of diabetic ketoacidosis among patients with type 2 diabetes mellitus treated with SGLT2 inhibitors and other antihyperglycemic agents. *Diabetes Res. Clin. Pract.*, 128:83–90.

Weinstein, R. B., Ryan, P., Berlin, J. A., Matcho, A., Schuemie, M., Swerdel, J., Patel, K., and Fife, D. (2017). Channeling in the Use of Nonprescription Paracetamol and Ibuprofen in an Electronic Medical Records Database: Evidence and Implications. *Drug Saf*, 40(12):1279–1292.

Weiskopf, N. G. and Weng, C. (2013). Methods and dimensions of electronic health record data quality assessment: enabling reuse for clinical research. *Journal of the American Medical Informatics Association: JAMIA*, 20(1):144–151.

Whelton, P. K., Carey, R. M., Aronow, W. S., Casey, D. E., Collins, K. J., Dennison Him-melfarb, C., DePalma, S. M., Gidding, S., Jamerson, K. A., Jones, D. W., MacLaughlin, E. J., Muntner, P., Ovbiagele, B., Smith, S. C., Spencer, C. C., Stafford, R. S., Taler, S. J., Thomas, R. J., Williams, K. A., Williamson, J. D., and Wright, J. T. (2018). 2017 ACC/AHA/AAPA/ABC/ACPM/AGS/APhA/ASH/ASPC/NMA/PCNA Guideline for the Prevention, Detection, Evaluation, and Management of High Blood Pressure in Adults: Executive Summary: A Report of the American College of Cardiology/American Heart Association Task Force on Clinical Practice Guidelines. *Circulation*, 138(17):e426–e483.

Whitaker, H. J., Farrington, C. P., Spiessens, B., and Musonda, P. (2006). Tutorial in bio-statistics: the self-controlled case series method. *Stat Med*, 25(10):1768–1797.

Who, A. (2013). Global brief on hypertension. *World Health Organization*.

Wickham, H. (2015). *R Packages*. O'Reilly Media, Inc., 1st edition.

Wikipedia (2019a). Open science — Wikipedia, the free encyclopedia. http://en.wikipedia. org/w/index.php?title=Open%20science&oldid=900178688. [Online; accessed 24-June-2019].

Wikipedia (2019b). Science 2.0 — Wikipedia, the free encyclopedia. http://en.wikipedia.org/ w/index.php?title=Science%202.0&oldid=887565958. [Online; accessed 09-July-2019].

Wikiquote (2019). Ronald fisher — wikiquote,. [Online; accessed 2-August-2019].

Wilkinson, M. D., Dumontier, M., Aalbersberg, I. J., Appleton, G., Axton, M., Baak, A., Blomberg, N., Boiten, J. W., da Silva Santos, L. B., Bourne, P. E., Bouwman, J., Brookes, A. J., Clark, T., Crosas, M., Dillo, I., Dumon, O., Edmunds, S., Evelo, C. T., Finkers, R., Gonzalez-Beltran, A., Gray, A. J., Groth, P., Goble, C., Grethe, J. S., Heringa, J., 't Hoen, P. A., Hooft, R., Kuhn, T., Kok, R., Kok, J., Lusher, S. J., Martone, M. E., Mons, A., Packer, A. L., Persson, B., Rocca-Serra, P., Roos, M., van Schaik, R., Sansone, S. A., Schultes, E., Sengstag, T., Slater, T., Strawn, G., Swertz, M. A., Thompson, M., van der Lei, J., van Mulligen, E., Velterop, J., Waagmeester, A., Wittenburg, P., Wolstencroft, K., Zhao, J., and Mons, B. (2016). The FAIR Guiding Principles for scientific data management and stewardship. *Sci Data*, 3:160018.

Yoon, D., Ahn, E. K., Park, M. Y., Cho, S. Y., Ryan, P., Schuemie, M. J., Shin, D., Park, H., and Park, R. W. (2016). Conversion and Data Quality Assessment of Electronic Health Record Data at a Korean Tertiary Teaching Hospital to a Common Data Model for Dis-tributed Network Research. *Healthc Inform Res*, 22(1):54–58.

Yuan, Z., DeFalco, F. J., Ryan, P. B., Schuemie, M. J., Stang, P. E., Berlin, J. A., Desai, M., and Rosenthal, N. (2018). Risk of lower extremity amputations in people with type 2 diabetes mellitus treated with sodium-glucose co-transporter-2 inhibitors in the USA: A retrospective cohort study. *Diabetes Obes Metab*, 20(3):582–589.

Zaadstra, B. M., Chorus, A. M., van Buuren, S., Kalsbeek, H., and van Noort, J. M. (2008). Selective association of multiple sclerosis with infectious mononucleosis. *Mult. Scler.*, 14(3):307–313.

Zaman, M. A., Oparil, S., and Calhoun, D. A. (2002). Drugs targeting the renin-angiotensin-aldosterone system. *Nat Rev Drug Discov*, 1(8):621–636.

Index

Made in United States
North Haven, CT
19 December 2021

13302748R00259